The Tufts
University Guide to
TOTAL
NUTRITION

◆ Revised and Updated ◆

The Tufts University Guide to TOTAL NUTRITION

◆ Revised and Updated ◆

STANLEY GERSHOFF, PH.D.
Dean Emeritus of the Tufts University School of Nutrition

with Catherine Whitney and the Editorial Advisory Board
of the *Tufts University Diet & Nutrition Letter*

HarperPerennial
A Division of HarperCollinsPublishers

HarperCollins books may be purchased for educational, business, or sales promotional use. For information, please write: Special Markets Department, HarperCollins Publishers, Inc., 10 East 53rd Street, New York, NY 10022.

FIRST HARPERPERENNIAL EDITION

Designed by Alma Hochhauser Orenstein

ISBN 0-06-271588-7 (hc)
ISBN 0-06-273316-8 (pbk.)   **174422**

96 97 98 99 v/RRD 10 9 8 7 6 5 4 3 2 1

Dedicated to William H. White, whose vision made this book possible;
and to the scientists and researchers whose work has led
to a greater understanding of human nutrition in our time.

And to Dr. Jean Mayer, a passionate advocate for human growth
and nutritional responsibility.

Contents

PART THREE:
NUTRITIONAL LIFE-CYCLES 183

Acknowledgments

The development of this book depended on the efforts of many people. I thank in particular my literary agent, Jane Dystel, who was instrumental in the book's conception and who gave many long hours to assure its smooth development; Carol Cohen, a talented and enthusiastic editor whose instincts about appealing to the popular market have always been on target; Robert Wilson, the dedicated editor for the revised edition; and Catherine Whitney, the writer who transformed the scientific information into practical, readable advice for consumers.

The staff of the *Tufts University Diet & Nutrition Letter* have supported this work in countless ways. The late Bill White fought to make the book a reality and contributed considerable time to defining its direction and content. Deborah White has used her experience with popular media and her strong marketing skills to assure the book a wide reading. The newsletter staff have been most generous in allowing me access to the excellent material they have gathered and have helped keep the book up to date during its development. In particular, I am grateful for the assistance of Lawrence Lindner, Gail Zyla, Viola Roth, Marie Johnson, and the members of the newsletter's editorial board. I have appreciated the support and input of Marilyn Crim, M.D., Ph.D., assistant professor for nutrition, and Robert Nicolosi, Ph.D., visiting professor of nutrition.

I am grateful for the work of Maureen Callahan, the nutritionist who consulted on this book. In particular, Maureen's contribution in developing practical food plans and appealing menus was critical. I also thank others who contributed to portions of this book, including art designer John Schuler, who developed some of the charts and illustrations.

Tables, Charts, Illustrations

Quizzes

Introduction

Nutrition has been a human preoccupation since the beginning of time. Our prehistoric ancestors served as the "laboratory subjects" for many of the foods we eat today, testing the viability of everything that grew or moved on the earth's surface. Over time, the human diet in different parts of the world settled into relatively stable, safe consumption patterns.

It was not until the eighteenth century that scientists began to draw more specific links between food and function. And it wasn't until the twentieth century that vitamins were discovered as essential elements in the human diet.

Given the state of our nutritional understanding today, it is hard to believe that only one hundred years ago rickets was a very common disease among American young people, scurvy afflicted large numbers of sailors, iron deficiency was common even among the wealthy, and dental cavities were a fact of life for children.

Two hundred years ago, the average human life expectancy was thirty-five years. One hundred years ago, it was only forty years. But as a result of medical advances, improved nutrition, and better living conditions, a child born today in the United States has an average life expectancy of seventy-five years.

In some respects, the rapid growth of nutrition-related discoveries, the elimination of common deficiencies, and the breakthroughs in the prevention and management of diseases have fostered a population of people with very high expectations for scientific research. People today expect positive discoveries to be made overnight; they are impatient with the slow, grinding process of research. They are better informed than ever, bolstered by a wealth of books, magazines, newspapers, and television programs that focus attention on nutrition. Yet in some ways they are less well informed than ever, lost in a sea of what appear to be constantly conflicting "expert" opinions. There seem to be so many scientific controversies that they don't know whom to believe.

Therefore, it may surprise you to know that, when it comes to most facets of nutrition, there is hardly any controversy within the scientific community. Nutritional authorities in the United States and around the world have reached a clear consensus on many important aspects of nutrition—indeed, the recommendations of the 1988 Surgeon General's Report on Nutrition and Health were born of that consensus. In fact, in November 1990, the Department of Agriculture and the Department of Health and Human Services issued a joint report on dietary guidelines, developed by a panel of scientists and nutritional authorities, that further substantiated these recommendations.

The media are always ready to give full play to the "discovery" of a new magic potion. For example, although the scientific community is in complete agreement that laetrile is not a vitamin and does not cure cancer, laetrile continues to be promoted as a cure, and cancer victims continue to spend precious time and money traveling to Mexico to receive treatments. However, not all the blame for disinformation should be attributed to charlatans or the media. Sometimes, in the desire to publish their work quickly, scientists and their public relations associates let information leak out prematurely and in ways that confuse both the media and the public.

When it comes to false or unsupported claims, the scientific community is often at a disadvantage. Few scientists are willing to spend their limited research time and resources to prove to public satisfaction that a quack remedy will not cure cancer or a variety of other ailments—although sometimes they are forced to do this when unproven claims are made by other scientists. The more meaningful task is in the discovery of medical or nutritional links that might work.

Consumers are easily persuaded by false claims because they grow so impatient with the slow process of research. (Of course, research doesn't seem so slow when you consider that most of the essential discoveries have been made in the past century.) The human body is a complex organism with thousands of possible interactions. Every time scientists discover a previously unknown contribution of one nutrient, their discovery has the potential for illuminating the metabolic roles of other nutrients. Before making a recommendation concerning food or nutrient therapy, however, scientists must not only rule out potentially detrimental interactions but must also examine factors such as age, sex, environment, hereditary patterns, and potentially harmful practices, such as smoking. These factors are examined by studies on animals and human beings. Sometimes they take place over a period of many years, because long-term effects must be taken into account.

People who are confused about what to believe can use the following guidelines to judge the validity of a nutritional claim. A statement should probably be considered questionable if:

◆ The claim sounds too good to be true. Consumers should take a skeptical view of diets, herbs, vitamins, minerals, enzymes, or "special foods" promoted as simple "cures" for, or "dramatic relief" from, a host of ills. Most scientists speak in terms of treating or reducing the risk of a disease rather than curing it. Furthermore, although dietary factors such as fat can play a role in the development of heart disease, cancer, and other disorders, anyone who suggests that diet alone is to blame for most ailments and that nutritional supplements offer a remedy is leading you astray.

◆ A promoter repeatedly refers to unproven remedies as "alternatives" to medically proven treatments and/or belittles established medicine. Physicians in the medical community generally welcome new treatment options, provided that such options are supported by solid research. If an "alternative" has not been accepted by legitimate health-care providers, it's because sufficient research is lacking or, even worse, the treatment has proved to be dangerous.

◆ Anecdotes and testimonials alone are used to support a claim. To measure the effectiveness of treatments, scientists rely on carefully controlled experiments, not random comments from consumers who use them before they're rigorously tested. Often, claims are made based on the personal experience of the author—hardly a reliable way to make pronouncements for the general population. It takes a good deal of time and careful study to determine if the seeming effects of a food or drug actually are what they're said to be.

◆ The recommendation limits variety. Human beings need protein, carbohydrates, fat, and a number of essential vitamins and minerals in order to grow and develop. Diet prescriptions that are based on excluding essential foods or that focus on one or several "special" foods are not valid. In effect, these dietary theories take us back to the "dark ages" of nutritional understanding, when deficiencies were rampant. Likewise, the "more is better" philosophy is fallacious. Vitamin and mineral megadoses can often lead to toxicity and negatively influence the absorption of other nutrients. Overdoing the use of a positive substance, such as fiber, will lead to problems.

◆ It contradicts consensus. At times, it becomes fashionable to mistrust the scientific and health establishment—as though there were an establishment in the sense that we all got together in a room and formulated proclamations. In fact, there is no formal establishment in the field of nutrition. Rather, the things we know about food and its functions have emerged over time as the consensus of scientists and other experts. It is absurd to heed the advice of self-proclaimed outsiders, many of whom have no training whatsoever in the disci-

plines they are evaluating. It can be frustrating for those of us who work in this field to see consumers listening to people who preach misinformation when there is so much that we know. Granted, some erroneous recommendations seem to be benign; although they won't help you, they probably won't hurt you either. But others are not so harmless and can lead to health problems that might easily have been avoided.

It is our hope that this book will provide you with a reliable, commonsense guide to nutrition. It contains hundreds of suggestions for better eating; it includes data on the most current scientific research underway, both here at Tufts and elsewhere; and it offers advice for people who are "average" as well as for people who have special concerns and needs.

We also hope that, in the process of reading and using this book, you will begin to experience some of the excitement about the possibilities that exist for human nutrition as we approach the end of the twentieth century. Good nutritional practices can improve the lives of many millions of Americans, and we look forward to the time when they are available to every person in the world as well. It will be a different planet indeed when that dream is realized.

Stanley Gershoff, Ph.D.
January 1996

PART ONE

The Fundamentals of Good Food

When you sit down at the dinner table, you probably don't look at the food and exclaim, "That protein smells delicious!" or "Please pass the vitamin C." Rather, what you see is food that has been prepared in a certain way. The aroma and presentation influence your reaction, as do the setting of the meal, the people with whom you share it, and a variety of other factors, including your food preferences, how hungry you are, and the way you live. These factors are all important to the practice of good nutrition. Together, they affect what foods you consume and how you consume them.

Nutrition—the dos and don'ts of healthful eating—may seem like an abstract concept to us. In fact, nutrition principles are based on the simple common sense of nature. It is not abstract at all.

The saying "You are what you eat" was originally coined as an admonition to those who might feast on fatty foods or ingest empty calories. But it is not exactly true that we are what we eat. A more accurate way to state the principle is: In order to reach our greatest potential for growth and development and to maintain good health, we must consume nutritious foods.

But what does that mean? What constitutes a nutritious diet? We begin this discussion by describing the fundamental design of food and how it nourishes your body.

The simplest way to define food is to say that it is the plant and animal products we ingest that enable our bodies to operate. It accomplishes this function in three ways: by supplying energy, by providing the building blocks to support growth and tissue repair, and by delivering the nutrients necessary to keep our metabolic systems running smoothly.

The components of food that supply calories primarily consist of three elements: carbon, oxygen, and hydrogen. Carbohydrates and fat are composed of these elements. Protein is composed of these three plus nitrogen and sulfur, which sets it apart from other nutrients in the roles it plays.

When we eat food, the nutrients aren't immediately available.

But once we start chewing, our bodies' food-conversion mechanisms kick into action in a remarkable way. The diagram below demonstrates, for example, how the body might process a peanut butter and jelly sandwich. First, the protein, carbohydrate, fat, vitamins, and minerals must become separated by the process of digestion. The pipeline for food processing is called the gastrointestinal (GI) tract. The GI tract is a tube containing somewhat elastic muscles that in an adult would measure about 26 feet in length if stretched completely straight. But the GI tract is not straight; it is a twisted pipeline made up of pouches and tubes, including the mouth, esophagus, stomach, small intestine, and large intestine. Through the process of peristalsis (contractions) and digestion, food moves through the pipeline and is pulverized and lubricated so that it becomes finely divided and

How Food Moves Through the GI Tract

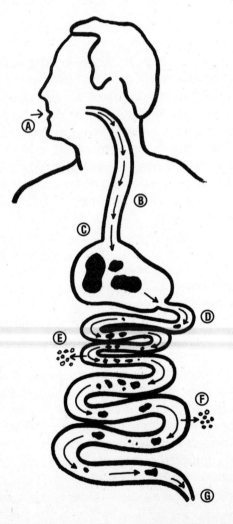

(A) Mouth: Chewing and saliva reduces food to a soft wad. Breakdown of carbohydrate begins.

(B) Esophagus: Muscles propel saliva-lubricated food down to stomach.

(C) Stomach: Stomach has about a 2-quart capacity. Food is churned into liquid mass. About every 20 seconds, some of this mass is released into the small intestine.

(D) Small intestine: Chemical activity breaks down protein, fat, carbohydrate.

(E) Nutrients now pass into the bloodstream to feed and fuel cells.

(F) Large Intestine: Beginning with the colon, water and salts pass into the bloodstream, leaving undigested waste for excretion.

(G) Anus: Exit for fecal waste. The entire process takes 1 to 2 days.

suspended in a watery, mushy solution. At various points in the digestive tract, hydrochloric acid from the stomach, bile from the liver, and enzymes from the mouth, stomach, pancreas, and small intestine are added.

The walls of parts of the GI tract are permeable, allowing nutrients to pass through them into the bloodstream. These nutrients consist of amino acids from protein, fatty acids from fats and oils, simple sugars from carbohydrates, and vitamins and minerals. As nutrients are absorbed, the bloodstream and lymphatic system transport them to the cells. But not all the material in food is absorbed. The nutrients the body needs to pass through the walls of the small intestine, and the waste material is passed on to the large intestine for excretion.

Each of the various food compounds has specific roles to play in our bodies. Once the various nutrients enter the cells, they go to work performing their unique functions, which are described in the following sections.

Protein: The Body Builder

We need dietary protein to provide and replenish the protein that is the structural core of the human body. Protein can accurately be called "the stuff of life," as it is at work in every cell of the body. In fact, about one-fifth of our total weight is protein—one-half of it in muscle, one-fifth in bone and cartilage, one-tenth in skin, and the rest in other tissues and body fluids.

Protein performs the most important jobs in the body, including all three of the functions of nutrients:

◆ Protein is essential for growth and the repair and formation of new tissues.

◆ Proteins are the regulatory agents for our important body processes, because all enzymes and many hormones are proteins. They are useful in transporting nutrients and oxygen through the body. Because antibodies and other components of our immune system are proteins, they play a major role in fighting diseases.

◆ Protein is a source of energy.

The Makeup of Protein

Protein consists of a variety of nitrogen-containing compounds, called amino acids, that are linked together in different, genetically controlled sequences. There are 22 separate amino acids, and the sequence in which they appear in a protein defines its biological activity. For example, even though liver proteins are made of the same amino acids as muscle proteins, the different ways they are linked allows them to perform separate functions.

Chemically, amino acids are absorbed into the body and rebuilt into various proteins through what is called a peptide linkage. When you eat protein-containing foods, the digestive enzymes in the intestines—some of which come from the pancreas—break the proteins down, first into peptides (small groups of amino acids) and finally into amino acids. The amino acids are absorbed through the intestines, and the body then builds them up again, under genetic control, in the various sequences that define the functions they will serve.

Thirteen of the amino acids can be manufactured in the human body. But nine of the amino acids needed to make up the body's protein cannot. We must eat protein to supply these nine essential amino acids. If we don't, our bodies cannot function. That's why dietary protein is an essential nutrient.

The essential amino acids are histidine,

isoleucine, leucine, lysine, methionine, phenyl-alanine, threonine, tryptophan, and valine. The term "essential" is somewhat misleading. All of the amino acids are necessary for good health. But because the body doesn't produce these nine, they must be consumed in the foods we eat; they are an essential part of the human diet. If your diet lacks even one of these amino acids, you can't produce enough new protein, and you will suffer muscle and other tissue loss within a day or two. In addition, many of the amino acids support other body functions. For example, tryptophan is converted into the B vitamin niacin and into the neurotransmitter serotonin, which influences alertness and mood. Likewise, histidine is converted into his-tamine, a compound associated with allergic reactions. Methionine is involved in the synthe-sis of substances that affect the transport of fat from the liver.

Anyone who is even vaguely familiar with nutrition can list a wide variety of foods that are significant sources of protein. But not all pro-tein food sources are equal when it comes to supplying the nine essential amino acids. Because we must have adequate amounts of all nine of them, it is important to know the differ-ence between complete proteins and incom-plete proteins.

Complete proteins contain all nine essential amino acids in sufficient quantities. Incomplete proteins lack or have limited amounts of one or more of the essential amino acids; by them-selves, they cannot support the body's growth and maintenance.

In general, animal proteins are more com-plete than plant proteins. While the proteins in meat and other animal products are not exactly the same as the proteins in the human body, they are similar enough in composition that they're likely to provide essential amino acids in the ratios needed. However, don't assume that this is always the case. Gelatin, for example, is a particularly poor protein source; it lacks or has inadequate amounts of several essential amino acids.

Proteins from vegetable sources (which include grains and legumes) are usually incom-plete. By itself, a vegetable food that lacks or has insufficient quantities of one or more of the nine essential amino acids cannot adequately support the body's upkeep. However, it is pos-sible to combine incomplete proteins to make up a complete protein. Some incomplete pro-teins are "complementary," making up for one another's deficiencies by forming a complete protein when eaten within a few hours of each other or even in the same day.

Unfortunately, in many parts of the world, single grains that contain incomplete proteins are the primary protein source for the popula-tion. In some less developed countries, 70 per-cent of the protein consumed is derived from incomplete sources like wheat. However, it is rare that people eat only a single source of pro-tein; if there is adequate food, different grains can be combined with vegetables, legumes, and small amounts of animal products to create complete protein patterns. One good example is a meal pattern that has evolved in Latin America, where two complementary protein sources, rice and beans, are eaten together.

Protein deficiencies are rarely a problem for North Americans, who tend to consume a wide variety of foods. However, people who go on fad diets that emphasize one or two foods with incomplete proteins (such as rice) are putting themselves in danger.

Good Sources of Complete Protein

Animal products, which contain complete pro-teins, provide a major part of the nine essential amino acids in the American food supply. These include meat, fish, poultry, eggs, milk, and cheese. Of course, these foods are not sim-ply "pure" protein; they are rich sources of vita-mins and minerals and may also contain fat and cholesterol. You can benefit from the protein without consuming excessive amounts of fat

HIGH PROTEIN VEGETABLE COMBINATIONS

lentil soup with corn bread
rice and kidney bean casserole
peanut butter on whole-wheat bread
corn tortillas with pinto beans
vegetable-tofu stir fry over rice
navy bean and potato soup with rye bread
peanut and sesame seed snack mix
rice cakes with peanut butter
chile with a side of whole-wheat bread
chick peas or black-eyed peas with corn bread

Or Use Small Amounts of Animal Protein:

spaghetti with tomato meat sauce
shredded chicken or pork with stir-fried vegetables
cereal with low-fat milk
spinach salad sprinkled lightly with bacon and hard-cooked egg
vegetable clam chowder
bean tortillas with shredded cheese topping
meatless chili bean soup, topped with shredded cheese
baked potato with low-fat yogurt and chives
potato and egg salad
macaroni casserole with tuna or grated cheese
split pea soup with diced ham

and cholesterol, or too many calories, if you follow some of the practical guidelines that are discussed in other sections of this book.

Combining Incomplete Protein Sources

But what if you want to restrict your consumption of animal products? Does this necessarily mean that you will suffer protein deficiencies? Not necessarily, since you probably eat many complementary foods without even thinking about it. An incomplete protein source like corn, for example, is low in the amino acids tryptophan and lysine. Beans are high in tryptophan and lysine but low in methionine, which corn has in sufficient amounts. Therefore, if your diet includes both corn and beans, it con-

tains all the essential amino acids. On the other hand, soy beans and many nuts contain all the essential amino acids. We now have available isolated soy protein concentrates that are as complete as the best animal proteins.

You can also create a high-quality protein meal by adding a very small quantity of an animal food to an incomplete protein. For example, cereal with milk or spaghetti with a little ground beef or grated cheese will supply the essential amino acids in the necessary quantities.

(Note that fresh, dry, or sprouted kidney, navy, pinto, and soy beans contain substances that can interfere with the digestion of proteins. To be on the safe side, make sure that these and other dried beans are thoroughly cooked—heat deactivates the inhibitors and helps deactivate flatulence, too.)

How Much Protein Do We Need?

Anyone who has access to and consumes a variety of foods shouldn't have a protein deficiency. And, although it has been suggested that North Americans consume too much protein, few people suffer from too much protein. The exceptions are people who deliberately choose a diet very high in protein or those who, because of kidney and liver problems, should restrict the amount of protein that they eat. In fact, because our bodies store very limited amounts of protein, we need to eat it every day to prevent muscle breakdown and lapses in other bodily functions.

Many Americans, however, have inflated views of how much protein they need. This misconception is reinforced by high-protein diets that are advertised as providing special benefits. For example, one currently popular diet theory states that the amino acid tryptophan converts to an alertness-related neurotransmitter, so animal protein should be eaten in abundance when we need to stay alert.

◆ NUTRITION QUIZ ◆
Do You Know the Truth About Protein?

Most people know that protein is essential, but there are many misconceptions about how much the body needs and what are the best sources. Take this true-or-false quiz to see if you know the facts.

1. Most Americans eat more than enough protein.

2. Proteins that come from animals contain all the essential amino acids the body needs.

3. As adults age, they require less protein.

4. High-protein diets are not recommended for the obese.

5. Red meats are better protein sources than poultry or fish.

6. Athletes need significantly more protein than nonathletes.

ANSWERS

1. True. Most Americans consume much more than their requirement for protein. For example, the RDA for a 130-pound woman is easily met by eating three ounces of lean meat, one slice of bread, one-half cup of cottage cheese, and 1 cup of milk.

2. True. Animal proteins are considered "complete," meaning that they contain the needed amounts of the nine essential amino acids your body must get from food. Vegetables, particularly grains, are not complete sources of protein; they lack essential amino acids or do not contain them in sufficient quantities to meet your body's needs. Only by eating a variety of complementary vegetables (e.g., rice and beans) can you receive a complete protein source.

3. False. Current thinking is that the RDA for protein remains the same on a weight basis throughout adulthood. Some investigators think that because of changes in the body's efficiency in using protein, the elderly might require more—and recent studies support the claim that the protein RDA for the elderly is low. However, because calorie needs decrease as we age, it is wise for the elderly to select low-fat sources of protein.

4. False. High-protein, low-carbohydrate, very low-calorie diets can be effective for weight loss in obese people (those who are approximately 25 percent or more above their normal weight range). After an initial water loss, significant amounts of fat are also lost. However, these diets can be hazardous and are recommended only for people whose obesity places them at high risk for heart disease or Type II diabetes. And they should always be undertaken with medical supervision.

5. False. Red meats tend to be higher in fat, so the percentage of protein on an ounce-for-ounce basis is lower than in fish or poultry.

6. False. Although an athlete may need slightly more protein during the initial stages of training or competition, that need is not very great. Because most Americans already consume more than enough protein, chances are the increased need has already been met by a normal diet.

Another popular notion is that because protein is needed for the development of muscle, a high-protein diet will make a person muscular. These ideas are unproven, or at least gross oversimplifications that can lead to trouble when people take them literally. As eagerly as we might seek "magical" effects from food, the simple fact remains that only by eating a balanced variety of foods can we get all the nutrients we need in the amounts we need them.

In fact, consuming an overabundance of protein can be expensive and inefficient. Our bodies are not able to store the amino acids they can't use, so the excess is used either for energy or converted to fat. Consider, too, that the waste products from excess protein metabolism are lost in the urine. Overconsumption can place a strain on the kidneys. Furthermore, the fat and cholesterol content of many high-protein foods can place you at risk for heart disease if you eat too much of them.

The amount of protein most people need is approximately 8 or 9 percent of their total calories, with needs being highest during periods of growth, such as childhood. For women who are pregnant or lactating, they are even higher. Americans consume an average of 12 to 14 percent of their calories in protein, yet we could eat even more—say, 20 percent—and still be healthy.

As we've pointed out, most Americans, if they have access to a variety of foods, don't have to worry about not getting enough protein. However, if you are concerned, it is easy to calculate your individual protein requirement by weight. If you look at the breakdowns of Recommended Dietary Allowances (RDAs) in Chapter 7, you will find guidelines that cover 18 standard profiles. These guidelines aren't meant to be taken as rules. But they're useful in determining the general range of nutrients appropriate for a person of your age or special circumstances.

If you want to develop an even more personal version of your daily protein requirement, here's how: The current recommendation for adults over the age of 19 is 0.8 of a gram of protein per kilogram of body weight. (A kilogram is equal to 2.2 pounds.) By making the following calculations, a 130-pound adult woman can estimate her daily protein requirement:

130 pounds ÷ 2.2 = 59 kilograms

59 kilograms ¥ 0.8 grams = 47 grams of protein

47 grams ¥ 4 (calories per gram) = 188 calories

Note that this is only a few grams different from the RDA. It can easily be met within the structure of a normal diet. But counting protein grams isn't a simple matter of weighing high-protein foods, because they contain other components as well. Get into the habit of reading labels to familiarize yourself with the protein content of common foods. And be aware that few foods are perfect sources of the nutrients they provide. For example, a 3-ounce lean round cut of beef, broiled, has 179 calories, with 26 grams or 104 calories contributed by protein. Most of the remainder is fat and water, plus a variety of vitamins and minerals.

We provide the following breakdowns for those who are interested in calculating or who need, for specific health reasons, to calculate their intake more precisely. But we stress that, for most people, a general awareness of the content of various foods will provide the tools they need to formulate a well-balanced diet. It is hardly our suggestion that you carry a pocket calculator to count your grams of protein each day. As a matter of fact, failing to consume your requirement on occasion for a day or two will not have a long-term effect on your health. And most people don't have to worry about this at all.

THE PROTEIN CONTENT OF COMMON FOODS

Serving of Food	Grams of Protein
Meats	
ground beef, 3 oz. broiled	21
beef round bottom, 3 oz., broiled	25
beef tenderloin, 3 oz., broiled	22
ham, 3 oz., roasted	18
veal, 3 oz., round, broiled	23
Poultry	
chicken, 3.5 oz., roasted	27
turkey, 3.5 oz., roasted	28
capon, 3.5 oz., roasted	29
Seafood	
salmon, 3.5 oz., baked/broiled	27
halibut, 3.5 oz., broiled	21
mackerel, 3.5 oz., broiled	22
flounder, 3.5 oz., baked	30
bluefish, 3.5 oz., baked/broiled	26
tuna, 3.5 oz., canned in water	28
swordfish, 3.5 oz., broiled	28
scallops, 3.5 oz., steamed	18
Dairy Products	
milk, 1 cup, whole/low-fat/skim	8
buttermilk	8
yogurt, 8 oz., low-fat, plain	12
yogurt, 8 oz., low-fat, fruit	9
cheese, 1 oz., cheddar	7
cream cheese, 1 oz.	2
cottage cheese, cup, low-fat	15.5
eggs, 1 large, boiled	6

Source: U.S. Department of Agriculture (figures are approximate).

2

Carbohydrates: Our Nutrient Staple

Many Americans born after World War II grew up believing that protein was the equivalent of dietary manna, while carbohydrates were secondary to health. In fact, for some time, carbohydrate foods were widely believed to be leading culprits in excess weight gain. Fortunately, as consumer education about nutrition has grown, Americans have opened their eyes to the benefits of many foods high in complex carbohydrates.

The Complex Carbohydrate Story

The most basic form of carbohydrate is that of the simple sugars, the most important of which are glucose, fructose, and galactose. Simple sugars are small compounds that have six carbons. In the same way that amino acids are the builiding blocks of protein, simple sugars are the building blocks of the complex carbohydrates (the starches).

Each simple sugar is called a monosaccharide. When it is chemically combined with another simple sugar, the result is a disaccharide. The most common disaccharide is ordinary table sugar, or sucrose, which is composed of one unit of glucose and one unit of fructose. Another disaccharide, maltose, is composed of two units of glucose. And lactose, the disaccharide found in milk, is composed of one part glucose and one part galactose.

When more than two glucose molecules are joined, they form a more complex carbohydrate called a polysaccharide. When they occur in plants, polysaccharides are known as starches; in animals, they are called glycogens. Polysaccharides are the form in which plants and animals store carbohydrate energy. They contain anywhere from 300 to 1,000 glucose units linked together, and it is the nature of the links that determines whether a polysaccharide is starch or glycogen.

The Dietary Role of Carbohydrates

From a nutritional standpoint, plant starch is the most important source of complex carbohydrates. There is very little glycogen in animals, but there's a great deal of starch in plants.

When we eat complex carbohydrates, the

digestive enzymes in the mouth and intestines break down the polysaccharides into disaccharides and, ultimately, into glucose. It is glucose that is absorbed into the system and converted into energy.

If complex carbohydrates are broken down and absorbed as sugar, why are we so concerned about the importance of eating starch? Why not just eat glucose? Starch differs from simple sugars in a very important way. When we eat simple sugars—in sweets or in table sugar—these literally are "empty calories," because there's nothing else in the sugar. It doesn't carry other nutrients. If you eat a pound of hard candy, all you've eaten is sucrose. There are no vitamins or minerals. (Honey and brown sugar are not more healthful; those sources of sugar add almost negligible amounts of nutrients.) There's a big difference between eating a bowl of sugar and a bowl of rice, because when you eat rice you're also getting protein, minerals, and vitamins.

To illustrate, let's compare a small baked potato with an ounce of gum drops. Both contain about 100 calories, but they come in very different packages. The potato, rich in glucose in the form of starch, provides about one-half of the RDA for vitamin C, along with small amounts of protein, B vitamins, about six minerals, and fiber. The gum drops, whose glucose is contributed as the disaccharide sugar sucrose, supplies the same amount of energy (calories) but no other nutrients in significant amounts.

What about fruit, which contains the sweetest-tasting sugar, fructose? Fruit does not contain a substantial amount of complex carbohydrates, but that does not make it nutritionally undesireable. Because fruit is mostly water (91 percent of the edible part of a watermelon, for example, is water), its fructose concentration is relatively low and therefore does not drive up the number of calories or make the fruit taste overly sweet. And the fruit has fiber. Moreover, like starchy foods, many fruits come packed with vitamins A and C and contain some minerals.

Are Starchy Foods Fattening?

It used to be that if you wanted to lose a few pounds, you cut out bread, pasta, rice, and potatoes. But today these very foods (without the rich toppings) are considered to be the best foods to include in any diet. Starch has no more calories than protein—just four per gram. And, unlike some high-protein foods such as meat and dairy products, most starchy foods are almost fat free.

But there's another reason starch is good for weight control. It appears that the process of metabolizing carbohydrates uses more energy (calories) than metabolizing fat. Some research has shown that as many as 25 percent of the excess calories we take in as carbohydrates are used to convert the carbohydrates to body fat. This means that only about 75 percent of the extra carbohydrate calories are "added on" as body weight. By contrast, only 3 percent of excess fat calories are needed to convert dietary fat to body fat, and a full 97 percent of extra fat calories wind up "on the body."

How Much Carbohydrates Should We Eat?

Carbohydrates are abundant in our food supply. The many nutritional benefits of foods that contain them lead most health professionals to recommend that 50 to 60 percent of our calorie intake be contributed by carbohydrates, and that most of them be complex carbohydrates rather than simple sugars.

It wasn't very long ago that complex carbohydrates accounted for a large percentage of our daily diet. At the beginning of the twentieth century, Americans consumed 40 to 50 percent of their calories this way. But today complex carbohydrates make up only 20 to 25 percent of the average American's diet. The decrease is largely the result of our becoming more affluent. We have turned to relatively expensive animal foods, such as meat and poultry, for our protein and away from the less expensive carbohydrate-containing grains and legumes that once played a greater role in meeting our protein needs.

Good sources of complex carbohydrates include all vegetables, cereal, rice, bread, pasta, nuts and seeds, grains, and legumes. It is best to consume a variety of high-carbohydrate foods to ensure that you get adequate amounts of the vitamins and minerals you need.

Does Sugar Cause Problems?

There is ample evidence that humans are born with a "sweet tooth." In tests conducted with newborns, researchers sought to discover what their automatic, untrained response might be to various substances. When a drop of water was placed on the babies' tongues, they showed no response. A drop of sour substance caused them to scrunch up their faces. Salt made them cry. And when a drop of sugar was placed on the babies' tongues, their faces relaxed into a contented expression.

Sugar has been called the culprit for everything from heart disease to cancer to diabetes to hyperactivity in children. But some years ago, a panel of scientists at the Food and Drug Administration, known as the Sugar Task Force, concluded that sugar does not directly contribute to any health problems other than dental cavities.

The main concern we have about sugar is that its overconsumption can indirectly lead to other problems, such as obesity, and that it supplies no nutrients. A teaspoon of sugar used to sweeten a cup of coffee or tea contains only 16 calories and is relatively harmless. But when it is one of the main ingredients in a product such as soft drinks, candy, sugar-coated cereal, or ice cream, the picture changes. A 12-ounce can of sugar-sweetened soda, for instance, contains about 10 teaspoons of sugar, or 160 calories' worth. Sugar also contributes more than a fourth of the calories in a small slice of chocolate cake. Similarly, it takes about 4 teaspoons of sugar—totaling 64 calories—just to sweeten 1 ounce of chocolate, which is naturally bitter in taste. In other words, sugar can add a substantial number of calories to food. And these calories are "empty"—they supply nothing in the way of vitamins or minerals.

But that's not all. Many of the foods people like because of their sweet taste are also loaded with fat. For example, a number of popular candy bars are about 25 percent fat by weight.

So, although sugar is not an inherently bad food—and can even be good in proper moderation—it's appropriate to use caution in its consumption.

HAVE A HIGH-CARBOHYDRATE DAY

Statistics show that the average American consumes only 20 to 25 percent of his or her daily calories in the form of complex carbohydrates, only half the amount most health professionals recommend. This one-day menu adds up to about 1,800 calories, with 53 percent of them from complex carbohydrates, 30 percent from fat, and 17 percent from protein.

Food	Carbohydrates (grams)
Breakfast	
1 cup cornflakes	21.7
1 cup 2% milk	11.7
banana	13.4
1 slice whole-wheat toast	11.4
1 tsp polyunsaturated margarine	0
1 cup orange juice	12.9
Lunch	
roast beef sandwich, with	
2 oz. lean roast beef	0
2 slices rye bread	24.0
lettuce	0
medium tomato	1.8
1 tbsp mayonnaise	0.4
1 cup black bean soup	19.8
1 cup grapes	7.9

Food	Carbohydrates (grams)
Mid-afternoon snack	
1 medium apple	21.1
Dinner	
3 oz. baked, skinless chicken breast	0
2 pieces corn on the cob	44.6
1 cup cooked green beans	4.9
2 tsp polyunsaturated margarine	0
tossed salad, with 1 cup lettuce, and	
1 cup each of carrots, mushrooms,	
tomato, celery	7.2
1 tbsp French salad dressing	2.7
After-dinner snack	
2 oatmeal raisin cookies	17.8
1 cup 2% milk	11.7

3

Fiber:
A Dietary Bonus from Plants

It may surprise you to know that fiber is not a substance with nutritive value. The word "fiber" is used to describe a variety of substances in plant foods that may have no relationship to one another except for the fact that they are not digested. Fiber is not necessary for life and growth, but it does perform a useful role in the digestive process and may contribute other benefits.

Fiber comes in two forms. Water-insoluble fibers, which make up the structural parts of plant cell walls, include substances like cellulose, hemi-cellulose, and lignin, which are found primarily in whole-wheat products, wheat bran, and fruit and vegetable skins. Water-soluble fibers come primarily from fruits, vegetables, beans, and oats, and they include pectins and gum, some of which are extracted for use as food additives. All plant foods contain some combination of the various types of fiber. For example, fruits and vegetables contain cellulose as well as pectin; in general, fruits are higher in pectin, and vegetables have more cellulose.

Fiber's Problem-Solving Qualities

Because fiber is not necessary to human nutrition, what true benefits can it really have? There is very good evidence that fiber serves a number of problem-solving functions in the body:

◆ The chemical nature of fiber (especially the insoluble kind) enables it to pick up water, which adds bulk to the stool and enhances the transit time of undigested foods through the GI tract. There are several advantages to this. First, when you have soft, bulky stools, there is less trauma to the bowel. In the case of hemorrhoids (swollen, distended veins in the rectal area), the larger, softer stools that result from eating foods high in water-insoluble fiber (such as wheat bran) may lead to less strain during defecation.

◆ There is also evidence that fiber protects against a common condition in the GI tract called diverticulosis. This disease is characterized by pouches that develop in weak areas of the large intestine. It is believed that a low-fiber intake might increase the likelihood of this problem's developing because the muscles of the intestine become "out of shape" as a result of insufficient stimulation. Until recently, fiber was not recommended for people with diverticular disease. But now a high-fiber diet and sometimes coarse wheat bran are recommended to relieve the accompanying constipation. (However, a high-fiber diet is not advised for complicated cases in which there is intestinal bleeding, perforation, or abscess.)

◆ There is some evidence that certain types of fiber—namely those in fruits, vegetables, and oats—can decrease blood lipids (fats) and therefore reduce the risk of heart disease. Some studies have reported that the soluble fiber found in oat bran and dried beans is effective in lowering blood cholesterol. Several years ago, these studies received enormous unwarranted media coverage. And oat bran was being sold in all kinds of products, with heavy advertising promotions. We believe that oat fiber has a real anti-cholesterol effect, but it is a relatively small effect, and one would be foolish to think that oat bran or any other dietary component is the answer to cholesterol problems. Other studies have revealed that pectin and guar—a type of gum—can also reduce blood cholesterol.

Potential Benefits Still Being Researched

It appears that the health benefits of fiber may reach even further. However, these speculations are as yet based on limited data, and much more research must be done before scientific conclusions can be made. There are two areas of current speculation:

◆ *Diabetes aid.* Accumulating studies demonstrate that dietary fiber can improve the control of blood sugar and decrease insulin requirements for some people with diabetes. Some doctors have found that diets high in both fiber and complex carbohydrates can effectively lower blood sugar. This result can be achieved with many different fiber sources, including legumes, whole-grain products, fruits, and vegetables. Some people with Type II diabetes have been freed from oral medication and insulin injections altogether. However, not all doctors have had favorable results, and under no circumstances should a person with

diabetes try such a diet without medical supervision.

◆ *Cancer prevention.* Some studies suggest that cancer of the colon, which is one of the most common malignancies in the Western world, with a 50 percent mortality rate, may be related to a low intake of fiber. Cancer of this portion of the large intestine is virtually nonexistent in areas of the world where the dietary fiber intake is high.

Fiber is thought to protect against colon cancer by increasing the bulk of stools, thereby diluting potential cancer-causing agents. Fiber may also bind some carcinogens so that they're less available to cause damage. In addition, because fiber can move waste material through the intestines more quickly, it may give carcinogens less time to work.

The fiber–cancer connection has received a great deal of attention, but the data are still so scanty that it is premature to assume that there is a direct link. Because there is not valid scientific evidence about the effect of fiber in protecting against cancer, the Food and Drug Administration (FDA) will not allow food manufacturers to advertise their high-fiber products as being helpful in reducing the risk of cancer.

Can Fiber Aid Weight Loss?

Fiber's weight-reducing properties were first promoted by companies that marketed supplements containing guar gum and cellulose. Fiber, they suggested, provides bulk that makes you feel full faster and slows down the rate at which your stomach empties. Another theory holds that because high-fiber foods usually require more chewing, you'll eat more slowly, and therefore less.

There is some evidence that slower eaters actually do consume less in the long run. And high-fiber, low-calorie fruits and vegetables are good fillers, whose bulk may help you eat less of other foods. In these indirect ways, foods high in fiber may help some people who want to lose weight.

However, fiber supplements are another matter. Although researchers are studying the weight-control effects of fiber supplements containing guar and other substances, the FDA has no evidence that guar is safe or effective for long-term weight loss. Keep in mind that aside from the harmless small amounts of guar gum used as thickeners in some processed foods, guar is not present to any substantial degree in foods. It is not known what, if any, potential problems might arise from using it as a regular dietary supplement.

Even if the FDA deems guar-containing supplements safe, do not be misled by the extravagant claims of some promoters about fiber's near-magical weight-loss benefits. These supplements are just one more weight-loss gimmick. Rather than trying to "trick" yourself into not feeling hungry, you would be wiser to concentrate on creating a balanced diet of nutritious foods and enroll in a regular program of exercise.

Too Much of a Good Thing

It seems to be characteristic of the American temperament to embrace a nutrition concept with such enthusiasm that we go overboard. But it is not necessarily true that if a substance is good for us, more of it will be better. And this is the case with fiber.

Overconsumption of fiber-rich foods is hardly a problem for most Americans. The typical adult consumes only about 15 grams a day, far short of the National Cancer Institute's recommendation of 20 to 30 grams. But with the easy availability of fiber supplements, as well as packages of raw wheat and oat bran, you should be careful not to overdo it on these fiber products. Such profuse and concentrated doses may undercut the natural processes of the GI tract and interfere with your body's absorption of

important nutrients. Fiber has a binding effect on substances that pass into the intestines, and too much fiber may bind minerals such as calcium, iron, and zinc, causing them to be lost in the stool rather than absorbed into the bloodstream.

Too much fiber can also be harmful when large doses are taken without adequate amounts of liquids. Your intestines can become blocked with indigestible matter.

Finally, there is concern that some people (especially growing children and those with poor appetites) may fill up too fast when they consume fiber supplements or concentrated sources of fiber and, as a result, may eat less than they need of nutrient-rich foods.

We suggest that you depend on a variety of fiber-rich foods for your daily intake. To obtain the most accurate fiber figures, nutrition scientists at the Tufts University School of Medicine scrutinized the various ways of analyzing the fiber content of food and then chose from the best methods to devise a list of the fiber content of thousands of items. This state-of-the-art research base is now used in many studies.

Good Fiber Sources: Eat a Variety!

High-fiber foods include whole-grain breads, cereal, and pasta (including wheat, rye, and oat products); brown rice, fruits, and vegetables; dried beans (legumes); and nuts and seeds. Refined grain products are low in fiber because the fibrous grain husk is removed during processing.

Ounce for ounce, vegetables and fruits have less fiber than grains because of their high water content. And not all vegetables are high in fiber. Iceberg lettuce, for example, has very little fiber, whereas peas have a great deal. Following is a list of good fiber sources. We suggest that you get your daily fiber from several of these sources.

A WIDE VARIETY OF FIBER-RICH FOODS

Food	Serving	Fiber (grams)	Food	Serving	Fiber (grams)
Bread			Figs, dried	2	7.4
Bran muffin	1	4.0	Orange	1 medium	2.8
Cracked-wheat bread	2 slices	2.4	Pear	1 medium	4.0
Pumpernickel bread	2 slices	3.2	Raisins	5 tbsp	3.0
Whole-wheat bagel	1	2.7	Raspberries	1 cup	9.2
Whole-wheat bread	2 slices	3.2	**Vegetables/Legumes**		
Grains			Broccoli, cooked	1 cup	5.0
Barley, dry	1 oz.	2.1	Brussels sprouts, cooked	1 cup	5.0
Brown rice	1 cup	3.0	Corn, sweet, cooked	1 cup	4.7
Wheat bran	1 oz.	11.3	Green peas, cooked	1 cup	3.1
Cereals			Kidney beans, cooked	1 cup	9.7
All-Bran	1 oz.	8.5	Lentil beans, cooked	1 cup	9.0
Bran Buds	1 oz.	7.9	Lima beans, cooked	1 cup	7.4
100% Bran	1 oz.	8.4	Green peas, cooked	1 cup	5.0
Corn Bran	1 oz.	5.3	Pinto Beans, cooked	1 cup	8.9
Fruits			Spinach, cooked	1 cup	6.5
Apple	1 medium	3.2	String beans, raw	3 oz.	3.4
Banana	1 medium	3.0	**Nuts**		
Blueberries	1 cup	3.0	Almonds	1 oz.	5.0
Blackberries	1 cup	4.5	Peanuts	1 oz.	2.5
Cranberries	1 cup	4.0	Pecans	1 oz.	2.0

4

Fat:
Good News and Bad News

For most people, the word "fat" is associated with a number of negatives, especially heart disease and obesity. But, in itself, fat is not bad. It's a fundamental part of the body's structure and operation, as are protein and carbohydrates.

Actually, the word "fat" is a misnomer. The real term for body substances that won't dissolve in water is lipids. Technically, lipids are more than fats, although they are primarily fats. Lipids also include several hormones, sterols (one being cholesterol), waxes, and other substances.

Like carbohydrates, fats are composed of carbon, hydrogen, and oxygen, but their structure is different from that of carbohydrates. One very important difference is that fats contain much less oxygen in their molecules. The lower amount of oxygen in relation to carbon results in fats being a more concentrated source of energy. In effect, when the body burns fat it produces more than twice the number of calories than when it burns the same amount of protein or carbohydrate. That is why one gram of fat is equivalent to nine calories, whereas one gram of carbohydrate or protein is equivalent to only four calories.

How Fats Are Constructed

The chemical structure of fats starts with a framework of linked carbon atoms. To this framework, called glycerol, three fatty acids are attached. This structure is called a triglyceride. In fat, each carbon atom forms bonds with another carbon atom and usually with hydrogen or oxygen atoms. Many of the carbon atoms form bonds with two carbon and two hydrogen atoms.

◆ If no hydrogens are missing from the structure of a fatty acid, it is called saturated. Animal fats found in meat and dairy products are high in saturated fatty acids, as are plant oils such as coconut oil and palm oil.

◆ If one pair of hydrogens is missing from the structure of a fatty acid, it is called a monounsaturated fatty acid. Avocado fat and olive oils are mostly composed of these.

◆ If two or more pairs of hydrogens are missing from the structure of a fatty acid, it is called a polyunsaturated fatty acid. Most vegetable oils (including safflower and sunflower) and fish oils are composed of polyunsaturated fatty acids.

Our bodies have the capability to synthesize saturated fatty acids, but not certain important polyunsaturated fatty acids. For this reason, we must consume these polyunsaturated fatty acids in our diets. That's why they are called essential fatty acids and should account for no less than 2 percent of our daily calories to avoid a deficiency. However, most Americans don't have to worry about this.

Usually, higher levels are recommended because the consumption of these fats as replacements to saturated fats tends to lower blood cholesterol. Three fatty acids have been found to be most essential: linoleic, arachidonic, and linolenic. Of these, linoleic is most important, as the other two can be made from it. Linoleic acid is present in high quantities in corn, safflower, and soybean oils.

Essential fatty acids are necessary for maintaining healthy cell walls, for normal cholesterol metabolism, and in the formation of important cell regulators called prostaglandins, hormone-like compounds that are involved in a wide variety of functions, such as regulation of blood pressure and blood coagulation.

In our food supply, no fats and oils are completely composed of saturated, polyunsaturated, or monounsaturated fatty acids. Most contain all three in some ratio; it's the makeup of this ratio that makes a food "high in saturated fat" or "high in polyunsaturated fat." In the following table, common cooking oils are broken down to show the ratio of the fatty acids. Canola oil is the least saturated; coconut oil is the most saturated. (Note that the totals do not add up to 100 percent, because these items also contain small amounts of other substances.)

The Role of Fat in a Healthful Diet

Every body cell contains some form of lipid, and lipids perform critical roles in the body. They store energy, support the cell walls, and store or circulate the fat-soluble vitamins: A, D,

FATTY ACID BREAKDOWN OF COMMON OILS

	Saturated (%)	Monoun-saturated (%)	Polyun-saturated (%)
Coconut	87	6	2
Corn	13	24	59
Cottonseed	26	18	52
Olive	13	74	8
Palm	49	37	9
Palm Kernel	81	11	2
Peanut	17	46	32
Safflower	9	12	75
Sesame	14	40	42
Soybean	14	23	58
Sunflower	10	20	66

E, and K. For this reason, we need some fat in our diets, especially the polyunsaturated kind that the body can't make on its own. Fat is a necessary source of energy, and it also helps to make the foods we eat palatable. But it is widely believed that Americans consume too much fat.

Health officials have called for a reduction of all types of fat, especially saturated fat, in the American diet. Evidence supports the relationship between excessive fat intake and a number of chronic conditions:

◆ *Obesity.* Because fat sources usually contain little water and take up less volume than protein or carbohydrate, we can eat more fat without feeling full. And because of its chemical nature, fat contains more calories per gram than other foods. It also takes less energy to store excess fat calories as body fat than those that come from carbohydrates and protein. So it may be easier to get fat on a high-fat diet.

Obesity increases the risk for high blood pressure and consequently for stroke. It is also associated with an increase in blood cholesterol, which is associated with heart disease. In addition, obesity is a critical causal factor in Type II diabetes, the most common form of diabetes.

◆ *Cancer.* There is compelling evidence that certain kinds of cancer—specifically colon, bladder, breast, and prostate—are more prevalent in people who have high-fat diets.

◆ *Heart Disease.* There is an enormous amount of data to support the premise that a high intake of saturated fat raises blood cholesterol levels and increases the risk of heart disease. Saturated fat is highest in animal foods, and dietary cholesterol is found only in animal foods. Animal foods and hydrogenated processed foods are the major sources of saturated fat in the American diet.

Many authorities now suggest that, for most people, the maximum percentage of daily calories from fat should be 30 percent, with the bulk of these calories coming from unsaturated fats and not more than 10 percent of total daily calories coming from saturated fats. We have broken down the ratios for average diets in the accompanying table.

In general, the more liquid a fat is at room temperature, the less saturated it is. But what about nonliquid foods such as margarine that are made from vegetable oils high in polyunsaturated fatty acids? Many prepared foods are hydrogenated, a process that, in effect, hardens a liquid oil. If margarine were not hydrogenated or partially hydrogenated, it would be a puddle of liquid at room temperature. Unfortunately, hydrogenating makes a fat more saturated. Your best compromise is to choose margarines and similar products that list a liquid oil as the first ingredient. These are somewhat less saturated than those that list a hydrogenated or partially hydrogenated fat as the first ingredient.

The Trans Fatty Acid Controversy

Butter or margarine? It used to be an easy decision. Butter, made from animal fat, was saturated. Margarine, made from vegetable oils, was not—and therefore constituted a more healthful

RECOMMENDED DAILY FAT INTAKE

Daily Calories	Calories from Fat	Fat (grams)	Saturated Fat (grams)
1,000	300	33.3	11
1,200	360	40	13
1,500	450	50	17
1,800	540	60	20
2,000	600	66.6	22
2,500	750	83	28
3,000	900	100	33

choice. But recent research suggests that the matter may not be so cut and dried, after all.

The controversy went full throttle when epidemiologists at Harvard University's School of Public Health published an opinion paper in a scientific journal saying that a type of fat in many margarines is a significant contributor to heart disease risk—more significant than the saturated fat in butter and other animal products. This fat, technically known as trans fatty acids, is formed when liquid fats such as sunflower, safflower, or soybean oil are hardened via a process called hydrogenation. The physical structure of some of the polyunsaturated fatty acids becomes altered so that their effect on blood cholesterol is similar to that of saturated fatty acids.

The Harvard scientists postulated that trans fatty acids raise the blood levels of "bad" LDL cholesterol (low density lipoproteins), just as saturated fats do. But they also said that trans fatty acids might cause even more damage than saturated fat because they lower the "good" HDL cholesterol (high density lipoproteins) as well.

What's the real story? Should people stop eating margarine? Might butter actually be a more healthful choice? Not so fast, say most of the researchers in the field. According to Alice Lichtenstein, DSc., a Tufts heart disease researcher, the Harvard report has done a tremendous disservice to consumers by misrepresenting the facts. Although she acknowledges that trans fatty acids do raise blood cholesterol,

Dr. Lichtenstein cautions that the number of studies is quite small, and the studies do not unanimously show that trans fatty acids both raise LDL and lower HDL cholesterol. Furthermore, because trans fatty acids make up only about 2 percent of the calories most people consume (and only a small portion of the fatty acids in margarine), they are far less troublesome than saturated fats, which account for an estimated 15 percent of Americans' calories.

The bottom line is that concern about trans fatty acids should not send you back to butter. If you really want to curb the "bad" fat in your diet, concentrate on cutting down on saturated fats and where possible replacing margarine with mono- and polyunsaturated oils. And, instead of splitting hairs on which fat is better or worse, moderate your intake of all fats.

Trimmer Beef Is a Reality

In recent years, the warnings about highly saturated fat and cholesterol in beef have led to a steady decline in consumption—a fact that has finally hit home for beef producers and retailers. A number of steps have been instituted within the beef industry to make beef a leaner choice for the American consumer.

The search for leanness starts on the ranch, where many ranchers are cross-breeding their stock with cattle that are naturally lean or are importing genetically lean breeds from Europe. In addition, many ranchers now leave their cattle in the feedlot for shorter periods of time, resulting in less-fatty beef.

The efforts do not end on the ranch. At packing houses, supermarkets, and neighborhood meat stores, butchers are trimming away more of the "separable" fat—that is, the layer of fat surrounding the beef. The half inch or more of external fat that butchers once left on beef has been reduced to a quarter inch or less.

Manufacturers are experimenting with developing meat products that are lower in fat. For example, the Omaha, Nebraska–based ConAgra food firm introduced Healthy Choice Extra Lean Ground Beef, which contained only a fraction of the fat found in other varieties of ground beef—130 calories and 4 fat grams in a 4-ounce serving as opposed to 351 calories and 30 fat grams in regular ground beef. To achieve this result, ConAgra blends ground beef with a substance called LEANesse, a fat substitute prepared with oat flour. Upon heating, LEANesse changes into a gel that mimics the texture and mouth feel of fat.

In 1987, the U.S. Department of Agriculture (USDA) developed new beef labeling standards which required that beef labeled "lean" or "low fat" could not contain more than 10 percent fat by weight. "Leaner" or "light" meat, which once meant anything retailers wanted it to mean, now must contain less than 10 percent fat or be 25 percent lower than usual—the "usual" being an actual meat cut with which it can be compared. The exception to the grading system is ground beef. The USDA also changed the grade for leaner cuts from "good" to "select," hoping to give lean beef a classier name, especially given that the fattiest cuts are graded "choice." One new direction of research may permanently change the fat profile of our nation's meat supply. Biotechnology may enable meat producers to genetically alter the makeup of an animal to make it naturally leaner. The time is coming when, rather than being considered an impediment to a low-fat diet, beef might be one of the best sources of high-quality, low-fat protein.

5

The Two Faces
of Cholesterol

Cholesterol is a lipid, present in every cell, that is used by your body to make some very important things happen. For example, cholesterol contributes to the formation of sex hormones (estrogen and testosterone), skin oils, digestive juices (bile), vitamin D, and the sheaths that protect nerve endings. It is also necessary for the development of each cell and is an important component of the membranes that hold cells together. Cholesterol differs from fat in its carbon and hydrogen configuration. Our blood cholesterol levels are dependent in part on the dietary cholesterol we consume in food.

We don't need to consume cholesterol, as our bodies are capable of manufacturing all we need; our livers produce it at the rate of one to two grams each day, using acetate, a product derived from the metabolism of glucose, amino acids, and fats.

Cholesterol travels back and forth from liver to cells by way of the bloodstream. But because it cannot move through the bloodsteam on its own, it must be carried. The carriers of cholesterol are called lipoproteins.

Lipoproteins, produced in the liver from protein products, are distinguished by their density. One might view high-density lipoproteins (HDLs) as strong carriers that remove cholesterol from each cell and deliver it safely to the liver for processing. Low-density lipoproteins (LDLs) can't "grab" as much cholesterol from the cells, and, on the way to and from the liver, they tend to have "accidents" and drop cholesterol along the way. This is what distinguishes "good" HDL cholesterol, the kind processed in your liver, from "bad" LDL cholesterol, which is left behind in the blood vessels.

The cholesterol deposited in the blood vessels contributes to plaque formation. As plaque builds up, it hardens and closes off the arterial pathway (in other words, it causes a type of hardening of the arteries), slowing the flow of blood. If too much plaque builds up, the flow of blood can stop completely. In an artery that supplies blood to the heart, this can cause a heart attack. In an artery that supplies blood to the brain, it can cause a stroke.

What Happens to the Cholesterol We Eat?

Although we do not need to eat cholesterol, most of us do. Every food that comes from an animal contains some cholesterol, including eggs (one of the highest contributors), cheese, meat, milk, poultry, and fish. Plant foods and plant oils do not contain any cholesterol.

Some of the cholestrol we consume or synthesize is incorporated into cell structures, where it has essential functions. Some is converted into biologically important compounds such as sex hormones and vitamin D. Some is broken down metabolically or excreted in the bile through the intestines. And finally, cholesterol can be deposited in tissues, particularly in the arteries, where it represents a major health risk.

The High-Risk American Diet

Because Americans consume so much fat and dietary cholesterol, there is much concern among medical professionals and nutritionists about the risks associated with high cholesterol levels in the blood. In fact, heart disease is the leading cause of death among Americans. The National Institutes of Health reports that the average American currently consumes between 450 and 500 milligrams of dietary cholesterol per day, a great deal higher than the 300 milligram maximum recommended by the American Heart Association and other health agencies (see Chapter 18). Cholesterol-rich foods that raise total cholesterol levels include eggs, organ meats (such as liver), whole milk, cheese, ice cream, butter, and red meat. However, more than cholesterol itself, the real culprit is saturated fat. Cholesterol-containing foods are often high in saturated fat, and fat is even more important in raising total blood cholesterol levels than dietary cholesterol. Saturated fats decrease the body's ability to break down cholesterol.

Polyunsaturated fats are believed to lower cholesterol by increasing its excretion and breakdown and decreasing its synthesis in the liver. Polyunsaturated fats are highest in vegetable oils like safflower, sunflower, corn, soybean, and cottonseed.

Some researchers believe than monounsaturated fats are more healthful than polyunsaturated fats. Monounsaturated fats also may cut down the risk of hardening of the arteries. The foods that contribute the most monounsaturated fat to our diets are olive and canola oils.

But can you really count on diet to lower the risk of high blood cholesterol? Some people are able to lower their blood cholesterol to acceptable levels by changing their diets. The National Cholesterol Education Program recommends that this be done in two steps. Step one involves lowering one's intake of saturated fat to 8 to 10 percent of total calories, overall fat to 30 percent or less of total calories, and cholesterol to less than 300 milligrams per day. If this does not work, step two calls for a further reduction of saturated fat to 7 percent of daily calories and cholesterol to less than 200 milligrams per day. Weight reduction for overweight people helps lower cholesterol. Physical activity can help raise HDL levels, too.

Diet is always the first line of defense. If these methods don't work, however, drug therapy can be very effective. In a study coordinated by the Heart Disease Prevention Clinic in Minneapolis, scientists placed each of 100 people with moderately high blood cholesterol on a reduced-fat diet and a cholesterol-lowering drug (lovastatin), first separately and then at the same time. They found that lovastatin led to a 27 percent average drop in blood cholesterol while the low-fat diet resulted in only a 5 percent reduction. In addition, lovastatin lowered proportionately more LDL cholesterol, while diet simultaneously lowered both HDL and LDL.

Although the results of this study might seem discouraging for people who want to lower their cholesterol dietarily, keep in mind that it does not necessarily present a full picture. The diets of study participants were not supervised, and people might have been consuming higher-fat foods than they reported. Furthermore, they were not counseled about weight loss, which can lower blood cholesterol levels; or exercise, which raises HDL levels; or stress reduction, also believed to lower blood cholesterol.

It is true that some people need the help of

THE FAT AND CHOLESTEROL CONTENT OF COMMON FOODS

	Amount	Total Fat (grams)	Choles-terol (grams)		Amount	Total Fat (grams)	Choles-terol (grams)
Beef [1]				flounder fillet	3 oz./85 g	.68	41.0
well-marbled	3 oz./85 g	27.2	79.9	shrimp meat	3 oz./85 g	.65	127.5
lean cuts	3 oz./85 g	10.5	77.3	oysters	3 oz./85 g	.8	187.0
salami	1 slice	8.8	14.0	tuna in oil	3 oz./85 g	17.4	47.0
bologna	1 slice	6.5	13.0	tuna in water	3 oz./85 g	2.5	53.5
hot dog	1	16.8	22.0	**Milk**			
pot pie	8 oz./225 g	22.7	38.0	whole	1 cup/244 g	9.0	34.0
pork chop (without bone)	3 oz./85 g	13.1	75.0	2% fat	1 cup/246 g	4.9	22.0
ham	3 oz./85 g	22.6	48.0	1% fat	1 cup/246 g	2.5	15.0
sausage	2 oz./53 g	25.0	39.0	light cream	1 cup/240 g	49.4	158.0
Lamb				whipped cream	1 cup/60 g	22.0	51.0
leg	3 oz./85 g	13.8	55.3	**Cheese**			
Chicken				blue	1 oz./28 g	7.8	24.0
breast with skin	3 oz./90 g	4.5	74.0	cheddar	1 oz./28 g	9.0	28.0
skinless breast	3 oz./80 g	2.0	53.0	Swiss	1 oz./28 g	7.8	28.0
leg and skin	2 oz/53 g	3.3	47.0	American	1 oz./28 g	6.2	25.0
pot pie	8 oz./225 g	25.9	29.0	cottage, 1% fat	4 oz./112 g	10.8	92.0
Turkey				cottage, 2% fat	4 oz./112 g	42.8	192.0
skinless light meat	3 oz./85 g	1.2	51.0	**Eggs**			
skinless dark meat	3 oz./85 g	4.3	64.0	white	1 large	0.0	0.0
Seafood				yolk	1 large	30.6	213.0
cod fillet	3 oz./85 g	.25	42.5	**Fats**			
pink salmon	3 oz./85 g	3.10	29.8	butter	1 tbsp./14 g	11.3	35.0
				vegetable-oil margarine	1 tbsp./14 g	12.2	0.0

[1] Meats are trimmed and cooked

cholesterol-lowering drugs. But the average person can improve his or her cholesterol profile with diet.

The Niacin Controversy

The B vitamin known as niacin, or nicotinic acid, has received a good bit of publicity for its ability to lower cholesterol. It is important to note that in the studies in which niacin was shown to be effective, it was used as a drug under medically supervised conditions, some-times in combination with other drugs and therapies. Such use is a far cry from recommending that people purchase niacin supplements and treat themselves with high doses (a recommendation made in at least one well-known cholesterol-lowering diet program). Niacin toxicity, which can result with levels above the RDA, can have a number of troubling side effects. The most common is the so-called niacin flush—intense reddening and itching of the face and upper body. More severe side effects might include gastrointestinal problems, abnormal liver functioning, and elevated blood sugar levels.

Is There a Fish Oil Benefit?

Research still in the early stages suggests that fish oils, which contain omega-3 fatty acids, may lower blood triglycerides and ultimately lead to less plaque buildup in arteries.

The fat in fish is polyunsaturated (if it were saturated, it would harden in cold water), but fish oils are constructed differently from other polyunsaturated oils, their primary fatty acids being eicosapentaenoic acid (EPA) and docosahexaeonic acid (DHA), which have characteristics that are very different from those of plant oils.

Omega-3 fatty acids favor thin, less sticky platelets, increasing the time it takes blood to coagulate, with the result that the development of clots at the point of plaque buildup in the arteries may be avoided.

The caution to apply when considering any possible health benefits of fish oils is that the misuse of the oils can result in problems with excessive bleeding and anemia and may increase the possibility of stroke. It's harder for thin, "unsticky" blood to clot when it's supposed to.

It is probably healthful to eat moderate amounts of fish high in omega-3 fatty acids. Even if omega-3 fatty acids turn out to be less instrumental in lowering blood cholesterol than some believe them to be, fish is still an excellent source of protein and much lower in fat than other cholesterol-containing foods.

Fish and other marine foods that are good sources of omega-3 fatty acids include the following:

Albacore tuna	mussels
anchovies	pollock
bluefish	rainbow trout
clams	salmon
cod [1]	sardines [2]
crab	scallops
halibut [1]	striped bass
herring [1]	trout
lake trout	whiting
mackerel [2]	

[1]Because cod and halibut are good sources of omega-3 fatty acids, some people have assumed that consuming cod liver oil or halibut liver oil is a cheap and efficient way to get fish oils. But these products may contain high levels of vitamins A and D, which can be extremely toxic when consumed in large quantities.

[2]Often these fish are prepared in a manner that makes them high in sodium, saturated fat, and calories. Pickled herring is high in sodium and, when it's accompanied by sour cream, high in saturated fat and calories. Mackerel is often smoked and dried, making it high in sodium. And tuna and sardines are not always packed in fish oils; frequently, vegetable oils are used, increasing their fat and calorie content.

6

Vitamins and Minerals: Nature's Delicate Balance

Vitamins and minerals are a relatively new discovery. Until the beginning of the twentieth century, most medical experts believed that the only things necessary for a good diet were protein, fat, and carbohydrates. But in the 1890s, a series of studies suggested that there were other materials in food that were essential to health.

The first to be identified was vitamin B-1, the chemical composition of which included an amine. Consequently, in 1912, the word "vitamine" was coined, meaning "an amine necessary for life." As the years went by, it became obvious that there were many of these substances, that some were fat-soluble (absorbed with and stored in body fat), that others were water-soluble, and that most of them were not amines. Eventually, the "e" was dropped from the word, and these substances came to be known as vitamins.

There are 13 known vitamins, 9 water-soluble and 4 fat-soluble. They are organic compounds composed almost entirely of carbon, oxygen, and hydrogen, and they are essential in minute amounts for the normal functioning of the body.

Many people would be surprised to learn how little of the material in food consists of vitamins. For example, if you were to remove the water from the diet of an average adult, he or she would consume about one and one-third pounds of food each day. Of this amount, only about one-tenth of a gram (or 100 milligrams) would consist of vitamins. But their lack of weight should not imply a lack of importance, as we could not survive without vitamins in our diet.

While some scientists at the turn of the century were busy discovering the biological activities of vitamins, others were concentrating on unraveling the mysteries of minerals. The role of minerals in the diet is a vastly complex matter, and even today many things are not known. Early in the study of minerals it was determined that, because our bones are composed of calcium and phosphorus, those minerals needed to be in the diet. Similarly, there was early evidence of the need for minerals such as magnesium, sodium, and potassium. These became known as macrominerals. However, as investigators and their analytical equipment grew more sophisticated, it became clear that other minerals, such as iron and iodine, were needed in very small amounts in the diet; these became known as trace minerals.

Scientists are continuing to learn about the role vitamins and minerals play in the diet, how they interact with one another, and the potential they may have for reducing the risk of chronic disease. The Recommended Dietary Allowances (see Chapter 7) are based on what is currently known about our daily need for vitamins and minerals, in addition to protein.

Water-Soluble Vitamins

There are nine water-soluble vitamins—eight B vitamins and vitamin C. In the preparation of foods, some water-soluble vitamins can easily be washed away or destroyed by light and heat. In the body, most are not stored very well and need to be replenished frequently.

You might be perplexed by the way in which the B vitamins are identified. Why is there B-1, B-2, B-6, and B-12, but no B vitamins with intermediate numbers? The numbering system resulted from the way the B vitamins were discovered. At various times during the first half of the twentieth century there were reports of materials that were given numbers like B-7 and B-8. But more careful study revealed that the substances either were not vitamins or that the researchers were looking at compounds that had already been identified and given a number or name. In recent years, there have been unscientific claims that substances like pangamic acid and laetrile were B vitamins. But neither of these materials is a vitamin, nor is either a medication with any demonstrable value.

Vitamin B-1 (Thiamin)

Thiamin is an essential dietary component. Because it is poorly stored in the body, deficiency symptoms will show up very quickly if it is not consumed.

The primary role of thiamin is to help convert carbohydrates into energy. It travels through the bloodstream to every part of the body. When thiamin is not present, the deficiency causes loss of energy, nerve damage, muscular weakness, and, in extreme cases, paralysis and heart failure. The severest form of thiamin deficiency, the disease beriberi, is rare in the United States except in chronic alcoholics.

Among the most important sources of thiamin is whole-wheat products, where the bran is retained. Pork, liver, and peas are also good sources. In addition, many flour and grain products in the United States are fortified with thiamin, along with other vitamins and minerals.

Food must be stored and prepared properly in order to maintain thiamin levels. Thiamin is sensitive to heat and, like some other water-soluble vitamins, is easily leached out of the food and into cooking water.

Vitamin B-2 (Riboflavin)

Riboflavin is an essential nutrient that plays a role in a large number of enzyme interactions that are designed to convert the food we eat into energy. When it is absent from the diet, a variety of pathologic changes occur, causing dry, scaly skin, cracks on the lips and corners of the mouth, and extreme sensitivity of the eyes to light. In many animal species, chronic riboflavin deficiency leads to cataract formation.

Fortunately, riboflavin is abundantly available in the food supply—in meats, fish, whole-grain foods, milk products, vegetables, and legumes, as well as products fortified with B vitamins. Because it is rapidly destroyed with exposure to sunlight, these foods are best stored in a pantry, in bins, and, when perishable, in the refrigerator to avoid nutrient loss.

Niacin

The B vitamin called niacin (or, sometimes, B-3) is an essential nutrient that either must be present in the diet or formed in the body from the amino acid tryptophan, found in proteins. Like riboflavin, niacin helps living cells generate energy from food. Its nutritional value was discovered in 1938 when it was found to cure the deficiency disease known as pellagra. In advanced cases, pellagra leads to severe mental impairment, hallucinations, and delirium. It also causes inflamed mucus membranes, with swelling in the tongue and mouth, and diarrhea. In the 1930s, approximately 200,000 Americans a year suffered from pellagra, and about 10,000 of them died from it. It was most often seen in poor people on corn-based diets that were lacking both niacin from food as well as tryptophan.

In addition to the niacin that is formed from tryptophan, niacin is present in foods such as whole grains, milk products, and liver.

In supplement form, niacin is sometimes prescribed to lower blood cholesterol, and, for reasons hard to support scientifically, it has gained popularity as an energy and strength booster. In vitamin supplements and fortified food, niacin is usually provided in its derivative, niacinamide, when consumed in large doses. Unfortunately, its consumption does not affect blood cholesterol.

As previously mentioned, megadoses of niacin (that is, excessive consumption above RDA levels) can be dangerous, leading to liver damage, ulcers, and high blood sugar. Commonly, large doses of niacin also cause rashes and stinging sensations in the skin. As concern with high blood cholesterol has mounted, many people have taken it upon themselves to self-prescribe megadoses of niacin supplements, not realizing that in large doses vitamins like niacin become drugs with potentially dangerous side effects.

Vitamin B-6

Also called pyridoxine, vitamin B-6 is used by the body in protein metabolism, helping to synthesize amino acids and to break them down so they can be converted to other compounds or to energy. It is important in many diverse roles, including the synthesis of muscle protein, hemoglobin, insulin, and the antibodies necessary to defend the body against infection.

Acute vitamin B-6 deficiency, which rarely occurs in humans, is accompanied by convulsions and severe anemia.

Vitamin B-6 is available in a wide variety of common foods, including meats, fish, nuts, beans, whole-wheat products, and some fruits and vegetables.

Traditionally, it was believed that there was no danger of toxicity from B-6 because it was a water-soluble vitamin whose excess was thought to be excreted out of the body. But evidence in recent years shows that B-6 toxicity might be a problem. According to a report in the *New England Journal of Medicine*, large doses of vitamin B-6 may cause severe nervous dysfunction. Dr. Herbert Schaumburg and colleagues from 4 prestigious medical centers described the symptoms of 7 adults who had been taking large doses of vitamin B-6—from 2,000 to 6,000 milligrams—for periods ranging from 2 to 40 months. This amount exceeded the RDA for B-6 by 1,000 to 3,000 times. The symptoms that developed included unstable gait and numbness of the feet, which eventually became so severe that a cane had to be used for walking. With time, numbness in the hands also occurred, and there was an impairment in the sensations of touch and temperature, as well as joint position. The afflictions were so severe that four of the patients were considered to be seriously handicapped. But when the B-6 supplements were stopped, the symptoms subsided.

It is not known at what levels toxicity begins. However, as early as 1964 it was reported that the ingestion of 200 milligrams of vitamin B-6 per day for 33 days by healthy young men resulted in metabolic and physiologic abnormalities. Further, the men in the experiment became dependent on the vitamin at this dosage level, thus increasing their requirement for it.

More recently, scientists have reported the development of problems associated with high doses taken by women to relieve premenstrual symptoms. Although there is no firm scientific evidence that vitamin B-6 relieves Premenstrual Syndrome (PMS), its use in treatment became popular during the 1980s. Only one out of four well-controlled studies suggested a positive effect, and this was at relatively low levels. Vitamin B-6 is now being recommended as a treatment for carpal tunnel syndrome. But it's easy to overdose on the amounts available in a single pill. In the mid-1980s, researchers from the University of California School of Medicine, San Francisco, reported that 2 women experienced severe nervous system problems after taking 500 milligrams of B-6 daily, 1 for 8 months and the other for 2 years. One woman who consumed only 200 milligrams a day for 3 years had similar symptoms. Furthermore, 13 other people who consumed at least 2,000 milligrams daily all experienced neurological changes.

Folacin

The B vitamin called folacin, or folic acid, is required for DNA metabolism and plays an important role in genetic functions such as cell division and tissue growth. Folacin is also involved in the formation of hemoglobin in red blood cells.

Folacin is available in abundance in many foods, including liver, kidneys, dark-green leafy vegetables, fruits, and beans and peas. However, because folacin is easily destroyed by oxidation, the vitamin may be lost in the cooking and processing of foods.

Pregnant women need to be particularly attentive to getting their RDA of folacin because

GOOD B-6 SOURCES

bananas
cabbage
yeast
wheat bran
wheat germ
peppers
beef
liver
kidney

it is needed to produce the genetic material of cells. Absence of folacin can lead to anemia in pregnant women, miscarriage, and infants born with deformities. Some studies suggest that neural tube defects in babies may be related to poor folic acid metabolism of their mothers during pregnancy. There are currently about 2,500 infants born with spina bifida in the United States each year, caused by lack of this vitamin. Some experts in the U.S. Public Health Service now recommend that women of childbearing age consume twice the RDA of folic acid to prevent birth defects. However, suggestions that foods be fortified with folic acid have been opposed because of side effects. One problem is that folic acid can mask the anemia symptoms of a vitamin B-12 deficiency. There have been cases in which people taking large amounts of folic acid in supplement form did not exhibit the blood symptoms of a vitamin B-12 deficiency, so they first became aware of the vitamin B-12 lack when they developed severe neurological damage. New research has shown that as many as 3 in 10 senior citizens may be consuming inadequate amounts of folic acid, as well as of vitamins B-6 and B-12. An examination of 1,200 older adults at the Human Nutrition Research Center on Aging at Tufts University found that those who had low blood concentrations of folic acid, B-6, and B-12 tended to have high blood levels of the amino acid homocysteine, which has been associated with heart disease.

Vitamin B-12

Vitamin B-12 is also known as a cobalamin because it contains cobalt. Like folacin, B-12 is important for DNA metabolism. It also assists in red blood cell formation and maintenance of the central nervous system.

There are no plant food sources for vitamin B-12. However, certain microorganisms can make the vitamin, and this fact has formed the basis for the commercial production of B-12. Some fermented foods, such as soy sauce, miso,

GOOD FOLIC ACID SOURCES

green leafy vegetables
peas
oranges
carrots
eggs
bananas
avocado
whole wheat flour
yeast
liver

and tempeh, may have some vitamin B-12 that results from the action of microorganisms used in the fermentation process.

For certain people, consuming the required amounts of vitamin B-12 won't necessarily guarantee that they are absorbing enough of the vitamin. In order to absorb vitamin B-12, people need a substance, called intrinsic factor, that is produced by the lining of the stomach. Some people with congenital stomach abnormalities or who have experienced stomach surgery may not be able to produce intrinsic factor. It has also been discovered that one in five people over age sixty have less stomach acid and cannot fully absorb B-12. The result of vitamin B-12 deficiency is a disease called pernicious anemia, which is characterized by anemia followed by severe neurological abnormalities. It can be treated with periodic vitamin B-12 injections or vitamin B-12 capsules. (Other alleged benefits of vitamin B-12 injections as energy boosters are completely unsupported by scientific evidence.) Vitamin B-12 is abundant in many animal foods that are common in our diets, such as milk and milk products, eggs, and fish. Vitamin B-12 is also found in liver, kidney, and muscle meats.

There have been no reported cases of people suffering from vitamin B-12 toxicity. But this fact does not in any way lend validity to its use by injection as an energy booster. The average adult needs only 3 micrograms of the vitamin daily to maintain the required level, and there is no evidence that normally healthy people will benefit from greater amounts.

Pantothenic Acid and Biotin

Requirements for the B vitamins pantothenic acid and biotin have not been determined, because deficiencies have never been observed except in experimental settings. Pantothenic acid, which is essential for synthesizing and metabolizing fats and the formation of hormones and cholesterol, is widely distributed in plant and animal foods. Safe and adequate daily dietary ranges have been set for pantothenic acid at 4 to 7 milligrams, but there is little need to be concerned about deficiency if you're eating a relatively balanced diet.

Biotin aids in the formation of fatty acids and carbohydrate metabolism. In addition to being present in many of the same foods from which we receive the other B vitamins, biotin is also manufactured by microorganisms in our intestinal tracts. Safe and adequate daily dietary ranges have been set at 100 to 200 micrograms, but deficiency is very rare. There is an undigestable protein in egg white that binds biotin, making it unavailable, but unless one is consuming very large quantities of egg white, it is unlikely that its consumption will affect biotin needs.

Vitamin C: Ascorbic Acid

The function of vitamin C was first discovered in 1747 by a British physician, James Lind, who found that the bleeding gums, loose teeth, anemia, and skin hemorrhaging characteristic of scurvy could be eliminated by eating citrus fruits. Vitamin C was not actually extracted from fruits and vegetables until 1928; it was not synthesized in the laboratory until the 1930s. Only during the past twenty years, in the wake of a large number of health claims, has the market for vitamin C supplements emerged.

Scientists are not certain exactly how vitamin C works, but it is believed to be involved in the formation of collagen, a protein-based substance necessary for healthy bones, teeth, skin, and tendons.

Vitamin C also appears to play a role in the

◆ NUTRITION QUIZ ◆
Do You Know Your B's?

The B vitamins are essential to good health. Do you know how to maximize their potential? Take this test and find out.

1. The B vitamins are numbered up to twelve. But how many actually are there?
   a. 5   b. 8   c. 12   d. 20

2. True or false? Roasted, fried, and broiled meats retain more B vitamins than braised or stewed meats.

3. Which of the B vitamins is most readily destroyed in cooking?
   a. B-6   b. B-2   c. pantothenic acid   d. thiamin

4. Deficiency of which of the B vitamins causes anemia?
   a. riboflavin and biotin   b. niacin and pantothenic acid   c. folacin, B-12, and B-6

5. One of the best sources of B vitamins is
   a. organ meats   b. citrus fruit   c. yellow vegetables

6. True or false? Rice and flour are good sources of the B vitamins.

7. Women on oral contraceptives may need added
   a. thiamin   b. riboflavin   c. B-6   d. folacin

8. Strict vegetarians are likely to get too little
   a. biotin   b. B-12   c. niacin   d. thiamin

ANSWERS

1. (b) The eight are thiamin (B-1), riboflavin (B-2), niacin, B-6, folacin, B-12, pantothenic acid, and biotin. Food faddists have dubbed laetrile as B-17 and pangamic acid as B-15, but they are not vitamins, and health claims made about them are false.

2. (True) Also, meats cooked rare lose fewer B vitamins.

3. (d) Thiamin is the most fragile, followed by B-6 and pantothenic acid.

4. (c) B-12 deficiency creates pernicious anemia; deficiencies of folacin and B-6 also lead to anemia.

5. (a) Organ meats are one of the best sources of the vitamins—particularly liver and kidney.

6. (True) But because milling and polishing remove so much of the vitamins, flour and rice in the United States are usually enriched with thiamin, riboflavin, and niacin.

7. (Possibly all) But there are data indicating a need for additional B-6 and folacin.

8. (b) There is no vitamin B-12 in plant foods.

healing of wounds, resistance to infection, the metabolism of some amino acids and folic acid, and the body's ability to absorb iron properly.

Scurvy, the vitamin C deficiency disease, is rarely seen in the United States, except in infants who consume nothing but cow's milk or in alcoholics and elderly people who are malnourished. All you need to prevent scurvy is a scant 10 milligrams of vitamin C a day—the amount in one-sixth of an orange. The remaining vitamin C consumed contributes to the body's stored reserve of approximately 1,500 milligrams.

A variety of factors may alter the need for vitamin C. Cigarette smokers have been discovered to have low blood levels of vitamin C. For them, the requirement may be as much as 50 percent greater than for nonsmokers. Age and sex may also alter vitamin C absorption. Women appear to break down and absorb the vitamin differently from the way men do. In particular, women who take birth control pills may need more vitamin C, as well as more B-6 and folacin.

Vitamin C, which is present in semen in very high concentrations, seems to play a role in the development of DNA. Dads-to-be should get plenty of vitamin C and avoid unhealthful habits like smoking.

It has been shown that environmental stresses, such as work in a very hot climate, may increase vitamin C requirements. In one study, South Africans working in very hot mines needed considerably more than the RDA to maintain normal levels of the vitamin. But this is an extreme case—it does not imply that people need to increase vitamin C when the seasons change. In the United States, people usually consume more vitamin C–containing fruits, vegetables, and drinks during the summer months. Incidentally, single nutrient doses of vitamin C will not ward off head colds.

Vitamin C is concentrated in some foods, particularly fruits, vegetables, and some fortified foods such as fruit drinks. When you select foods for their vitamin C content, remember that their value can be greatly altered by the way they are processed, cooked, and stored. Vitamin

C is vulnerable to air and heat, and because it is water-soluble, it leaches out of food into cooking water. The best way to lock in the vitamin is to cover containers of juice and cut fruits and vegetables with lids, foil, or plastic wrap. Avoid premature chopping or paring, because the more surfaces that are exposed to air, and the longer they are exposed, the greater the loss of the vitamin. If possible, keep the skins intact on foods like potatoes and apples. And remember that the outer leaves of foods such as lettuce typically contain the most vitamin C.

There are some concerns associated with megadoses of vitamin C. Although the vitamin, at RDA levels, helps fight infection, high doses have been shown to interfere with the white blood cells' ability to kill bacteria. It can also interfere with the absorption of copper. Some people who megadose on the vitamin have suffered gastrointestinal side effects such as nausea and diarrhea.

Pregnant women who take vitamin C in excessive amounts may give birth to babies with unusually high vitamin C requirements, a condition known as "rebound scurvy." There have been incidents reported in which women who took more than 400 milligrams per day during pregnancy had babies who developed scurvy when they were fed normal amounts of the vitamin.

Vitamin C megadoses can obscure the results of some medical tests. People with diabetes who take high doses may get false negative results when the Testape method is used for measuring sugar in the urine. On the other hand, too much vitamin C can yield false positive results when the Clinitest method is used. Finally, megadoses of vitamin C can interfere with the drugs heparin and coumadin, both used to keep blood from clotting.

Fat-Soluble Vitamins

Four vitamins—A, D, E, and K—are fat-soluble, meaning they are not soluble in water. They are stored in the body's fat and are transported to cells by blood, often attached to proteins. Unlike water-soluble vitamins, they are not excreted in the urine but remain in the body until they are broken down. This increases the potential for toxicity, because it's easier for the body to build up stores of the fat-soluble vitamins.

Vitamin A

Vitamin A, or retinol, is needed for the maintenance of a wide variety of body cells. As a result, a deficiency of this vitamin results in abnormalities in the skin and in bone development and to problems in the respiratory, urogenital, and gastrointestinal tracts. Because many of the cell membranes that form a barrier against invasion by microorganisms rely on vitamin A for their structural integrity, its deficiency leaves people more susceptible to infection. Vitamin A also plays a special metabolic role in our vision, and its deficiency affects how well we see, particularly in the dark. Severe deficiency can even lead to blindness.

Studies conducted during the past few years suggest that the vitamin A precursor, beta-carotene, may play a role in diminishing the risk of some cancers, in particular lung cancer (see Chapter 20), as well as heart disease. Although the studies are promising, the connection has yet to be firmly established, and a recent study of Finns who smoked heavily was negative.

A number of animal foods are rich in vitamin A; these include cheese, eggs, butter, chicken, and liver. Plants don't contain vitamin A, but yellow, orange, and some dark-green leafy vegetables and fruits—such as carrots, cantaloupe, spinach, and broccoli—contain beta-carotene, which is converted to vitamin A in the body. Margarines and some other foods are fortified with vitamin A.

If you eat excessive amounts of carotene-rich foods, your skin can turn yellow, a condition that is harmless. However, taking doses of vitamin A itself in supplements that greatly exceed the RDA can be dangerous, because your body stores excessive amounts of the vitamin in your liver. In fact, the federal government has restricted the dosage allowed for vitamin A capsules. Symptoms of toxicity include fatigue, severe headaches, blurred vision, insomnia, loss of body hair, menstrual irregularities, skin rashes, and joint pain. In severe cases, excess consumption can lead to brain and nervous system damage, abnormal bone growth, and liver damage.

Vitamin D

Vitamin D is crucial in the formation of bones and teeth. The nutrient aids in the absorption and utilization of calcium. Vitamin D deficiency is manifested in children who have stunted bone growth, bone malformations (rickets), and malformed teeth. In adults, vitamin D deficiency, called osteomalacia, may lead to a tendency for bone fractures and muscle spasms.

For the majority of us, vitamin D–fortified milk is the most practical way to meet our dietary needs, although people who live in the South can easily get it from the sun. The few other foods that provide vitamin D are not usually consumed in great enough quantities. Sun exposure results in the formation of the vitamin in the skin; for many people it is the primary source of vitamin D.

Because vitamin D enhances the body's absorption and utilization of calcium, excessive amounts of vitamin D supplements may result in irreversible calcification of soft tissues. The pathological changes can be particularly serious if they occur in the heart, kidneys, or lungs. They can also worsen the condition of people suffering from osteoporosis.

Vitamin E

The exact nature of the function vitamin E plays in the body is still unclear. However, it is known to act as an antioxidant—that is, it protects other substances from destructive oxidative reactions. For example, oils or fats, particularly those that are polyunsaturated, are subject to oxidative changes that lead to rancidity. The same kind of chemical changes take place in body tissues, so vitamin E requirements are increased by the consumption of diets high in polyunsaturated fats. Fortunately, many of these fats are rich sources of the vitamin. Vitamin E also protects the walls of the red blood cells from becoming fragile. Thus, the vitamin appears to make the cell membranes more stable, and it prevents tissues from becoming damaged.

Most American diets meet the RDA for vitamin E because it is so widely distributed in foods. Some people who have deficiencies in their ability to absorb and digest fats (such as those with liver disease) may require supplements of vitamin E or other fat-soluble vitamins, even though their diets appear adequate. Some scientists are saying people should take 400 I.U. of vitamin E a day to protect them against chronic disease. But most people do not need vitamin E supplements, because the vitamin is abundant in vegetable oils, whole-grain products, wheat germ, liver, nuts, and leafy green vegetables.

In recent years, a number of health claims have been made concerning the value of vitamin E supplements as protectors against heart disease and cancer. And there have been new studies indicating that vitamin E might serve as a protection against some cancers or may enhance the immune response to certain diseases. However, in a 1994 published study of 29,000 male smokers in Finland, vitamin E did not seem to offer any protection against the development of lung cancer. And those who swallowed vitamin E supplements were more likely to die of a hemorrhagic stroke. The bottom line is that the value of taking single nutrient supplements is still uncertain.

Vitamin K

Vitamin K is essential for the synthesis of at least 4 of the 13 proteins needed to make blood

BEST BETS FOR BETA-CAROTENE

green and yellow vegetables
fruit
carrots
eggs
fortified dairy products
liver

clot. Without it, blood would fail to coagulate at the site of an injury, and the victim could bleed to death. Recent studies have examined the role of vitamin K and found it to be important in the metabolism of the amino acid glutamic acid, which affects bones and other tissues.

The RDA for vitamin K was established in 1989. Setting a dietary requirement for the vitamin was complicated by the fact that the vitamin is synthesized in large amounts by intestinal bacteria. Vitamin K–rich foods include dark-green leafy vegetables such as brussels sprouts, lettuce, broccoli, spinach and kale; liver; egg yolks; and herbal tea and green tea.

People taking antibiotics may be at risk for vitamin K deficiency because antibiotics can destroy the intestinal bacteria that produce it. The case for this likelihood was made in a report in the *Journal of the American Medical Association*. Researchers at a hospital in Galveston, Texas, discovered 42 patients on antibiotics who developed bleeding disorders, all of which were linked to a deficiency in vitamin K.

A variety of conditions may result in a malabsorption of vitamin K. As a result, surgeons and dentists usually do a medical history before operating or extracting teeth to determine if a patient is vitamin K–deficient. In some cases, blood clotting tests may be conducted.

Infants are particularly susceptible to vitamin K deficiency because their immature digestive tracts do not contain any of the vitamin K–producing bacteria, and breast milk is a poor source of the nutrient. For this reason, infants frequently receive an injection of vitamin K at birth.

◆ NUTRITION QUIZ ◆
Are You Vitamin C Savvy?

Have you learned how to separate fact from fiction about one of our most important nutrients? Take this test and find out.

1. Vitamin C megadoses are helpful in preventing, but not curing, the common cold. True or False?

2. Chemical vitamin C, made in a laboratory, is as effective as "natural" vitamin C, as extracted from rose hips. True or False?

3. Exercise increases the body's need for vitamin C. True or False?

4. It is harmless to take large doses of vitamin C because the body takes what it needs and excretes the rest. True or False?

5. Potatoes are a good source of vitamin C. True or False?

6. Vitamin C deficiency affects the ability of wounds to heal. True or False?

7. Men need more vitamin C than women. True or False?

ANSWERS

1. False. Despite repeated attempts, carefully controlled studies have not been able to demonstrate that vitamin C megadoses have any significant effect either in preventing or in curing the common cold. Although some studies have reported that the vitamin has a slight effect on decreasing the severity of cold symptoms, over-the-counter pharmaceuticals do a better job.

2. True. Vitamin C that has been extracted from a plant has exactly the same chemical structure as vitamin C that is chemically synthesized in a laboratory. The body cannot tell the difference between the two forms.

3. False. Exercise does not affect the body's requirement for vitamin C.

4. False. There are enough reports of harmful effects of megadosing to suggest a need for caution in consuming very large amounts of vitamin C or any other nutrient.

5. True. White potatoes, in particular, are a good source. One medium potato offers about one-third of the daily requirement for the vitamin. However, the more potatoes are whipped, the more vitamin C is lost.

6. True. The healing process involves many factors, one of them being proper nutrition, which includes vitamin C because it is necessary for the formation of collagen, a type of connective tissue. The need for vitamin C appears to increase significantly during recovery from surgery, injuries, and severe burns.

7. False. The RDA is the same for both men and women, under normal circumstances. Pregnant and lactating women need more.

In 1994 when former vice president Dan Quayle was hospitalized with a blood clot in his lungs, there was a question about whether or not the culprit was too *much* vitamin K–rich foods. However, diets rich in vitamin K won't cause blood clots in healthy people. There has to be something else going on—such as a cancerous tumor, a blood disorder, or an injury to a vein. It is true that vitamin K can somewhat hamper the effectiveness of anticoagulant medicines, but physicians and dietitians hardly ever recommend that blood clot patients eat less vitamin K–rich foods. Rather, they emphasize keeping the consumption of these foods consistent and similar to what is usually eaten at home so doctors can adjust the drug dosage accordingly.

The Truth About Antioxidants

Antioxidants are vitamins that are thought by some scientists to ward off diseases such as cancer, heart disease, cataracts, rheumatoid arthritis, and more. Scientists are heartened by the potential of vitamins C and E and beta-carotene and are aggressively studying their promise as disease fighters.

What is the theory behind antioxidants? Simply put, these substances fight against toxic compounds in the body that can injure cells. These compounds, called free radicals, can damage DNA and interfere with the body's immune response. Antioxidants eliminate free radicals.

Vitamins C and E and beta-carotene all work to deactivate free radicals. But they accomplish their tasks in different ways. For example, because vitamin C is water-soluble, it floats around in the watery inner part of the cells and takes care of free radicals in that area. Vitamin E, which is fat-soluble, stays within the fat-containing cell membranes that surround the cells. And beta-carotene appears to act in places that have what is called a low oxygen tension, such as the capillaries of muscle tissue.

Scientists are now investigating the potentially protective role of substances in plant foods called phytochemicals. Phytochemicals protect plants from sunlight, but they might also have beneficial effects for people. For example, a phytochemical in broccoli called sulforaphine has been shown to prevent breast cancer in laboratory animals. Similar tests have been done on substances in tomatoes and other plant foods.

It's a long way from laboratory studies to conclusions—not to mention the development of synthetic forms of phytochemicals. The best advice is still to find your antioxidants in food.

A number of epidemiological studies show that the consumption of diets high in antioxidants (which usually include lots of fruits and vegetables and are low in fat) is associated with lower incidences of cancer, heart disease, and other degenerative afflictions. That makes sense when you consider that free radicals harm DNA, which is essential in cell division and the transfer of genetic information. Antioxidants may play a role in preventing heart disease because LDL cholesterol undergoes oxidation in the blood vessel walls.

In recent years, there has been much publicity about antioxidants, and although there are promising results in early studies, full human trials have yet to be conducted. Nothing would please us more than to be able to report that a large dose of one or several nutrients would confer major health benefits. But before we can safely do that, several standards must be met:

◆ The supplement must be proven effective.

◆ There is no danger of toxicity or other ill effects.

◆ The appropriate dose has been determined.

None of these conditions has been met for antioxidants. Instead, the results of promising early research have been distorted—by scientists, the media, and those who have economic interests in the sale of antioxidants. The result has been public confusion.

For good reason, people have grown cynical about health claims that offer more than they deliver. They need to know that the process of scientific study is slow and careful, and it may be some time before we understand the full effects of antioxidants. In the meantime, there are plenty of nutritious dietary ways to get your vitamins C and E, and beta-carotene.

For more information on the potential role of antioxidants in cancer prevention, and for a list of antioxidant foods, see Chapter 20.

Macrominerals

Minerals are inorganic dietary elements that are necessary for health. Some are required in relatively large amounts (called macrominerals) and some in smaller quantities (called trace minerals), but the amount required does not imply the degree of importance to the diet. They are all essential.

Three macrominerals have been found to be essential in established amounts and are included in the RDAs. These are calcium, magnesium, and phosphorus. Three others—potassium, sodium, and chloride—are also essential, functioning as agents that help maintain the body's fluid balance. But because requirements for these three minerals vary markedly under conditions that affect body-water loss (such as sweating), RDAs have not been established for them.

Calcium, magnesium, and phosphorus are complementary minerals that work together metabolically. In addition, each one performs particular functions in the body.

Calcium

Calcium is known to be essential for building bones and teeth and for maintaining bone strength. Much research has been done on the role of calcium in preventing bone loss, or osteoporosis, especially in women. Although the adult RDA is set at 800 milligrams, the requirement for youths is listed at 1,200 milligrams to support their growth. A special national task force has recommended 1,500 milligrams a day for some people, especially women.

However, large numbers of Americans do not consume even the RDA for calcium—particularly adults, and especially women over 50, who frequently consume less than half the RDA. Many people avoid calcium-rich dairy foods because of their high fat content, even though low-fat dairy products contain equally high levels of calcium. Strict vegetarians who have eliminated dairy products from their diets have few food sources for calcium, and supplements are often recommended to help them meet their daily requirements. Like other mineral nutrients, calcium in supplements always comes in combination with other chemicals, because pure minerals are often not chemically stable. The most common forms are calcium carbonate, calcium lactate, calcium gluconate, dicalcium phosphate, and oyster shell (basically calcium carbonate). Current evidence suggests that the body absorbs each of these almost equally well. They can be purchased in tablet, capsule, powder, or liquid form. However, not all are equal from a practical standpoint. For example, whereas calcium carbonate contains 40 percent calcium, calcium gluconate contains only 9 percent. And some natural sources like bone meal and dolomite may be contaminated with heavy metals like lead or mercury.

D. Mark Hegsted, M.D., visiting professor of nutritional biochemistry at Tufts and professor emeritus at Harvard University, has expressed the need for caution when fortifying foods with calcium, pointing out that there is still no final proof that a high-calcium diet can definitely prevent osteoporosis.

Epidemiologic studies show that in countries in which consumption of high-protein dairy products (and therefore calcium) is high, such as the United States and New Zealand, the incidence of hip fractures is greater than anywhere else in the world.

Further, recent studies indicate that, after menopause, even supplementation with high doses of the mineral (2,000 milligrams or more per day) may not be particularly effective in slowing bone loss. In fact, scientists report in the *New England Journal of Medicine* that, in the early years after menopause when the rate of bone loss is greatest, administration of the hormone estrogen may be much better at "saving" bone than large doses of calcium.

Several factors must be considered in discussing the calcium requirements of the elderly. One is that protein foods, which Americans consume in much higher quantities than they need, may cause an increase in the amount of calcium excreted in the urine, potentially affecting calcium requirements. Research has also shown that osteoporosis may be affected by heredity or related to a lack of weight-bearing exercise and is not a condition that can be avoided simply by consuming more calcium.

It is important to be educated about the various effects of available calcium supplements, because not all are equally advantageous. Calcium carbonate is the substance that contains the highest concentration of calcium. Sources of calcium carbonate include some antacids and ground oyster shells. The calcium in "natural" and synthetic forms are practically the same as in dietary supplements containing calcium carbonate.

Although it's true that the body needs small amounts of acid to absorb calcium, antacids taken in the recommended dosages will not upset the acid balance needed for absorption. A majority of over-the-counter antacids, such as Rolaids, DiGel, Maalox, Mylanta, and Gelusil, do not contain calcium carbonate. They contain aluminum instead. Dosages larger than the recommended limit can bind phosphorus and increase calcium excretion, increasing the risk for bone disease, especially for the elderly.

A number of calcium supplements come with other nutrients, in particular vitamin D, which is needed for the body properly to absorb and metabolize calcium. With these supplements, it is important to be sure that you don't exceed the RDA for vitamin D in order to satisfy the RDA for calcium, because an overdose of vitamin D has toxic side effects.

There may be negative effects for some people who consume large amounts of calcium. The use of large amounts of calcium supplements may increase the incidence of kidney stone disease. In one major study conducted at the Massachusetts General Hospital, it was found that about 5 percent of patients with kidney stone disease stopped making kidney stones when their calcium intakes were decreased. However, too *much* calcium is rarely a problem in American diets.

Phosphorus

Phosphorus is needed to build and strengthen bones and teeth and is also involved in the formation of genetic material, cell membranes, and many enzymes. It is very important in energy metabolism. It is not common for Americans to suffer phosphorus deficiencies because it is abundant in meats, and also because Americans consume large amounts of soft drinks that contain phosphoric acid. But the ratio of calcium to phosphorus in the diet is important to proper bone formation, and nutritionists are growing increasingly concerned about the declining ratio of calcium to phosphorus, particularly in the diets of American children, who consume large quantities of soft drinks, sometimes as a replacement for milk.

Phosphorus deficiency, which leads to bone pain, weakness, and appetite loss, can be caused by an overuse of antacids over a long period of time.

Magnesium

Magnesium, a component of many enzyme systems, is particularly important to the normal functioning of nerves and muscles. When inadequate amounts of magnesium are present in the diet, symptoms include weakness, muscle spasms, irregular heartbeat, and leg cramps. Ordinarily, magnesium deficiency is rare in healthy people, as magnesium is found in so many vegetables, grains, and legumes. However, alcoholics frequently appear deficient in this mineral. Because magnesium salts are often poorly absorbed, they act as cathartics, attracting water to the GI tract.

Many years of animal and human studies on the effects of magnesium have led scientists to conclude that relatively small amounts of the mineral will prevent most people with a history of recurrent calcium oxalate kidney stone disease from making new stones.

Sodium, Potassium, and Chloride

Many people think of sodium as a nonnutritious dietary element, but it's actually an essential mineral that acts, in combination with potassium and chloride, to maintain the balance of our body fluids. Sodium mainly operates in the fluid outside cells, and potassium mainly operates in the fluid inside cells. Recently, there have been several cases of seizures in sodium-deficient infants whose mothers fed them bottled water confusingly labeled so that it appeared to contain nutrients infants needed—including sodium.

Sodium cannot be stored or manufactured in the body and must be consumed in food. It is available in vegetables, animal foods, and some drinking water, and our bodily requirement of 200 milligrams a day is easily satisfied from these sources. However, the average American consumes less than one-half of his or her sodium this way. The remainder comes from the sodium compounds that are used as flavoring agents in processed foods, and to a lesser degree from table salt.

Excessive sodium intake upsets the fluid balance in the body and can cause a number of serious problems. One danger of too much sodium is that it draws water and potassium out of the cells, where it is needed to maintain the electrolyte balance.

A related effect of excessive sodium is a condition called edema, which is the collection of water in and around body tissues. Women have a tendency to retain sodium and suffer mild cases of edema prior to the start of their menstrual periods, and many pregnant women suffer from the condition.

For some people, especially the elderly, African Americans, and those already afflicted with high blood pressure (hypertension), sodium can be dangerous, as it is associated with high blood pressure. Sensitivity to salt seems to increase with age, which may help to explain why Americans' blood pressures tend to rise as they grow older. In the few societies in which very little salt is consumed, hypertension is rare, and blood pressure does not rise with age.

Even people who are not salt sensitive will show at least some blood pressure response to increased amounts of dietary salt. For those who are salt sensitive, the benefits of decreasing sodium in the diet can be tremendous. As a case in point, one-third of a group of hypertensives at Indiana University's Hypertension Research Center lowered the levels of sodium in their diets and in only seven months were able to cut down on the amount of blood pressure medication they required.

Nutritionists agree that, salt sensitive or not, most Americans could benefit from cutting down on the amount of salt they sprinkle on food and by limiting high-sodium processed foods, which account for 80 percent of our salt intake.

GOOD CALCIUM SOURCES

low-fat or non-fat milk
low-fat or non-fat cheese
low-fat or non-fat cottage cheese
low-fat or non-fat yogurt
sardines with bones
canned salmon with bones
spinach
soy beans
certain antacids like Tums

Trace Minerals

Trace minerals are crucial to health, serving as catalysts for many life-sustaining cellular processes. Yet only in the past 35 years have scientists begun to understand the metabolic function they play in humans.

There are 4 essential trace minerals for which RDAs have been established. They are iron, zinc, iodine, and selenium. The RDA for selenium was just established in 1989. There are 5 others for which RDAs have not yet been determined but that are known to be important and for which "safe and adequate" daily ranges of intake have been estimated. These are copper, manganese, fluoride, chromium, and molybdenum. At least 5 to 7 others are known to be needed in amounts that have not yet been quantified. No doubt these numbers will change as further research is conducted. Zinc was added to the RDAs as recently as 1974, and the 6 for which ranges have been given were included only in 1980. Scientists are still in the process of identifying and quantifying important trace minerals, and it is likely that new discoveries will be made in the coming years. For example, there is evidence that selenium and arsenic, clearly poisonous at high levels, are essential at small levels. And there even appears to be a need for minerals such as nickel and silicon, the latter being one of the most prevalent elements on the planet.

Because trace minerals find their way into so many different types of food, it might seem that Americans, who have such an abundant food supply, need not be concerned about getting sufficient amounts. What's more, each of us has built-in homeostatic biochemical mechanisms that, up to a point, make it possible to more efficiently absorb the minerals and other nutrients we consume when we are deficient in them. We are also somewhat protected from toxicity by our ability to store or excrete those we consume in greater quantities than we need.

Still, as researchers dig deeper into the questions of trace element nutrition, it is clear that our food sources and eating patterns are such that many of us are not eating adequate amounts of the trace minerals. There is much still to learn about how trace minerals interact with one another and with other nutrients to help maintain health and prevent disease.

However, it is important to remember that minerals, vitamins, and other nutrients do not operate independently of one another. It is not enough to concentrate on the intake of any one, because their proper functioning depends on maintaining the delicate balance among them.

Iron

Iron is absorbed through the intestines and picked up by the bloodstream. About 70 percent of the iron we absorb ends up in hemoglobin, a protein that releases oxygen to body cells for energy production and other metabolic functions and gives color to the red blood cells. About 4 percent of absorbed iron goes into myoglobin, another protein that transfers oxygen, specifically to muscle cells. Some of the remaining iron is involved in important cellular chemical reactions responsible for energy metabolism. The amount of iron that the body absorbs depends primarily on the type and source of iron consumed. The intestines increase or decrease absorption according to the body's need. People who are iron deficient may absorb 2 to 3 times as much iron as those who have adequate levels.

Long-term iron deficiency results in iron-deficiency anemia, a condition in which the blood hemoglobin levels drop and red blood cells become small and pale. The symptoms of iron deficiency usually appear slowly and can include fatigue, irritability, headaches, lack of energy, and tingling in the hands and feet. In some cases, a bizarre craving called pica leads people to consume dirt, clay, ice, laundry starch, and other nonfood substances.

Anemia impairs the ability to do physical and possibly mental work. In one study, when anemic tea pickers were given iron supplements, they were able to pick far more leaves per day. And another study showed that anemic workers, who were originally seen as lazy and unintelligent by their supervisors, came to be viewed as more motivated, bright, and productive after they were given iron supplements. It is now thought that iron deficiency leading to anemia may negatively affect learning ability and the ability to fight infection.

There are many food sources for iron, but it is absorbed more efficiently from some foods than from others. Iron is best absorbed from animal foods, such as beef, beef liver, chicken, tuna, and shrimp. This iron is known as heme iron.

Iron found in plant foods, such as dried beans, nuts, whole grains, and dried fruits, is called nonheme iron and is absorbed less efficiently. Iron that is added to processed foods is much like nonheme iron.

It should be noted that tea and coffee contain substances that inhibit iron absorption, and that eating a vitamin C–rich food at the same meal with iron will enhance the absorption of nonheme iron. Moreover, the presence of heme iron in the meal will enhance the absorption of nonheme iron. For example, the nonheme iron content of beans in a bowl of chili will be better assimilated if the chili also contains even a little ground beef.

Blood loss caused by a heavy menstrual flow, gastrointestinal disease, surgery, and too-frequent blood donations can result in iron deficiency. The iron problems of young women are not simply due to loss of menstrual blood. Iron deficiency in a young woman may stem from a combination of low iron intake, heavy menstrual periods, repeated dieting, and too much caffeine. Recent studies have shown that the average American woman consumes only about 60 percent of the RDA for iron.

Although deficiency, not toxicity, is usually the problem with iron, toxicity can be seen in some people who have a hereditary defect that causes their bodies to store too much and also in people who ingest too much iron in supplement form. Recently, there has been controversy surrounding a study of 2,000 middle-aged men in eastern Finland which suggested that high iron levels were associated with increased risk of heart attack. The risk was more than doubled for those with the highest measurements, helping to make iron stores a greater predictor of heart attack in the study than several well-accepted factors such as high blood cholesterol and high blood pressure. Overabundance of iron can also manifest itself in liver damage and damage to other tissues. In addition, excessive amounts of iron can reduce the body's ability to use other trace minerals. Again, however, iron toxicity is usually not a problem for Americans.

Zinc

Zinc is the second most abundant trace mineral in the body next to iron, and it serves a number of functions vital to life. It is involved in the breakdown and utilization of carbohydrates and the synthesis of proteins. It is also required for the replication of DNA, the genetic material that determines the function of every living cell. Zinc is necessary for normal growth and development in children. It is also important for the health of such diverse cells as those of the taste buds, the lining of the GI tract, the immune system, and the retina of the eye, as well as for the production of sperm and the male sex hormone testosterone. The exact way in which zinc functions has not been determined, but, in part, it exhibits its effects by being an essential component of a variety of enzymes involved in cellular reactions.

The absorption of zinc from foods is affected by its interaction with other trace minerals and by the existence of absorption-impairing substances in some foods—most specifically, whole-grain foods and some soy preparations. Zinc is found in rich supply in meats and poultry (especially the dark meat), oysters, eggs, and legumes.

Because available zinc stores are limited and it is continually being excreted from the body in feces, sweat, and urine, inadequate dietary intake over an extended period of time can result in a state of chronic deficiency. This deficiency was first delineated in rural areas of the Middle East, where it produced a syndrome of stunted growth and impaired sexual development in boys.

Other manifestations of severe zinc deficiency include loss of appetite, impaired mental ability, emotional disorders, tremors, a slowdown in the healing of wounds and burns, poor night vision, loss of a sense of taste, and pustular skin rashes on the arms, legs, mouth, and genital region. The effects of a mild deficiency are more subtle. In children, there might be a less extreme form of physical retardation. In adults, there might be a decline in male sperm count, combined with a reduction in the amount of testosterone produced; a higher level of blood ammonia, which is a toxic by-product of the breakdown of protein; and the inability to maintain a constant body weight.

Zinc deficiency is rare in America, but it can be serious during pregnancy, resulting in prolonged gestation and labor and creating risks to the fetus toward the end of pregnancy.

Several groups of people run a risk of zinc deficiency. Heavy drinkers often suffer zinc deficiency because alcohol speeds the rate at which zinc is lost from the body in the urine. Drinking alcohol is particularly hazardous during pregnancy because it not only enhances zinc excretion but also impairs the transport of zinc across the placenta to the developing fetus. Indeed, fetal alcohol syndrome—a cluster of birth defects that include mental retardation in the children of women who drink excessively during pregnancy—is in part linked to the depletion of zinc in fetal tissues.

Some athletes run the risk of zinc deficiency because of the large amounts of zinc that are excreted in sweat. Studies of male long-distance runners disclosed that their average blood level of zinc was 20 percent below the normal value.

The problem may be heightened by the fact that endurance athletes often eat large quantities of high-energy carbohydrate foods, such as fruit, yogurt, bread, and pasta, none of which contains much zinc.

Vegetarians have a difficult time satisfying the RDA for zinc when their diets lack any animal protein or dairy products. Fruits and vegetables do not contain much zinc, and, although whole-grain foods are good sources, they contain substances called phytates that bind the mineral and impede its absorption into the body. Soy products may also contain large amounts of phytates, as well as phosphorous-containing substances that impair zinc absorption. For this reason, even if a vegetarian consumes the RDA for zinc, it may not be sufficient.

Women who are breast-feeding may need zinc supplements to assure that their milk contains adequate amounts of the mineral.

Zinc is not very toxic unless it is taken in high doses. In one study, 11 healthy men who consumed 300 milligrams of zinc daily (20 times the RDA) were studied for 6 weeks. The results, published in the *Journal of the American Medical Association*, indicated that zinc at that dosage level impaired the function of white blood cells—the cells that fight infection. Moreover, the volunteers' blood levels of HDL cholesterol, the type believed to protect against heart disease, were lowered. LDL cholesterol, the kind that predisposes people to heart problems, was raised.

Selenium

Selenium was identified as an essential nutrient in the 1950s. Before that, selenium was believed to be toxic at any level. Now it is known that selenium is crucial for the proper functioning of the heart muscle and protects against toxic doses of the heavy metals cadmium, mercury, and silver. In addition, the data presented in some very preliminary studies suggest that selenium may help ward off certain

◆ NUTRITION QUIZ ◆
Are You Iron-Rich?

1. Do you regularly consume meats?

   Red meats are the best sources of heme iron, and animal protein facilitates the absorption of nonheme iron. Poultry and fish contain heme iron, but the amount is lower. Liver is one of the richest sources, but it is very high in cholesterol. You can diminish the calorie-fat-cholesterol toll on most iron-rich proteins by selecting lean cuts, removing visible fat, and broiling the meat.

2. Are fruits and vegetables among your food favorites?

   Consuming foods rich in vitamin C—citrus fruits and juices, dark-green vegetables, cauliflower, cabbage, tomatoes, cantaloupe, and strawberries—can substantially increase absorption of nonheme iron. But you must consume them at the same time you eat the iron-containing foods.

3. Do you look for enriched products when you buy processed foods?

   Many refined products are enriched to include iron. For example, almost all processed flours, baking mixes, and cereals have added iron. When purchasing these products, check the labels to find those that have the most.

4. Do you ever cook in iron pans?

   When you cook acidic foods—such as tomato sauce—in iron pans, some of the iron leaches into the food, providing an additional iron source for your diet.

5. Are you a coffee or tea drinker?

   When consumed with a meal, coffee can decrease iron absorption by as much as 39 percent; tea can decrease absorption by 87 percent. The culprit is not caffeine but other substances in the beverages. Poor iron absorption occurs only when coffee or tea are consumed along with the iron source. And one study showed that including vitamin C in the same meal helps improve iron absorption.

6. Are you a high-fiber eater?

   If you normally consume very little iron but consume very large quantities of high-fiber foods, the bran and substances in the fiber can interfere with the absorption of iron. If your diet is well rounded, with adequate amounts of both iron and fiber, this factor isn't important.

forms of cancer. However, it is easy to reach a toxic level of selenium. High levels of selenium may increase dental cavities and cause skin lesions.

In 1989, selenium was added to the Recommended Dietary Allowances for Americans. It is found naturally in fish, meat, breads, and cereal.

Iodine

Iodine is part of the hormone thyroxine, produced by the thyroid gland. This hormone is important in the regulation of the body's metabolism. The RDA for iodine is only 0.15 mg, a smaller quantity than the recommendation for every vitamin except B-12. It is amazing how biologically important such tiny amounts of some nutrients can be.

A deficiency in iodine results in goiter, an enlargement of the thyroid as it tries to accommodate for the deficiency. A chronic deficiency will result in the destruction of the gland. Infants born to mothers who have iodine deficiency sometimes suffer from cretinism, characterized by retarded growth and mental development, as well as a low metabolic rate. Cretins have protruding abdomens, swollen features, thick lips, and enlarged tongues.

For a variety of reasons, some people may produce excess thyroxine. The condition is serious and may be treated by drugs that lower thyroxine levels. In some cases, the treatment may be to destroy the thyroid by radioactive iodine, as was the case with First Lady Barbara Bush, or to remove the thyroid surgically. Fortunately, thyroxine is synthesized inexpensively, and people lacking the hormone can restore normal function when they're given thyroxine orally.

The primary natural source of iodine is seafood, especially saltwater fish.

There was a time when goiter was epidemic in the midwestern United States because the soil was deficient in iodine. Today, most table salt in the United States is iodized, and the deficiency is virtually nonexistent.

Copper

Although RDAs for copper have not yet been determined, a "safe and adequate" intake of the mineral has been set at 2 to 3 mg per day for adults.

Copper is needed for the synthesis of hemoglobin, a central component of red blood cells; the manufacture of collagen, a protein that helps make up connective tissue; and the maintenance of the protective sheath that surrounds nerve fibers. Copper is also essential for the proper functioning of the heart.

Some recent evidence indicates that just a slight copper deficiency may cause an elevation in blood cholesterol levels. One researcher who placed a man on a low-copper diet found that his cholesterol level rose from 206 to 235 after only a few months. The man's cholesterol dropped back down to 200 once he resumed eating a diet with an adequate amount of copper.

Copper is available in whole-grain foods, liver, kidney, oysters, and nuts.

Other Important Trace Minerals

The functions of several other trace minerals have been studied.

Fluoride was the subject of heated debate in recent decades, when scientists announced that it plays a role in preventing dental cavities. Fluoride deficiency leads to dental decay and bone loss, and it might even be related to osteoporosis. Today, most tap water in the United States has been fluoridated, with the result that many American children are growing up free of dental cavities.

It appears that a form of chromium, called trivalent chromium, in a complex containing niacin and some amino acids, assists the activity of the hormone insulin in regulating glucose and lipid metabolism. Chromium may also play a role in helping to solve medical problems related to diabetes and heart disease, and it may be involved in DNA and RNA metabolism.

Sources of chromium include meat, cheese, brewer's yeast, dried beans, and whole-grain products.

Manganese is involved in protein and energy metabolism and is essential for normal bone structure and the functioning of the nervous system. To date, manganese deficiency has never been observed in humans. Sources of manganese include legumes and whole grains.

Molybdenum has been found to be a component of several of the body's enzymes, and it too has never been found to be deficient in humans. Molybdenum occurs in meats, grains, and legumes.

Water: The Most Important Nutrient

You won't find water listed on nutrient charts, but everyone knows that humans can't live without it. In fact, although we can survive for extended periods of time without many vitamins and minerals, it takes only a few days without water to lead to death.

Water is a colorless compound of hydrogen and oxygen that virtually every cell in the body needs to survive; it contains no calories. Even tissues that are not thought of as "watery" contain large amounts of this substance. For instance, water makes up about three-fourths of the brain and muscles, and bone is more than one-fifth water. In all, water accounts for about one-half to two-thirds of the body's makeup. Men have more water than women per pound, because they have proportionately less fat, and fat tissue holds less water than lean tissue.

One of water's many essential tasks as a solvent and carrier is to transport nutrients and oxygen to all parts of the body through the blood and through the lymphatic systems. In addition, it plays an important role in maintaining body temperature; the heat released when we lose water through perspiration helps keep us cool. Water also removes metabolic waste by way of urine and sweat, lubricates the joints,

gives form to the cells, surrounds and protects a fetus, and serves as the medium for thousands of life-supporting chemical reactions that are constantly taking place inside our bodies.

The average adult consumes and excretes about two-and-a-half to three quarts of water each day. People who live in hot climates or whose jobs or hobbies involve strenuous physical exercise need to consume more. In many cases, thirst is a good indicator of when the body needs water. It is regulated by the sodium concentration in the blood; when the sodium level of blood rises, receptors in the brain's hypothalamus gland trigger a thirst sensation. In addition, "thirsty" blood draws water from the salivary glands, which accounts for the dry mouth. When there is a need for water, the kidneys excrete less urine.

But thirst cannot always be relied on as the perfect indicator of water requirements. It is possible to quench your thirst without putting back into your body the amount of water you need. That's the reason you're advised to drink 6 to 8 glasses of fluid every day, whether you're thirsty or not. This recommendation has special implications for the elderly, as they are less likely than younger people to get adequate thirst signals when their bodies need water. People who eat high-salt or high-protein diets have an increased need for water to maintain electrolyte balance and to help their kidneys flush out the excess salt and the waste products of protein metabolism. Drinking water past the point of thirst also reduces the risk of dehydration for people who live in extremely hot climates, as well as for athletes and laborers who sweat excessively. It's almost impossible to take in too much water, as the body is very efficient at getting rid of what it doesn't need.

Most of the water we consume comes from beverages, including juice, milk, and soft drinks. Coffee, tea, and alcoholic beverages also supply water, but these substances are diuretics and increase loss of water through the kidneys at the same time they replenish it.

Solid foods also contribute substantially to our

daily water intake. Most fruits are more than 80 percent water, and even foods that don't seem juicy or moist supply us with large amounts. For example, cooked lean beef is 60 percent water, bread is about one-third water, and butter is roughly 15 percent water. In addition, when foods are metabolized to provide energy, significant amounts of water are produced.

Is all water the same? Water is always composed of two parts hydrogen to one part oxygen, but the composition of the water we drink is affected by where it comes from and how it is processed. It can be hard or soft, carbonated or still, "natural" or "modified." The source of water might be buried deep within the earth's surface, or it might be a reservoir or pond. Because water is an excellent solvent, it often contains minerals.

Many people believe that bottled water is safer than tap water, and the subject is open to debate. Following are differences between the two.

Tap Water

Public water systems provide 90 percent of the American population with drinking water. Close to half of our municipal tap water comes from surface water, such as rivers and streams. The rest comes from groundwater, including wells, springs, and aquifers, which are areas of porous rock, sand, or gravel that are fed by rain and snow. In some regions the water is naturally hard, meaning it contains comparatively high concentrations of minerals, notably calcium and magnesium. Soft water has higher levels of sodium. You can find out how hard or soft your water is from your water utility.

Many people prefer soft water for a number of reasons. It makes soap lather better and leaves less of a ring around the tub. It also gets clothes cleaner. Some municipalities (and individuals) soften their water by removing calcium and magnesium and adding sodium, in what is known as an ion exchange process. From a nutritional standpoint, this practice has drawbacks. For one thing, our diets are already quite high in sodium and, although the levels in most water supplies don't add up to much, we don't need more, especially at the expense of minerals, like calcium and magnesium.

Water may pick up undesirable metals like lead from the pipes. Lead is more soluble in hot water than it is in cold water, so if you have a lead pipe problem, you should only use cold water for drinking and cooking, and run it awhile before use.

Along with the differences in mineral concentration, water has varying levels of heavy metals, microorganisms, and organic compounds. These must be filtered out (or, in the case of microorganisms, killed by disinfection) to the point where they do not endanger human health. The filtering process is nothing new; humans have been cleaning their drinking water for thousands of years. Pictures of water-clarifying apparatus have been found on Egyptian walls that date back to 1500 B.C., and a Sanskrit quotation from as early as 200 B.C. refers to appropriate methods for filtering water.

Concern for the purity of drinking water remains high today. The composition of water that comes out of the tap is regulated by state and local law and by the Environmental Protection Agency (EPA) under the provisions of the Safe Drinking Water Act of 1974, a law that sets minimum quality standards for drinking water. One of the agency's requirements is that tap water must be treated, if necessary, to prevent contamination from bacteria, ensuring against outbreaks of waterborne diseases. Several amendments to the Safe Drinking Water Act have strengthened the provisions for water filtering and have added provisions for better protection of our groundwater resources.

Much of the tap water in the United States is disinfected with chlorine. Although chlorine kills many bacteria, it has been found to react with organic compounds to form what are known as trihalomethanes, which are suspected of causing cancer or genetic mutations that promote cancer. For this reason, the EPA restricts

Check Your Vitamin-Mineral IQ

How much do you know about which foods are the best sources for the vitamins and minerals you need? Rate the following foods in order of their quality in providing nutrients: 1 = best source, 2 = medium source, 3 = least effective source.

FOR VITAMIN C
a. apple
b. grapefruit
c. banana

FOR IRON
a. cheddar cheese
b. round steak
c. cod

FOR VITAMIN A
a. corn
b. asparagus
c. broccoli

FOR CALCIUM
a. skim milk
b. whole milk
c. plain yogurt

FOR VITAMIN B-12
a. kidney beans
b. lentils
c. peas

FOR THIAMIN
a. enriched white rice
b. mashed potatoes
c. cooked tomatoes

FOR VITAMIN E
a. butter
b. shortening
c. corn oil

FOR POTASSIUM
   a.   grapefruit juice
   b.   tomato juice
   c.   grape juice

FOR ZINC
   a.   beef liver
   b.   chicken breast
   c.   ground beef

FOR RIBOFLAVIN
   a.   orange juice
   b.   whole milk
   c.   beer

ANSWERS

Vitamin C (b, c, a). Grapefruit is rich in vitamin C, as are all citrus fruits. Apple-a-day adherents might be surprised to learn that apples are not rich sources of the vitamin.

Iron (b, c, a). Red meats are high in the form of iron that is readily used by the body. Dairy products tend to be low in the mineral.

Vitamin A (c, b, a). Deep green and orange color should be your guide in selecting plant foods for vitamin A.

Calcium (all three foods are equally good sources of calcium). Low-fat dairy foods maintain as much calcium as whole-milk foods.

Vitamin B-12 (none of these foods offers vitamin B-12). It's available only from animal sources.

Thiamin (a, b, c). Enriched grain products and whole grains are good sources of thiamin.

Vitamin E (c, b, a). Vegetable oils are the best sources. Although shortening and margarine contain E, some of it is lost in the processing.

Potassium (b, a, c). Tomato juice is the richest in potassium, but each of these foods contains significant amounts of the mineral.

Zinc (a, c, b). Beef liver has far more zinc than the other two. All red meats are considered good sources of the mineral.

Riboflavin (b, a, c). Milk is the only good source listed.

the level of trihalomethanes in municipal drinking water to 0.10 mg per liter, or 100 parts per billion. Scientists believe that at that level or below, water is perfectly safe for humans.

The EPA has also set limits for many other contaminants that are found in drinking water, including mercury, nitrate, and silver, as well as pesticides and radioactivity. It is the responsibility of the water utilities to monitor the level of contaminants in the water and periodically report to the state or, in some cases, the federal government. If the water is deemed unsafe to drink, consumers must receive notification through the media and be given instructions on necessary precautions, such as boiling their water or using bottled water.

The Centers for Disease Contorl has recently recommended that people with weakened immune systems take special precautions with tap water to avoid parasite infection. People with HIV infection, cancer patients, and others may want to boil tap water, use filtration systems, or drink bottled water.

Should You Drink from the Well?

Recent warnings by the Environmental Protection Agency state that some 5 million Americans who drink water from private wells may be exposed to dangerously high levels of lead. The potential hazard stems from certain types of submersible well pumps—four-inch-round fixtures installed under water inside the well. These devices have fittings made of brass, a metal alloy consisting mainly of copper, zinc, and 2 to 7 percent lead. As the submerged pipes soak, the lead in the brass can leach into the water and contaminate it before it reaches the faucet.

Water circulated to homes via these pumps may contain as much as 770 parts per billion of lead—51 times the EPA's limit of 15 parts per billion. Pumps less than a year old are particularly hazardous because the brass releases the largest amounts of lead during the first year of use. Pumps made entirely of stainless steel and plastic pose no risk.

The EPA advises homeowners with submersible brass pumps to have their water tested for lead. The EPA's Safe Drinking Water Hotline (1-800-426-4791) provides information about local laboratories certified to test water.

The Fluoride Factor

It has been more than 50 years since Grand Rapids, Michigan, became the first town to fluoridate its water supply. Since then, it has been well established that fluoride helps strengthen teeth and prevent cavities, and fluoridation has been endorsed by several health organizations, including the American Dental Association and the American Medical Association. Yet many municipal water supplies remain unfluoridated. Part of the reason is the efforts of antifluoridation activisits, who use the nonsensical arguments that fluoride promotes cancer, sickle-cell anemia, and even AIDS.

It is true that dental fluorosis, a harmless, if unsightly, mottling of the teeth, has been seen in communities where the *naturally* occurring fluoride in the water is more than several parts per million. But when fluoride is *added* to water, it is in much lower concentrations, and children who live in areas where the water is fluoridated have many fewer cavities than those who don't.

Further, there is no evidence that properly fluoridated water is injurious to the public's health.

To find out if your tap water is fluoridated, you can contact your local water department or the state board of health. Based on the amount of fluoride in your water, your dentist should be able to tell you whether your child needs fluoride supplements. The American Dental Association recommends that in areas where the fluoridation concentration is less than 0.7 parts per million children be given fluoride supplements from birth to 13 years of age.

Bottled Water

Minimum standards for the quality of bottled water are set by the Food and Drug Administration (FDA) and match the standards set for municipal water supplies. There are several different types of bottled water.

◆ *Natural water* is water that has been unmodified by mineral addition or depletion.

◆ *Naturally sparkling water* has enough carbon dioxide to be bubbly without the introduction of outside chemicals.

◆ *Sparkling water* has been made effervescent by the injection of carbon dioxide from an outside source.

◆ *Spring water* naturally flows out of the earth at a particular spot and is bottled at or near its source. Like natural water, it is not altered by the addition or deletion of minerals.

◆ *Drinking water* is usually noncarbonated, or still. It is generally used as an alternative to tap water, although its sources might be the municipal water supply.

◆ *Purified water* has been demineralized. When it is vaporized and recondensed it is called distilled water.

◆ *Mineral water* is an imprecise term because, with the exception of purified and distilled, all water has minerals. According to the International Bottled Water Association, mineral water contains not less than 500 parts per million (about one-eighth teaspoon per quart) of total dissolved minerals.

◆ *Seltzer* is usually tap water that has been injected with carbon dioxide.

◆ *Club soda* is also artificially carbonated, but it contains added salts and minerals. The FDA regulates club soda, seltzer, and naturally sparkling water under the guidelines for soda water (like colas), not bottled water. Manufac-turers may add up to 0.02 percent caffeine and 0.5 percent alcohol by weight.

For more information on water and water safety, refer to Chapter 13.

Supplements: Separating Myth from Reality

Certain vitamin and mineral substances have been popularized as having near-magical qualities in preventing or curing disease, improving performance, or otherwise benefiting people, usually in higher than recommended dosages. It is easy to see why consumers might be attracted to the idea of popping a pill to eliminate stress, cure baldness, become more sexy, or protect against cancer.

What are the facts behind the many myths about supplement taking? How can you decide whether or not you need supplements? The first thing to consider is if you might be at risk for nutrient deficiencies that could warrant supplementation. Fortunately, most people in the United States get all the nutrients they need from the abundant food supply.

Several groups of people might need supplements.

◆ If you are frequently on a low-calorie diet, as are many women and adolescent girls, you may need a multivitamin/mineral supplement, particularly if your usual diet includes no more than 1,200 calories. In fact, government surveys have shown that many American women have low intakes of vitamins A, C, and B-6, calcium, iron, and magnesium. Because of menstrual losses, women also have difficulty obtaining enough dietary iron.

◆ Heavy smokers and drinkers may also have special needs. Regular smoking increases the need for vitamin C. In addition, heavy alcohol consumption can increase the need for vitamins B-6 and B-12, thiamin, riboflavin, and folic acid, as well as magnesium and zinc. The increased need of alcoholics is partly metabolic and partly because a large consumption of non-nutritive calories in the form of alcohol precludes the consumption of adequate amounts of nutritious foods.

◆ Because the physiological changes of pregnancy and lactation increase the need for a number of nutrients, pregnant or nursing mothers should ask their physicians about the possible need for a supplement. Many authorities believe that pregnant women need supplements of iron and folic acid. And if they don't eat well, a combination vitamin/mineral supplement may also be in order.

◆ Some elderly people don't get enough of the nutrients they need from food, because they can't physically get the food they need, can't financially afford it, are unable to prepare it, or don't absorb it well. Problems with chewing or swallowing, digestive disturbances, and medications can contribute to changes in an elderly person's appetite and eating habits that might also lead to nutrient deficiencies.

◆ Drug-nutrient interactions may lead to vitamin/mineral deficiencies. The risk is greater for people who have marginal diets or who have diseases or injuries that may increase nutrient needs. Both over-the-counter and prescription drugs can alter your nutritional requirements. If you take a lot of aspirin, for example, you may need more vitamin K. And the continuous use of antacids can increase the need for some minerals. Ask your physician or pharmacist whether there are drug-nutrient interactions with the medication you use regularly.

Even if you fall into any of these nutritionally risky categories, it is best to try to get your missing nutrients from natural food sources before you start taking supplements. But when considering supplements, the first rule of thumb is to avoid taking doses of isolated nutrients unless they have been prescribed for a specific medical reason. One possible exception is calcium, because multivitamin/mineral supplements do not supply much of this nutrient. But large amounts of some nutrients can upset the balance of other nutrients in the body. For example, too much vitamin C may interfere with copper metabolism, and calcium supplements may interfere with the normal absorption of iron. In addition, as we have seen, large doses of some nutrients can produce toxicity.

In selecting a supplement, the sensible guide is to choose a combination multivitamin/mineral supplement that contains a variety of vitamins and minerals in amounts no greater than 100 percent of the RDA. Because it is unlikely that your body needs more than that, the high-potency supplements are of little value.

Supplement labels express nutrient levels in two ways: One is a quantity measure—for example, milligrams (mg) or International Units (IU); the other is the percentage of the U.S. Recommended Daily Allowance (USRDA). Whereas Recommended Dietary Allowance (RDA) values vary according to sex, age, and certain circumstances, the USRDA generally represents the highest value for any group (see Chapter 7). However, the RDA, not the USRDA, is a more appropriate standard for children and pregnant and lactating women.

Don't be fooled into thinking that expensive supplements are best. Given two choices with the same nutrients, the less expensive one will meet your needs just as well. Added ingredients such as choline, inositol, and PABA only increase the cost. Except for people with special medical needs, there is no dietary need for them.

There are a number of prevailing myths regarding supplement use. Let's look at what they are and at the facts behind them.

Myth: Supplements are necessary because people's nutrient needs vary and the RDAs can't always account for individual needs.

The Facts: The RDAs do take individual variations into account. The Food and Nutrition

Board of the National Academy of Sciences sets the RDAs above actual requirements for most people so that the needs of all healthy people are satisfied, even those with larger than average requirements. The RDAs are designed not only to protect against deficiency diseases but also to allow nutrients to be stored in tissues. In effect, this provides insurance against periods of poor nutrition that many of us experience at one time or another in our lives.

Myth: Water-soluble vitamins must be replaced every day because they are not stored in the body.

The Facts: Although water-soluble vitamins are not retained in the body as long as fat-soluble vitamins, they are preserved in organs and tissues for weeks, months, and sometimes years, depending on the vitamin. If they weren't, there would be a high incidence of vitamin-deficiency disease in the United States, because many people go for short periods without consuming adequate amounts. Specifically, several weeks must go by without vitamin B-1 before symptoms of thiamin deficiency occur, and about 5 years of vitamin B-12 deprivation must pass before signs of a vitamin B-12 deficiency develop. Even symptoms of scurvy won't occur for about 16 weeks if a healthy person consumes no vitamin C.

Myth: Megadoses of vitamin C will prevent and cure colds.

The Facts: The notion that large doses of vitamin C can prevent or cure colds has been popular since Linus Pauling first published *Vitamin C and the Common Cold* in 1970. But scientific studies have not confirmed Dr. Pauling's assertions. For example, after pooling the data from 8 well-designed scientific studies on ascorbic acid and colds, Dr. Thomas C. Chalmers of New York's Mount Sinai Medical Center concluded in the *American Journal of Medicine* that people who took vitamin C rather than a placebo had only about one-tenth fewer colds per year. And

their colds lasted an average of one-tenth less time than those of people who took a placebo in place of a supplement.

Myth: If you're tired or run down, vitamin B-12 supplements will boost your energy.

The Facts: Some practitioners of vitamin therapy give vitamin B-12 shots to their patients, and many people report feeling more energetic as a result. However, there is no proof that B-12 can cure fatigue, except in cases of pernicious anemia. Most Americans have many years' worth of vitamin B-12 stored in their livers, so a vitamin B-12 shot or pill is like a drop in the river.

Myth: Zinc supplements will cure impotence or otherwise improve sexual performance.

The Facts: That zinc has been touted as a sexual aid probably stems from the finding that some adolescent boys in the Middle East suffered from stunted growth and arrested sexual development as a result of deficiency in the mineral. When the young men were given zinc supplements, they began to grow again and to mature sexually. But zinc deficiency and subsequent supplementation with that mineral have nothing to do with an otherwise healthy man's sexual potency.

Myth: Vegetarians need a variety of supplements to compensate for the absence of meat in their diets.

The Facts: According to Albert Sanchea, Ph.D., of Loma Linda University, an institution in southern California where much of the nation's research on vegetarianism is conducted, the supplement needs of vegetarians vary according to the regimen. People who avoid only red meat do not need supplements because poultry and fish provide all the nutrients that red meat does. Lacto-ovo vegetarians—those who avoid all meat, poultry, and fish but do eat dairy products and eggs—do not need supplements either. However, strict vegetarians, who do not eat any kind of dairy food, eggs, meat, poultry, or fish, should gauge the amount of vitamin B-12 they are consuming from foods fortified with B-12 and consult a qualified health professional about their need for supplements of this nutrient, as well as calcium, iron, and zinc.

Myth: People with drinking problems should take vitamin supplements to balance the negative effects of alcohol.

The Facts: Excessive amounts of alcohol are toxic to the liver, and the damage cannot be reversed by vitamin or mineral supplements. Although a supplement might supply some of the nutrients missing from the diets of people with drinking problems as well as some of the nutrients they are not absorbing properly, supplementation will ultimately prove meaningless if heavy alcohol consumption is continued.

Curbing Supplement Abuse

Annual sales of vitamin and mineral supplements have grown substantially during the past decade. Consumers spend billions of dollars each year on nutrients in the form of pills and foods that are overfortified with nutrients, a matter that has caused concern among physicians and scientists because megadoses of some of these substances can cause adverse side effects. Many people don't realize that taking high doses of nutrient supplements is a risky practice that can amount to a form of over-the-counter drug abuse.

The FDA is currently prohibited from setting upper limits on allowable levels of vitamins and minerals unless adverse effects can be clearly demonstrated. In the past, the agency has had no means of keeping track of adverse reactions. In fact, during the 1970s, in response to pressure from the supplement industry, health food stores, and private citizens, Congress prohibited the FDA from interfering with the sale or dosage regulation of supplements unless such negative reactions were proven. But as the nation's doctors begin to record their patients' use of supplements, more information is becoming available. Now doctors are encouraged to report adverse reactions to vitamin and mineral pills to the FDA, just as they do for drugs.

The practice of taking nutrients in pill form is becoming so widespread that four major health organizations—the American Dietetic Association, the American Institute of Nutrition, the American Society for Clinical Nutrition, and the National Council against Health Fraud—have issued a joint statement warning Americans about the unnecessary and sometimes unsafe use of vitamin and mineral supplements.

In 1986, a panel formed by the American Dietetic Association established initial guidelines about when supplement use turns to abuse. Panel members agreed that they saw no harm in taking daily multivitamin/mineral preparations that contained 100 percent of the RDA. However, they documented serious side effects from higher doses of certain nutrients. For example, vitamin A, if taken at a daily level of 25,000 IU—a level believed by many vitamin enthusiasts to be safe—may cause permanent liver damage after 7 to 10 years of use.

Recently, panic was created by the FDA's threat to issue a crackdown on vitamin and mineral supplements—making them available by prescription, limiting their potencies, and restricting access to proof about their potential health benefits. But the real intention of the FDA is to assure that supplements are held to the same standards of accuracy as food labels. For example, the FDA is concerned about supplements' sporting health claims for which there is scant or no scientific evidence.

The FDA's interest in supplement-label accuracy created a huge stir among supplement manufacturers, a number of whose labels make unproven and sometimes outlandish claims that their products can be used to treat everything from AIDS to baldness to impotence to epileptic seizures to cancer. To protect their vested interest, the supplement industry backed the formation of an organization called the National Health Alliance, which launched a campaign of scare tactics to fight the FDA. To date, the supplement lobby has effectively slowed down any congressional action, so for now labels remain untouched—whether they're accurate or not.

The best solution is to be an educated consumer. If you are in the habit of taking a multi-vitamin/mineral supplement containing RDA levels of nutrients every day, we wouldn't presume to tell you to stop taking it or to suggest that it doesn't really make you feel better. We would encourage you only to consider it a supplement, not a substitute, for the rich variety of vitamin- and mineral-packed foods available in the American diet.

7

The Recommended Dietary Allowances

The Recommended Dietary Allowances (RDAs) are standards that the federal government sets for the daily intake of various nutrients. They're considered to be adequate quantities for practically all healthy people.

The RDAs are based on the recommendation of the nutrition scientists who compose the Food and Nutrition Board of the National Academy of Sciences–National Research Council. They are defined as "the levels of intake of essential nutrients considered, in the judgment of the Food and Nutrition Board on the basis of available scientific knowledge, to be adequate to meet the known nutritional needs of practically all healthy persons." The RDAs are reestablished approximately every 5 years. The latest RDAs were published in 1989. As of this publication, revised RDAs are due.

To arrive at these recommendations, the Food and Nutrition Board appoints committees of scientists to review scientific literature from around the world on the nutrient requirements of people, paying particular attention to new findings since the last RDAs were published. The research they look at includes studies of individuals who are deficient in particular nutrients and those who are not. They also consider studies in which scientists have determined nutrient requirements in groups of people of different ages and sex.

From these and other studies, the committee can estimate the average daily requirement for each nutrient. Of course, people vary in their needs, so before the scientists come up with a final number, they increase the figures to account for the needs of people with high requirements. The figures also allow for the body's inefficient use of certain nutrients as they appear in particular foods; for example, the RDA for iron allows for the fact that only about 10 percent of the iron we eat is absorbed.

The RDA values for nutrients vary according to age and sex and are also altered for pregnant and breast-feeding women. In total, there are 15 different recommendations by age (2 for infants, 3 for children, 5 for males 11 years and older, and 5 for females 11 years and older), in addition to the 3 special categories of pregnant women, breast-feeding women in the first 6 months, and breast-feeding women in the second 6 months.

The nutrients for which RDAs exist are protein, most fat- and water-soluble vitamins, and 7 minerals. For most groupings, there is considered to be a "reference," or typical, person for whom recommendations are made. For example, the "reference" woman for ages 15 to 18 years is 5 feet, 4 inches tall and weighs 120 pounds. Obviously, not all women are this size. And some nutrient requirements, such as those for the B vitamins, depend on size.

The RDAs are not intended to be requirements; they are merely offered as guidelines for meeting the needs of most people. Common sense should be your guide as you review the RDAs. If you were to consume less than a particular nutrient's RDA for a day, a week, or even a month, you would probably do yourself no harm. However, the risk increases with time, depending on how much below the RDA you go, and the state of your stores of the nutrient. Also, many people safely consume more than the RDA, although the RDA committee states that its members have seen no evidence of benefits gained from overconsumption. In some cases, toxicity can result when consumption greatly exceeds the RDA, particularly for fat-soluble vitamins such as A and D. The most recent recommendations include the suggestion that cigarette smokers consume 100 mg per day of vitamin C.

What the RDAs Don't Cover

RDAs exist for nutrients when there are reliable, quantifiable data. But there are essential nutrients for which these data do not exist. For a number of vitamins and minerals, "safe and adequate" ranges have been devised by the RDA committee. These figures give the minimum amounts believed to prevent deficiencies and the maximum amounts believed to be needed and, in the case of potential toxicity, safe.

Another essential nutrient for which there is no RDA is water. It's difficult to specify an ideal amount because needs vary greatly according to climate, activity level, and the amount of salt consumed. In addition, certain illnesses and medications, as well as high-protein diets, can markedly increase the amount of water one

should drink. Fortunately, except for elderly people and athletes, thirst is usually a reliable indicator that the body's water level has fallen too low. (See Chapter 25 for further information on the nutritional needs of athletes and Chapter 17 for dietary guidelines for the elderly.)

Beside lacking numbers for various substances classified as "required" nutrients, the RDAs also do not list such food components as fiber or water. Nor do they address many pertinent issues, such as how much salt intake is suggested, the number of calories, or the amount of complex carbohydrates, fat, and dietary fiber that is needed for a healthy diet. As far as these other components are concerned, Tufts agrees with the recommendations presented in the 1989 report by the National Research Council, *Diet and Health: Implications for Reducing Chronic Disease Risk.* According to the report, which was based on a review of more than 5,000 studies, by following the council's guidelines Americans could reduce the risk of heart disease by at least 20 percent and also reduce the risk of cancer, strokes, high blood pressure, osteoporosis, liver disease, and obesity. The recommendations include:

◆ Limit fats to 30 percent of daily calories, with saturated fats making up no more than 10 percent of total daily calories.

◆ Maintain dietary cholesterol intake below 300 mg daily.

SAFE AND ADEQUATE NUTRIENT RANGES

Biotin	100–200 ug
Pantothenic acid	4–7 mg
Copper	2–3 mg
Manganese	2.5–5 mg
Fluoride	1.5–4 mg
Chromium	0.05–0.2 mg
Molybdenum	0.15–0.5 mg
Sodium	1,100–3,300 mg
Potassium	1,875–5,625 mg
Chloride	1,700–5,100 mg

◆ Consume at least 55 percent of daily calories in the form of carbohydrates, mostly complex.

◆ Consume the RDA for protein, but no more than twice that amount.

◆ Avoid the use of vitamin and mineral supplements unless necessary—instead consume the daily requirements in the form of a varied diet.

◆ Limit daily alcohol intake to less than 1 ounce, the equivalent of 2 beers or 2 small glasses of wine; women should limit alcohol intake to 1 drink per day.

Key

μ = microgram (1 millionth of a gram)
mg = milligram (equal to 1,000 micrograms)
g = gram (equal to 1,000 milligrams)
kg = kilogram (equal to 1,000 grams)
Heights and weights are averages based on the "reference" person in the particular category.

THE 18 RDA BREAKDOWNS

I. INFANTS—BIRTH TO 6 MONTHS
HEIGHT: 24 INCHES   WEIGHT: 13 POUNDS

Fat-Soluble Vitamins

Vitamin A	Vitamin D	Vitamin E	Vitamin K
375 μg	7.5 μg	3 mg	5 μg

Water-Soluble Vitamins

Vitamin C	B Vitamins					
	Thiamin	Riboflavin	Niacin	B-6	Folacin	B-12[1]
30 mg	0.3 μg	0.4 mg	5 mg	0.3 mg	25 μg	0.3 μg

Minerals

Calcium	Phosphorus	Magnesium	Iron	Zinc	Iodine	Selenium
400 mg	300 mg	40 mg	6 mg	5 mg	40 μg	10 μg

Protein 13 g

2. INFANTS—6 MONTHS TO I YEAR
HEIGHT: 28 INCHES   WEIGHT: 20 POUNDS

Fat-Soluble Vitamins

Vitamin A	Vitamin D	Vitamin E	Vitamin K
375 μg	10 μg	4 mg	10 μg

Water-Soluble Vitamins

Vitamin C	B Vitamins					
	Thiamin	Riboflavin	Niacin	B-6	Folacin	B-12
35 mg	0.4 μg	0.5 mg	9 mg	0.6 mg	35 μg	0.5 μg

[1]The recommended dietary allowance for vitamin B-12 in infants is based on average concentrations of the vitamin in human milk. The allowances after weaning are based on energy intake (as recommended by the American Academy of Pediatrics) and consideration of other factors, such as intestinal absorption.

THE 18 RDA BREAKDOWNS (cont.)

Minerals

Calcium	Phosphorus	Magnesium	Iron	Zinc	Iodine	Selenium
600 mg	500 mg	60 mg	10 mg	5 mg	50 mg	15 µg

Protein 14 g

3. CHILDREN—1 TO 3 YEARS
HEIGHT: 2'11"   WEIGHT: 29 POUNDS

Fat-Soluble Vitamins

Vitamin A	Vitamin D	Vitamin E	Vitamin K
400 µg	10 µg	6 mg	15 µg

Water-Soluble Vitamins

Vitamin C	B Vitamins					
	Thiamin	Riboflavin	Niacin	B-6	Folacin	B-12
40 mg	0.7 µg	0.8 mg	9 mg	1.0 mg	50µg	0.7 µg

Minerals

Calcium	Phosphorus	Magnesium	Iron	Zinc	Iodine	Selenium
800 mg	800 mg	80 mg	10 mg	10 mg	70 mg	20 µg

Protein 16 g

4. CHILDREN—4 TO 6 YEARS
HEIGHT: 3'8"   WEIGHT: 44 POUNDS

Fat-Soluble Vitamins

Vitamin A	Vitamin D	Vitamin E	Vitamin K
500 µg	10 µg	7 mg	20 µg

Water-Soluble Vitamins

Vitamin C	B Vitamins					
	Thiamin	Riboflavin	Niacin	B-6	Folacin	B-12
45 mg	0.9 µg	1.1 mg	12 mg	1.1 mg	75 µg	1.0 µg

Minerals

Calcium	Phosphorus	Magnesium	Iron	Zinc	Iodine	Selenium
800 mg	800 mg	120 mg	10 mg	10 mg	90 µg	20 µg

Protein 24 g

5. CHILDREN—7 TO 10 YEARS
HEIGHT: 4'4"   WEIGHT: 62 POUNDS

Fat-Soluble Vitamins

Vitamin A	Vitamin D	Vitamin E	Vitamin K
700 µg	10 µg	7 mg	30 µg

Water-Soluble Vitamins

Vitamin C	B Vitamins					
	Thiamin	Riboflavin	Niacin	B-6	Folacin	B-12
45 mg	1.0 µg	1.2 mg	13 mg	1.4 mg	100 µg	1.4 µg

THE 18 RDA BREAKDOWNS (cont.)

Minerals

Calcium	Phosphorus	Magnesium	Iron	Zinc	Iodine	Selenium
800 mg	800 mg	170 mg	10 mg	10 mg	120 mg	30 µg

Protein 26 g

6. ADOLESCENT MALES—11 TO 14 YEARS
   HEIGHT: 5'2"   WEIGHT: 99 POUNDS

Fat-Soluble Vitamins

Vitamin A	Vitamin D	Vitamin E	Vitamin K
1 mg	10 mg	10 mg	45 µg

Water-Soluble Vitamins

Vitamin C	B Vitamins					
	Thiamin	Riboflavin	Niacin	B-6	Folacin	B-12
50 mg	1.3 µg	1.5 mg	17 mg	1.7 mg	150 µg	2.0 µg

Minerals

Calcium	Phosphorus	Magnesium	Iron	Zinc	Iodine	Selenium
1,200 mg	1,200 mg	270 mg	12 mg	15 mg	150 mg	40 µg

Protein 45 g

7. ADOLESCENT FEMALES—11 TO 14 YEARS
   HEIGHT: 5'2"   WEIGHT: 101 POUNDS

Fat-Soluble Vitamins

Vitamin A	Vitamin D	Vitamin E	Vitamin K
800 µg	10 µg	8 mg	45 µg

Water-Soluble Vitamins

Vitamin C	B Vitamins					
	Thiamin	Riboflavin	Niacin	B-6	Folacin	B-12
50 mg	1.1 µg	1.3 mg	15 mg	1.4 mg	150 µg	2.0 µg

Minerals

Calcium	Phosphorus	Magnesium	Iron	Zinc	Iodine	Selenium
1,200 mg	1,200 mg	280 mg	15 mg	15 mg	150 mg	45 µg

Protein 46 g

8. ADOLESCENT MALES—15 TO 18 YEARS
   HEIGHT: 5'9"   WEIGHT: 145 POUNDS

Fat-Soluble Vitamins

Vitamin A	Vitamin D	Vitamin E	Vitamin K
1 mg	10 µg	10 mg	65 µg

Water-Soluble Vitamins

Vitamin C	B Vitamins					
	Thiamin	Riboflavin	Niacin	B-6	Folacin	B-12
60 mg	1.5 µg	1.8 mg	20 mg	2 mg	200 µg	2.0 µg

THE 18 RDA BREAKDOWNS (cont.)

Minerals

Calcium	Phosphorus	Magnesium	Iron	Zinc	Iodine	Selenium
1,200 mg	1,200 mg	400 mg	12 mg	15 mg	150 mg	50 μg

Protein 59 g

9. ADOLESCENT FEMALES—15 TO 18 YEARS
   HEIGHT: 5'4"   WEIGHT: 120 POUNDS

Fat-Soluble Vitamins

Vitamin A	Vitamin D	Vitamin E	Vitamin K
800 mg	10 μg	8 mg	55 μg

Water-Soluble Vitamins

Vitamin C	B Vitamins					
60 mg	Thiamin	Riboflavin	Niacin	B-6	Folacin	B-12
	1.1 μg	1.3 mg	15 mg	1.5 mg	180 μg	2.0 μg

Minerals

Calcium	Phosphorus	Magnesium	Iron	Zinc	Iodine	Selenium
1,200 mg	1,200 mg	300 mg	15 mg	12 mg	150 mg	50 μg

Protein 44 g

10. ADULT MALES—19 TO 24 YEARS
   HEIGHT: 5'10"   WEIGHT: 160 POUNDS

Fat-Soluble Vitamins

Vitamin A	Vitamin D	Vitamin E	Vitamin K
1 mg	10 μg	10 mg	70 μg

Water-Soluble Vitamins

Vitamin C	B Vitamins					
60 mg	Thiamin	Riboflavin	Niacin	B-6	Folacin	B-12
	1.5 μg	1.7 mg	19 mg	2.0 mg	200 μg	2.0 μg

Minerals

Calcium	Phosphorus	Magnesium	Iron	Zinc	Iodine	Selenium
1,200 mg	1,200 mg	350 mg	10 mg	15 mg	150 mg	70 μg

Protein 53 g

11. ADULT FEMALES—19 TO 24 YEARS
   HEIGHT: 5'4"   WEIGHT: 128 POUNDS

Fat-Soluble Vitamins

Vitamin A	Vitamin D	Vitamin E	Vitamin K
800 μg	10 μg	8 mg	60 mg

Water-Soluble Vitamins

Vitamin C	B Vitamins					
60 mg	Thiamin	Riboflavin	Niacin	B-6	Folacin	B-12
	1.1 mg	1.3 mg	15 mg	1.6 mg	180 μg	2.0 μg

THE 18 RDA BREAKDOWNS (cont.)

Minerals

Calcium	Phosphorus	Magnesium	Iron	Zinc	Iodine	Selenium
1,200 mg	1,200 mg	280 mg	15 mg	12 mg	150 mg	55 µg

Protein 46 g

12. ADULT MALES—25 TO 50 YEARS
HEIGHT: 5'10" WEIGHT: 174 POUNDS

Fat-Soluble Vitamins

Vitamin A	Vitamin D	Vitamin E	Vitamin K
1 mg	5 µg	10 mg	80 mg

Water-Soluble Vitamins

Vitamin C	B Vitamins					
	Thiamin	Riboflavin	Niacin	B-6	Folacin	B-12
60 mg	1.5 mg	1.7 mg	19 mg	2.0 mg	200µg	2.0 µg

Minerals

Calcium	Phosphorus	Magnesium	Iron	Zinc	Iodine	Selenium
800 mg	800 mg	350 mg	10 mg	15 mg	150 mg	70 µg

Protein 63 g

13. ADULT FEMALES—25 TO 50 YEARS
HEIGHT: 5'4"   WEIGHT: 136 POUNDS

Fat-Soluble Vitamins

Vitamin A	Vitamin D	Vitamin E	Vitamin K
800 µg	5 µg	8 mg	65 µg

Water-Soluble Vitamins

Vitamin C	B Vitamins					
	Thiamin	Riboflavin	Niacin	B-6	Folacin	B-12
60 mg	1.1 µg	1.3 mg	15 mg	1.6 mg	180 µg	2.0 µg

Minerals

Calcium	Phosphorus	Magnesium	Iron	Zinc	Iodine	Selenium
800 mg	800 mg	280 mg	15 mg	12 mg	150 mg	55 µg

Protein 50 g

14. ADULT MALES—51-PLUS YEARS
HEIGHT: 5'10" WEIGHT: 170 POUNDS

Fat-Soluble Vitamins

Vitamin A	Vitamin D	Vitamin E	Vitamin K
1 mg	5 µg	10 mg	80 µg

Water-Soluble Vitamins

Vitamin C	B Vitamins					
	Thiamin	Riboflavin	Niacin	B-6	Folacin	B-12
60 mg	1.2 µg	1.4 mg	15 mg	2.0 mg	200 µg	2 µg

THE 18 RDA BREAKDOWNS (cont.)

Minerals

Calcium	Phosphorus	Magnesium	Iron	Zinc	Iodine	Selenium
800 mg	800 mg	350 mg	10 mg	15 mg	150 mg	70 µg

Protein 63 g

15. ADULT FEMALES—51-PLUS YEARS
HEIGHT: 5'4"   WEIGHT: 143 POUNDS

Fat-Soluble Vitamins

Vitamin A	Vitamin D	Vitamin E	Vitamin K
800 µg	5 mg	8 mg	65 µg

Water-Soluble Vitamins

Vitamin C	B Vitamins					
	Thiamin	Riboflavin	Niacin	B-6	Folacin	B-12
60 mg	1 µg	1.2 mg	13 mg	1.6 mg	180µg	2.0 µg

Minerals

Calcium	Phosphorus	Magnesium	Iron	Zinc	Iodine	Selenium
800 mg	800 mg	280 mg	10 mg	12 mg	150 mg	55 µg

Protein 50 g

16. PREGNANT WOMEN

Fat-Soluble Vitamins

Vitamin A	Vitamin D	Vitamin E	Vitamin K
800 µg	10 µg	10 mg	65 µg

Water-Soluble Vitamins

Vitamin C	B Vitamins					
	Thiamin	Riboflavin	Niacin	B-6	Folacin	B-12
70 mg	1.5 µg	1.6 mg	17 mg	2.2 mg	400 µg	2.2 µg

Minerals

Calcium	Phosphorus	Magnesium	Iron	Zinc	Iodine	Selenium
1,200 mg	1,200 mg	320 mg	30 mg	15 mg	175 mg	65 µg

Protein 60 g

17. LACTATING MOTHERS, FIRST SIX MONTHS

Fat-Soluble Vitamins

Vitamin A	Vitamin D	Vitamin E	Vitamin K
1.3 mg	10 µg	12 mg	65 µg

Water-Soluble Vitamins

Vitamin C	B Vitamins					
	Thiamin	Riboflavin	Niacin	B-6	Folacin	B-12
95 mg	1.6 µg	1.8 mg	20 mg	2.1 mg	280 µg	2.6 µg

THE 18 RDA BREAKDOWNS (cont.)

Minerals

Calcium	Phosphorus	Magnesium	Iron	Zinc	Iodine	Selenium
1,200 mg	1,200 mg	335 mg	15 mg	19 mg	200 mg	75 µg

Protein 63 g

18. LACTATING MOTHERS, SECOND SIX MONTHS

Fat-Soluble Vitamins

Vitamin A	Vitamin D	Vitamin E	Vitamin K
1.2 mg	10 µg	11 mg	65 µg

Water-Soluble Vitamins

Vitamin C	B Vitamins					
	Thiamin	Riboflavin	Niacin	B-6	Folacin	B-12
90 mg	1.6 µg	1.7 mg	20 mg	2.1 mg	260 µg	2.6 µg

Minerals

Calcium	Phosphorus	Magnesium	Iron	Zinc	Iodine	Selenium
1,200 mg	1,200 mg	340 mg	15 mg	16 mg	200 mg	75 µg

Protein 62 g

8

Red Flags in the Food Supply

Some people approach nutrition as though they were entering a mine field in which danger lurks at every turn. Others find themselves caught up in a constant swirl of confusion as they try to sort through the bombardment of conflicting information. Nutrition experts seem to be constantly flip-flopping on whether or not certain substances are good, bad, or indifferent. In particular, there are 3 areas of dietary concern that are the subject of ongoing study and speculation. They have to do with caffeine, alcohol, and other nonnutritive substances, such as additives and food substitutes. (A fourth and sometimes related concern regarding safety and the use of pesticides is addressed in Chapter 13.) All 3 of these so-called "red flags" are part of the everyday lives of a majority of Americans. For millions of people, caffeine, in the forms of coffee, tea, and soda, is a necessary part of the day, as is an evening cocktail or a glass of wine at dinner. And nearly all of us consume additives to some extent.

Like many areas in the complex world of nutrition, we find some ambiguity in the evidence about the relative dangers or benefits of these substances. Our basic recommendations are threefold: first, that you take to heart the advice of health professionals; second, that you

keep the information, especially about additives, in perspective and avoid placing "good or evil" labels on them; and third, that you consider this material in light of the other information contained in this section on the constituents of a well-balanced, healthful diet.

Sorting Out the Caffeine Controversy

After more than 30 years of research, the reviews are still mixed on the relative hazards and benefits of caffeine, the substance millions of Americans depend on for a quick energy boost. During the past decade, many people have cut back on caffeine because of the speculation that it might be a contributor to a variety of health problems, including heart disease, cancer, fibrocystic breast disease, and birth defects. Recent reports conclude what we have long suspected—that it is possible to become caffeine dependent. The question remains, is this dependency harmful?

The most well-publicized studies have linked caffeine consumption with heart disease. But the studies are far from conclusive, as it is nearly impossible to do controlled research on the effects of solitary substances.

One widely reported study tracked the coffee-drinking habits of more than a thousand male graduates of Johns Hopkins Medical School for up to 25 years.

Thomas A. Pearson, M.D., Andrea LaCroix, Ph.D., and their colleagues found that the more coffee the men drank, the higher the incidence of heart disease. At greatest risk were those who drank at least five cups a day; their rate of heart disease was two-and-a-half times the rate for men who did not drink coffee.

The researchers' findings took into account the effects of smoking, high blood pressure, and variations in blood cholesterol when the men were young—all factors that might enhance the susceptibility to heart disease. But the analysis did not take into account exercise, stress, or diet, three further aspects that play a role in heart health but that are difficult to measure over the course of many years. So it is possible that the heavy coffee drinkers were under more pressure, exercised less, or ate more fatty foods than the other men. Further, the study lumped together those who drank 5 cups of coffee a day with those who consumed very large quantities—10 to 20 cups a day. It was also difficult to isolate caffeine as the culprit because coffee contains many other chemical substances.

Other attempts to study the effects of caffeine have had similar drawbacks. Many have not defined the size of a cup when evaluating coffee drinking or compared findings about caffeinated-coffee drinkers with findings about decaffeinated-coffee drinkers. Results are also clouded when the method of brewing is considered. For example, a group of Norwegian coffee drinkers was found to have increased levels of blood cholesterol. But in Norway, people tend to add coffee grounds directly to boiling water and steep them for some time, so the results of that study are not necessarily applicable to Americans who use automatic drip coffee makers, instant coffee, and electric percolators.

For the time being, there is no definitive evidence that moderate amounts of caffeine are a problem for most people, but it is easier to evaluate the facts when you understand what happens to caffeine after you've consumed it.

What Exactly Is Caffeine?

Caffeine is one of a group of compounds called methylxanthines that occur naturally in more than 60 species of plants. The most familiar sources of caffeine are coffee beans, cola nuts, cocoa beans, and tea leaves. Coffee is the United States' greatest source of caffeine, with soft drinks ranked second, followed by tea and chocolate.

Many people are unaware of all the places caffeine shows up. It is also found in some cold medications, allergy pills, diet pills, and headache remedies. Sometimes coffee is used as a flavoring agent in baked goods, frozen desserts, and puddings.

Foods and beverages containing caffeine are often consumed as "pick-me-ups" to get that extra lift that helps you have a sharper focus in performing mental and physical tasks. These "upper" effects stem from caffeine's ability to act as a stimulant to the central nervous system. In this respect, the caffeine levels in one or two cups of coffee can increase alertness. Caffeine can also cause a number of other reactions, depending on how much you consume, how high your caffeine tolerance is, and other individual factors. It can increase heartbeat and urine production, and it can open up some blood vessels while constricting others. Caffeine promotes the stomach's output of acid. However, because decaffeinated coffee also produces acid secretion, there are other substances in coffee apart from caffeine that are responsible for this.

What Are Caffeine's Risks?

People who consume large amounts of caffeine may experience insomnia, heartbeat irregularities, and diarrhea. Even moderate consumption of caffeine can lead to irritability, headaches, trembling, and nervousness. In fact, a symptom likened to an anxiety neurosis, termed "caffeinism," has been shown to disappear in people who eliminate caffeine-containing foods and beverages from their diets. But because caffeine's effects are highly individual, it may cause problems for some people and not for others. People who are used to consuming a fair amount tend to develop a tolerance and become less susceptible to caffeine's effects.

Children may be more vulnerable to caffeine-related problems, particularly through some sodas that contain only about one-third the caffeine of coffee but still enough to create problems. Laurence Finberg, M.D., former chairman of the committee on nutrition at the American Academy of Pediatrics, recommends that children who drink soda consume no more than two 12-ounce cans of caffeine-containing soda a day.

Caffeine can pose problems for certain people on medications. This was discovered when Dr. Michael Simmons and his colleagues at UCLA found that caffeine from as little as three cups of coffee increased the potency of asthma medications containing theophylline, as this substance is structurally similar to caffeine.

Controversy about the effects of caffeine have focused on certain types of medical problems:

Caffeine and birth defects: The Food and Drug Administration (FDA) has advised that pregnant women avoid or use sparingly foods that contain caffeine, because caffeine passes through the placenta and enters the unborn infant's body. This warning is based on research conducted by the agency that showed that caffeine, when fed to rats, caused birth defects and delayed bone development in fetuses. It is not known how these findings might apply to humans, but the FDA issued the warning because of the widespread use of caffeine-containing beverages in the United States.

Many researchers criticized one of the FDA's studies because the rats were force-fed exceedingly high amounts of caffeine. In a later study, the rats were given varying levels of caffeine in their water throughout the day. Ultimately, no birth defects were seen unless the pregnant rats consumed caffeine levels equivalent to that contained in 18 or more cups of coffee a day.

In early 1982, a team of Harvard scientists published in the *New England Journal of Medicine* their study on the effects of caffeine on the outcome of pregnancy in more than 12,000 women. The researchers found no link between the amount of coffee consumed and birth defects. Additional studies in the United States and Finland reached the same conclusion. However, a newer study indicates that caffeine consumption may boost the chance of a woman's miscarrying. The study, which was conducted at the Montreal University–affiliated Saint-Justine Hospital, found that women who drank three or four cups of coffee a day in the month prior to conception had nearly twice as great a risk of losing their babies as those who drank less than half a cup a day. During pregnancy itself, as little as one-and-a-half to two cups a day (or five cups of tea or four cans of caffeinated cola) doubled the possibility of miscarriage. Three to four daily cups of coffee nearly tripled the risk. Although these studies are not conclusive, why take a chance? Pregnant women, or women who are planning to become pregnant, should be on the safe side and limit their caffeine consumption.

There is early evidence that caffeine may also contribute to infertility in some women. Researchers at the National Institute of Environmental Health Sciences of the National Institutes of Health studied a group of women who were trying to get pregnant. Those who consumed more than 100 milligrams of caffeine a day (comparable to one cup of coffee or two cans of caffeinated soda) were only half as likely to become pregnant in a given month as women who consumed less caffeine. Age, frequency of sexual intercourse, alcohol use, and smoking were all factored into the study. Although the study is far from conclusive, women who want to get pregnant might consider cutting down on caffeine consumption.

Caffeine and nursing babies: Again, there is no firm evidence relating caffeine consumption to problems for the babies of breast-feeding mothers. In fact, one study showed that there was little caffeine pass-along to babies of coffee-drinking mothers. Ceston Berlin Jr., M.D., and colleagues from the Hershey Medical Center in Pennsylvania studied the metabolism and transfer of caffeine in 15 nursing mothers who had been instructed to drink their preferred caffeine-containing beverage in the usual amounts. Thirteen women were accustomed to drinking one to three cups of coffee a day, and two were used to drinking six cups of coffee a day. On the day of the study, the amount of caffeine the women consumed at one time ranged from 36 to 335 milligrams. The caffeine in their breast milk was measured over the course of 12 hours, and their infants were fed according to their usual schedules. To determine how much caffeine was reaching the babies, the researchers tested their urine.

Four of the mothers who drank less than 100 milligrams of caffeine had none in their breast milk. Caffeine rapidly appeared in the milk of the other mothers and peaked within an hour, yet none was detected in the urine of the babies. The researchers estimated that only 0.06 to 1.5 percent of the caffeine the mothers drank was available to the infants. Their conclusion was that "the modest use of caffeinated beverages does not appear to present a hazard to the nursing infant." However, researchers acknowledged that the mothers in the study consumed a single dose of caffeine, and they raised the possibility that frequent intakes, particularly in amounts greater than 150 milligrams, might cause a cumulative effect.

Caffeine and fibrocystic breast disease: Fibrocystic breast disease is a painful, noncancerous breast condition that occurs in approximately 10 to 20 percent of women. Some evidence suggests that removing all methylxanthines, including caffeine, from the diet helps control or cure the painful breast lumps, but the evidence is not yet conclusive.

One study of 323 women with the condition and nearly 1,500 without it showed no association between the consumption of caffeine and benign fibrocystic disease.

Caffeine and heart disease: Researchers at Ohio State University Hospital investigated the role caffeine might have in producing arrhythmias, which are irregular heartbeats. After receiving the amount of caffeine in two cups of brewed coffee, three heart patients experienced an increased heart rate, and six patients had arrhythmias. Three of the healthy volunteers also had arrhythmias after receiving coffee. The researchers concluded that caffeine has the potential to induce heartbeat irregularities, especially in patients with existing heart problems.

Another study examined coffee consumption and its effects on blood cholesterol in more than 14,500 Norwegian men and women. The study concluded that as coffee consumption increased, so did blood cholesterol levels. For those who drank one to four cups of coffee a day, blood cholesterol was more than 5 percent higher than that of non–coffee drinkers. And those who drank nine or more cups a day showed blood cholesterol levels that were about 14 percent higher than those of people who drank less than one daily cup of coffee.

The Norwegian study created such a stir that a public health warning was issued in Germany. It also caused a storm of criticism from research and medical groups. Criticisms included charges that the study failed to account fully for such factors as stress and certain other dietary components that can affect blood cholesterol. Further, although two groups found an association between coffee or caffeine consumption and blood cholesterol, three other research groups did not. Some experts believe that the different results obtained from laboratory to laboratory might in part be related to the way coffee is grown and prepared.

Researchers at the Johns Hopkins Medical Institutions in Baltimore challenged the Norwegian study, based on the way coffee is prepared. Their study of 100 men suggested that when prepared with a filter in an automatic machine, coffee is less harmful for those with high cholesterol than when it is boiled without a filter.

Although subjects who drank four six-ounce cups of filtered coffee every day for two months did experience a slight rise in cholesterol, most of that was in HDL, or "good," cholesterol, not in the harmful LDL cholesterol.

Beware the Gourmet Coffee Trend

Although Americans have always loved their coffee, the fast-growing trend in gourmet coffee outlets has brought this love affair to a new level. Today, more than 4,500 coffee outlets serve up exotic brews across the country—a number that is expected to double by the end of the 1990s. The biggest chain, Starbucks, has been opening coffee bars at the rate of two a week. Gloria Jean's Coffee Bean has more than 200 outlets. The Coffee Beanery sells its brew in 31 states.

More consumers are also preparing special coffee beverages at home, with the advent of products like Nescafé's Cappuccino, Maxwell House's Cappuccino Mocha, and a growing variety of General Foods' International Coffees. All told, specialty coffee blends and flavored beans account for nearly $2 billion in sales per year.

Many people use specialty coffee drinks as flavorful replacements for rich desserts. But some coffee beverages are made with enough milk and syrup to give them more fat and calories than traditional desserts. A large Café

Mocha from Starbucks, for example, contains 409 calories and 31 grams of fat—about 100 more calories and three times the fat of a wedge of devil's food cake with chocolate icing, or 180 more calories and twice the fat of a half cup of Haagen-Dazs super premium ice cream. Add whipped cream and you're approaching 500 calories and 40 grams of fat.

Mocha beverages tend to have the most fat and calories in all the gourmet coffee shops, in part because they contain a good deal of milk (up to 11 ounces in a large cup), plus a one- to three-ounce dose of chocolate syrup.

But a latte doesn't necessarily fall far behind. For example, a latte from The Coffee Beanery, made from whole milk and topped with whipped cream and grated milk chocolate, contains about 350 calories and 20 grams of fat.

Cappuccino tends to run relatively low in calories and fat, as long as you don't add whipped cream. For example, a large cappuccino at Au Bon Pain, made with 2% fat milk, has 156 calories and 6 grams of fat. Of course, in many coffee bars you can avoid fat and calories altogether by asking that your drink be made with skim milk.

Believe it or not, specialty coffees actually contain less caffeine than regular coffee purchased in cans from the supermarket. That's because they are made from arabica beans, which impart a stronger taste but less caffeine than the robusta beans used in many commercial brands. If the coffee is dark roasted, even more caffeine is burned off the beans.

What About Decaffeination?

Traditionally, products have been decaffeinated using an agent called methylene chloride. Although this substance is still allowed by the FDA, many companies have turned to safer methods. Methylene chloride, which is used to extract the caffeine from coffee beans, has been found to cause cancer when inhaled in large amounts by laboratory animals.

WATCH WHAT'S IN YOUR CUP

Coffee, black	Caffeine[1] (mg)
Dunkin' Donuts	
Small (10 oz cup holding 8 oz of coffee)[2]	104 mg caffeine
McDonald's	
Small (6 oz)	60 mg caffeine
Starbucks	
Short (8 oz cup holding 5.8 oz of coffee)[2]	81 mg caffeine
Gloria Jean's Coffee Bean	
Small (8 oz cup holding 6.3 oz of coffee)[2]	82 mg caffeine
The Coffee Beanery	
Small (8 oz cup holding 7.7 oz coffee)[2]	100 mg caffeine
Au Bon Pain	
Small (10 oz cup holding 9 oz of coffee)[2]	171 mg caffeine

Espresso

Starbucks	
Solo (0.7 oz)	57 mg caffeine
Gloria Jean's Coffee Bean (2.7 oz)	51 mg caffeine
The Coffee Beanery (2.4 oz)	84 mg caffeine
Au Bon Pain (2.6 oz)	130 mg caffeine

	Calories[3]	Fat[1] (g)
	with skim/2% fat/whole milk	

Cappuccino

Starbucks			
Short (8 oz)	57	57/79/99	0/3/5
Grande (16 oz; contains 2 shots of espresso)	114	143/200/249	1/8/13
Gloria Jean's Coffee Bean (made with 2% fat milk only)			
Small (8 oz)	51	68	3
Large (16 oz; contains 2 shots of espresso)	102	136	5
The Coffee Beanery			
One size only (8 oz)	84	54/76/94	0/3/5
Au Bon Pain (no whole-milk option)			
Small (10 oz; contains 1/2 shot of espresso)	65	71/99	0/4
Large (16 oz)	130	111/156	1/6

Latte

Starbucks			
Short (8 oz)	57	68/90/114	1/4/6
Grande (16 oz; contains 2 shots of espresso)	114	146/195/247	2/8/13
Gloria Jean's Coffee Bean (made with 2% fat milk only)			
Small (8 oz)	51	76	3

WATCH WHAT'S IN YOUR CUP (cont.)

Large (16 oz; contains 2 shots espresso)	102	166	6
The Coffee Beanery			
One size only (16 oz)	84	151/211/263	1/8/14
Au Bon Pain (no whole-milk option)			
Small (10 oz; contains ½ shot of espresso)	65	81/113	0/5
Large (16 oz)	130	121/170	1/7

Cafe Mocha

Starbucks			
Short (8 oz)	57	156/175/195	11/13/15
Grande (16 oz; contains 2 shots of espresso)	114	324/365/409	21/27/31
Gloria Jean's Coffee Bean (made with 2% fat milk only)			
Small (8 oz)	51	222	4
Large (16 oz; contains 2 shots of espresso)	102	312	7
The Coffee Beanery			
One size only (12 oz)	84	232/267/296	1/6/9
Au Bon Pain Hot Mocha Blast (no whole-milk option)			
Small (10 oz; contains ½ shot of espresso)	65	120/153	1/5
Large (16 oz)	130	200/249	1/7

Cold coffee beverages

Starbucks Iced Cafe Mocha			
Tall (12 oz)	57	201/235/271	11/16/19
Gloria Jean's Coffee			
Bean Iced Mocha (made with 2% fat milk only)			
Medium (12 oz)	51	282	6
Au Bon Pain Iced Mocha Blast (no whole-milk option)			
Medium (16 oz)	130	180/221	1/6

Specialty coffee beverages from the supermarket (prepared with water)

General Foods International Coffees			
Italian Cappuccino (8 oz)	35	50	2
Nescafe			
Cappuccino Authentic (8 oz)	100	90	3
Maxwell House			
Cappuccino Coffee (8 oz)	117	80	1

[1]Values for caffeine content are based on samples of coffee and espresso bought in Massachusetts, New Hampshire, and New Jersey. They are intended as ballpark estimates rather than definitive numbers.

[2]The cup is not big enough to hold the specified number of ounces of coffee plus milk. Thus, up to 2 ounces for milk are left at the top.

[3]A shot of hazlenut, vanilla, or some other type of syrup squirted into, say, a latte can add at least another 40 calories. And putting whipped cream on top of any beverage will add in the neighborhood of 60 calories and 5 grams of fat. A gram of fat contains 9 calories. Someone following an 1,800-calorie diet should average no more than 60 grams of fat a day.

Because the chemical has been banned in hair spray, why is the FDA allowing its use in coffee? According to FDA officials, the amount of methylene chloride in decaffeinated coffee is negligible. Even if someone drinks as many as five five-ounce cups of coffee a day, there is only a one in a million chance that that person's risk of cancer will increase. However, public-interest groups disagree with this line of thinking, arguing that even minimum amounts of a substance associated with cancer risk should not be used, especially if safe alternatives are available.

Some coffee producers are doing just that. They are using ethyl acetate, a substance that occurs naturally in fruits and vegetables, to extract the caffeine from coffee beans. Ethyl acetate is also used to decaffeinate tea.

Others use a combination of water and carbon dioxide or water and coffee oils that have been pressed from other coffee beans.

The Pros and Cons of Drinking Alcohol

Recent reports that drinking in moderation may actually be good for you have created quite a stir. According to some studies, having one or two drinks a day may protect people from developing heart disease. But there are many limitations to the research picture. For one thing, behavioral studies are difficult to measure. For example, in one study, the categories used were "teetotaler," "moderate drinker," and "heavy drinker." There was no effort to distinguish a person who had never consumed alcoholic beverages from, say, a recovering alcoholic who did not currently drink. Nor do the studies take into account other factors, such as cigarette smoking, which, in combination with alcohol, appears to increase risk factors substantially.

Another study, analyzing data on approximately 5,000 adults from Framingham, Massachusetts, over a 22-year period, revealed that men who had one or two drinks a week had a lower mortality rate than heavy drinkers or those who did not drink at all. However, these studies are not considered conclusive, as other factors might be at play. For example, it is possible that men who drink in small amounts tend to have lifestyles or personalities that increase longevity.

Then there is the famous "French paradox"—the reason why the high-fat French diet doesn't seem to raise the numbers of people suffering heart disease. A popular theory that the intake of fat in the French diet seemed to be counteracted by drinking red wine boosted wine sales in the United States. The theory was that moderate consumption of red wine (one to three glasses per day) flushed away the platelets that cling to artery walls and cause blood to clot. Many cardiologists support the consumption of wine in moderate amounts, but researchers warn that the reasons for low incidence of heart disease among the French may be linked to other factors, such as the tradition of eating the largest meal of the day at midday. Furthermore, experts are wary about promoting greater wine consumption in the United States, where the ill effects of alcoholism far outweigh other considerations.

MEASURE YOUR CAFFEINE INTAKE

Say "caffeine" and most people think coffee. Yet caffeine is present in a host of other products Americans consume, as the list below shows.

	Milligrams of Caffeine
Drip-brewed coffee (6 fl oz)	130–180
Instant coffee (6 fl oz)	50–130
Decaffeinated coffee (6 fl oz)	2–6
Tea, steeped 3 minutes (6 fl oz)	36
Cola, soft drink, regular and diet (12 fl oz)	46
Hot cocoa (6 fl oz)	4
Chocolate milk (8 fl oz)	6
Cadbury milk chocolate (1 oz)	15
Dannon coffee-flavored yogurt (8 oz)	45
Excedrin (2 tablets)	130
Anacin (2 tablets)	64

Even if moderate drinking were shown conclusively to reduce the risk of heart disease, most health professionals would be hesitant to make an across-the-board recommendation because there are plenty of reasons not to drink. For example, research indicates that people who have one to three drinks a day have a 60 percent higher risk of developing oral cancer than nondrinkers. For people who drink that amount and smoke one to two packs of cigarettes a day, the risk is three times greater than for smokers who do not drink. Furthermore, given the fact that there are an estimated 18 million Americans with alcohol problems, health professionals are not anxious to promote drinking.

Nevertheless, among people who do drink, some research indicates that beer may benefit certain individuals. Johns Hopkins Medical Institutions sponsored a widely publicized study on the drinking habits and illnesses of 17,000 people. Alex Richman, M.D., and his colleagues found that people who preferred beer over other alcoholic beverages said they were ill much less often than the researchers expected. They had fewer medical visits, spent fewer days sick in bed, and lost fewer days from work or school. Those who drank one or two beers a day reported the lowest incidences of illness. Once the level reached 35 beers a week, the apparent health benefits were eliminated. People in the study who drank different alcoholic beverages—namely, wine and distilled spirits—reported being ill only 1 to 2 percent less than expected, so it may be that some ingredient in beer other than alcohol helps keep beer drinkers healthy. However, these studies shouldn't lead to the conclusion that it's a good idea to drink beer.

There's simply not enough data available to warrant the statement that a couple of drinks a day can be considered beneficial to health. In order to understand fully the role of alcohol in the diet, it is important to know what happens in your body once it is consumed.

What Does Alcohol Do?

Unlike protein, fat, and carbohydrates, all of which must pass from the stomach to the small intestine before being absorbed into the bloodstream, about 20 percent of the alcohol we consume goes directly from the stomach to the blood. That's because alcohol molecules are so small that the intestine does not need to break all of them down into smaller components before they enter the circulatory system. Most of the remaining alcohol that does not pass straight from the stomach to the blood goes through the wall of the small intestine.

In the bloodstream, the body handles alcohol (or, more precisely, ethyl alcohol or ethanol) much as it would a drug, quickly setting about its elimination. About 3 percent leaves the body unmetabolized via urine, perspiration, and through breathing. The rest, formerly thought to be almost exclusively metabolized by the liver, is now believed to be processed in significant amounts in the stomach and small intestines of men after it is consumed. Much less is metabolized this way in women, so if the same amount of alcohol is consumed by men and women of the same size, more gets into the bloodstream of women. Because usually men are larger than women, these two factors make women less able to "hold their liquor" than men.

Because the intestine can metabolize only about seven grams (or a quarter of an ounce) of alcohol an hour, it starts to accumulate in the bloodstream and affect the brain and other organs if it's consumed at a faster rate. In the brain, alcohol acts as a narcotic, actually putting nerve cells "to sleep." This anesthetic effect begins in areas of the brain that control behavior, which is why people who are drinking tend to be less inhibited.

As blood alcohol levels rise, other brain centers become depressed. The result is that speech becomes slurred, vision blurred, and walking difficult. If one drinks to the point of passing out, it means that the entire conscious brain has effectively "dozed off." It's even possible to shut down the brain's unconscious centers, such as those that control breathing and heart rate, if enough alcohol is consumed.

Alcohol: The Nutritional Issues

According to the Surgeon General's Report on Nutrition and Health, "social" drinkers do not seem to suffer any notable nutritional deficiencies. The report cited two important studies. In one, three groups of nonalcoholics kept diaries of what they ate and drank over a period of 6 to 12 months, and 79 percent of them reported consuming alcohol on half or more of the days. For 22 percent of the drinkers, alcohol contributed approximately 10 percent of average daily calories; for another 23 percent, it contributed from 5 to 10 percent of daily calories. Alcohol accounted for less than 5 percent of daily calories for the remaining 55 percent. It was found that, as the proportion of calories from alcohol increased, the protein intake underwent little change, and the overall quality of the diet could not be related to the consumption of alcohol.

In a second study, conducted with upper-middle-class people in southern California, it was found that alcohol did not replace calories derived from other nutrients.

The surgeon general concludes that nutritional issues are not pressing for the average healthy person who consumes moderate amounts of alcohol.

But what constitutes a "moderate" amount of drinking? For one thing, alcohol's effect is highly individual; its influence depends on your body size, your metabolism, what or whether you've eaten recently, and the medication you're taking, if any. If consumed with food, one or two drinks usually won't cause major problems (unless you're driving a car). But what constitutes a drink? Many people don't measure the ounces of alcohol they pour and might be consuming far more than one or two.

Alcohol is also loaded with calories, and they're "empty" calories in that they provide no nutrients. Take note of the approximate calorie count of your favorite drinks, listed in the accompanying tables.

Who Should Avoid Alcohol?

Although a drink or two a day probably won't cause problems for most normal people, there are several categories of people who should proceed with caution or avoid alcohol consumption altogether. These include:

◆ *Pregnant women:* Many authorities, including the U.S. Surgeon General and the

HOW MUCH ALCOHOL IS IN A DRINK?

Beverage	Amount Equal to One Ounce of Absolute Alcohol
80-proof liquor	two 1.5-oz. shots
beer	two 12-oz. cans or bottles
sherry	two 3-oz. glasses
table wine	two 4-oz. glasses

WILL DRINKING MAKE YOU FAT?

Drink	Amount	Approximate Calories
beer or ale	12 oz.	150
light beer	12 oz.	100
liquor (gin, rum, brandy, bourbon, scotch, vodka)		
80 proof	1.5 oz.	100
100 proof	1.5 oz.	125
champagne, dry	3 oz.	80
cold duck wine	3 oz.	90
cordials, liqueurs	1 oz.	80–120
wine (dry red, white, rosé)	6 oz.	130–150
light wine	6 oz.	90
eggnog, with 1 oz. rum	1 cup	235
hot toddy or grog, with 1 shot of liquor	1 cup	115
hot buttered rum	1 cup	260

American Medical Association, feel that it is best for mothers-to-be to avoid alcohol, because it reaches the unborn baby's blood at the same concentration as the mother's within 15 minutes of her taking a drink. At very high levels of chronic intake, alcohol causes a number of defects, known collectively as fetal alcohol syndrome. But even moderate drinking may be linked to miscarriages, stillbirths, and low birth weight.

◆ *Breast-feeding mothers:* There are some theories that new mothers who are having difficulty breast-feeding should have a glass or two of wine to help them relax. However, alcohol can be counterproductive to this end because it can inhibit the "letdown" reflex that leads to milk secretion. The alcohol also passes into the mother's milk. And although the level of alcohol in the milk is lower than in the mother's blood, the infant can become intoxicated even if the mother has had only a couple of drinks. For these reasons, nursing mothers should avoid alcohol or be sure to consume it several hours before nursing time.

◆ *People on medication:* Because alcohol can have the same effect as a drug when it is consumed, it is wise for people taking any form of medication to check with their physicians before drinking. Even a single drink may increase or decrease the potency of some medications.

◆ *People with diabetes:* They should consult with their doctors before drinking even in moderate amounts, because alcohol can interfere with blood sugar metabolism. In addition, it can raise blood triglycerides. These fats, which may increase the risk of heart disease if they're excessively high, tend to be already elevated in people with diabetes, especially if their blood sugar is poorly controlled. Small amounts of alcohol may also interact with oral medication, such as Diabenese, used to lower blood sugar, and result in flushing, nausea, rapid heartbeat, or impaired speech.

◆ *People with high blood pressure:* Drinking appears to be associated with the development of hypertension. Researchers at Stanford University found that as alcohol intake increased, so did blood pressure in a group of men age 20 and older. The alcohol–blood pressure connection was strongest after the age of 50. For women, alcohol intake was linked to high blood pressure only after age 50. Other studies have shown that, in some hypertensive people, an increase in alcohol intake definitely causes an increase in blood pressure. Thus, alcohol not only may be involved in the development of hypertension, but it may also aggravate an existing condition.

In November 1989, a federally mandated warning label appeared on all containers of liquor, wine, and beer. The warning reads:

Consumption of alcoholic beverages impairs your ability to drive a car or operate machinery and may cause health problems.

According to the surgeon general, women should not drink alcoholic beverages during pregnancy because of the risk of birth defects.

Alcoholic Malnutrition

The nutritional balance in chronic alcoholics is upset both because they consume fewer nutrients and because excessive amounts of alcohol impede the proper absorption and utilization of the nutrients they do consume. Studies have shown that hospitalized alcoholics who derived 30 percent or more of their daily calories from alcohol showed signs of protein malnutrition, as well as deficiencies in calcium, iron, vitamins A and C, and the B vitamins (in particular B-12), thiamin, and riboflavin.

In addition to symptoms associated with a poor diet, the alcoholic suffers a variety of symptoms related to the effects alcohol has on the absorption, metabolism, storage, and excretion of many nutrients.

It was once believed that the organ and tissue damage often seen in chronic alcoholics, such as cirrhosis of the liver, was primarily caused by the long-term effects of nutritional deficiencies. By the 1960s, however, medical experts had reached the conclusion that many of the clinical consequences of alcoholism were the direct result of the toxic effects of alcohol itself.

There is much that remains unknown about the specific relationship between alcoholism and the activity of nutrients in the body. Most of the studies have focused on indigent alcoholics, who make up only 5 percent of the alcoholic population, and whose lifestyle and general eating patterns differ greatly from those of the average, more healthy population. Furthermore, the indigent alcoholics studied have been almost exclusively male.

Avoiding the Post-Party Blues

Many of America's favorite holiday and celebrative occasions take place around food and abundant drinking, and it is a common plight for even the most moderate of drinkers to succumb to the festivities and imbibe "one too many." It's easy to see how this can happen when you consider that it takes an average-size man about 2 hours to burn off the 14 grams of alcohol contained in one drink. Three or four drinks over an evening's time can present problems, especially in a person not accustomed to drinking. Ironically, the body builds a tolerance for alcohol consumption, so the light drinker becomes drunk on less alcohol than the heavy drinker.

If you drink, it is best not to do so on an empty stomach. Food acts as a kind of barrier between the alcohol and the stomach wall, decreasing the absorption there. Food also postpones the emptying of the stomach's contents into the small intestine, where most of the alcohol is absorbed into the bloodstream. And food appears to stimulate enzymes in the stomach and small intestine that help break down some of the alcohol before it reaches the bloodstream and travels to the brain.

Diluting drinks can also help. Although sparkling water and other carbonated mixers—as opposed to plain water and juices—can hasten alcohol absorption, this is more likely to happen on an empty stomach. "Nursing" a drink is another good way to avoid getting drunk. Or alternate alcoholic drinks with club soda, juices, or water.

Once alcohol enters the bloodstream, there is no way to speed up its metabolism. Drinking coffee, taking cold showers, or walking around the block may wake you up, but they will not make you less inebriated. For full sobriety, nature must take its course.

Of course, if you do have too much to drink, you're likely to be saddled with the infamous "morning after" hangover. The metabolic reasons for the headache, nausea, irritability, and fatigue that drinkers suffer when they've had too much are not understood, although the accompanying thirst is the result of alcohol's diuretic effect.

It is possible that some types of liquor bring on more serious hangovers than others. One study showed that, in descending order, brandy, red wine, rum, whiskey, white wine, and gin caused the worst hangovers. This difference in the after-effects of alcohol might be caused by congeners, a large number of diverse chemicals that are the by-products of distillation and fermentation. It appears that the more congeners a liquor has, the worse the hangover.

One myth holds that taking aspirin helps diminish the effects of alcohol on the system. But researchers have discovered that taking aspirin before consuming alcohol actually slows alcohol's travel time through the body. The reason appears to be that aspirin interferes with the ability of a stomach enzyme (gastric alcohol dehydrogenase) to break down alcohol before it has a chance to enter the blood stream and travel to the head.

Can Nonfoods Be Beneficial?

In addition to coffee, tea, and alcohol, we consume many other substances that contain no naturally occurring nutrients. Many of them are added to foods to preserve, color, flavor, stabilize, or replace substances lost in processing. Others are designed as substitutes for foods that, for a variety of reasons, some people are unable or unwilling to eat in their natural form. The most common examples of food substitutes are artificial sweeteners and, more recently, artificial fats.

Many people assume that our food supply would be more healthful without these nonnutrients. It is in response to this assumption that many food manufacturers label their products with terms such as "no preservatives" or "no artificial ingredients." But do artificial food substances necessarily compromise the nutritional quality of our diets? Scientists who have devoted many years to the study of this question have found that, for the most part, FDA-approved additives do not. The choice is left up to you. However, before you jump on the "no additive–no substitute" bandwagon, it is important that you understand all sides of the issue, including some surprising nutritional benefits of additives and substitutes.

The Additive Debate

It is estimated that nearly 3,000 chemical and natural substances are added to foods during processing, and the federal government keeps close tabs on their use. The Food, Drug, and Cosmetic Act was passed by Congress in 1938, prohibiting the marketing of foods containing toxic substances. Since that time, amendments have been passed to clarify specific issues, such as the 1958 Food Additive Amendment, which stated that no additive could be used in any amount that had been shown to cause cancer in animal or other studies. However, the Food Additive Amendment exempted 670 substances that were classified as "Generally Recognized as Safe" (GRAS), based on scientific studies and other data. GRAS substances were not always trouble-free, however. Saccharin had to be taken off the list in the early 1970s when it was found to cause cancer in laboratory animals.

Many consumers are alarmed by the intimidating words that appear on food labels and are loath to consume products that contain such scary-sounding ingredients as "L-lysine monohydrochloride" or "apocarotenal." What they might not know is that many of these are naturally occurring substances. L-lysine monohydrochloride, for example, is simply a form of the amino acid lysine, a building block of protein that is in short supply in most grains. Apocarotenal is a member of the carotene family of plant pigments found throughout nature, some of which are converted by the body into vitamin A.

Over the years, there have been a number of hotly staged controversies over particular additives, and a number of them have been removed from the food supply. However, in spite of the questions that still remain, we do know that, as a category, additives are not "bad." In fact, overall, they have a number of benefits:

◆ Additives prevent spoilage and the accompanying bacterial ailments associated with eating spoiled foods.

◆ Additives allow a year-round supply of nutritious fruits and vegetables that would otherwise be available only during a given season.

◆ Foods containing certain additives may be tastier and of a consistent quality.

◆ Foods fortified with vitamin and mineral additives help some people, who might otherwise suffer deficiencies, meet their daily requirement for essential nutrients.

◆ Overall, they make more foods available in greater varieties to more people.

Much as the natural-food enthusiasts might hope for unprocessed, additive-free foods, in the long run it appears that most additives do more good than harm. According to a major report prepared in 1989 by the Committee on Diet and Health of the National Research Council, there are no data to support the opinion that Americans suffer nutritionally from the presence of nonnutritive substances in their diets. In fact, the committee noted, "Exposure to individual nonnutritive chemicals, in the minute quantities normally present in the average diet, is unlikely to contribute to the overall cancer risk to humans in the United States. The life span of humans in Western countries is steadily increasing, and age-specific mortalities from most common cancers such as breast and colon cancer show no increases (or decreases) over the past generation. These facts suggest that our society as a whole is not facing a health crisis posed by environmental agents." Nevertheless, the debate goes on regarding certain additives common to the American food supply.

After many years of debate, the FDA banned the use of sulfite preservatives in fresh fruits and vegetables (except potatoes), but it appears likely that they'll continue to be allowed elsewhere. Almost half the adverse reactions to sulfites, including hives, shortness of breath, and even death, have been linked to their use in fruits and vegetables, mostly in salad bars—and these are most commonly experienced by asthmatics. The FDA estimates that about 80,000 to 100,000 people in the United States are sensitive to sulfites. However, products that contain at least 10 parts per million of sulfites are required to state their presence on the label. Look for the names sulfur dioxide, potassium metabisulfite, sodium metabisulfite, potassium bisulfite, sodium bisulfite, or sodium sulfite on the ingredients list.

Concern over sulfites in wine and beer (put there to prevent the growth of molds and bacteria) have led the Federal Bureau of Alcohol, Tobacco, and Firearms, which monitors these products, to require labels that say "contains sulfites" on cans and bottles.

Nitrates, additive substances that inhibit the growth of bacteria that cause botulism in foods and are used for curing bacon and other processed meats, have also been the subject of debate because, during frying and digestion, nitrates are converted to nitrosamines, which have been shown to cause cancer in laboratory animals. At present, there has been no action taken to discontinue their use.

Some people may choose to avoid foods containing certain additives because they add to the sodium content of foods or because they believe they have food sensitivities to these substances. Monosodium glutamate (MSG) is one such substance. MSG, which is the sodium salt of glutamic acid, naturally occurs in many foods, such as tomato sauce and cheese. It is also frequently used as a flavor enhancer.

Sugar Substitutes: How Sweet?

Perhaps the most concerted effort related to nonfood substances has been focused on artificial sweeteners. In the early 1950s, the FDA approved an artificial sweetener called cyclamate. Cyclamate-sweetened foods and beverages became popular, as did a cyclamate-based artificial sweetener called Sweet 'n Low.

Cyclamate, sometimes combined with saccharin, became the country's most popular sugar substitute, sweetening canned goods, baked goods, bacon, toothpaste, mouthwash, lipstick, and cereal, as well as diet and nondiet beverages. It wasn't until 1969 that the FDA banned cyclamate, after research showed that it caused bladder tumors in laboratory rats who were fed large amounts. Saccharin then became the substitute of choice and also the subject of continued controversy after laboratory rats, also fed large amounts of the substance, developed bladder cancer.

In 1981, the FDA approved a new sugar substitute, aspartame, marketed as NutraSweet. Aspartame comprises the amino acids aspartic acid and phenylalanine, which are found in large quantities in most proteins. Today, many products contain aspartame, but it too has been the subject of some controversy. Various claims have been made concerning possible side effects from aspartame, but they have failed to stand up under careful scientific investigation. To date, most of the antiaspartame evidence has been anecdotal, not scientific. That is, people said they developed headaches or other symptoms, but there was no independent verification of the claims. In fact, when researchers at Johns Hopkins Medical Center conducted a double-blind study, using aspartame and placebos, the subjects taking aspartame reported no more headaches than those taking placebos.

The FDA has set guidelines regarding an acceptable daily intake (ADI) for aspartame, and research has shown that most people consume well below the ADI. For example, a 150-pound adult would have to drink about 17 cans of soda sweetened with aspartame to reach the ADI: a 40-pound child would have to drink 4 to 5 cans.

There is also concern about the effects of the amino acid phenylalanine on a particular group of people who lack the enzyme to metabolize it normally. The condition, called phenylketonuria, or PKU, is rare, but the danger exists that children with PKU could suffer neurologic damage from aspartame. (They suffer similar damage from eating protein foods.) Because of this, aspartame products contain the warning, "Phenylketonurics: Contains Phenylalanine." For people who do not have this condition, there is no evidence that moderate amounts of aspartame in the diet are harmful.

In 1988, the FDA approved a new artificial sweetener for use in dry-food products and for sale in powder and tablet form. The new sweetener, marketed under the name Sunette, is known as acesulfame K. According to the FDA, four long-term animal studies showed no toxic effects from the substance. But the Center for Science in the Public Interest disputed this finding with two studies. In one, rats fed acesulfame K developed more tumors than those who were not given the substance. In another study,

a group of diabetic rats experienced a rise in blood cholesterol after being fed the sweetener. The results of these tests are still being examined by scientists to determine their validity.

If you're concerned about the potential dangers of artificial sweeteners, you might ask yourself why you're using them. Chances are, you're interested in their "calorie-saving" properties. But as you swig your artificially sweetened soda, consider this: Several studies have demonstrated that people who "save" calories by drinking artificially sweetened sodas usually add them elsewhere. So far, no one has shown that people who substitute sugar (only 16 calories a teaspoon) for these substances lose more weight than other people.

Nonfat Fats

Manufacturers are also currently testing several different kinds of fat substitutes, which include both synthetic varieties and substitutes made from naturally occurring food substances. Olestra, being tested by Procter & Gamble, is composed mainly of sucrose and vegetable oil, bonded together into molecules that are too large to be digested. Because it cannot be digested, it adds no calories. It has been suggested that it might inhibit the absorption of cholesterol from other foods, but this is yet to be fully determined, and it may reduce the absorption of fat-soluble vitamins.

Simplesse, produced by the manufacturers of NutraSweet, is composed of whey protein from milk or egg whites. Unlike Olestra, it's utilized by the body but reduces calorie consumption because it can replace 27 calories of fat with 4 calories of high-quality protein.

Although these "fake fats" are still open to scrutiny, they certainly have the potential to provide real benefits in helping people cut down on fat. One caution might be that, if people can eat as much as they want of ice cream, candy, rich sauces, and the like, might this not lead to their cutting down on high-carbohydrate, high-fiber foods? Human nature being what it is, if the artificial fats are approved and catch on, medical experts and nutritionists will probably need to reestablish firmly the necessity of eating a variety of wholesome foods.

There are many gray areas concerning food additives and substitutes, and the FDA's reviewing process of currently available products moves very slowly. However, we agree with the FDA that the majority of additives are safe and play an important role in our diets. In fact, the FDA ranks additives last on a list of things to be concerned about in food, with such issues as bacterial contamination and nutrient deficiencies ranking higher.

Designer Foods: Good or Bad?

When the FDA announced that it was giving manufacturers the green light to produce genetically engineered foods, many consumers were confused about what that meant, and a bit dismayed by the concept.

First, a definition. Genetically engineered food is food in which a "foreign" gene (or genes) has been added or which has been otherwise manipulated. Every source of food, plant as well as animal, contains strands of genes known as DNA, which determine all of the food's characteristics. When a scientist genetically engineers a food, he or she splices a new gene into one of the DNA strands from another food source, or inserts a gene that was synthesized in a laboratory. The extra gene might help a food stay fresh longer, taste better, or remain more resistant to insects before being harvested, thus reducing the need for pesticides.

Because the goal of genetic engineering is to produce better, more healthful, more abundant food, what's the problem? Supporters of genetic engineering see it simply as an extension of traditional breeding techniques in which, for instance, two different types of lettuce are "mated" so that the crunchiness of one and the flavor of the other will come together in the next lettuce generation.

However, critics of genetic engineering argue that it represents a significant departure from the breeding experiments of the past, and that the safety of a new or foreign gene cannot be assumed until it has been tested as thoroughly as any food containing a new additive.

Equally disturbing to many people is the FDA's policy that genetically engineered foods need not be labeled as such unless a food is noticeably different from what consumers would expect. "Without labeling, mixing and matching genes may be very disruptive for many people who have chosen or learned to eat certain foods for religious, moral or health reasons," says Sheldon Krimsky, Ph.D., professor of urban and environmental policy at Tufts University and head of the board of the Council for Responsible Genetics.

Dr. Krimsky points out that some vegetarians might not want to eat even a single gene contributed by an animal, and some Jews and Muslims might not want to eat any genetic material from a pig. Dr. Krimsky also notes that many people are allergic to or intolerant of certain foods and that genetic engineering may inadvertently transfer allergenicity from one food to another.

Although genetically engineered foods are only now making an appearance in stores, in the form of spoil-resistant tomatoes, their existence clearly will emerge as an issue in the next decade. Responsible consumers can be alert to the introduction of these foods and lobby for appropriate testing and labeling.

COMMON FOOD ADDITIVES AT A GLANCE

Category	Examples	Dietary Contribution
		(+) = positive role (-) = other considerations
Preservatives	BHA, BHT, calcium propionate, sodium Benzoate, sorbic acid, sodium nitrate, sulfites	+Increase food shelf life +Prevent spoilage of perishable foods +Increase availability +Sometimes add nutrients (calcium propionate is a good source of calcium) - Nitrates can be converted into nitrosamines in the body - Being studied as a factor in cancer - Sulfites cause reactions in some people, especially asthmatics; banned in fresh fruits and vegetables (except potatoes)
Flavoring agents	Spices, essential oils, MSG, vanillin, limonene, GMP	+Replace natural flavors lost in processing +Enhance flavors +Create new flavors - Some people sensitive to MSG - GMP, found in many prepared soups, converts to uric acid in the body and should be avoided by people with gout or other excess–uric acid diseases
Coloring agents	Annatto, caramel, beta-carotene, dyes	+Provide rich colors that consumers associate with foods (e.g., yellow butter, green mint) - Five dyes have been approved as safe; others have been banned—red dyes no. 2 and no. 4
Sweeteners	Saccharin, aspartame	+Noncaloric sweetening - Possible cancer link to saccharin; products must contain warning - Aspartame may cause symptoms in people with genetic disorder known as phenylketonuria
Emulsifiers	Lecithin, monoglycerides, diglycerides, polysorbates	+Prevent separation of oil and water +Enhance flavor +Retard spoilage - Polysorbates are limited by the FDA, contain very small amounts of carcinogens
Texturizers and stabilizers	Gelatin, pectin, carrageenan, cellulose gum, modified starches, sodium alginate	+Add "body" and thicken foods +Improve flavor/texture +Prevent canned foods from separating - Safe in small quantities; in larger amounts might replace needed nutrients

PART TWO

Eating Better in America

Food is basic to life, but many factors dictate what we eat, how our food is prepared, and the ways we incorporate eating into our social rituals. We do not eat simply to fuel our bodily operations; if that were the case, we might already have developed nutrition capsules to circumvent the complex business of procuring, preparing, and eating food. Instead, eating is a central and valued human activity whose contexts include custom, religion, family tradition, health, pleasure, and lifestyle.

In recent times, the availability of nutrition information has heightened consumer awareness of the ways food relates to health and fitness. This is a positive trend, but sound nutrition does not exist in a vacuum. There can exist no fixed list of good foods or bad foods. Nor is there a simple set of rules that can guarantee a perfect nutritional balance that applies to everyone. Nutrition goals must encompass the full range of social, psychological, historical, and economic considerations with which people live.

If there is flexibility in the idea of what good nutrition is, there are firm statements we can make about what good nutrition is not:

Good nutrition is not torture: It does not mean deprivation or being forced to eat foods one dislikes. The "no pain, no gain" philosophy of health is not only unnecessary, but also it often leads to a reverse effect. The fact is that good nutrition can coexist with the pleasure of eating.

Good nutrition is not a magic formula: We cannot guarantee a certain level of health or longevity by virtue of what we eat. It's true that there are scientific judgments about certain foods. These dietary guidelines help us make choices, but they are not rigid standards that apply to every individual in every situation.

Good nutrition need not be costly: It does not require the purchase of special foods, expensive supplements, or unusual appliances. A healthful diet can easily be maintained on even a modest food budget.

Good nutrition is not dull: Some people see nutrition as a clinical eating experience, at odds with the notion that food gives pleasure.

But sound nutritional advice can be expressed in ways that allow people to enjoy food fully without constantly analyzing it.

In our daily lives, nutrition is a dynamic force, not a static one. It is an exercise in problem solving, a way of taking into account all our needs and evolving an eating style that fits them.

Making Better Choices

Our lifestyles dictate many things about the way we eat, and these lifestyles are determined by a variety of factors—family, ethnic background, the influence of media, daily schedules, and peers. There is no reason most people can't develop a diet that both suits their lifestyles and meets all of their nutritional needs.

For example, as we examine what people eat, we see that almost everyone consumes food from grains, primarily wheat, rice, and corn. These foods may differ in the way they are prepared, but they supply basically the same kind of nutrients. A corn tortilla and a bowl of spaghetti aren't that different in their nutritional effects; neither are a serving of rice and a slice of bread. Their consumption reflects our diet preferences, but none of the choices are superior to the others.

Good nutrition boils down to making the best possible choices in your diet from the selections that are realistically available. We know, for example, that Americans spend nearly $15 billion every year on frozen foods. The best nutritional approach is to determine which frozen foods make the best choices. We also know that at least one-third of all Americans patronize a restaurant (half of them "fast" food restaurants) at least once a day. The best nutritional approach describes how to make choices from restaurant menus.

It's too bad that good nutrition is often associated with rigidity, guilt, and denial. According to a survey by the American Dietetic Association, almost two out of every five people in the United States believe that following a balanced diet means giving up foods they like. No wonder so many people are discouraged from healthful eating!

However, the essence of a healthful diet is much simpler and far less agonizing than most people think. In fact, it can be summed up in nine words: More plant foods, fewer animal foods, and more exercise.

Nutrition in the Real World

Consumer confusion is the natural fallout of a health industry that stresses information over practical application. Consumers are assaulted with facts, theories, warnings, and impressions about diet but are usually left with very little in the way of simple, realistic guidelines for eating that can be followed in the normal course of life.

Practical nutrition relates to people and the ways they live. In this section, we focus on the lifestyles of Americans. We provide hundreds of practical guidelines for purchasing and preparing healthful foods. Because more than half the foods Americans eat come in packages, we describe how to read package labels for nutrition. We address the very real concerns people have about the safety of the food supply. And we offer practical advice for the millions of people who eat out in restaurants. More than anything, this section will debunk the myth that painful sacrifices must accompany healthful eating.

9

A Healthy Cook's Kitchen

If you are a lover of gourmet cooking and eating, or even simply a lover of food, you may wonder if your enjoyment of culinary delights is at odds with your desire for nutritious cuisine. The good news is that adopting healthful cooking techniques need not doom you to tiny portions of bland foods. On the contrary, foods prepared with nutrition in mind can satisfy the most exotic palate. Once you discover the simple techniques and have the right tools on hand, it can be fun to learn the many ways you can imaginatively prepare foods that provide good nutrition balance and that are low in calories, fat, cholesterol, and sodium—without sacrificing the pleasure of eating.

The Food Pyramid: The Picture of Nutrition

To get across the essence of a balanced diet quickly and easily, in 1992 the U.S. Department of Agriculture replaced the four-food-group pie chart, used since the 1950s, with a new Food Guide Pyramid.

The pyramid illustrates at a glance the food groups that should be included in a healthful diet, and the recommended proportions of each food.

As the illustration demonstrates, the bread, cereal, rice and pasta group at the base of the pyramid ranks as the largest section. That's because grain-based foods, rich in complex carbohydrates, should make up the bulk of the diet. Fats, oils, and sweets take up the least space at the pyramid's narrow tip, just as they contribute to the least number of calories in a healthful meal plan. The Food Guide Pyramid is a useful tool for menu planning. Although the basic advice remains the same, many people find that this graphic representation makes it easier to assure a well-balanced diet.

Small Changes Go a Long Way

Changes in your cooking style can provide you and your family with a diet that may protect against heart disease, hypertension, and possibly cancer. It can also help you to restrict calories while you eat hearty portions of foods that are tasty and good for you.

The way you set up your kitchen for healthful cooking depends on your personal living style, your family makeup, and your particular health and fitness concerns. Even if you're a minimalist cook, you can add quality to your meals (both nutritionally and in terms of taste)

Food Guide Pyramid
A Guide to Daily Food Choices

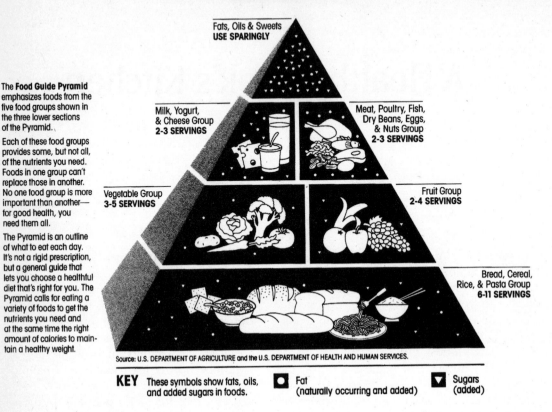

The **Food Guide Pyramid** emphasizes foods from the five food groups shown in the three lower sections of the Pyramid.

Each of these food groups provides some, but not all, of the nutrients you need. Foods in one group can't replace those in another. No one food group is more important than another—for good health, you need them all.

The Pyramid is an outline of what to eat each day. It's not a rigid prescription, but a general guide that lets you choose a healthful diet that's right for you. The Pyramid calls for eating a variety of foods to get the nutrients you need and at the same time the right amount of calories to maintain a healthy weight.

Fats, Oils & Sweets
USE SPARINGLY

Milk, Yogurt, & Cheese Group
2-3 SERVINGS

Meat, Poultry, Fish, Dry Beans, Eggs, & Nuts Group
2-3 SERVINGS

Vegetable Group
3-5 SERVINGS

Fruit Group
2-4 SERVINGS

Bread, Cereal, Rice, & Pasta Group
6-11 SERVINGS

Source: U.S. DEPARTMENT OF AGRICULTURE and the U.S. DEPARTMENT OF HEALTH AND HUMAN SERVICES.

KEY These symbols show fats, oils, and added sugars in foods.

● Fat (naturally occurring and added)

▼ Sugars (added)

with some basic planning and preparation. It's not necessary to overhaul completely your diet and totally restock your kitchen overnight. Begin by making small changes. If you find it difficult, for example, to juggle many nutritional recommendations at once, choose one or two that are particularly important and focus on them, adding other changes over time. Don't forget that food can be fun. If you approach dietary changes with a heavy heart and feelings of deprivation, your good intentions aren't likely to last. When you're making food substitutions, be sure to choose the foods you enjoy.

You'll be pleasantly surprised to learn how easy it is to incorporate nutrition into your day without making any drastic changes. In fact, the simplest substitutions can dramatically improve your food intake. To demonstrate, if you were to make certain minor changes in your cooking, your calorie savings would be quite substantial, and nearly all the calories saved would be from fat.

Stock Your Kitchen for Health

You can have a nutrition-at-your-fingertips kitchen once you stock your larder with supportive cooking ingredients and diet-conscious cooking aids. Chances are, you will already have on hand some of the items we'll talk about here, but maybe you've never understood their benefits.

The following information and checklists will

FAT-SAVING SUBSTITUTIONS

Substitute	For	Calories Saved
1 cup low-fat milk (1%)	1 cup whole milk	50
1 cup skim evaporated milk	1 cup heavy cream	640
1 cup plain low-fat yogurt	1 cup sour cream	375
1 cup blended low-fat cottage cheese	1 cup sour cream	305
1 cup plain low-fat yogurt	1 cup regular mayonnaise	1,455
1 cup part-skim ricotta cheese	1 cup whole-milk ricotta cheese	90
1 cup white sauce, made with low-fat milk, 2 tablespoons flour, no fat	1 cup whole-milk white sauce made with 2 tablespoons flour and 2 tablespoons butter	250
1 cup diet margarine	1 cup regular margarine	205
1 cup reduced-calorie mayonnaise	1 cup regular mayonnaise	480

establish some ground rules for your healthful kitchen. Start slowly and gradually to set up your kitchen, experimenting with cooking ingredients and equipment to find those that suit you best. We're not going to tell you that all of them are essential for every kitchen. It really depends on how much you cook and the kinds of foods you like to eat. And even if you don't do a lot of home cooking, you're sure to find some quick and easy ways to improve both the nutrition and the enjoyment you get from your diet.

Fill Your Pantry with Nature's Best

Most people who cook stock their kitchens with a certain number of "cooking basics," such as flour, sugar, and rice. Start with an examination of your kitchen's staples to find the items for which you can substitute better choices.

Here are some suggestions:

◆ Long- or short-grain brown rice without the bran removed is more healthful than white rice, primarily because of its high fiber content.

◆ Whole-grain flours (such as whole wheat, buckwheat, rye, and oat flour) are more healthful than refined grains, primarily because they're high in fiber. These flours are also a very good source of B vitamins, as is fortified white flour. Some, like soy flour, are excellent sources of protein. Be aware that these drier, heavier flours may change the way you prepare recipes that call for refined flours. Some cooks find that a satisfying compromise is to mix a whole grain flour half and half with a refined flour.

◆ Legumes (beans, peas, and lentils) are good sources of protein for those who want to reduce their fat intake by sometimes substituting a nonmeat main course. Legumes can also be good sources of B vitamins, nonheme iron, and calcium. Use them to make hearty soups and stews, casseroles, and salads. The most commonly used legumes include black beans, black-eyed peas, kidney beans, lentil beans, lima beans, navy beans, pinto beans, soy beans, split peas, and whole peas. (Be sure to store legumes in tightly covered containers in a cool, dry place to preserve nutrients and prevent rancidity.)

◆ Most vegetable oils—such as safflower, sunflower, corn, and especially canola—are high in polyunsaturated and monounsaturated fats which are more healthful. The exceptions (notably palm and coconut oils) are rarely used in home cooking. Vegetable oils will last up to one year, and olive oil six months, if stored at room temperature. With refrigeration, they will last a month or two longer.

◆ Use sparingly those condiments that are high in sodium and/or fat. Worcestershire sauce, soy sauce, and bouillon are examples of condiments with a particularly high sodium

◆ NUTRITION QUIZ ◆
Test Your Food Savvy

With all the new findings about fish oil and fiber, the controversies about calcium, the recommendations about fat, and the myriad other nutrition notes that cross your path every day, it's hard to keep track of some of the basic facts and figures about nutrition. Take this quiz to assess your nutrition knowledge.

1. Which of these foods is highest in fat?
   (a) 1 tablespoon of peanut butter (b) 1 cup of sunflower seeds (c) 5 shortbread cookies

2. For adults, the recommended dietary allowance for calcium is:
   (a) 800 milligrams (b) 1,000 milligrams (c) 1,500 milligrams

3. Which fish is highest in omega-3 fatty acids?
   (a) salmon (b) rainbow trout (c) haddock

4. Spinach is a particularly good source of:
   (a) calcium (b) vitamin A (c) iron

5. Which is the best source of water-soluble fiber?
   (a) wheat bran (b) oat bran (c) oatmeal

6. Which of the following foods is richest in the iron the body absorbs most efficiently (heme iron)?
   (a) iron-fortified cereal (b) red snapper (c) tofu

7. A baked potato best meets our need for:
   (a) vitamin C (b) vitamin B-6 (c) protein

8. Which of these nuts contains the least fat?
   (a) peanuts (b) macadamia nuts (c) chestnuts

ANSWERS

1. (b) Although all foods listed are high in fat, sunflower seeds top the list with more than 15 grams (equal to 135 calories) in a 1-cup serving. One tablespoon of peanut butter contains approximately 8 grams of fat. Five shortbread cookies have 11.5 grams.

2. (a)—with a caveat. The current RDA for calcium is 800 milligrams for adults, with the exception of pregnant women and breast-feeding mothers, whose allowance is recommended at 1,200 milligrams per day. Some experts believe these women should take 1,500 milligrams per day.

3. (a) Salmon, one of the richest sources of omega-3 fatty acids, contains 1 to 2 grams in a 3-ounce serving. Fresh rainbow or brook trout is also a rich source of omega-3 fatty acids, with nearly 1 gram in a 3-ounce portion. All three fish mentioned are good, low-calorie sources of protein.

4. (b) Spinach, like other darker salad greens, packs more nutrients than the light-colored varieties such as iceberg lettuce. It is richest in vitamin A because it is high in beta-carotene, which is converted to vitamin A in the body. A 1-cup serving provides more than 100 percent of the RDA. Contrary to popular belief, spinach is not a very good source of iron or calcium.

5. (b) Oat bran (the outer husk or shell of the oat grain) is the richest source of water-soluble fiber. Oatmeal, which is huskless, has only about half as much soluble fiber as the bran portion. Wheat bran contains mainly insoluble fiber, which increases the bulk of the stool and helps prevent constipation.

6. (b) Animal foods (fish, meat, and poultry) contain heme iron, of which the body absorbs roughly 25 percent. Cereals, grains, and vegetables contain nonheme iron, of which the body absorbs only 3 to 8 percent. But when foods with nonheme iron are eaten in combination with foods that contain heme iron, the amount of iron that is absorbed from them increases.

7. (a) One medium-sized potato (with many of its nutrients concentrated just under the skin) contains more than a third of the body's daily requirements for vitamin C. Potatoes are also a good source of vitamin B-6, providing more than 20 percent of the RDA for this nutrient. In addition, they supply 6 percent of the RDA for protein, along with smaller amounts of other nutrients.

8. (c) Three small chestnuts contain only 29 calories and less than 1 gram of fat. Sixteen shelled, roasted peanuts, which weigh the same amount, have 85 calories, 65 of which come from fat. Macadamia nuts top the list. Six of them contain 109 calories, nearly all of which come from fat.

content. Mayonnaise and cream-based sauces have a high fat content. Better choices include vinegar, tomato paste, lemon juice, lime juice, and mustard. Ketchup is moderately high in sodium (unless you choose a no-salt brand) and it usually contains sugar, but it's okay for use in small amounts.

Lose the Fat, Keep the Satisfaction

It won't surprise you to hear that chemists have found fat to have a pleasing "mouth feel." It not only helps dishes stay moist, but it also adds flavor and provides a smooth texture. But with a little care, you can reduce the fat without compromisng the taste and texture. Here are some simple suggestions:

◆ Use heavy iron skillets as well as heavy pans with nonstick coatings. These allow you to cook with less oil than other pans because they conduct heat more evenly. Vegetable-oil cooking spray helps, too. It can make a thinner pan as stick resistant as a heavy one.

◆ Add less oil than recipes call for when browning meat. Many recipes call for up to a tablespoon of oil per serving. But as a general rule, you need only about a teaspoon per serving. (Be sure to use measuring spoons. What seems like a mere "drop" of oil can be much more!)

◆ Stir-fry instead of still-fry. Quickly cooking thinly cut food over high heat while stirring frequently allows you to get by with less oil. And if you heat the pan and the oil first, you can use even less oil.

◆ Seal in juices and flavor with foil. Fish will stay wonderfully moist this way. Place each fillet on a sheet of foil, top with slices of green pepper, onion, and tomato, then seal individual pouches and bake or grill. For barbecued chicken, coat skinless pieces with barbecue sauce in a baking pan, cover with foil, and bake at 350 degrees, then remove the foil for the last 10 to 15 minutes to get a "baked" finish.

◆ Marinate to moisten and tenderize leaner cuts of meat, or chicken and fish. Try the following marinades to introduce flavors without adding much fat. For teriyaki-style beef, use two parts soy sauce and one part sesame oil, with garlic, ginger, scallions, and a pinch of sugar. For Mediterranean-flavored seafood, use equal parts lemon juice and olive oil plus a sprinkling of fresh herbs. For chicken, use equal parts lime juice and olive oil plus garlic and pepper.

◆ Top pasta, rice, and vegetable dishes with a tablespoon or two of Romano, Parmesan, or feta cheese. These varieties have as much fat as other cheeses, but because they are so flavorful, a little bit goes a long way.

Cut the Salt and Add Flavor

We have become so accustomed to the flavor of salty foods that many people assume they wouldn't enjoy food without having the salt shaker handy. In reality, by using salt as your primary flavoring agent, you are not only increasing your daily sodium intake, you are also potentially masking the flavors of many foods, not to mention missing out on the wonderful taste enhancement that herbs and spices can provide.

If the world of herbs and spices is a new one for you, you're in for a treat. The range of flavors is as varied as you want it to be. The accompanying table lists common spices, along with the foods they most perfectly complement.

Liquid flavorings (extracts) can also add zest

GETTING LESS FAT WITH ANIMAL PROTEIN

Although animal foods are generally fattier than plant foods, it is definitely possible to choose at least some high-protein foods of animal origin—which also supply plenty of other nutrients—and limit fat at the same time.

	Protein(g)[1]	Fat(g)[2]	Total calories
1 cup whole milk	8	8	150
1 cup skim milk	8	0	86
3½ oz roasted chicken with skin	27	14	239
3½ oz roasted chicken without skin	29	7	190
3 oz broiled T-bone steak (choice cut)	24	9	182
3 oz broiled top round steak (select cut)	27	5	156

[1] A gram of protein contains 4 calories
[2] A gram of fat contains 9 calories

to foods, reducing the necessity of adding sugars or sauces that are high in fat and calories. Just a drop or two of these intense flavors can punch up a salt- or sugar-free dish. You can purchase common extracts in the supermarket (usually in the baked-goods section), but for the more exotic varieties, you may have to try specialty bakeries, mail order catalogs, or gourmet shops.

Extracts are usually sold in tiny bottles that contain from two to four ounces, but a little bit goes a long way. They may be used in a wide variety of creative ways.

If you enjoy ethnic cooking or like to make your own sauces and dressings, note that these ingredients are often used to create favorite seasonings:

◆ *Barbecue seasoning*: celery seeds, cayenne, clove, coriander, garlic, nutmeg, onion, chili powder, hickory flavor

◆ *Cajun spice*: paprika, garlic, onion, cumin, chilis, oregano, parsley, pepper, basil, thyme, marjoram, rosemary, cayenne pepper.

Stir-Fried Beef with Broccoli and Red Pepper

3/4 pound top round steak
1 teaspoon sugar
1 teaspoon cornstarch
1 tablespoon reduced-sodium soy sauce
1 tablespoon dry sherry

Sauce

1-1/2 teaspoons cornstarch
1/8 teaspoon crushed red pepper
1 tablespoon reduced-sodium soy sauce
2 garlic cloves, minced
1/2 cup water
1 tablespoon canola oil
4 cups broccoli florets, thinly sliced lengthwise
1 large celery rib, thinly sliced at an angle
1 medium-size red bell pepper, cut into small squares
3 scallions, white and green parts, minced

Partially freeze steak, about one hour. (To save time, freezing can be omitted, but it makes slicing much easier.) Trim fat from meat; cut steak lengthwise in half and crosswise in thin strips. In a large bowl whisk sugar, 1 teaspoon cornstarch, 1 tablespoon soy sauce, and sherry. Add beef and toss to combine; let stand (marinate) 20 minutes, tossing occasionally.

In a small bowl whisk sauce ingredients; set aside.

Heat oil in a large nonstick skillet or wok over medium-high heat until hot. Add beef, half at a time, and stir-fry until meat is no longer pink on the outside. As beef cooks, remove to a plate.

Add broccoli, celery, and 2 tablespoons water to skillet; stir-fry until crisp-tender, about 4 minutes. Add red pepper and scallions; stir-fry until crisp-tender, about 2 minutes. Whisk sauce again; add to skillet, and stir-fry until lightly thickened. Return beef and juices to skillet and heat through. Serve immediately. Makes four servings.

Nutrition information per serving

calories: 237
sodium: 329 milligrams
fat:[1] 8 grams
Plus one cup cooked white rice
calories: 501
sodium: 333 milligrams
fat: 9 grams

[1]One gram of fat contains nine calories. Someone following an 1,800-calorie diet should average no more than 60 grams of fat a day. The National Academy of Sciences recommends a daily sodium limit of 2,400 milligrams.

◆ *Curry*: cumin, coriander, cayenne, tumeric, fenugreek, garlic, ginger, cloves, pepper.

◆ *Italian seasoning*: savory, oregano, marjoram, sage, thyme, sweet basil, rosemary.

◆ *Mexican seasoning*: chilis, garlic, onion, paprika, cumin, bay, parsley, oregano, celery seed, cayenne.

◆ *Pizza seasoning*: onion, fennel, oregano, garlic, basil, parsley, marjoram, celery flakes, thyme.

◆ *Poultry seasoning*: marjoram, parsley, savory, sage, thyme.

◆ *Salad seasoning*: basil, tarragon, dill, chervil, parsley.

◆ *Salsa*: onion, celery, parsley, cumin, garlic, oregano, cayenne pepper.

While you're spicing up your diet, be careful that you don't inadvertently choose seasonings that contain large amounts of sodium. These include:

◆ *Garlic salt*: 1,850 mg in 1 teaspoon. (Use garlic powder, which contains only 1 mg of sodium per teaspoon.)

◆ *Meat tenderizer*: 1,750 mg in 1 teaspoon.

◆ *Onion salt*: 1,620 mg in 1 teaspoon. (Use onion powder, which contains only 1 mg of sodium per teaspoon.)

Note: Salt substitutes don't contain sodium, but they don't taste just like salt either. You might enjoy experimenting with the wide variety of spices and seasonings that are available.

Easy Ways to Incorporate Fruits and Vegetables

Many Americans are still eating far less than the recommended five servings a day of fruits and

TRY FLAVORS YOU LIKE IN THESE WAYS

Almond	
Anise (licorice flavor)	
Apricot	added to dessert recipes
Blackberry	added to plain seltzer
Blueberry	added to coffee
Cherry	mixed with yogurt
Chocolate	rubbed into meats before cooking
Cinnamon	
Clove	mixed into salads
Lemon	added to milk
Lime	added to vegetable dishes
Maple	mixed into fruit compotes
Mint	added to vanilla ice cream or ice milk
Orange	
Peppermint	dashed into plain tea
Raspberry	added to cold fruit and vegetable soups
Root beer	
Spearmint	mixed with yogurt dips
Strawberry	
Vanilla	
Walnut	

vegetables. Perhaps this is because they feel that incorporating more produce into the diet is simply too inconvenient and time consuming. Or maybe a lot of items, particularly vegetables, just don't appeal to people's taste buds. But eating lots of fruits and vegetables need not be a grim, time-consuming task. There are many little tricks for slipping in produce unobtrusively.

First of all, eating enough produce doesn't have to require a wholesale dietary change. Keep in mind that a single serving doesn't amount to much. Just one-half cup of cut-up produce or small-sized fruit (about 15 grapes, a slice or two of fresh pineapple, or half of a fresh broccoli spear) makes a serving. A cup of leafy greens, less than can comfortably fit on a salad plate, makes for a full-size portion. So do six ounces of fruit or vegetable juice or a single apple or pear.

Think of eating five servings a day as a diet tune-up rather than a major overhaul. For example, instead of replacing other foods you

SPICE UP A LOW-SALT DIET

Allspice	fish, eggs, soups, stews, carrots, tomatoes, winter squash	Ginger	poultry, pork, fish, fruit
Anise	poultry, coleslaw, desserts, baked goods	Horseradish	beef, fish, green salad
		Marjoram	beef, poultry, fish, eggs, eggplant, summer squash, tomatoes
Basil	beef, poultry, lamb, fish, eggs, soups, green beans, green salad, peas, spinach, summer squash, tomatoes, zucchini	Mint	beef, lamb, fish, carrots, peas, spinach, fruit
		Mustard seed	beef, pork, green salad, beans
Bay leaves	poultry, fish, soups, spaghetti, tomatoes	Nutmeg	poultry, fruit, desserts, baked goods, cottage cheese
Caraway seed	asparagus, cabbage, carrots, green beans, fruit, baked goods	Onion	beef, poultry, fish, soups, eggs, salads, tomatoes
Cardamom	poultry, cabbage, fruit	Oregano	eggs, soups, green salad, tomatoes, pasta dishes
Celery seed	beef, pork, fish, eggs		
Chervil	poultry, fish, eggs, soups, carrots, green salad	Paprika	poultry, fish, coleslaw
		Parsley	beef, poultry, pork, lamb, fish, soups, salads, peas
Chives	beef, poulty, fish, soups, cottage cheese	Poppy seed	green salad, fruit, baked goods
Cinnamon	poultry, pork, lamb, fruit, desserts, baked goods	Rosemary	poultry, lamb, fish, pasta, spinach, potatoes, fruit
Clove	poultry, pork, fish, tomatoes	Sage	beef, poultry, fish, eggplant, peas, tomatoes, rice, pasta
Coriander	pork, zucchini		
Cumin	beef, eggs, beans	Savory	fish, eggs, green beans
Dill	lamb, fish, soups, carrots, coleslaw, green salad, peas, summer squash, tomatoes	Sesame seed	poultry, bread, salads, casseroles
		Tarragon	poultry, pasta, fish, green salad
		Thyme	poultry, fish, soups, carrots, peas, tomatoes
Fennel	fish		
Garlic	beef, pork, lamb, poultry, fish, beans, rice, salads		

like with produce, why not add produce to those foods you already enjoy? If your favorite sandwich is chicken salad mixed with a little mayonnaise, consider chopping some green pepper into it the next time you make it. And before you add the top piece of bread, add a layer of sliced cucumbers or tomatoes.

Sandwiches are actually among the easiest dishes to add produce to without feeling like you're on a rabbit-food diet. Add lightly sautéed mushrooms, onions, and green peppers to a roast beef or turkey sandwich. Or add a tangy coleslaw, made with low-fat dressing, to sliced chicken and cold meat sandwiches. Simply mix shredded cabbage with equal parts reduced fat or fat-free mayonnaise and plain nonfat yogurt seasoned with basil and thyme.

Just as vegetables tend to blend well into sandwiches, fruits work great with desserts. Just scoop frozen yogurt into a melon half or top a bowl of frozen or plain yogurt with mixed fruits, raisins, and nuts. Top baked goods with sliced fruits in season, adding a drop of orange juice for extra moisture.

Nutrition-Wise Kitchen Tools

The tools you use for cooking can be nutritional helpmates. The equipment you buy depends to a large extent on how much time you spend in the kitchen and the kinds of foods you tend to prepare.

There are literally hundreds of cooking mate-

Savory Salad Sandwich

Heat 2 teaspoons olive oil in a nonstick skillet.
Mix in ⅔ cup each finely chopped mushrooms and onions.
Cover and cook over low heat until softened, about 5 minutes.
Remove from heat and mix in 1 garlic clove, minced, 1 10-ounce package of frozen spinach,
   thawed with the water squeezed out, and 2 tablespoons grated Parmesan cheese.
Serve on an English muffin and top with tomato slices.

rials from which to choose, from basic essentials to luxury appliances to colorful but not particularly useful gadgets. Stocking your kitchen with health-enhancing cooking tools will not guarantee good nutrition, but some tools will enable you to make small changes in your everyday meal preparation that, over time, can add up to a more nutritious diet. Every healthful kitchen should have the following basics:

Nonstick Pans

Use. All-purpose pans for sautéing meats and vegetables, "frying" eggs, and making omelettes.

Nutrition benefit. Allows foods to be fried with the use of very small amounts of butter or oil. You may also use a nonstick vegetable spray.

Vegetable Steamer

Use. An inexpensive, usually metal, insert that, when placed inside of cooking pots, holds vegetables above the water. Vegetables are cooked with a moist steam heat.

Nutrition benefit. Limits the nutrient loss that occurs when vegetables are submerged in water while cooking.

Kitchen Scale

Use. Weighing food portions—usually meat, poultry, fish, and cheese. A small, inexpensive postage-style scale (for weights of 1 to 10 ounces) is sufficient.

Nutrition benefit. Many people have trouble calculating portion sizes, often overestimating the amount of food that constitutes a four- or five-ounce serving. A scale can be particularly helpful if you're watching your calories and/or want to better control your intake of fatty foods.

Blender or Food Processor

Use. Mixes, purees, chops, slices, and grates foods. Food processors are equipped for more purposes than blenders and are better at tasks such as very fine grating and chopping.

Nutrition benefit. These devices can simplify home cooking and make nutritional drinks, soups, and vegetable-pureed gravy stock.

Juicer

Use. Squeezes and liquefies fresh fruits and vegetables, creating fresh juice.

Nutrition benefit. A juicer makes it easy to keep fresh fruit and vegetable juices available.

Egg Coddler

Use. Cooks eggs in a style similar to poaching.

Nutrition benefit. There's no need to use butter or oil. Coddling is easier than poaching and allows spices and other chopped ingredients to be added to the egg.

Wok

Use. Stir-frying meats and vegetables.

Nutrition benefit. A little oil is used, but not as much as is required for pan frying, and the intense heat cooks foods fast. This is a very healthful way to cook vegetables, because the longer they cook, the more nutrients are depleted.

Skimmer/Strainer

Use. Removes congealed fat from the tops of stews and soups that have been stored in the refrigerator or freezer. Also allows skimming of fat from the top of broths while cooking. (You can do this with a spoon, too, but a skimmer makes it easier.)

Nutrition benefit. Substantially reduces fat content and reduces the number of calories in soups and stews.

Microwave Oven

Use. Fast cooking for most foods.

Nutrition benefit. Because moist heat is used, there is no need to use butter or oil. Also, the fast cooking and the need for less water help preserve vitamins and minerals in foods.

Hot-air Popcorn Popper

Use. Pops corn.

Nutrition benefit. Keeps popcorn snack low in calories and free of fat, as no oil or butter is required.

Grill

Use. Adds flavor and substance to meats, fish, and vegatables.

Nutrition benefit. A grill adds a special smoky richness to cooking, with a minimum of fat.

Nonstick Skillet

Use. The same as a cooking pot.

Nutrition benefit. A nonstick skillet allows you to bake, fry, sauté, or boil meat, poultry, fish, and vegetables with much less fat. Also, it allows vegetables to cook without added water, preserving water-soluble nutrients that might be leached out during cooking.

Sharp Knife

Use. Food preparation.

Nutrition benefit. A sharp knife can mean the difference between cooking healthfully and not. It helps to cut up vegetables quickly and easily for stir-frys and salads. And the thinner you can cut meat, the less you will tend to use.

One Key to Nourishment Lies in the Cooking

Even if you've carried home grocery bags full of "healthful" foods, it's possible to at least partially sabotage your good intentions by using the wrong method of cooking. Begin to train yourself to think of the process of preparation as an integral part of what makes a food "good." For example, rather than thinking "A potato is nutritious," think "A potato baked in its skin is nutritious." The methods you use to prepare your foods can make a big difference in their nutritional value. And the preferred methods do not necessarily take more time; in some cases, they take less. Following is some cooking wisdom for your favorite foods.

Keep Fruits and Vegetables Packed with Nutrients

◆ Before cooking begins, fresh vegetables must be washed thoroughly, even when you buy them "washed" in the supermarket. As you remove all dirt, you will also remove surface pesticides.

◆ Run vegetables in a heavy stream of water whether they're to be cooked or eaten raw. Scrub hard-surfaced items with a vegetable brush. Separate the leaves of leafy vegetables and immerse them in a sinkful of water. Lift them out while the dirty water drains, repeating the process more than once if necessary. Avoid soaking vegetables, as doing so promotes a loss of nutrients.

◆ As you prepare your vegetables for cooking, minimize chopping and peeling, as vitamins are lost when the surface is exposed. Using a sharp knife, cut vegetables into uniform pieces so they will all cook at the same rate. Try to cook vegetables with jackets and skins intact, peeling afterward. Be sure to cover and refrigerate anything you don't use right away.

◆ When vegetables are being cooked, their enemies are light, heat, air, and water. Light destroys the B vitamin riboflavin, as well as vitamin A; heat wreaks havoc with vitamin C, thiamin, and folic acid; air breaks down vitamins C, E, and K; and water leaches out water-soluble vitamins and some minerals. The result to shoot for with any cooking method is vegetables that are tender to crisp, not soggy or mushy. You can accomplish this goal using any of the following procedures: Cook in a pan with a tight-fitting lid, using only a small amount of water in the bottom. For best results, bring water to a boil, add vegetables, cover, and quickly return to the boil. Then lower heat and gently cook for a few minutes.

◆ Steam using a vegetable steamer, in a pot with a lid that fits. Don't allow the vegetables to touch the water or pack them so tightly that steam can't circulate.

◆ Stir-fry a dish for a family of four with only a tablespoon or two of oil. Make sure the oil is hot (but not smoking) before you add the vegetables.

◆ Pressure cook, following the directions on the appliance. Be careful not to overcook, or you'll lose both nutrients and crisp texture. Young, tender vegetables don't work well in a pressure cooker.

◆ Microwave with one or two tablespoons of water in a covered, microwave-safe container. The microwave creates a moist, hot atmosphere that conducts heat from one area to another. You'll need to experiment for different types of vegetables and quantities.

◆ The least effective cooking method for retaining nutrients in vegetables is to boil them in large quantities of water. However, if you do this, save the water for use in soups, stews, and gravies to recover some of the vitamin and mineral loss.

◆ Once your vegetables are cooked, serve them right away; nutrient loss occurs when they sit on a warming tray or at room temperature. In fact, two- to three-day-old leftovers can lose as much as half their vitamin C.

◆ Acids, such as vinegar and lemon juice, will not destroy nutrients, but it is better to add them after cooking to avoid a hard-textured surface on the vegetables.

◆ Keep vegetables whole until you're ready to cook them, in order to preserve water-soluble vitamins (Bs and C).

◆ Nutrients are lost when you peel the skins from vegetables. Try to cook them with the skins on. For example, one medium-sized baked potato has two grams of fiber, almost twice as much as a peeled potato.

◆ If you're concerned about the sodium content of canned vegetables, you can rinse some of the salt away with water.

◆ Use chicken broth or tomato juice, rather than butter, to cook vegetables.

◆ Broccoli and leafy green vegetables like collard greens, kale, and mustard greens are good sources of calcium. Use them to supplement other calcium sources, such as dairy foods, to meet your daily requirements.

◆ To improve your iron absorption from plant foods, serve iron-rich foods with foods rich in vitamin C, such as oranges, tomatoes, and broccoli. Vitamin C aids the absorption of iron.

◆ Boost the fiber content of breakfast cereal by slicing a banana on top; one medium-sized banana contains two grams of fiber.

◆ Use fruit as a sweet, nutritious staple. Mix fresh fruit as a topping for unsweetened cereals, waffles, and baked goods (like angel food cake).

Use Methods That Cook Meat Lean

◆ Good ways to cook meat and poultry include roasting, baking, broiling, and stir-frying. These methods require the addition of little or no fat and even help drain off some of the fat contained in the meat. With the development of crisping trays and other specialty microwaving dishes, it is becoming more common to microwave meats. Microwaving is also a low-fat method.

◆ Roasting is a dry-heat cooking method. Beef, pork, and lamb usually won't require basting because of their fat content, which renders them self-basting.

◆ If very lean items require basting, use nonfat substances like wine, vinegar, and lemon juice. Be sure to place the meat on a rack in the roasting pan so that excess fat can drip away during cooking. Baking is also a dry-heat cooking method for meat, poultry, fish, and casseroles. Some baking dishes (such as glass bakeware) require greasing to prevent food from sticking.

◆ Broiling is done under very high, direct heat. Be sure to place meat on a rack that allows the fat to drip away during cooking. If you choose to marinate the meat before cooking, try fruit juices like lemon, lime, or grape, or dry wine.

◆ Trim the obvious fat from meat and remove the whitish fat pads from under the skin in poultry, as well as removing the skin itself. One fatless method for browning meat and poultry is to pan-broil them in nonstick pans.

◆ The least healthful methods of preparing meat and poultry are frying and batter frying. Also, if you stew meat or slow-cook it in a Crockpot, reduce the fat content by skimming the top of the broth occasionally while it's cooking.

◆ Use a light basting sauce for cooking meat, such as lemon juice or wine.

◆ Use oven bags to keep lean meat and poultry from drying out during cooking. Available in supermarkets, they can be used in both conventional ovens and microwaves.

◆ If you broil regular (that is, not lean) hamburger meat well done on a grill that allows fat to drip off, you'll end up with as little fat as you'd get from using lean ground beef, which is more expensive.

◆ To cut the grease in fried chicken, minimize the cooking time. Fat absorption is related to the time food spends in oil. After cooking, set the chicken on a paper towel to absorb surface fat. Better yet, don't fry. Pull the skin off before baking or broiling. Crispy baked chicken can be made by dipping chicken into water, lemon, skim milk, egg white, or low or nonfat yogurt, then rolling it in unsalted cracker crumbs before baking. This method works well even if you pull off the skin before dipping.

◆ Create delicious, nutritious, and less caloric poultry stuffings by using larger amounts of fresh vegetables, such as celery, carrots, mushrooms, and onions, to supplement the bread.

◆ Light meat on chicken and turkey contains less fat than dark meat, and also fewer calories. (A 3-ounce serving of light turkey meat has 25 fewer calories than a similar serving of dark meat.)

◆ Rather than purchase processed luncheon meats, which are often high in fat and sodium, make your own sandwich fillings by baking turkey breast with the skin removed. Or look for low-fat versions of your favorite cold cuts.

◆ For Mexican tacos and burritos, substitute home-cooked pinto beans for chopped beef. (Beware of commercial brands of pinto beans, because they're usually cooked in lard.) For homemade pizzas, replace high-fat cheese with a combination of part-skim mozzarella and freshly grated Parmesan.

◆ Create a lower-fat, lower-cholesterol omelette by using more egg whites than egg yolks. For example, a three-egg omelette can be made with the whites of three eggs and the yolk of one.

Enhance the Value of Fish

It appears that eating one or two fish meals a week may cut the risk of cardiovascular disease for some people. Both lean and oily fish varieties are good; some of the oils in fish like salmon, trout, and mackerel, known as omega-3 fatty acids, may be associated with a lowered risk of heart disease.

Prepare fish with an eye to protecting its health benefits. The amount of fat that a fish naturally contains should determine the way it is cooked. Fattier fish, such as salmon and trout, can be grilled or broiled. Leaner fish, such as flounder and haddock, do better with moist cooking methods, such as poaching or microwaving. Incorporate these tips into your fish preparation:

◆ The mistake cooks make most often is to overcook fish, rendering it dry and tough. You can tell when fish is ready simply by looking at it: Once it loses its translucence and becomes opaque, it is probably ready. Test it with a fork; if it is flakey to the touch, remove it from the oven.

◆ Use low-fat ingredients to make a delicious liquid for poaching. The best include tomato juice, lemon or lime juice, and wine. Vegetable bouillon is also a good low-fat option, although it is higher in sodium than the others. When poaching, keep the heat at a temperature that just barely simmers the liquid, and cover the pan with a lid.

Pasta Made Perfect

With its impressive range of shapes, sizes, and colors, pasta can really jazz up your table. And because pasta is free of saturated fat and cholesterol, it makes for a nutritious, satisfying meal.

◆ Rinsing after cooking tends to wash away nutrients, particularly the B vitamins, so pasta should never be rinsed unless a recipe specifically calls for rinsing.

◆ Because pasta is eaten with either a sauce or dressing, you'll want to be attentive to the ingredients in the sauce you choose. A creamy, high-fat sauce can severely undercut pasta's natural low-fat properties. Use simple tomato, vegetable, or fish sauces and take advantage of the many seasonings that enhance the flavor of pasta.

◆ Use low-fat cottage cheese, skim milk, or yogurt instead of sour cream for flour and whole-milk sauces. Whenever possible, use margarine or oil instead of butter.

◆ To keep down the calories, flavor pasta with the sauce—don't drown it.

Delicious Diets Full of Beans

High in protein, vitamins, and fiber, and low in salt and fat, beans taste great in soups, salads, and casseroles. Because of their high protein content, beans are often used as a main-course meat substitute for people who are interested in reducing fat and cholesterol.

◆ Before cooking beans, rinse them well and remove misshapen or discolored beans.

◆ Most beans need to be presoaked before cooking. If you place them in a large pot of cold water and let it stand overnight, beans will soften yet retain their shape. A quicker method can be used if you don't care about the beans' breaking apart in water. Place them in a saucepan and cover with water by about two inches. Bring to a boil over medium heat, then simmer for two to three minutes. Turn off the heat, cover, and let stand for one to two hours before cooking. Be prepared to cook the beans for a while before you add other ingredients. As they cook, remove with a strainer the residue that floats to the top of the water, and add water as needed so that the beans are always covered. A slight cracking in the skin usually indicates that the beans are done. Of course, the foolproof method is to taste the bean. When beans are cooked whole, they should be tender, but not mushy.

◆ Bean eaters often complain of problems with gas after a meal. To eliminate some of the gas-forming ingredients, drain the water after beans have finished soaking, refill the saucepan with fresh water, and simmer until tender.

◆ If you are not accustomed to eating beans, incorporating them gradually into your diet will give your intestines a chance to adapt to this new carbohydrate source and help cut down on gas problems. You can also try a product called Bean-o, a liquid that you sprinkle on beans just before eating. It contains an enzyme that prevents the development of gas.

Make Your Own Hearty Soups

Many people shy away from making soups from scratch because they think it's too time consuming or complicated. But homemade soups can be relatively easy to prepare and are worth the effort from the standpoints of both taste and nutrition. These basic techniques are all you need to know to prepare mouth-watering and super-healthful soups.

◆ Make your stock by simmering vegetables, bones, and spices together in water over a gentle heat, barely boiling. Stock is easy to make, because ingredients don't have to be measured and almost any vegetable is suitable: onions, carrots, and flavorful but otherwise discarded parts like celery tops, tomato, and potato peels, and parsley stems.

◆ Leave vegetables and trimmings in large pieces. Add bones (shank and knuckle bones have the most flavor, but others, including poultry carcasses, make delicious stock), bay leaves, and a few crushed peppercorns. Cover with water in a large pot and simmer for an hour or two.

◆ "Degrease" the stock before use by chilling it and then lifting off the hardened top (fat) layer. Alternately, fat-free broth can be made by omitting bones and meat, and fat-reduced broth can be made by trimming the fat as closely as possible before cooking.

◆ If making broth from scratch takes more time than you want to spend, commercial broths—also called consommé, bouillon, or broth—can be used. They come bottled, canned, or in concentrated dry cubes or granules. Be aware, though, that many commercial stocks are quite salty and high in fat. As a rule of thumb, check to see that "chicken broth" or "beef broth" is listed as one of the first ingredients on the label, not salt or animal fat.

◆ After you have prepared the stock, sauté chopped onions, garlic, and celery in a large kettle, using a little olive oil. You can minimize the amount of oil you need to use by covering the vegetables during part of the sauté to retain moisture and prevent sticking. Then add your stock.

◆ Plan on an assortment of goods for substance. By including beans, peas, or other

Couscous with Kidney Beans, Carrots, and Zucchini

⅔ cup unsalted chicken stock or reduced-salt canned broth, fat removed (chill the unopened
    can in the refrigerator, remove the lid, and lift off the fat)
1 large garlic clove, put through a press or minced
2 tablespoons lemon juice
salt, optional
pepper to taste
1 tablespoon olive oil
1 large onion, thinly sliced
1 (16-ounce) can red kidney beans, rinsed and drained
1 medium (½ pound) zucchini, diced
2 cups thinly sliced carrots, cut at a slant
1 cup couscous

    In a measuring cup or small bowl stir broth, garlic, lemon juice, salt (if desired), and pepper.
    In a large nonstick skillet heat oil. Add onion and cook over medium heat, stirring occasionally, until softened, about 5 minutes. Add kidney beans, zucchini, and carrots. Stir the broth mixture and pour over vegetables; mix with a large spoon. Cover and simmer until vegetables are tender, about 10 minutes.
    Meanwhile, in a medium size saucepan bring 1⅔ cups water to a boil. Sprinkle couscous over top. Cover, remove from heat, and let stand 5 minutes.
    Fluff the couscous with a fork, transfer to individual serving plates, and spoon vegetables over top. Makes 4 servings.

Nutrition information per serving

calories: 380
fat[1]: 4 grams
sodium without added salt[2]: 59 milligrams

    [1]One gram of fat contains nine calories. Someone following a 1,800-calorie diet should average no more than 60 grams of fat a day.
    [2]The National Academy of Sciences recommends a daily sodium limit of 2,400 milligrams.

legumes in the same soup with grains and vegetables you increase the fiber and protein value of your soup. A little meat, poultry, or seafood will then go a long way.

◆ Time your additions to the soup pot according to how long items take to cook. Raw meats (which should be quickly browned beforehand) and long-cooking grains and vegetables should go in first. To preserve texture and nutrients, add fresh or frozen fast-cooking vegetables shortly before serving.

◆ Always simmer the soup gently; a vigorous boil will break up the ingredients and cloud the mixture, as well as diminish the flavor. You can tell that you've got a good simmer when the bubbles that form in the bottom of the pot rise slowly, barely breaking the surface. Once simmering, the pot can be left on its own.

◆ Add seasonings during the second half of cooking because they intensify as liquid evaporates. Fresh herbs, such as parsley, dill, thyme, oregano, and marjoram, may be left whole and tied together in what is known as a bouquet garni, for easy removal, or they may be chopped and sprinkled into the soup.

◆ To thicken the soup, add a little grated raw potato, barley, peas, rice, oatmeal, or oat bran, then simmer a bit longer. Pureed vegetables can also be used to thicken a soup.

Dress Your Salad Well

Many a salad has been marred by an overdose of dressing, tipping the fat and calorie balance from modest to excess by its richness. As many calorie watchers know, even the simplest vinaigrette has up to 100 calories per tablespoon, and a single tablespoon doesn't go far on the average salad.

The problem is that most salad dressings are laden with fat, and fat calories mount quickly. To be sure, a number of reduced-fat versions are available commercially. A few are delicious, but some are high in salt, and other rely on tasteless gums and fillers as replacements for oil.

Why not try making your own salad dressing? It's easy to prepare one that is both tasty and high in quality ingredients. Good oil, fine vinegar, and fresh seasonings are all readily available in supermarkets. The rich flavor of these select ingredients allows less to taste like more, and that helps you keep the fat and calorie content of your salads under control.

Picking Your Ingredients

For oil, choose one that is labeled "unrefined," "virgin," or "cold-pressed." It will have more color and taste of the grain, nut, or seed from which it originated, making a more savory dressing. (The more often the oil is "pressed," the more it loses its original composition.) In addition to unrefined olive oil, sesame seed oil

Yellow Pea and Spinach Soup

Yield: 8 servings, just under 1 cup each per serving
Calories: 130
Fat: 18
Sodium: 211 mg
Fiber: 3.6 g
1 cup chopped onion
2 tsp minced garlic
2 tsp olive oil
1 cup yellow split peas, washed
4 cups chicken broth (no added salt)
2 cups water
10 oz. package frozen, chopped spinach
1 tsp salt (optional)
1 tsp pepper

Sauté onion and garlic in olive oil in a large pot, covered. Add yellow split peas, chicken broth, and water. Bring them to a boil, then lower heat and simmer for 30 minutes. Add spinach, salt, and pepper and continue simmering for 30 more minutes.

Barley-Vegetable Soup

Pearled barley is sold in regular and quick-cooking forms which can be substituted for each other in recipes. If you use the quick-cooking kind for this soup, reduce the simmering time to 20 minutes or until the barley is tender.

1 tablespoon canola or corn oil
1 cup chopped onion
1 cup diced carrots
1 cup diced celery
2 large garlic cloves, put through a press or minced ¾ cup pearled barley
1 (13¾-ounce) can reduced-salt beef broth, fat removed (chill the unopened can in the refrigerator, remove the lid, and lift off the fat)
6 cups water
salt, optional
pepper to taste
1 teaspooon thyme leaves
1 (10-ounce) package frozen corn
½ cup (tightly packed) chopped fresh parsley

In a Dutch oven or large pot heat the oil. Add onion, carrots, celery, and garlic; mix with a large spoon. Cover and cook over low heat until onion is softened, about 5 minutes.

Add barley, broth, water, salt (if desired), and pepper. Crumble thyme between fingers into pot. Cover and bring to a boil. Reduce heat and simmer until barley is tender, about 55 minutes.

Add corn: simmer 5 minutes longer. Stir in parsley. Makes 6 servings, about 1½ cups each.

Nutrition information per serving

calories: 185
fat:[1] 3 grams
sodium (without added salt):[2] 53 milligrams.

[1]One gram of fat contains nine calories. Someone following an 1,800-calorie diet should average no more than 60 grams of fat a day.
[2]The National Academy of Sciences recommends a daily sodium limit of 2,400 milligrams.

and nut oils like hazelnut and walnut are especially rich. Granted, these oils tend to be more costly. But you can make them stretch further by blending them with a neutral-tasting but more economical oil like soybean, corn, safflower, sunflower, or canola.

Today's markets feature a wide variety of flavorful vinegars that will spark up a dressing. Delicious varieties include balsamic and rice- or fruit-flavored versions, such as raspberry, blueberry, or black currant. Fine red and white wine vinegars also make rich dressing flavors.

You might also make a habit of using fresh seasonings to enrich the flavor of your dressing. For example, try minced garlic clove instead of garlic powder or salt. Whenever possible, use fresh herbs instead of dried. Good salad choices include basil, chervil, chives, coriander, dill,

Try These Three Lean Dressings

Each one is rich in taste and texture, but lighter in calories and sodium than regular commercial brands. To further cut fat, change the ratio of vinegar or lemon juice to oil, as described above.

Raspberry Vinaigrette

Calories: 50/tbsp
Sodium: 60 mg/tbsp
1 tbsp raspberry vinegar
1 tbsp cider vinegar
4 tbsp vegetable oil (olive oil)
3 tbsp water
1 minced garlic clove
1 tsp Dijon mustard
1 tsp. salt
freshly ground black pepper to taste

Creamy Italian

Calories: 40/tbsp
Sodium: 40 mg/tbsp
1 tbsp lemon juice
2 tbsp vegetable oil (olive oil)
4 tbsp low-fat yogurt
1 tsp oregano
1 tsp salt
freshly ground black pepper to taste
1 tsp sugar (optional)

Light Russian

Calories: 40/tbsp
Sodium: 40 mg/tbsp
1 tbsp rice vinegar
2 tbsp vegetable oil
1 tbsp ketchup
1 tbsp water

fennel, marjoram, mint, oregano, parsley, rosemary, summer savory, tarragon, and thyme.

Making Your Dressing

If you want to reduce significantly the fat and calorie content of your dressing, replace one-half or more of the oil or fat in traditional recipes with low-fat ingredients or "expanders." In noncreamy dressings, use fruit juices (like tomato or lemon), water, ketchup, or broth for part of the oil. For creamy dressings, use low- or nonfat yogurt, buttermilk, or cottage cheese instead of mayonnaise, sweet cream, or sour cream. For a smooth texture, swirl the dressing briefly in a blender or food processor. These techniques add body without sacrificing flavor.

If you want to cut calories even further, increase the ratios of substitute ingredients. A good rule of thumb is to start with a 1:2 ratio of vinegar or lemon juice to oil, then add varying amounts of "expanders," anywhere from about one-half to two times the volume of the vinegar and oil components.

Better Ways to Dress Your Meals

Sauces and dressings don't have to spell high fat and calories. There are many ways to sauce up your foods healthfully:

◆ Create a pasta sauce from the saved juices of fish, scallops, clams, chicken, or vegetables. Add spices and tomato paste.

◆ Reduce the calories in coleslaw or salad dressing by "cutting" mayonnaise with low-fat yogurt.

◆ Four ounces of cottage cheese (with 1 percent milk fat) has only 83 calories and can be used with seasonings for vegetable dips or fruit toppings.

◆ Instead of sour cream, use plain yogurt, seasoned with pepper or other spices, as a topping for a baked potato or fresh fruit.

◆ Reduced-calorie and reduced-fat mayonnaise has 50 percent fewer calories than regular and is acceptable in salads and dressings.

◆ Cook with a nonstick vegetable spray instead of oil.

◆ In lasagna recipes, substitute whipped low-fat cottage cheese with Italian seasonings for ricotta cheese.

Guilt-Free Desserts

Contrary to popular belief, the dessert portion of your meal doesn't have to mark your nutritional demise. It's easy to satisfy your sweet tooth using less fat and sugar than dessert recipes usually call for. Compare, for instance the traditonal apple pie in the accompanying box with a slimmer, crustless version.

There are many other ways to make the eating of dessert a healthful as well as happy occasion. Here are some of our favorite tips:

◆ When you're baking cookies, muffins, pie fillings, puddings, and fruit crisps, reduce the sugars (including white and brown sugar, honey, and molasses) to half the amount called for in traditional recipes. Although sugar supplies tenderness and volume, many recipes can withstand a substantial reduction without sacrificing results. Experiment.

◆ To enhance the impression of sweetness while avoiding the sugar calories, use more sweet-tasting spices like cinnamon, nutmeg, and allspice. Intense flavorings like vanilla, almond, and rum extract can also enhance flavor.

◆ Cut the fat content by decreasing the amount of added margarine, butter, shortening, or vegetable oil by a fourth to a third of what is called for in dessert recipes. For example, if a recipe calls for one cup of margarine, use two-thirds of a cup. Fat makes products tender and light in texture, but it can often be reduced without ruining the taste. As a general guide for minimal fat content in cakes and cookies, use no more than two tablespoons of fat per cup of flour. (Drop cookies may be more successfully adapted than rolled cookies, which can become hard to roll out when they're low in fat.) For muffins and quick breads, use one to two tablespoons of fat.

◆ Add fruits and vegetables to baked goods in place of some of the fat. Mashed ripe bananas, grated carrots, applesauce, canned pumpkin or squash, raisins, prunes, figs, and dates all add their own natural moistness and sweetness—along with fiber, vitamins, and minerals.

◆ When possible, use only egg whites, not the whole egg, in cooking; the whites contain no fat or cholesterol.

◆ Instead of icing, which is typically high in fat and sugar, sprinkle on cinnamon and sugar before baking cupcakes; this will make a low-calorie, crunchy, sweet topping. Or try topping gingerbread, spice, or plain cake with hot spiced applesauce.

◆ To replace some of the fiber and other nutrients lost during the milling of refined flours, use whole-grain flour for half the all-purpose or white flour called for in a recipe. Because whole-grain flour is heavier, this technique works better in cookies, quick breads, and muffins than it does in cakes. You can also make your own exotic blends: rolled oats, barley, rice, or uncooked hot cereal can be quickly ground in a food processor and will give baked goods interesting variations in taste.

Apple Pie Bakeoff

Traditional Apple Pie

standard double crust made from:

2 cups flour
⅔ cup shortening
1 teaspoon salt
⅓ cup water
4 cups sliced, peeled apples
⅔ cup sugar
½ teaspoon cinnamon
⅛ teaspoon nutmeg
1 tablespoon lemon juice
1 tablespoon butter

calories (⅛ pie): 380
fat: 19 grams
sodium: 300 milligrams

Low-fat Apple Pie

4 cups sliced, peeled apples
1 tablespoon lemon juice
2 tablespoons flour
6 tablespoons brown sugar
¼ cup water
2 tablespoons margarine, melted
½ cup rolled oats
1 teaspoon cinnamon

Toss apples with lemon juice, flour, and 2 tablespoons sugar. Pour into one-quart baking dish that has been sprayed with vegetable cooking spray. Add water. Combine margarine, remaining sugar, rolled oats, and cinnamon. Spread over the apples. Bake at 350 degrees until the apples are tender—about 25 minutes.
calories (⅛ pie): 139
fat: 3 grams
sodium: 35 milligrams

◆ Substitute soft low-fat frozen yogurt for ice cream. Add chopped fresh fruit to plain yogurt instead of serving ready-made fruit-filled brands.

◆ If you do purchase flavored yogurt brands, note that plain flavors such as vanilla, coffee, and lemon contain less sugar than the fruited brands.

10

The Nutritional Shopping Cart

If you're like 70 percent of Americans, you make one or two major trips to the local supermarket each week. Once inside, you juggle a number of variables in making choices, including quality, convenience, nutrition, taste, presentation, and price. Even though supermarkets are becoming bigger and expanding the number and variety of products, there is no need for you to be intimidated by the prospect of shopping for good food. It would be absurd to think that responsible shopping requires careful scrutiny of the 20,000-plus products in a given store. In fact, you probably have only 10 to 20 items on your shopping list, and many of these (particularly the nonperishable ones) don't even show up every week.

To a large degree, the nation's supermarket chains are attempting to respond to their nutrition-conscious public. One important way this response is being demonstrated is in consumer education. For example, some chains use shelf-labeling programs and recipe boxes to alert consumers to foods that are low in calories, sodium, cholesterol, and fat.

Manufacturers are getting involved, too. One effective program, jointly sponsored by the National Livestock and Meat Board and the Food Marketing Institute, provides point-of-purchase information on the nutritional makeup of various cuts of meat, along with suggestions for preparation and cooking. And the National Dairy Board sponsors a calcium education program that includes booklets keyed to different age groups, with information about specific dairy products.

These are positive signs that nutrition is gradually becoming an integral part of the food shopping experience. But the primary responsibility for filling the shopping cart with the best variety of healthful foods still rests with the customer. The following sections provide practical advice and information that will make that task easier.

A Word About Commercial Fat-Free Foods

Cakes, cookies, frozen desserts, salad dressings, mayonnaise—is there any food you *can't* buy in a fat-free version? The trend in commercially available fat-free foods has been welcomed by consumers. Research shows that two out of three adults currently eat some low-fat or reduced-fat products. Although this trend is generally a good one, you should be aware that the proliferation of reduced-fat products in supermarkets is not the key to a healthful diet. One reason is that those items tend to replace foods that are not nutritional mainstays in the first place. Cakes, cookies, mayonnaise, and sour cream are not rich sources of vitamins, minerals, complex carbohydrates, fiber, or any other substances you need in your diet.

So, low-fat foods aren't necessarily healthful foods.

Furthermore, the new low- and nonfat items on the grocery shelves don't help Americans make the necessary shift to higher proportions of plant-based foods. So, when you're shopping low-fat at the supermarket, keep in mind that the goal is a healthful balance. Low-fat isn't enough!

Begin with a Good List

Your shopping trip will be more nutritionally effective if you use a little creativity in your shopping list.

First, set it up by category. For efficiency, the categories should follow the layout of your supermarket. Place your list in a handy location so that you can add items as you notice you need them.

When you create menus for the week, keep your list nearby and write down the ingredients you'll need. On your shopping list, these ingredients should appear in the form in which you'll actually be buying them. For example, if a recipe calls for four cups of milk, write "one quart" on the list.

If you have trouble keeping track of the best nutritional selections while you're shopping, include the information right on your list. You might want to create a symbol system to remind yourself about the nutritional characteristics you're looking for in certain foods. For instance, dairy foods might be checked for fat and cholesterol, breads for fiber, and sauces for sugar and sodium. If you know that certain brands meet your nutritional standards, write the brand names on your list.

Tip Sheets for Smart Shoppers

Dairy Products

NUTRITIONAL BENEFITS

Milk products are excellent sources of protein, calcium, certain B vitamins, and vitamin A. Low-fat milk is usually fortified with vitamin A (because fat-soluble vitamins are lost in the defatting process), and most milk is fortified with vitamin D (which aids the absorption of calcium). According to government figures, milk and milk products account for more than 75 percent of the calcium available in our food supply.

Calcium intake is considered one of the major factors in the prevention of osteoporosis (the loss of bone mass that most commonly afflicts postmenopausal women). One cup of low-fat (1%) milk contains 300 milligrams of calcium.

NUTRITIONAL CAUTIONS

Whole-milk dairy products are high in saturated fat, a problem for those concerned with blood cholesterol levels. The high fat content shows up in the calorie total, too. For example, 8 ounces of low-fat (1%) milk has 100 calories, compared with 150 calories for whole milk. Hard cheeses such as cheddar, made from whole milk, typically contain more saturated fat than meat products. Cheeses made from skim milk have less fat; the leanest are cottage cheeses made with 1% fat, although there is relatively little calcium in cottage cheese. Fortunately, there are low-fat substitutes for nearly all high-fat dairy products, and these are becoming the staples of the average household.

SHOPPING TIPS

◆ If you're eliminating cream in order to cut your fat intake, don't use nondairy substitutes. They're frequently made with palm and coconut oils, both high in saturated fat. Nonfat dry milk or 1% liquid skim milk are acceptable alternatives.

◆ If milk cartons are stacked in the display case, select the ones near the bottom. Those on top may not be getting cooled properly. Always check the "sell by" date on the carton.

◆ Buy milk right before you're ready to pay. The less time it remains unrefrigerated, the better.

◆ Flavored yogurts, such as vanilla or coffee, contain some sugar, and the fruit-filled brands contain even more. They also have more calories, up to 250. You're better off buying plain yogurt and adding fresh fruit.

BEST CHOICES

Milk
　　skim milk (no fat)
　　low-fat (1%)
　　buttermilk

Cottage Cheese
　　low-fat
　　dry-curd

Yogurt
　　low-fat, plain
　　nonfat, plain

Eggs

NUTRITIONAL BENEFITS

Eggs are a good source of high-quality protein, as well as a good source of vitamin A and several other micronutrients.

NUTRITIONAL CAUTIONS

Eggs are extremely high in cholesterol. One egg contains about 213 milligrams, more than half the limit suggested for one day. (Because the cholesterol is all in the egg yolk, however, the whites can be used for cooking without adding cholesterol.)

According to recent studies, raw eggs and partially cooked eggs have been known to cause salmonella poisoning, and you can't be 100 percent certain of avoiding this risk. To protect yourself, avoid eating raw eggs contained in foods like egg nog and key lime pie. Be sure that the eggs you buy are not cracked or dirty. If the white is thin and runny and the yolk does not hold together when you crack the egg, it may not be perfectly fresh.

SHOPPING TIPS

If you notice cartons of eggs sitting in the supermarket aisle, waiting to be shelved, do not buy them from that store. Eggs can easily spoil if they're left unrefrigerated.

Always open the egg carton and take a look before you put it into your cart.

Check for cleanliness and wholeness; if even one egg is cracked, select a new carton.

If eggs aren't on your list because of their cholesterol content, you might want to try one of the cholesterol-free egg substitutes, usually located in the frozen-food section. Or look for the product called "Just Whites," which is a powder that consists of egg whites. (If you can't find "Just Whites" in your area, you can order them by calling 1-800-773-8822.)

Beef and Poultry

NUTRITIONAL BENEFITS

Meat and poultry are among the highest-quality sources of protein available, and meat and poultry are also good sources of iron and the B vitamins. Shifting to leaner cuts of beef can yield many benefits, including a higher concentration of the B vitamins, iron, phosphorus, and zinc. For example, the riboflavin and iron content in 100 grams of beef ranges from about 10 to 20 percent of the RDA, with increased concentration in the leaner cuts.

Poultry is a high-quality protein source that

CHICKEN VS. BEEF

	Chicken, Roasted (no skin)	Ground Beef, Broiled (17% fat by weight)
Serving	1.5 oz.	1.5 oz.
Calories	70	115
Protein	13.5 g	11.5 g
Fat	1.5 g	117.5 g
Calories from fat	19%	159%
Sodium	27 mg	131.5 mg

is leaner than beef, especially if the skin is removed before cooking. For example, a chicken breast without the skin is only 131 calories, with 6 grams of fat and 64 milligrams of dietary cholesterol. Although the cholesterol total does not change when the skin is added, the fat total nearly doubles and the number of calories shoots up to 229.

Lean cuts of pork, trimmed of excess fat, can be a good choice, too. Pork producers herald it as "the other white meat."

NUTRITIONAL CAUTIONS

Because certain cuts are very high in fat (and calories), beef can be a nutritionally expensive way to get your protein if you don't stick with lean cuts. In a study by the USDA, beef was found to be the primary source of fat for most age and sex groups, particularly adult males.

Many Americans should probably cut their beef intake, and all should be conscious of selecting leaner cuts and trimming visible fat. Like all organ meats, liver is high in fat and cholesterol, although it is a very good source of iron and vitamins.

Beware of ground meat which can harbor E. coli bacteria. Ground meat should always be cooked thoroughly to make sure that any potential bacteria is killed.

SHOPPING TIPS

Examine meat for visible fat, including marbling, the thin white streaks of fat that run throughout the meat. Choose those that have the least.

Check the "sell by" date to see how fresh the meat is. Hold the package to your nose and smell. It is easy to judge freshness by smell. If you think it smells "funny" but aren't sure, choose another package.

Know the meaning of the grades that are assigned to meat cuts at the slaughterhouse, according to USDA guidelines. Grades are assigned on the basis of fat content and texture. They are: Prime (usually has the most fat and is also the most tender); Choice (moderately fatty and tender; the grade most commonly sold in supermarkets—94 percent of the beef graded by the USDA is graded "Choice"); and Select (lean).

Memorize the grading terms. They tend to be misleading and often cause consumer confusion. In one national study, consumers were asked to identify which grade of beef had the least amount of fat: 56 percent said Prime! Examples of the difference: A cut of chuck blade from the Select grade, braised, has 13 percent less total fat and saturated fatty acids and 7 percent fewer calories than a Choice cut of chuck. A Select grade indicates that the cut is almost 20 percent lower in calories and has only two-thirds the fat and saturated fatty acids of a Prime cut. In addition, the Agriculture Department now permits beef with 10 percent fat or less to be called lean or low-fat, and beef with 5 percent fat to be called extra-lean. Watch for these cuts in the supermarket meat case.

If you can afford it, choose ground round instead of ground chuck, or ask the butcher to grind the meat for you from the round cut of the beef which is leaner.

Self-basting turkeys are often injected with oils high in saturated fat. You might be better off creating your own basting liquid with polyunsaturated oils or margarine.

Because meat spoils easily, don't buy portions that are wrapped in damaged containers, with broken wrap or crushed plastic.

MEAT CHOICES

Beef
    lean round
    lean shoulder
    lean rump
    lean sirloin tips
    ground round
    veal (cuts with no visible fat)

Lamb
    leg

Nutrition Note: Kosher Meat

Kosher meat is determined by the method of slaughter. Rather than the usual method (which involves blood being spilled), the kosher technique involves drawing the blood from the animal through a salting process. For this reason, kosher meats have a much higher sodium content than nonkosher meats. Small amounts of sodium can be removed by soaking beef in water for an hour or so; this method is ineffective for chicken.

Pork
    center cut ham (high in sodium)
    loin chops
    pork tenderloin

Poultry
    chicken broiler
    turkey (not self-basting)
    cornish game hen

Processed Meats

NUTRITIONAL CAUTIONS

Although processed meats have plenty of convenience benefits, they really don't have any sterling qualities nutritionally. On average, they provide only about half the protein value of nonprocessed meats and are very high in fat and sodium.

SHOPPING TIPS

If you do buy processed meats occasionally, note that some varieties are better than others, particularly lean brands of turkey and ham. Incidentally, government regulations require that meat products designated as "light," "lite," "leaner," or "lower fat" must have at least 25 percent less fat than a comparable product. Foods labeled "light" or "lite" may also have less sodium, calories, or filler than a comparable product. Compare the labels.

Most packaged meats wouldn't be recommended for a person watching calorie, cholesterol, sodium, or saturated fat content. However, some are definitely better than others. For example, a slice of Oscar Mayer bologna fashioned from beef and pork has about 90 calories, with 72 of them from fat, and 300 milligrams of sodium. On the other hand, a slice of Oscar Mayer smoked turkey breast has only about 20 calories, with half of them from fat, and 290 milligrams of sodium.

Turkey has found its way into the cold-cut section, providing a low-fat, low-calorie substi-

CHOOSING THE LEANEST MEATS AND POULTRY

Meat (3 oz. cooked)	Calories	Fat (%)	Cholesterol (mg)	Protein (% RDA)
sirloin tip roast, trimmed of fat	156	33	69	38
top loin steak, trimmed of fat	163	36	65	38
ground chuck	240	57	87	37
lamb chop, loin cut	184	41	81	40
leg of lamb, sirloin	175	41	79	38
veal chop, loin cut	192	36	135	44
veal cutlet, round cut	150	37	112	34
chicken breast, trimmed of skin	131	24	64	36
ham	191	26	[1]	51
pork tenderloin	142	26	78	38

[1]Figures not available

tute for everything from bologna to salami to ham to hot dogs. If you buy any of these products, look for the turkey version. It will save you fat, calories, and sometimes sodium.

Fish and Shellfish

NUTRITIONAL BENEFITS

Fish and shellfish are excellent sources of high-quality protein, as well as of several vitamins and minerals. Fish is generally low in fat, but even the fattier varieties may provide a benefit because they contain omega-3 fatty acids.

For a long time, shellfish were crossed off many shoppers' lists because of their relatively high cholesterol content. But what researchers formerly took to be cholesterol in mollusks (clams, oysters, mussels, scallops, and squid) is really a composite of several different kinds of sterols, and many of these are noncholesterol sterols that may actually inhibit cholesterol absorption. Even the cholesterol in crustaceans (crab, shrimp, lobster, crayfish) is relatively low. For example, a 1-pound Maine lobster contains only about 140 milligrams, and Alaska king crab contains a scant 42 milligrams per 3 ounce serving. Add the benefits of low calories and fat, and shellfish can be considered a very healthful main course.

NUTRITIONAL CAUTIONS

Certain fish preparations are high in sodium. Salted, dried, and smoked fish such as smoked salmon and dried, salted mackerel should be limited by those concerned with sodium levels. Pickled fish, such as pickled herring, may be high in both sodium and calories, especially if it is in a creamed sauce.

Caviar is a rich fish food prepared by mixing the black, gray, or golden eggs of sturgeon with salt. A 1-ounce serving (one rounded tablespoon) contains almost 72 calories, nearly two-thirds of them fat. It also contains more than 400 milligrams of sodium and about 170 milligrams of cholesterol.

A composite crab product called surimi is commonly sold in supermarkets as an inexpensive substitute for crab. Although it has low levels of fat and cholesterol, it can contain up to eight times the sodium found in raw shellfish as a result of added salt and MSG.

Many people are currently concerned about the condition of our waters, particularly freshwater outlets near major industrial areas. Yet incidents of contamination from fish have been rare; most reports have involved mollusks and shellfish eaten raw. According to the Centers for Disease Control and Prevention, there is a very low incidence of seafood-related illness—only one in a million servings (excluding raw mussels, clams, and oysters).

Proper refrigeration before cooking and thorough cooking eliminates most of the potential danger. Popular wisdom suggests eating raw mollusks and shellfish only during cold-weather months, when the water temperature falls and there is less chance of bacteria. There may be some truth to this, but there's no guarantee that raw mollusks and shellfish will be without infection, regardless of the season.

Pregnant women, or women who might become pregnant, should be aware that although PCBs were banned from use in 1979, they continue to linger in waters in which they were once dumped, as well as in the tissues of species such as salmon, swordfish, and lake whitefish. PCBs, when consumed in large enough quantities, have been associated with harmful effects to fetuses. A second concern for women of childbearing age is mercury, the poisonous metal released into waters by burning fuels and industrial waste. Mercury accumulates in the bodies of larger fish that live for many years—such as tuna, shark, and swordfish. Although it is unknown how much mercury might cause fetal damage, pregnant women should probably cut back on their consumption.

SHOPPING TIPS

The best way for fish to be sold is inside glass cases, unwrapped on ice. If you can, buy from markets that display it this way, rather than purchase the prewrapped fish that is located at one end of the meat counter in most supermarkets.

Don't buy prewrapped fresh or frozen fish if there are any breakages in the package.

Smell fish before you buy it. If fish is fresh, it won't smell "fishy."

When buying a whole fish, check for yellowing along the cut line, which indicates deterioration. A fresh whole fish will have bulging eyes, firm flesh, and a light, almost translucent, color.

When you buy fresh lobster and crab, buy only live ones. Because bacteria grow very quickly, it's always best to eat these fish as soon as possible after they're cooked.

Use caution when buying prepared fish dishes from deli or gourmet departments. Never buy cooked fish if it's displayed next to raw fish, because bacteria can be transferred from the raw to the cooked.

BEST CHOICES

The difference between lean and fatty fish is a matter of a few calories. All of these varieties are good choices nutritionally.

Lean
    cod
    flounder
    haddock
    monkfish
    sea bass
    pike
    whiting

Moderately Lean
    bluefin tuna
    halibut
    mullet
    red snapper
    swordfish

Fattier
    salmon
    albacore tuna
    mackerel
    bluefish
    herring
    shad
    trout

Mollusks
    abalone clams
    cuttlefish
    blue mussels
    oysters
    scallops
    squid

Crustaceans
  D1
  crab
  crayfish
  lobster
  shrimp

Canned Fish

NUTRITIONAL INFORMATION

Canned sardines, tuna, and salmon can enhance your diet if you take certain precautions. Sardines and salmon canned with soft, edible bones are a good source of calcium. Three ounces of sardines with bones contain 371 milligrams of calcium, and 3 ounces of salmon with bones contain 167 milligrams of calcium.

Canned tuna is a staple of many American diets, but canning in oil increases the total fat content by 200 to 500 percent compared with canning in water.

SHOPPING TIPS

◆ Canned tuna labeled "white" is made only from the albacore species and is flakier and less fishy tasting than "light" tuna, which can come from a variety of species. The word "light," in this case, has no nutritional significance. It simply refers to color.

◆ The difference between oil-packed and water-packed tuna is roughly the following: A 3-ounce serving of oil-packed tuna contains about 300 calories and 20 grams of fat; the same serving of drained oil-packed tuna has about 200 calories and 8 grams of fat. A 3-ounce serving of water-packed tuna has 131 calories and only about 1 gram of fat.

◆ Canned fish is generally high in sodium: a 3-ounce serving of tuna can contain more than 600 milligrams. Some of the sodium can be washed away by rinsing the tuna in a colander, and many companies are now selling low-sodium canned fish.

◆ Boneless canned salmon doesn't have the calcium benefits of salmon with bones.

◆ Deeper-colored salmons are highest in fat and contain more omega-3 fatty acids and calories. Chinook, or king salmon, is the most oily; pink salmon is paler and has less oil; chum is the least oily. (Prices usually correspond to the oil content, with Chinook being the most costly, chum the least.)

Fresh Fruit

NUTRITIONAL BENEFITS

Fruit is relatively low in calories and sodium, high in carbohydrates and fiber, and a good source of some essential nutrients—particularly vitamins A and C and potassium. Because Vitamin C enhances the absorption of iron, it can also boost the benefits of iron intake from other foods.

NUTRITIONAL CAUTIONS

Dried fruits are higher in calories than fresh fruits because they contain less water and are more concentrated. For example, 10 dates contain 200 calories, so, if you're watching calories, you may choose to get your potassium and iron elsewhere.

Avocados are high in fat, even though it is unsaturated, and in calories: One avocado contains about 300 calories. Because avocados supply only small amounts of vitamins A and C, the B vitamins, and potassium, you might want to limit your intake.

SHOPPING TIPS

◆ For most fresh fruit, a week is the upper limit for storage before it begins to spoil. Buy fruit only in quantities you can easily consume.

◆ Many fruits—such as bananas, pears, peaches, and plums—might not be quite ripe when you buy them. Allow them to ripen naturally by keeping them at room temperature.

FRESH FRUIT SHOPPING GUIDE

Fruit	Best Season	Nutrients
apples	year-round	good fiber; some potassium
apricots	late spring to midsummer	excellent vitamin A
bananas	year-round	excellent potassium; some vitamin A
blueberries	July–August	vitamin C, iron, fiber
cantaloupe	summer	excellent vitamins A and C, potassium
cherries	June–July	vitamins A and C
figs	summer–early autumn	excellent fiber, potassium; some iron
grapefruit	year-round	excellent vitamin C, potassium, good vitamin A (pink)
grapes	year-round	fiber
honeydew melon	summer–early autumn	good vitamin C, potassium
kiwifruit	spring–autumn	excellent vitamin C
kumquats	winter	good vitamin C; some potassium
lemons	year-round	excellent vitamin C
limes	year-round	excellent vitamin C
mangoes	late spring–summer	excellent vitamin A; some potassium, folic acid
nectarines	July–August	vitamin A, potassium; some vitamin C
oranges	autumn–spring	excellent vitamin C, potassium, folic acid
peaches	summer–early fall	vitamin A; some potassium
pears	late summer–winter	potassium, fiber
pineapples	year-round	good vitamin C
plums	summer	vitamin A, some fiber
raspberries	summer	good vitamin C, folic acid
strawberries	late spring	excellent vitamin C; some potassium, folic acid
tangerines	early winter	excellent vitamin C; some vitamin A
watermelon	late spring–summer	vitamins A and C

◆ Vitamins A and C are easily destroyed in storage; eat your A- and C-rich fruits right away to get the most out of them.

◆ If possible, pick berries and cherries from a bin, rather than buying them in prewrapped packages that don't allow examination.

Canned/Frozen Fruit

NUTRITIONAL INFORMATION

Canned or frozen fruit can be used as a substitute for out-of-season fresh varieties. Frozen is usually preferable, because canned fruits sometimes contain added sugar or sugary liquids. Generally, those that don't will be labeled "unsweetened," "packed in its own juices," or "packed in fruit juice."

Fresh Vegetables

NUTRITIONAL BENEFITS

A satisfying variety of fresh vegetables is available year-round in the supermarket. Most vegetables are low in calories, and many are excellent sources of essential nutrients, including fiber, vitamins A and C, and potassium.

NUTRITIONAL CAUTIONS

Vegetables easily lose their nutritional punch. To ensure that the nutrients aren't lost in the cooking process, follow the preparation and cooking guidelines in Chapter 9.

SHOPPING TIPS

◆ Try to purchase fresh vegetables at least twice a week to assure that you get the freshest

BUY FRUITS AT THEIR BEST

How do you know what to look for when you're examining fruit for quality? Follow these general guidelines to choose top-notch fresh fruits:

Fruit	Look For
apples	strong color, firm texture, no bruises or soft spots
apricots	golden yellow, plump, and firm; avoid if soft to the touch
bananas	firm, not fully yellow
blueberries	plump with strong color, no signs of mold
cantaloupe	no stem, coarse skin, slightly soft, fresh odor
cherries	fresh stems, plump, bright, rich color
grapefruit	heavy for their size (indicates juiciness)
grapes	rich color, plump, firmly attached to stem
honeydew melon	creamy white surface with waxy texture
kiwifruit	hard texture indicates they're not ready to eat; ripe kiwifruit is just barely soft
lemons	heavy for their size (indicates juiciness), rich yellow color, relatively smooth
limes	heavy for their size (indicates juiciness), shiny skin
mangoes	orange-yellow to red skin, barely soft
nectarines	firm, slightly unripened; avoid if hard, dull, or shriveled
oranges	heavy for their size (indicates juiciness), firm, with relatively smooth (not spongy) surface
peaches	fairly firm—just a bit soft
pears	firm, but not hard; avoid if shriveled near the stem
pineapples	heavy for their size (indicates juiciness); deep-green, fresh-looking leaves; fragrant aroma; flat, almost hollow "eyes"
plums	slight shine, good color, barely soft to the touch
raspberries	rich, scarlet color, plump, cool, dry, free from mold or bruises
strawberries	bright red color, green caps in place, no signs of mold
tangerines	strong, bright color, heavy for their size (indicates juiciness)
watermelon	smooth surface, filled-out shape, dull green color

available. The fresher the vegetables, the more nutrients are available to you.

◆ In general, the darker the vegetable, the richer it is nutritionally. For example, pale, small carrots have far less vitamin A than mature, bright-orange carrots. Dark-green leafy vegetables, like spinach and leaf lettuce, are better nutritionally than light greens, like iceberg lettuce.

◆ Sometimes vegetables are marked for sale because they are old or damaged. After produce has been sitting around unrefrigerated for a few days, levels of vitamins A and C drop substantially.

Canned/Frozen Vegetables

NUTRITIONAL INFORMATION

Canned and frozen vegetables can be good substitutes for fresh vegetables, providing almost the same nutritional value. They are a good substitute for out-of-season varieties.

Overall, more nutrients are preserved in freezing, since they're flash-frozen right after harvest to preserve nutrients. The water in canned vegetables tends to leach out some of the nutrients. Always check the labels on packaged vegetables, particularly canned; the sodium content is usually high. Beware the frozen varieties with added cream or cheese sauces; they're high in calories and fat.

FRESH VEGETABLE SHOPPING GUIDE

Vegetable	Best Season	Nutrients
artichoke	spring	fiber, potassium, folic acid
asparagus	spring	vitamins A and C, niacin, folic acid, potassium, iron
beans (green)	late spring–summer	fiber, vitamin A, potassium; some protein, vitamin C, calcium
beets	year-round	potassium, folic acid
broccoli	year-round	calcium, potassium, iron, vitamins A and C, fiber, folic acid, niacin
Brussels sprouts	autumn–winter	fiber, vitamins A and C, folic acid, potassium, iron, protein
cabbage	year-round	vitamin C, fiber, potassium, folic acid
carrots	year-round	vitamin A, potassium
cauliflower	year-round	fiber, vitamin C, folic acid, potassium; some protein, iron
celery	year-round	potassium
corn	late spring–summer	vitamin A (yellow), potassium, protein
cucumbers	year-round	minor source of nutrients
eggplant	year-round	potassium
greens	year-round	vitamins A and C, fiber, iron, calcium, B vitamins
lettuce (romaine or other dark, leafy variety)	year-round	vitamins A and C, folic acid, iron, calcium
mushrooms	year-round	potassium, niacin, riboflavin
onions	year-round	minor source of nutrients
peas (green)	spring–early summer	fiber, vitamin A, protein, potassium, B vitamins
peppers (sweet)	year-round	vitamins A and C, fiber, potassium
potatoes	year-round	protein, vitamins B and C, potassium
spinach	year-round	iron, vitamin A, fiber, potassium; some vitamin C, protein
squash (summer)	year-round	fiber, potassium, vitamins A and C, niacin
squash (winter)	year-round	fiber, vitamin A, niacin, potassium, iron, protein
sweet potatoes	year-round	vitamin A; some protein, fiber
tomatoes	late spring–summer	vitamin C, iron, protein

Legumes (Dried Beans, Peas, Lentils)

NUTRITIONAL BENEFITS

Legumes are excellent nutritional bargains. Their high protein content makes them a healthful substitute for meat, and they have the added advantage of being high in fiber.

Legumes also supply essential minerals and vitamins, including iron, zinc, magnesium, phosphorus, thiamin, and niacin, as well as vitamin B-6. And legumes are a good source of complex carbohydrates.

Tofu, or bean curd, is one of the highest-protein vegetable foods. Tofu is made by mixing soybean milk with a mineral stabilizing agent—the process is not unlike that used to make cheese. Although tofu's taste and texture don't lend to its being a stand-alone food, it is often used to supplement other foods. Tofu has no taste of its own so it picks up the flavor of the ingredients with which it is mixed, making it ideal for soups, casseroles, dips, and salads. Depending on how it's processed, tofu may be high in calcium, but use sparingly because it's also high in fat.

NUTRITIONAL CAUTIONS

By themselves, legume proteins are considered "incomplete" in that they lack certain amino acids the body needs to get from food. If you use them frequently as a meat substitute,

BUY VEGETABLES AT THEIR BEST

When you examine vegetables in the produce department for freshness and quality, follow these guidelines:

Vegetable	Look For
artichokes	olive green, plump, tightly attached greens
asparagus	firm spears, compact tips; avoid if yellowing or if tips are flaking
beans (green)	firm, fresh, and bright color; avoid limp or overbulging jackets
beets	deep purple-red color, firm, smooth
broccoli	dark color, tightly compacted clusters of buds, firm (not thick) stalks
cabbage	heavy, solid head; strong color (green or red) on outer leaves
carrots	strong orange color, healthy-looking greens
cauliflower	white or creamy-white clusters; solid, firm heads; fresh green leaves
celery	thick, crisp, healthy stalks; avoid limp, bruised, or cracked stalks
corn	healthy green husks; golden, smooth silk ends
eggplant	heavy for size, rich dark-purple color
greens	crisp green leaves, small stems
lettuce (romaine or another dark, leafy variety)	bright color; crisp texture for romaine, otherwise tender; avoid brown-edged leaves and stems and brown ribs
mushrooms	tightly closed "veil" (underside); cream-colored, white, or light brown; no bruises
onions	dry and firm (not mushy), no soft spots or cuts
peas (green)	firm, crisp pods with bright green color; avoid wilted or unfilled pods
peppers (sweet)	bright color (red, green, or yellow), no soft spots, relatively heavy for size
potatoes	well shaped, relatively smooth; no eyes, sprouts, soft spots, or bruises
spinach	dark-green color, crisp, smells like earth (not sour)
squash (summer)	heavy for size, strong color, noncoarse skin
squash (winter)	heavy for size, tough rind, stems attached
sweet potatoes	even skin color, firm; avoid if bruised, discolored, or cut
tomatoes	heavy for size, plump, firm, strong color, fresh smell

also include other foods in your diet such as rice, whole grains, wheat, some nuts, and seeds. These are rich in the two amino acids that legumes lack.

Some people find legumes difficult to digest and as a consequence suffer from intestinal flatulence (gas). Lentils, split peas, and lima beans are the most easily digestible. Introduce legumes gradually into your diet so that your intestines can adapt to them, and follow the cooking tips suggested in Chapter 9.

SHOPPING TIPS

◆ To ensure freshness, look for legumes with a bright color. Faded color indicates that they've been in storage too long.

◆ Cracks, pinhole marks, and discolorations are signs that the legumes may be less than fresh and may even be decaying.

◆ Buy legumes that are uniform in size and shape. They'll cook more evenly.

◆ Inspect the bag legumes are sold in to be sure that there are no cracks or tears. Exposure enhances decay.

◆ Tofu is best when it's purchased fresh out of a container of chilled water. You'll know it's fresh if it has a smooth texture and is odorless.

LEGUME SHOPPING GUIDE

Legume	Description	Common Uses
black beans	small, round, black	soups; main course with rice
black-eyed peas	small, round, off-white with small black "eye"	main course with rice
chick peas (garbanzos)	coarse, round, hard, tan	additions for salads and stews; base for Middle Eastern hummus
kidney beans	large, deep-red, kidney-shaped	chili; hearty soups; three-bean salad
lentils	small, round, flat, brown or red	soups; stews
lima beans	broad, flat, white	delicate flavor for soups and stews
pea (navy) beans	small, oval, white	soups; stews; baked beans
pinto beans	pink with brown dots	baked beans; soups; chili; salads; with rice
soybeans	small, round, hard, tan (highest protein content)	meat substitutions; ingredient in soups, salads, sauces, and casseroles

Grains

NUTRITIONAL INFORMATION

Nutrition experts recommend that grain-based foods make up at least half of our calories. There is a tantalizing selection of fiber-rich grains available that can add new varieties of taste and texture without adding many calories or fat.

SHOPPING TIPS

Although supermarkets don't normally stock a full range of grain products, you can usually find bulgur and couscous there. Bulgur is tan granules of crushed wheat that have a somewhat nutty flavor. It can be substituted for rice. Couscous is tiny, hay-colored granules of finely cracked wheat that taste soft and buttery and make a perfect bed for stews or a base for main-dish salads.

More exotic grain products will probably need to be purchased in a health food store. Often, they are available in bulk. These grains include:

◆ *Roasted buckwheat groats* (also known as kasha): small brown, pyramid-shaped bits, which botanically speaking are not grains but resemble them in looks and nutritional profile. They are served with meat and poultry.

◆ *Barley*: usually sold not in its whole-grain version but as refined or pearled barley. Like oats, a good source of soluble fiber.

◆ *Amaranth*: looks like golden poppy seeds. Cooks to a slightly crunchy porridge consistency with a subtle corn flavor. Works great as a breakfast dish topped with maple syrup.

◆ *Quinoa* (pronounced keen-wa): a tiny, mild-flavored grain that can be used as a substitute for rice. Be sure to rinse it thoroughly under cold running water to remove its bitter coating.

◆ *Millet*: rounded, ivory-colored beads that form a good base for meat or vegetarian dishes like chili.

Bread

NUTRITIONAL BENEFITS

Fiber-poor "white" bread is still the most common type sold in supermarkets (accounting for more than 60 percent of all bread sales). Whole wheat, rye, and multigrain breads can be excellent sources of fiber. Bread that has been fortified with a variety of vitamins and minerals may still be low in fiber.

A new product on the market provides the health benefits of fiber-rich flours with the lightness of white flour. It's called whole white wheat flour. It looks lighter and tastes milder than traditional wheat flours, with the additional benefit of performing like the lighter flours in baking.

NUTRITIONAL CAUTIONS

Almost without exception, white bread is low in fiber, because the refining process removes the bran (wheat's outer coating) and the germ (the kernel that is the seed of the new plant). As much as 90 percent of the fiber is lost with the removal of the germ and the bran.

SHOPPING TIPS

◆ Check the label to determine if you're getting a fiber-rich brand. The first ingredient should be whole wheat.

◆ Some brands are high in sodium. Choose low-sodium varieties.

BEST CHOICES

100 percent whole wheat
whole grain
multigrain, made with whole wheat
rye, made with whole wheat
oat
cracked wheat
whole white wheat
stone ground whole-wheat bagels
whole-wheat pita
whole-grain English muffins

Cereal

NUTRITIONAL BENEFITS

Cereals can be one of our best sources of fiber, in addition to being fortified with a number of vitamins and minerals. The primary cereal grains in our diets are made from wheat, corn, oats, barley, rye, and rice. They contain approximately 70 to 80 percent complex carbohydrates (starch), 7 to 13 percent protein, and very little fat. The whole grain contains vitamins, especially B and E, and various minerals—plus whatever the manufacturer adds in fortification. (Some manufacturers will add nutrients not ordinarily found in cereals, including vitamins A, C, and D.) Hot cereals, which are usually made from unrefined grains, are good natural sources of B vitamins, iron, zinc, and fiber.

Different fiber-containing cereals are composed of different parts of the cereal grain, making for variations in their nutritional content. Whole-grain cereals, for example, contain the fiber-rich bran portion of the grain as well as the germ, which contains vitamins and minerals. All-bran cereals, on the other hand, have the highest fiber concentration but lack the vitamin- and mineral-packed germ and must depend largely on fortification.

NUTRITIONAL CAUTIONS

You may choose a fibrous, vitamin- and mineral-packed cereal only to discover that it is heavily sugared and high in sodium. If you're trying to avoid sugar altogether, note that very few commercial brands are totally sugar-free. But check the labels, because some use less sugar than others. (If you are in the habit of adding sugar to unsweetened cereals, you may find that some brands contain less than you might add but are quite satisfying.) The fact that a cereal contains the entire RDA for certain vitamins and minerals does not necessarily guarantee that it is more healthful than one that is less fortified. For one thing, chances are that you'll get these vitamins and minerals in other foods throughout the day, especially if you eat a variety. Also, the fortification lure can mask other problems with the cereal, such as a high sugar, sodium, or calorie count.

It is also important to realize that even high-fiber cereals do not supply all the fiber you need in a day. Moreover, it's best to get fiber from a variety of sources, including fruit, vegetables, beans, and whole-grain breads.

◆ NUTRITION QUIZ ◆
How Well Do You Know Your Fruit?

1. What is the best-selling fruit in the United States year after year?

2. What popular "vegetable" is really fruit?

3. What is a drupe? Can you name three?

4. Name three fruits that are native to the continental United States.

5. Name six citrus fruits. Why are they such an important part of the American diet?

6. What popular fruit is actually an herb?

7. Can you tell if a watermelon is ripe by thumping it? By looking at the color of the rind?

8. Name a fruit—other than avocado—that is high in fat.

9. What noncitrus fruit contains more than 100 percent of the USRDA for vitamin C?

ANSWERS

1. Bananas—more than 5 billion pounds are sold each year, an average of 22.5 pounds per person.

2. The tomato—it is really the "blossom," or fruit, of the plant. Tomatoes are a fair source of vitamin C and also provide vitamin A.

3. A drupe is a fruit that has a large pod or seed in the center with fleshy pulp surrounding it—three examples are apricots, plums, and peaches.

4. Cranberries, blueberries, and concord grapes come from the continental United States—other than these three (and some minor berries), the fruits that Americans consume were originally imported from Central and South America, Asia, and Europe.

5. Orange, lemon, lime, grapefruit, tangerine, and ugli fruit (a hybrid of a grapefruit and tangerine)—citrus fruits are a major source of vitamin C.

6. The pineapple is an herb, or edible leaf—when a pineapple fruit is picked, another seed-leaf grows. The process is repeated time and again during the 50-year life span of the typical pineapple plant.

7. No and no—the only sure way to know if a watermelon is ripe is to see that the pulp is a rich red and the seeds are dark brown and black. Therefore, it's better to buy a watermelon that has already been cut, even if it's a little more expensive.

8. The coconut—a cup of coconut milk has about twice as much as the amount in a quart of whole milk.

9. The kiwifruit—it is only about the size of a large egg, but it has almost twice as much vitamin C as several varieties of orange.

SHOPPING TIPS

◆ Watch out for granola-style cereals, which often contain fat because oils have been added. Many use palm or coconut oils, which are highly saturated. Make sure the brand you choose is "low-fat."

BEST CHOICES

whole-grain puffed wheat, corn, and rice
shredded wheat
whole-grain wheat, oat, and rice flakes
oatmeal
mixed-grain hot cereal
low-fat granola

Pasta

NUTRITIONAL INFORMATION

Pasta is high in complex carbohydrates and can be a low-calorie, low-fat main course. It is high in protein and, when made from whole grains, is a good source of fiber. Pasta is also a good source of the B vitamins and iron.

Although pasta has long been considered a healthful dietary choice, reports in 1995 that pasta and other foods high in complex carbohydrates might make you fat caused great confusion in the marketplace. The bottom line is that, for most people, eating complex carbohydrates in moderation is not harmful. The key is moderation and a well-balanced diet. For some insulin-resistant people (see Chapter 21), complex carbohydrates may need to be limited.

Because pasta is rarely eaten without some kind of sauce, the ultimate nutritional benefits usually depend on the topping. Vegetable-based sauces, like those made with tomatoes, green peppers, onions, and mushrooms, will enhance the final product. Cream-based sauces made with large amounts of butter and rich cheeses can turn your healthful pasta meal into one that is loaded with fat and calories.

Rice

NUTRITIONAL INFORMATION

Like other grain-based products, rice is an excellent source of complex carbohydrates, protein, and, as long as the bran has not been removed, fiber. Polished, refined rice is the most common kind sold in the United States. Although it is often fortified to replace vitamins lost in the refining process, this does nothing to replace the fiber that is lost. Instant rice has undergone even more refining, making it the least nutritious. Brown rice (long- or short-grained) has more fiber.

Soups

NUTRITIONAL INFORMATION

Soup *is* good food. It's comforting, filling, inexpensive, easy to prepare, and in many cases loaded with nutrient- and fiber-rich vegetables and legumes. For example, a cup of Healthy Choice Country Vegetable Soup supplies more than 20 percent of the USRDA for vitamin A, more than 10 percent of the USRDA for vitamin C, and small amounts of B vitamins, protein, and fiber—all for 128 calories and just one gram of fat.

It wasn't that long ago that a serving of most of the canned and dried soups available in supermarkets contained 800-plus milligrams of sodium and plenty of fat. Fortunately, that has changed as manufacturers have grown more attentive to customer demand for more healthful products. For example, Healthy Choice, Health Valley, and Campbell's Healthy Request lines all contain fewer than 650 milligrams of sodium per cup. And Pritikin and Campbell's Special Request lines contain fewer than 200 milligrams.

Although some manufacturers continue to sell the high-fat, high-sodium varieties, they offer options as well. For instance, Campbell's still sells Chunky New England Clam Chowder with 13 grams of fat and 219 calories per cup. But it also sells a Healthy Request version that contains only 3 grams of fat and 100 calories.

Vegetable Oils and Margarines

NUTRITIONAL INFORMATION

All vegetable oils contain approximately the same number of calories (about 120 in a tablespoon), and they're all pure fat. But, for the sake of their health, many Americans have increased their consumption of vegetable fats and oils because animal fats are high in saturated fats.

One might think that all vegetable oils are more or less equally healthful, but that's not the case. Coconut oil, palm oil, and palm kernel oil all contain high levels of saturated fat. And all vegetable oils, when hydrogenated or partially hydrogenated, contain trans fatty acids.

Common oils include:

◆ Canola oil: monounsaturated oil used in cooking and salad dressings

◆ Safflower oil: highest in polyunsaturated fats; used mainly in margarine, salad dressing, and mayonnaise

◆ Sunflower oil: relatively tasteless; used in cooking oil, salad dressing, and margarine and for deep frying

◆ Corn oil: used for salad dressings, cooking oil, and margarine

◆ Soybean oil: the most highly consumed vegetable oil in the United States and the rest of the world, although much of its use is commercial; often used in margarines and shortenings; at home, you can use it for cooking and salad dressings

◆ Cottonseed oil: a preferred cooking oil (second most popular after soybean); used for cooking, salad oil, shortening, and margarine

◆ Sesame oil: pleasant tasting and durable; used for salad dressing, cooking oil, and margarine

◆ Peanut oil: peanutty taste and flavor; used for frying foods and salad dressings

◆ Olive oil: a good source of monounsaturated fat; popular for salad dressings and cooking but more expensive than most cooking oils; unrefined or "virgin" olive oil will be less processed and have a stronger flavor

◆ Palm kernel oil: used frequently in margarine; high in saturated fat

◆ Coconut oil: the highest in saturated fat; used in many snack and pastry foods

SHOPPING TIPS

◆ Bear in mind that saturated vegetable oils can have the same effect on cholesterol levels as animal fats because of trans fatty acids.

◆ Hydrogenation is a process that solidifies oils, thus making them more saturated. Hydrogenated or partially hydrogenated oils are used in many processed products (including margarine).

◆ The best margarine choices are those that list a liquid oil as the first ingredient. These products will be less saturated.

◆ Palm and coconut oils—both high in saturated fat—are frequently used by manufacturers for packaged products.

Sugar

All sugars are created equal when it comes to nutrition. Although sugar may not be the evil substance it has long been accused of being, neither does it add anything to the diet except calories. The more sugar in your diet, the less room there is for foods that supply essential nutrients. You will see sugar in various forms

A BUTTER–MARGARINE CHECKLIST

I tablespoon	Calories	Total fat(g)	Saturated Fat(g)	Sodium (mg)
Butter[1]	100	11	7.1	90–120

Stick margarine

I tablespoon	Calories	Total fat(g)	Saturated Fat(g)	Sodium (mg)
Blue Bonnet	90	11	2	95
Fleischmann's Light	80	8	1	80
Fleischmann's Move Over Butter	90	10	2	100
Imperial	100	11	2	105
Kraft Parkay	100	11	2	115
Premium Mazola	100	11	2	100
Promise	90	10	2	90
Promise Extra Light	50	6	<1	50
Promise Light	70	7	1	65

Soft tub margarine

I tablespoon	Calories	Total fat(g)	Saturated Fat(g)	Sodium (mg)
Fleischmann's Extra Light	50	6	1	55
Fleischmann's Light	80	8	1	70
I Can't Believe It's Not Butter[3]	90	10	2	90
I Can't Believe It's Not Butter[3] Light	60	7	1	110
Kraft Parkay Soft	100	11	2	105
Kraft Touch of Butter	60	7	1	110
Land O Lakes Country Morning Blend[2]	90	10	4	80
Land O Lakes Country Morning [2] Blend Light	60	6	3	90
Land O Lakes Spread with Sweet Cream	80	8	2	80
Mazola Extra Light	50	6	1	100
Promise	90	10	1	90
Promise Extra Light	50	6	<1	50
Promise Ultra	35	4	0	50
Shedd's Spread Country Crock Churn Style	60	7	1	55
Weight Watchers Country Cottage Farms Extra Light Spread	45	4	1	75

Liquid margarine

I tablespoon	Calories	Total fat(g)	Saturated Fat(g)	Sodium (mg)
I Can't Believe It's Not Butter	90	10	2	70
Kraft Parkay Squeeze Spread	80	9	1	115

[1]Contains 33 milligrams of cholesterol. All margarines listed contain 0 milligram of cholesterol unless otherwise indicated.

[2]A margarine-butter blend. One tablespoon contains no more than 10 milligrams of cholesterol.

[3]While all are referred to as margarine in this chart some of the items, technically speaking, are spreads. Margarine, by law, must be comprised of not less than 80 percent fat by weight. The fat content of spreads ranges from about 20 to 79 percent.

on the labels of products. Contrary to popular belief, among these varieties none is more healthful than any other.

Jams and Jellies

You'll find a wide variety of jams and jellies in the supermarket and, from a nutritional standpoint, these products are quite similar to one another. By law, anything called a jelly, jam, or preserve must be sweetened with sugar and contain 55 percent sugar by weight. When something other than sugar is used as a sweetener (like fruit juice), the product must be identified as a "spread" or "conserve." However, that doesn't necessarily make it lower in calories. For example, two teaspoons of Smucker's Simply Fruit red raspberry spread, which is sweetened with white grape juice, have 35 calories, the same number as are in two teaspoons of Smucker's red raspberry jam.

If you're interested in cutting calories, you might want to try a "low sugar" spread that has about half the sugar and half the calories of a regular spread.

Juices and Juice Drinks

You may be uncertain about how to choose the most healthful drinks, especially given that major companies, including Dole, Libby's, Minute Maid, Ocean Spray, and Welch's, are continuing to roll out fruit-based drinks to suit every taste. Some of these beverages are made of juice, with no added sugar or water. Others are only part juice (sometimes as little as 10 percent), with sugar and water as the main ingredients; they may not be good dietary additions.

These beverages are found in many parts of the store. They may be refrigerated alongside milk containers; bottled; boxed or canned in the dry-food aisle; or frozen. The first tip-off on what is in the container is whether the label calls it a juice, drink, or cocktail. Beverages labeled fruit "drink" or "cocktail" contain less than 100 percent juice.

Be sure to pay attention to the wording. Welch's, for example, make a blended juice drink that bears a label almost identical to its all-juice products.

Because ingredients must be listed in descending order by weight, drinks that list water and/or high fructose, corn syrup, or sugar before the juices have more water or sweeteners than juice. Also be aware that not all juice-flavored sparkling waters and seltzers are a simple blend of water and juice. Many flavored beverages are sweetened with sugar. Furthermore, the amount of juice in these drinks can be very small. Check the label for the percentage of juice.

Condiments

The condiment aisle is full of products that add pizzazz to a meal. But beware that condiments are not always benign extras. Some contain large amounts of fat, calories, and/or sodium. For instance, each tablespoon of tartar sauce (mayonnaise with chopped pickles) adds 70 calories, almost all of it from fat. Plain mayonnaise, at 99 calories a tablespoon, is almost 100 percent fat. Soy sauce, on the other hand, is virtually fat free, but just one tablespoon of the standard variety contains 1,029 milligrams of sodium. Ketchup is better in terms of sodium, with only 170 milligrams in a tablespoon. But because Americans pour 570 million bottles of ketchup a year onto everything from scrambled eggs to meatloaf, the sodium in ketchup is something to watch.

You don't have to give up your favorite condiments, but it is possible to use them more wisely. For instance, once in a while, in place of tartar sauce, purchase cocktail sauce, which is a low-fat mixture of ketchup, lemon juice, and horseradish. Chili sauce or salsa, used in Mexican dishes, is also low in fat and contains fewer than 20 calories per tablespoon. And mayonnaise can be "stretched" by mixing it with an equal amount of plain low- or non-fat yogurt.

THE COMPOSITION OF POPULAR CONDIMENTS

Condiment (1 tbsp)	Calories	Fat (g)	Sodium (mg)
chili sauce	16	trace	201
chutney, tomato	41	trace	34
cocktail sauce	20	trace	160
ketchup	16	0.1	170
mayonnaise	99	11	78
imitation mayonnaise	35	2.9	75
mustard	11	0.1	188
sweet-pickle relish	21	0.1	107
soy sauce	11	0	1,029
steak sauce	18	trace	149
sweet & sour sauce	32	trace	320
tartar sauce	75	8	182
teriyaki sauce	15	0	690
Worcestershire sauce	12	0	147

The new low-calorie or "light" mayonnaise products are created by adding water. The dilution gives them fewer calories and less fat per serving. Some brands are also low sodium.

Chutneys—low-calorie, low-sodium condiments made with fruits and vegetables—are available in supermarkets and go well as relishes on many sandwiches. Mustard is also a good choice, with only 11 calories per tablespoon and only a trace of fat.

The accompanying table shows how your favorite condiments stack up in terms of calories, fat, and sodium.

◆ NUTRITION QUIZ ◆
Be Rice Wise

Okay, so the Italians eat 59 pounds of pasta per person per year, as opposed to just 19 pounds per person in the United States. But are you aware that the Japanese eat 158 pounds of rice per person each year, compared to about 18 pounds in this country? Or that rice is a dietary staple for over half the earth's population?

And do you know how much more fiber brown rice has than white? Or what *converted* means? Test your rice 'IQ' with the following quiz.

1. True or false? Brown rice is much higher in fiber than white rice.

2. *True or false?* Brown rice comes in small boxes rather than big bags because it is not as popular as white rice and therefore does not need to be on hand in U.S. households in large quantities.

3. Rice is one of the complex-carbohydrate foods that the U.S. Dietary Guidelines says we should eat six to 11 servings of each day. A serving of (cooked) rice comes to (a) one-third cup (b) one-half cup (c) one cup.

4. The state that produces the most rice is (a) California (b) Arkansas (c) Louisiana.

5. The most popular rice in the United States is (a) long grain (b) medium grain (c) short grain.

6. *True or false?* Wild rice is a type of brown rice.

7. Converted rice is rice that has been (a) enriched with vitamins and minerals (b) parboiled (c) processed from the brown to the white variety.

8. *True or false?* Parboiled rice is rice that has been precooked and therefore has a shorter cooking time than other rice.

ANSWERS

1. *False.* A half cup of brown rice contains 0.2 gram of dietary fiber, while a half cup of white rice has in the neighborhood of 0.1 gram. Brown rice does have a bit more in the way of several nutrients, including fat, protein, calcium, phosphorus, and potassium. But in terms of the overall diet, the differences are negligible, just like the calorie difference between brown and white. Brown rice has 89 calories per half cup and white rice, 82.

2. *False.* Brown rice comes in small boxes because the oil in the bran portion (the bran is missing from white rice) can go rancid if it is kept around a long time before it is eaten. The USA Rice Council, a trade association headquartered in Houston, recommends storing brown rice in the refrigerator rather than the pantry if you plan to have it on hand longer than six months.

3. (b) A half cup of cooked rice is actually only a few heaping tablespoonsful.

Be Rice Wise *(cont.)*

4. (b) While Arkansas ranks number one, the second-highest producer of rice is California, followed by Louisiana, Texas, Mississippi, and then Missouri.

5. (a) Long-grain rice, incidentally, is four to five times as long as it is wide. Medium-grain rice is two to three times as long as wide. And the short-grain version is one to two times as long as wide.

6. *False*. Wild rice is an aquatic grass native to North America and grown largely in northern states such as Minnesota and Wisconsin.

7. (b) "Converted" is simply Uncle Ben's brand name for parboiled.

8. *False*. Parboiled rice has a *longer* cooking time than other rice, about 25 minutes. What the parboiling process does rather than precook is soak, steam, and dry the rice in such a way that it becomes translucent and shiny and has a cooking quality that allows it to separate easily for a fluffy rather than a mushier final product.

   Precooked rice, on the other hand, is rice that has been completely cooked and then dried. In the process it becomes more porous so that boiling water can penetrate the grains and rehydrate them (puff them up again) in a shorter time, approximately 5 minutes. To make matters a little more confusing, there's also precooked, parboiled rice that takes about 15 minutes to cook.

Learn the Language of Labels

Just about all packaged foods available in U.S. supermarkets are labeled with a Nutrition Information Panel. If you know how to read this label, it can be a useful guide as you design a balanced, healthful diet.

The Food and Drug Administration (FDA) first established nutrition labeling guidelines for a wide variety of goods in 1938. In recent years, Nutrition Information Panels printed on the packaging of many products have supplied detailed information about a product's nutrient content. These panels reflect the growing consumer interest in nutrition and increased awareness within the food industry of that interest.

In its 1988 report, the National Academy of Science's Board on Agriculture applauded producers, processors, and retailers for becoming more responsive to health trends. But the board urged further development of nutritional labels that allow consumers to make informed choices and recommended that manufacturers supply all the nutritional information desired, avoid misleading terms and descriptions, help consumers bridge the gap between information and application, and support their products with nutritionally helpful point-of-purchase materials.

In December 1992, the federal government finally approved legislation establishing the most extensive and consumer-oriented food labeling in the history of the country.

The New Food Labeling Guidelines

The new food label contains a good deal of information not previously included. It is attentive to issues of public health, including prevention of heart disease, cancer, osteoporosis, and high blood pressure. The new food labeling guidelines include the following:

◆ *Standardized serving sizes.* Formerly, if a product was high in fat, a company could make a serving size smaller to "reduce" its fat content. But now, serving sizes have been standardized based on food consumption surveys that reflect the amount of food people actually eat.

◆ *Saturated fat.* Eating this type of fat is particularly likely to result in clogged arteries, leading to heart disease. According to government guidelines, saturated fat should supply no more than 10 percent or one-third of all daily fat intake. Now, for the first time, labels must indicate how many grams of total fat are saturated.

◆ *Dietary fiber.* Americans currently fall woefully short in the fiber department, eating only about 15 grams a day when they should be consuming between 20 and 30 grams. The new labels, which are required to list fiber content, will help people figure out whether they are meeting their fiber goals.

◆ *Percentage Daily Values.* At first glance, these numbers make the new label look more complicated than ever. But the extra column actually makes shopping easier. On the basis of what experts deem 100 percent of the fat, saturated fat, cholesterol, sodium, carbohydrate, and fiber that should be consumed each day, the numbers indicate the percentage contributed by

a single serving of food. The Daily Value numbers are based on a 2,000-calorie diet—although the values for sodium and cholesterol are the same for everyone, regardless of the number of calories. And the Daily Values for those vitamins and minerals listed are taken from the RDAs for those nutrients. When it comes to fat, saturated fat, total carbohydrates, dietary fiber, and protein, values do vary with calorie consumption. Total fat should come to no more than a third of calories with 10 percent of that coming from saturated fat. Total carbohydrate is supposed to supply at least 60 percent of total calories. Fiber intake should be at least 11.5 grams per 1,000 calories. And protein values are based on 10 percent of total calories.

Serving sizes will be standardized to reflect the amount of foods people actually eat.

The list of nutrients includes those most important to the health of today's consumers, most of whom need to worry about getting too much of certain items (fat, for example) rather than too few vitamins or minerals, as in the past.

% Daily Values show how a food fits into the overall daily diet. They are based on a daily diet of 2,000 calories. Individuals may want to adjust the values to fit their own calorie intake.

The label will now tell the number of calories per gram of fat, carbohydrates, and protein.

Nutrition Facts

Serving Size 1/2 cup (114 g)	Servings Per Container 4

Amount Per Serving

Calories 260	Calories from Fat 120

	% Daily Value[1]
Total Fat 13g	20%
Saturated Fat 5g	25%
Cholesterol 30 mg	10%
Sodium 660 mg	28%
Total Carbohydrate 31g	11%
Dietary Fiber 0g	0%
Sugars 5g	
Protein 5g	

Vitamin A	4%	Vitamin C	2%
Calcium	15%	Iron	4%

		Calories	2,000	2,500
Total Fat	Less than		65g	80g
Saturated Fat	Less than		20g	25g
Cholesterol	Less than		300mg	300mg
Sodium	Less than		2,400mg	2,400mg
Total Carbohydrates	300g		375g	
Fiber			25g	30g

Calories per gram:

Fat 9	Carbohydrates 4	Protein 4

[1] Percent Daily Values are based on a 2,000-calorie diet. Your daily values may be higher or lower depending on your calorie needs.

New Rules on Health Claims

In the mid-1980s, Kellogg's caused considerable upheaval in legislative and food industry circles when it advertised that one of its bran-rich cereals might help prevent cancer. That's because by law, health claims linking a particular food to a reduced risk of a specific disease were forbidden—in large part because scientists had relatively little information about the relationship among foods, nutrients, and disease. To some extent, that picture has changed. Under the new labeling guidelines, claims for seven food–disease relationships may be made using statements, symbols (such as a heart), or descriptions. The food–disease relationships are:

◆ calcium and osteoporosis

◆ fat and cancer

◆ saturated fat and cholesterol/coronary heart disease

◆ fiber-containing vegetables, fruits, and grains and cancer/coronary heart disease

◆ sodium and high blood pressure

◆ folate and birth defects

◆ fruits and vegetables and cancer

However, very stringent rules have been established for using health claims. For example, just because a food is high in calcium doesn't mean it can be labeled as helping to prevent osteoporosis. The calcium must also be in a form that is easily absorbed. Moreover, manufacturers are not allowed to overstate the case. They are permitted only to say that a food "may" or "might" reduce the risk of disease, and they must also state that other factors, such as adequate exercise, play a role.

For the small proportion of Americans with sensitivities to particular substances in foods, ingredients will now become more specific. All color additives, for example, rather than being referred to by the word "colors," will have to be specified by name. And sources of ingredients called protein hydrolysates will have to be listed by name instead of generic titles like "flavorings." That's especially helpful for people on sodium-restricted diets because many of the protein hydrolysates are high in sodium.

What the Label *Won't* Tell You

Here's what the new label *won't* tell you:

◆ The levels of the B vitamins thiamin, riboflavin, and niacin (unless a food is fortified with those nutrients or a manufacturer makes a claim that they are present). Nutrient deficiencies are not the problem they were when the original labeling laws were devised. The greater danger today is one of dietary excess, which is why the new label emphasizes fat, cholesterol, sodium, and calories.

◆ Nutrition information on small packages. Any package smaller than 12 square inches (such as a small candy bar) does not have to provide nutrition information on the label. It does, however, have to provide an address or telephone number for consumers who wish to obtain it.

◆ Fat levels in children's foods. Labels on foods for children under age two may not carry information related to calories from fat and saturated fat. That's because the Food and Drug Administration wants to prevent parents from wrongly assuming that infants and toddlers should restrict fat intake. Fat is important during the first few years of life to ensure adequate growth and development.

◆ Nutrition information about food served in restaurants. Restaurant food is exempt from nutrition labeling, as are meals served on airplanes and in hospital cafeterias. Also exempt are foods served on-site (such as at a bakery or deli) and food sold by sidewalk vendors.

No More Label Fables

No longer will manufacturers be able to use words like "light" and "low-fat" whenever they wish. The FDA has set forth specific definitions for such eye-catching nutrition terms so that when consumers see them they will be able to trust what they read. The terms will prove particularly helpful to shoppers who don't like to scrutinize all the numbers on food labels but who want to pick up items that are lower in fat, cholesterol, or sodium as they walk through the supermarket aisles. These are the health claims and their federally mandated definitions:

◆ *Free* indicates that a product contains none or only negligible amounts of fat, saturated fat, cholesterol, sodium, sugar, and/or calories. But it must appear on a product that would otherwise contain these.

◆ *Low* may be used on foods that can be eaten frequently without a person's exceeding the dietary guidelines for fat, saturated fat, cholesterol, sodium, and/or calories. More specifically:

low fat: 3 grams or fewer per serving
low saturated fat: no more than 1 gram per serving
low sodium: fewer than 140 milligrams per serving
very low sodium: fewer than 35 milligrams per serving
low cholesterol: fewer than 20 milligrams per serving
low calorie: 40 calories or fewer per serving

◆ *Lean* and *extra lean* describe the fat content of certain meats, poultry, seafood, and game meats.

lean: fewer than 10 grams of fat, fewer than 4 grams of saturated fat, and fewer than 95 milligrams of cholesterol per serving.
extra lean: fewer than 5 grams of fat, fewer than 2 grams of saturated fat, and fewer than 95 milligrams of cholesterol per serving.

◆ *High* indicates that a serving of the food contains 20 percent or more of the Daily Value for a particular nutrient.

◆ *Good source* means that a serving of the food supplies 10 to 19 percent of the Daily Value for a particular nutrient.

◆ *Reduced* indicates that a product has been nutritionally altered and contains 25 percent less of a nutrient (such as fat) or of calories than the regular product. A reduced claim for a product cannot be made if the "regular" product already meets the requirements of "low" in that nutrient. In other words, a product that starts out "low calorie" cannot undergo a calorie reduction and then be called "reduced."

◆ *Less* signifies that a food contains 25 percent less of a nutrient than a comparable food. For example, pretzels could be labeled as containing 25 percent "less" fat than potato chips. ("Fewer" can be used in the same way.)

◆ *Light* means that calories in a nutritionally altered food have been reduced by at least one-third of what they were in the regular product, or the fat reduced by one-half. (If a food contains 50 percent or more of its calories in fat to begin with, it's the fat that must be reduced for a product to earn the "light" claim.) If the sodium is reduced in a food that is not low in fat and calories, the label must state "light in sodium." Bear in mind that "light" can also be used on labels to refer to the texture and/or color of a food, but the label must spell it out— for example, "light brown sugar."

◆ *More* indicates that a serving of food contains at least 10 percent more of the Daily Value for a nutrient than the regular food. The label on calcium-fortified orange juice, for example, could specify that the product contains "more calcium" than regular juice.

◆ *Percent fat free*, which must now be used only on foods that are low fat or fat free to begin with, is a reflection of the amount of the food's weight that is fat free. For example, if a serving of food weighs 100 grams and two of them come from fat, it can be labeled "98 percent fat free." But keep in mind that 98 percent fat free by *weight* is not the same as by *calories*. If the serving in question supplies 75 calories, the two grams of fat contribute 18 of them, which is 24 percent of the calories.

◆ *Other claims*: "No tropical oils," "Made with oat bran," and other claims that mislead the consumer into thinking a food contains (or doesn't contain) significant amounts of certain nutrients are prohibited under the new labeling law. For example, a manufacturer is not allowed to claim that a food is "made with oat bran" unless it contains enough oat bran to meet the definition requirements for a "good" source of fiber. And a product may tout "no tropical oils" only if it's low in saturated fat.

Heart-Smart Labeling

As helpful as the new labeling requirements are, many consumers still find it time-consuming and difficult to make on-the-spot judgments in the supermarket. The American Heart Association had this in mind when it developed the "On-Pack" program, whereby shoppers would see the organization's familiar heart-and-torch logo on the labels of various "approved" products.

WE'RE FIGHTING FOR YOUR LIFE

American Heart Association

At first glance, On-Pack seems like a perfect way to help consumers choose a heart-healthful diet. After all, items that bear the Heart Association's seal must be deemed consistent with its standards: less than 30 percent of calories as fat, less than 10 percent of calories as saturated fat, fewer than 300 milligrams of cholesterol daily, and fewer than 3,000 milligrams of sodium daily. But products carrying the Heart Association symbol must meet other criteria which can make particularly good choices for people trying to follow a diet low in saturated fat, especially since this excludes certain foods. For instance, an approved food must contain a certain proportion of iron, calcium, protein, fiber, or vitamins A and C. And it must contain the substance naturally, not through fortification. That criterion, sometimes referred to as "the jelly bean rule," keeps the Heart Association from placing its logo on foods such as jelly beans, which are low in fat and sodium, yet supply virtually nothing but calories from sugar.

The problem is, the rule also precludes the use of the Heart Association logo on jams, margarine, many candies, and even some fruit juices. And for the low-fat eater looking for an alternative to butter on bread and bagels, or a little something besides high-fat chocolates to satisfy a sweet tooth, jams, jelly beans, and hard candies are perfectly reasonable alternatives.

Also excluded from the On-Pack program are all foods whose manufacturers are owned by tobacco companies, their subsidiaries, or their parent companies, as it has been the Heart Association's long-standing policy to avoid any relationship with the tobacco industry. Although the policy may be laudable, the result is the exclusion of many heart-healthful foods made by giant food companies like Kraft and Nabisco.

Apart from these problems, critics of the seal also argue that the concept is essentially flawed. They point out that it gives the message that certain foods are fundamentally good or bad, depending on whether or not they carry the Heart Association's approval. But no food is good or bad; any item can be fit into a healthful diet with a bit of planning.

The Heart Association is trying to counter these arguments by requiring that approved products carry the following message: "This product is consistent with the American Heart Association dietary guidelines, when used as part of a totally balanced diet. . . . Diets low in saturated fat and cholesterol and high in fiber-containing grains, fruits, and vegetables, particularly soluble fiber, may reduce risk of heart disease." But all those words put the consumer back in the realm of fine print. Special logo or not, you still have to read most food labels carefully to familiarize yourself with the nutritional profiles of the products.

Fortification: For Better or for Worse?

If you're conscious of adhering to the basic guidelines of the RDAs, you might wonder: "Should I shop for food or for nutrients?" That's a pertinent question in light of the fortification boom. You've no doubt noticed that many products are "fortified" with vitamins and minerals, and the list is growing. Even Kool-Aid and some sodas have added vitamin C.

When foods were first fortified in the early 1940s, the intention was to correct specific deficiencies and to protect the public if food shortages arose because of World War II. Scientists added iodine to salt to combat goiter. Food manufacturers were encouraged to put a number of B vitamins into flour, bread, and ready-to-eat cereal products to prevent deficiency diseases. And milk was fortified with vitamin D to fight rickets, a condition that impairs bone formation. Because of efforts such as these, most deficiency diseases in the United States have been eradicated.

Fortification with vitamins and minerals has been so successful, in fact, that in 1982 the American Medical Association (AMA) recommended expanding the list of nutrients added

to foods and has offered guidelines that both the National Academy of Sciences and the Institute of Food Technology have endorsed. The AMA's basic suggestion is that any nutrient added to food should be one that a large group of people is not getting in sufficient amounts. In addition, the item selected for fortification should be a staple food for large segments of the population that is at risk. Finally, adding a vitamin or mineral should neither cause harm nor result in a nutrient imbalance when the food it fortifies is part of the regular diet.

Unfortunately, in today's competitive commercial environment, fortification often has more to do with marketing than with nutrition, and the outer limits of these guidelines are being stretched. It is difficult to see a pressing need to add B vitamins to soda pop, for example, considering that most Americans eat more than enough foods that are rich in B vitamins. The fortification trend makes it easy for food marketers to add particular nutrients to their products for the purpose of making them more salable, not necessarily better.

Are there any nutritional hazards to the fortification trend? Not directly, but the implications of product marketing have federal agencies concerned. For example, a calcium-fortified orange juice that is marketed as having the same amount of calcium as milk may lead consumers to believe that orange juice can replace milk. But if they choose orange juice as a milk substitute, they will shortchange themselves on a number of other important nutrients that milk provides, including protein, vitamins A and D, and riboflavin.

Furthermore, the abundance of "highly fortified" foods might be giving consumers the false impression that eating a few foods fortified with huge amounts of particular nutrients satisfies all their dietary needs. In fact, foods provide more than 40 essential nutrients, and even a heavily fortified product that supplies 100 percent of the RDA for 10 or 12 vitamins and minerals cannot foot the entire nutrition bill. Moreover, eating a fortified food does not fully compensate for eating "empty" foods, items filled mainly with calories, sugar, and fat.

Your best strategy is to eat a varied diet. Be attentive, but not tied, to the RDA guidelines. When you shop, focus on the Nutrition Information Panel and ingredients list, not the advertising claims. Never select a food based on its claimed percentage of RDA for certain nutrients until you've looked to see what else the product contains.

Beware Mixed Messages

The FDA places restrictions on most food labels, and the U.S. Department of Agriculture (USDA) monitors poultry and meat products, but there are plenty of gaps. Although the FDA requires that packages under its jurisdiction list ingredients in descending order according to the percentage of weight they contribute to the total, there is no requirement to list many of the additives used. Consequently, a "natural" product may be filled with artificial ingredients, and the consumer has no way to know.

It is a further complication that at times the FDA and the U.S. Department of Agriculture seem to be working at cross purposes. For example, certain USDA standards for meat and poultry labels make it harder for consumers to judge the health value of nonmeat items. For instance, the USDA requires that a meat or poultry product that is labeled "natural" contain no artificial colors, flavors, preservatives, or synthetic ingredients. However, the FDA has no standard for the use of the term "natural" in the foods it regulates, so baked goods, beverages, and other nonmeat and poultry products can claim to be "natural" without offering any evidence at all.

Until the federal standards for labeling become more complete, consumers are left to exercise as much caution as they can when they're shopping. Once again, it is important to read the nutrition panel and the ingredients list for true nutritional information.

Protectors of Our Food

The Food and Drug Administration (FDA), with regional offices throughout the country, monitors the safety of all foods and beverages (including their packaging) with the exceptions of meat, poultry, and alcohol. That includes lobster and other seafood, fruits, vegetables, and even rubber nipples on baby bottles, because they come into contact with food.

The U.S. Department of Agriculture (USDA) monitors the safety of meats and poultry, as well as that of any products that contain more than 2 percent poultry and 3 percent meat by weight. Inspectors who work for a branch of the USDA called the Food Safety and Inspection Service examine meat and poultry at approximately 8,000 plants in the United States where slaughtering, processing, and packaging occur.

The Environmental Protection Agency (EPA) indirectly protects meats, produce, and processed foods by setting standards for the amount of pesticide residue allowed on raw and processed foods, including animal feed. (Both the FDA and the USDA help to make sure that these requirements are met.) The EPA also sets standards for the safety of drinking water and monitors the safety of tap water throughout the country. (The FDA monitors bottled water.) The Bureau of Alcohol, Tobacco, and Firearms, which is a branch of the Treasury Department, is responsible for the safety of alcoholic beverages. It also works closely with the FDA and EPA on issues such as sulfites in the wine supply.

12

Balancing Lifestyle and Nutrition

Must the pursuit of a nutritional eating style necessarily be a time-consuming and costly venture? Not at all. It is possible for most Americans to balance the demands of their lifestyles with healthful diets. This is good news for the post–World War II generation, whose way of life is vastly different from that of their parents.

Today, more than two-thirds of adult women are in the work force, making two-career families the norm. Overall, Americans seem to be working harder than ever. New technologies for food packaging and preparation and the increase in outlets for prepared food have expanded the role of convenience foods in the American diet. Perhaps the greatest shift in American eating patterns is that many families no longer sit down to the table to share two or three "square" meals each day. In households where both adults work outside the home, breakfast is often a rushed affair, when it is not skipped altogether. (It is estimated that as many as 33 percent of Americans skip breakfast.) For lunch, there is the cafeteria, the "business lunch," the fast-food restaurant, or the quick cup of yogurt or sandwich at the desk. It is often just one of many hurried segments in a busy day. At school, the children are on their own; even if you've packed a nutritious lunch,

it is not unheard of for a child to trade a piece of fruit for a bag of potato chips, or simply to discard portions of the lunch. For dinner, convenience cooking and restaurant meals are common; many families and couples manage relaxed, home-cooked dinners together only a couple of nights a week or on weekends. Many people have abandoned three-meal-a-day patterns altogether. Data from the Continuing Survey on Food Intake conducted by the Department of Agriculture indicate that people are eating more frequently throughout the day, rather than confining themselves to set meals.

Healthful Eating for Active Americans

It may not always be clear how nutritional balance can be achieved when "eat and run" is the norm. But, in spite of changing styles, people are more attentive to nutrition than ever. Unfortunately, consumers often lack a practical understanding of how to incorporate nutritional concepts into convenience-oriented eating styles. For example, if you consume a number of small meals throughout the day (a practice sometimes called "grazing") rather than sitting down to full meals that include a balance of nutrients, how can you make certain that you're getting all the nourishment you need? Or, if you eat three meals a day but their content varies widely depending on your schedule or other factors, what adjustments can you make to satisfy both your lifestyle and your dietary requirements? The goal of your daily meal pattern, whatever it is, is to provide your body with its nutritional requirements. One meal per day, for example, is not a recommended way to eat, even if that meal is a very large one, containing a variety of nutrients. Eating at regularly scheduled periods throughout the day is a better way to keep your health and energy levels high, and six small well-balanced meals can be as good as three hearty ones.

Whatever your meal pattern, it's a good idea to examine the nutritional quality of your diet over a week's period. You can do this by keeping a precise diary of what you eat and comparing it with dietary guidelines to find out where you may be shortchanging yourself. This analysis will also tell you where you may be "overdoing it" on foods that are high in fat, sodium, and calories. Questions to ask about your week's food balance include the following:

◆ Are you getting enough calories, but not too many? The best way to determine this is to weigh yourself and then to compare your weight with the recommended range for your height and age (see chart in Chapter 23). Also be aware that other factors, such as the amount of exercise you do and certain illnesses, affect your calorie needs.

◆ Of your daily calories, is the percentage of fat calories 30 percent or less? Foods that are low in fat will help you limit your caloric intake. (To calculate the number of fat calories, multiply each gram of fat by nine.) Here's one simple way to balance your fat intake: If you plan to eat a high-fat lunch, such as a hamburger and fries, eat a light morning meal such as fruit and low-fat cottage cheese, then end the day with a lean meal of broiled fish, fresh vegetables, rice, and a tossed salad.

◆ Are you taking steps to reduce the amount of saturated fat in your diet? In addition to keeping your total fat calories at 30 percent or less of your daily intake, it is also advisable to limit the amount of saturated fat, which comes from animal products and from oils like coconut and palm, to no more than 10 percent. This is particularly important if you're trying to keep your blood cholesterol low.

◆ Are you keeping your sodium intake in check? If you're a snacker, sodium could be a problem; many popular snack foods are high in sodium. In addition, many convenience foods, including some dinners, contain high levels of sodium.

◆ Are you eating a variety of foods throughout the week? The greater the variety, the better the chance that your diet contains the essential nutrients in adequate amounts. Balance your diet using the Food Guide Pyramid shown in Chapter 9.

◆ Are you eating calcium-rich foods each day? Government surveys show that most Americans, particularly women, don't meet their calcium needs, and low-calcium diets may increase the risk of osteoporosis, or loss of bone mass. Good sources of calcium include milk, cheese, yogurt, sardines (unboned), and canned salmon (unboned). Broccoli, collards, and tofu can be good supplementary sources. If you're concerned about your fat and calorie intake, use low-calorie dairy foods.

◆ Are you eating enough fiber foods? According to the National Cancer Institute, most Americans fall short of the recommended levels of dietary fiber—about 20 to 35 grams per day. Water-insoluble fiber, or "roughage"— found in wheat bran, most vegetables, and whole-grain breads—is a digestive aid that promotes regularity and decreased the risk of colon cancer. Certain soluble fibers—found in oats, dried beans, and fruits and vegetables— seem to be a factor in lowering blood cholesterol.

The Cost of Healthful Eating

If you ask many people why they don't eat more healthfully, chances are they'll say that it's too expensive. According to a survey conducted by Princeton Survey Research Associates, some 4 in 10 consumers believe that fruits, vegetables, seafood, and the other components of a healthful diet would put too much of a dent in their budgets. But it doesn't have to be that way. When researchers affiliated with Pennsylvania State University and the Mary Bassett Research Institute gave nearly 300 men and women with high cholesterol levels a how-to home video on adopting low-fat diets, those whose blood cholesterol dropped the most after nine months actually *cut* their foods bills by an average of $1.10 a day—or more than $400 each year.

The first step to trimming food costs is to keep a one- or two-week tally of everything you eat. It sounds tedious, but putting things on paper can yield enlightening truths about spending patterns, even for those who are already adept at sticking to a budget. After a week or two, some basic dietary spending habits should emerge—and you might be surprised at what you learn. One woman found that between morning coffee, take-out lunches, and afternoon snacks she was easily spending $5.00 to $7.00 during most workdays. Yet, that same person said she'd feel extravagant spending $2.99 for a pint of strawberries at the supermarket in the dead of winter. As this example shows, there's a great deal of psychology involved in food purchases.

If you've been avoiding healthful eating because you fear its toll on your pocketbook, this research should help you see things another way. By following a series of practical suggestions, you can learn how to make good eating pay.

◆ Don't judge everything by price alone. If you live by yourself and dine out with friends a couple of times a week, the tab may be money well spent because the "return" on your investment is not only a meal but also the camaraderie that goes with the occasion. On the flip side, the lesser price of a fast-food meal gobbled down alone might not be worth it. The same goes for vending-machine or snack-shop purchases made during the working day. A bag of chips, a can of soda, and a candy bar can add a couple of dollars to your daily food bill—not to mention 600 calories and 22 grams of fat. On the other hand, six vanilla wafers, an eight-ounce container of orange juice, and a banana brought from home total only 79 cents and contain 335 calories and 5 grams of fat.

◆ Limit your meat, poultry, and seafood allowance to 6 ounces daily. Although the federal government advises people to eat no more than an average of 6 ounces of flesh foods, many Americans consume more on the order of 11 ounces, raising their food costs considerably. Consider a family of four in which two adults eat 3 ounces each of luncheon meat at noon and 8 ounces each of roast beef for dinner (about twice the recommended daily average), and two kids eat 3 ounces each of luncheon meat and 6 ounces each of roast beef. The total bill comes to $11.88. But limit everyone's portion size to 3 ounces per meal and the cost of the entire family's meat intake is just $6.60 a day.

As for seafood, you may be under the impression that fish is more expensive than meat and poultry. But consider this: Compare what you actually get with a pound of porterhouse steak at $5.99 versus a pound of haddock at $6.99. On the face of it, the haddock seems more expensive. But after you remove the steak's bone and trim away all visible fat you're left with only about three-quarters of a pound of meat, raising the price of the steak to $7.98 a pound—a dollar more than the haddock.

◆ Go with more grains. Grain-based foods, which are supposed to account for about half the calories in a healthful diet, tend to cost the least. The trick is to keep food simple. One pound of plain white rice costs 45 cents and contains less than a gram of fat and only a trace of sodium. Package it as Rice-a-Roni, however, and the price soars to $2.64 a pound. And, if you add the butter and milk the package recommends, the amount of fat and sodium soars to 4 grams and 670 milligrams, respectively.

◆ Eat at least five servings of fruits and vegetables a day. That's what experts recommend, but the average American eats about three servings a day. Price is often given as a reason. But if you think about produce as an alternative to typical high-fat snacks, the cost is relatively low. For example, a banana at 15 cents is cheaper and more healthful than a Snickers bar at 50 cents. Even a fruit cup in a cafeteria, at upward of $2.00, might be no more expensive than a piece of carrot cake. And it's certainly much more healthful.

◆ It's not necessarily "all or nothing." Let's say you have less than half an hour to make dinner between work and your child's ball game. You may be tempted to pick up burgers and fries, or fried chicken, mashed potatoes, and mayonnaise-soaked coleslaw at a fast-food outlet on your way home. But you can save money as well as fat by buying just the burgers or chicken at the fast-food outlet and serving them with pre-cut vegetables from the grocery store or potatoes "baked" in the microwave. A small two-ounce order of fries generally costs about $1 and has upward of ten grams of fat. A seven-ounce baked potato costs only 15 to 25 cents and contains just a trace of fat.

Be a Healthy Vegetarian

Vegetarianism has gone mainstream. No longer is it the domain of the soyburger or the seaweed sandwich. The vegetarian trend, which is up 30 percent since 1970, has opened the way for a proliferation of vegetarian restaurants, convenience-food products, and cookbooks that offer enticing meatless meals.

It is unlikely that the United States will become a vegetarian nation, but the trend has plenty to recommend it, as those who fill their plates with fruits, vegetables, and grains rather than with large quantities of animal foods place themselves at a lower risk for the most common American illnesses: heart disease, colon cancer, breast cancer, diabetes, hypertension, and obesity.

Some of the strongest evidence that a diet rich in plant foods and sparing of animal foods confers a variety of health benefits comes from observations of a group of Seventh Day Adventists, many of whom eat no animal flesh, although they may consume dairy products and eggs. Compared with those who eat the typical high-fat American diet, members of this sect who were tested had a dramatically lower rate of heart disease. One group of researchers in California found that the death rate from coronary disease in male members of this sect is as low as half of that found in the average California male. Undoubtedly, the fact that Seventh Day Adventists are also nonsmokers contributes to the health picture, because smoking is one of the risk factors for heart disease. But diet apparently plays an integral role, as the rate of heart disease among Seventh Day Adventists who are not vegetarians was found to be three times higher than that of their vegetarian counterparts. Their low-fat diets may also account for the fact that Seventh Day Adventists are only half as likely as other Americans to develop colon and rectal cancer. Their rate of cancer of the breast, prostate, pancreas, and ovaries is much smaller, too. Diets that favor fruits, vegetables, and grains, in addition to being low in cholesterol, are also high in fiber.

There are three kinds of vegetarian styles: Semivegetarians are those who dramatically cut back their meat, poultry, and fish intake, using them as sideline items rather than as a main course. Lacto-ovo vegetarians don't eat animal flesh but consume dairy products such as cheese and milk. Vegans consume no meat or dairy foods. Dietary needs vary for each group.

CASHING IN ON HEALTHFUL EATING

Those who have the fattiest diets generally tend to see the greatest cuts in cost after changing to a low-fat way of eating. Consider the following before-and-after example, which illustrates the cost-saving change possible for one person who participated in a recent fat-lowering study.

Before	Fat(g)	Approximate Cost
Breakfast		
6 fl oz coffee	0	$.03
1 tsp sugar	0.01	
Cream-filled doughnut	21	.35
Lunch		
Seafood salad hoagie made with an 8" roll, 4 oz seafood salad with mayonnaise, lettuce, tomato, and onion	15	1.53
1¼ oz bag Fritos corn chips	13	.31
2 (.8 oz) Reese's Peanut Butter Cups	14	.45
1 (12 fl oz) can Diet Pepsi	0	.65
Snack		
6 fl oz coffee	0	.03
1 tsp sugar	0	.01
2 (1 oz) Archway oatmeal cookies	6	.28
Dinner		
3 slices thick crust pizza with 2 meat toppings, extra cheese, thick crust	51	4.19
1 (12 fl oz) can Dr. Pepper	0	.65
Total	120	$8.49

After	Fat(g)	Approximate Cost
Breakfast		
6 fl oz coffee	0	.03
1 tsp sugar	0	.01
1½ cups raisin bran cereal	2	.28
8 fl oz 1% fat milk	3	.20
2 slices whole-wheat toast	2	.12
2 tsp jelly	0	.06
8 fl oz orange juice	trace	.20
Lunch		
Tuna salad sandwich made with an 8" roll, 3 oz water-packed tuna, 1 tbsp light mayonnaise, lettuce, and tomato	8	1.14
1 oz bag pretzels	1	.23
1 banana	trace	.15
8 fl oz 1% fat milk	3	.20
Snack		
6 fl oz coffee	0	.03
1 tsp sugar	0	.01
2 (1 oz) Archway oatmeal cookies	6	.28
Dinner		
2 slices thick crust pizza with mushrooms and green peppers	13	2.75
2 slices garlic bread	10	.24

CASHING IN ON HEALTHFUL EATING *(cont.)*

1 cup tossed salad made with lettuce, carrot, and red cabbage and 1 tbsp reduced-fat dressing	3	.27
1 (12 fl oz) can Dr. Pepper	0	.65
Snack		
8 oz hot chocolate	1	.08
Total	52	$6.93

Cutting Down on Meat

Many people have become semivegetarians because they've taken to heart the advice of organizations like the American Heart Association and the American Cancer Society to cut the fat in their diets. Just changing the proportions of plant foods to animal foods in your diet may automatically lower your fat intake. For example, a traditional 10-ounce steak intended for one person can easily be turned into two 5-ounce servings. The "hole" that's left on the plate can be filled with a heftier salad, a large serving of a cooked vegetable like broccoli or spinach, or even a second baked potato or a second piece of corn on the cob. Indeed, cutting out that 5 ounces of steak will result in your consuming 120 fewer calories as fat. Even if you add 2 teaspoons of margarine to a potato or corn on the cob, it will put back only 70 calories of fat—most of it unsaturated.

Cutting down on or even cutting out meat does not have to mean risking deficiencies of essential nutrients. Even small quantities of meat added to the main course of a meal can supply the nutrients you need. And dairy foods and eggs are a good source of complete protein, so lacto-ovo vegetarians are not at risk for protein deficiency.

Keeping a Nutrient Balance for Strict Vegetarians

The strictest vegetarians—a small minority called vegans, who abstain from eating both meat and dairy products—need to pay closer attention than others to their intake of certain nutrients in order to avoid deficiencies. For them, managing a healthful diet involves some savvy about the science of nutrition. Diets that do not include any animal foods often lack calories, along with essential vitamins and minerals, and are usually inadequate for growing children or others with special nutritional needs.

Vegans need to be aware that the proteins in plant foods, particularly grains and legumes, are not "complete." That is, one or another plant food by itself cannot provide the body with all the amino acids, the building blocks of proteins that humans require for building and maintaining body tissues. In order to be assured of getting complete proteins, vegans must consume a variety of incomplete proteins throughout the day. Eating red beans with rice, for instance, turns two sources of incomplete protein into one complete source. Split pea soup and a slice of rye bread makes for another full complement. (See Chapter 1 for more information about complete and incomplete protein sources.)

One nutrient vegans must consider more carefully than others is calcium, because dairy products are the best sources. It is hard to fulfill the dietary requirement for this nutrient from vegetables alone. Further, the calcium in plant foods may not be absorbed as readily as the calcium in animal foods. It's important to eat generous portions of calcium-containing vegetables. One large stalk of broccoli provides more than 10 percent of the recommended adult allowance. Collard greens and mustard greens supply appreciable levels, too. Small amounts of calcium can be found in other plant foods, but a diet dependent on plant foods for calcium is not likely to be adequate.

Vegans must also be careful to look for sources of iron in their diet. Fortunately, a wide variety of plant foods are iron rich. A cup of dried beans, peas, or lentils contains about 5 milligrams of iron, or just under one-third of the RDA of 15 milligrams for women, and half the RDA of 10 milligrams for men. But similar to calcium, the iron in plant foods is not well absorbed, something to consider in light of the fact that even many meat eaters lack iron in their diets. Making sure there's enough vitamin C in the diet will help, because vitamin C aids in the absorption of iron.

Vegans must pay particular attention to their intake of vitamin B-12 because that nutrient, without which pernicious anemia develops, is available naturally only in animal foods. One way to ensure sufficient vitamin B-12 is to eat cereals that have been fortified with the vitamin. However, strict vegetarians should consult a knowledgeable physician about taking vitamin B-12 supplements or multivitamin/mineral supplements that contain B-12, because fortified cereals and soy foods often do not contain the nutrient.

The same visit to the doctor should also include a discussion about whether supplements of vitamin D are necessary. People who do not drink milk may be at risk for a vitamin D deficiency because vitamin D–fortified milk is about the only food that contains adequate amounts of the vitamin. It is true that exposure to the sun allows the body to synthesize vitamin D, but not everyone, especially those living in northern climates, gets the amount of sunlight necessary to make all of the vitamin D the body needs. Further, there is increasing evidence that with age our ability to synthesize and metabolize the active form of vitamin D is diminished.

Making Meals Appetizing

The American imagination, accustomed to creating meals around meat, may falter at the prospect of making low-meat or vegetarian meals appetizing and hearty. But many ethnic cuisines have discovered the secret to using meat as a condiment rather than as a main course, or stretching small amounts of meat to go further. A Chinese stir-fry, for example, can utilize thin strips of beef or chicken or go without the meat altogether and still make for a hearty dish. Traditional pasta sauces don't need meat as an ingredient, or they can get by with small amounts.

Nutritious Nibbling

Consumers are snacking more than ever: Americans spend more than $12 billion each year on such items as chips, pretzels, popcorn, and pork rinds. No wonder the U.S. Department of Agriculture's Human Nutrition Information Service decided to design a handbook devoted specifically to tallying the fat, calories, and other nutrients in America's munchies.

Snacking does not have to mean throwing nutritional caution to the wind. Snack foods high in calories, salt, sugar, and fat are available in abundance, but there are plenty of healthful options that you can buy or make yourself.

Snack foods are often salty, and because salt is nearly half sodium, it's best to watch snack items like chips, salted nuts, salty crackers, and salted pretzels. Sugar-filled cookies, ice cream, and candy are often high in fat as well. For example, 72 of the 150 calories in a one-ounce Nestlé's Crunch Bar come from fat.

Can you avoid the calorie-fat-salt-sugar trap by purchasing "healthful" snacks? Health food stores offer plenty of foods like "natural" potato chips and "sugarless" candy bars. But, upon close inspection, you might find that these potato chips are fried in fat and laden with salt, just like supermarket brands. Granted, the potatoes in the "natural" brand may be fried in a less saturated oil, like safflower oil. But saturated or not, a 1-ounce, 150-calorie bag of potato chips still contains 60 percent fat calories, which hardly qualifies it as a "health food." One health food store markets a high-fiber candy bar, but the nutrition claims are misleading. Although the little bar does contain 5 grams of dietary fiber, fat makes up more than 35 percent of its calories. In fact, ounce for ounce, it has more fat than a Milky Way bar! Worse still, the candy's "nectar vanilla yogurt coating" is made with palm kernel oil. The candy bar also contains less than 7 percent of the USRDA for all the vitamins and minerals listed on its label. It's not that health food stores don't carry any nutritious snack. Just be sure to read the label before you buy.

Snacking can actually be a way to round out your meal plan, adding nutrients that you may not be getting enough of elsewhere in the day. Remember, a snack doesn't have to consist of a fatty, salty food. The only requirement is that it be quick, convenient, satisfying, and, of course, healthful. Here are some ideas for nutritious nibbling:

◆ Popcorn: What could be more all-American? And it's fast, fun, and good for you, too. If you make it in a hot-air popper, a cup of popcorn has only 27 calories. If you don't have a hot-air popper, you can pop a half cup of kernels in as little as a tablespoon of oil, which adds only 11 calories per cup of popped popcorn. Microwave varieties differ widely in the amount of fat and sodium, but many are relatively high in fat. However, check the packages of some of the new low-fat brands that manufacturers like Orville Redenbacher are producing.

◆ Graham crackers and milk: an old-fashioned afternoon snack that is still a good bet. Two graham crackers have only about 70 calories, and a glass of (1%) low-fat milk has about 100. Although the graham crackers add little nutritional value, this snack is an enjoyable way to help meet your daily calcium requirement because it includes milk.

◆ Fruit: Buy "convenience fruits" that are easy to carry in a briefcase or lunch bag. These include apples, peaches, oranges, pears, nectarines, and plums.

◆ Snack-size cans of unsweetened applesauce or fruit juice are a good bet, as are miniature boxes of raisins.

◆ Vegetables and dip: Because they are high in fiber, vegetables are filling, as well as a source of vitamins. Enjoy them alone or add low-fat cottage cheese stuffing or low-fat yogurt dip. A serving of low-fat yogurt has less than 150 calories. To make a tasty vegetable dip, stir in such seasonings as dill, caraway seeds, chili powder, mint, paprika, mustard powder, garlic, or pepper. Good vegetables for dipping include celery sticks, carrot sticks, cucumber slices, mushrooms, radishes, cherry tomatoes, broccoli or cauliflower florets, green or red peppers, and asparagus spears.

◆ Fruit and yogurt: Make your own fruit yogurt, adding bananas, diced apples, peaches, berries, and other favorites to low-fat, plain yogurt. This fresh snack will taste great, and it's much better than commercial fruit yogurts, which can have as many as 250 calories per serving and more sugar than fruit. Top your creation with cinnamon or even mix in a teaspoon of sugar, which has only 16 calories.

Fast and Frozen: The Right Choices

Americans spend nearly $15 billion every year on frozen dinners, and health-conscious consumers are finding that they don't have to sacrifice nutrition when they shop the frozen-food section. A wide variety of "diet" dinners are available, featuring portion and calorie control, low fat and cholesterol, and low sodium. And the numbers are growing.

How can you take advantage of the convenience benefits of frozen dinners and still eat healthfully? You can start by using the following criteria when choosing a frozen dinner:

◆ A maximum of 30 percent of calories from fat, the recommended level.

◆ No more than 600 milligrams of sodium—25 percent of the upper daily limit the National Academy of Sciences deems healthful.

◆ At least nine ounces of food.

Even a frozen meal that meets all of these requirements might be somewhat low in one or another essential vitamin or mineral, particularly vitamins A and C. Also, most frozen dinners do not provide the level of calcium recommended for keeping bones healthy. To make up for the lack of calcium, include one or two of these items in your daily menu: a cup of skim or low-fat (1%) milk, 1 ounce of low-fat hard cheese, a cup of yogurt, 2 cups of broccoli, or 4 ounces of salmon or sardines with bones.

You might also want to try adding one of the following side dishes to a frozen entree to add fiber and nutrients. Each contains from 100 to 200 calories:

◆ Spinach salad: 1 cup chopped spinach, 1 cup sliced mushrooms, wedged tomato, chopped hard-cooked egg, 1 tablespoon walnuts, 1 tablespoon low-calorie Italian dressing; 2 breadsticks.

◆ 1 cup steamed red and green cabbage sprinkled with caraway seeds; 1 cup pineapple chunks garnished with maraschino cherry and a sprig of mint.

◆ 4 asparagus spears; 1 cup sliced strawberries with a dollop of low-fat lemon or vanilla yogurt.

◆ 1 cup each shredded iceberg and romaine lettuce and 1 cup sliced mushrooms sprinkled with wine vinegar and a dash of basil; 1 cup red grapes with 1 ounce wedge of low-fat cheese.

◆ 1 cup cooked green beans tossed with 1 cup water chestnuts and 1 tablespoon toasted, slivered almonds; 1 sliced orange with ½ a sliced grapefruit.

◆ 1 small ear corn on the cob with 1 teaspoon margarine; 4" x 8" watermelon wedge.

◆ 1 cup steamed carrots dusted with parsley; 1 kiwifruit sliced into 1 cup water-packed fruit cocktail.

◆ 1 cup romaine lettuce, 1 cup cherry tomato halves tossed with 1 tablespoon low-calorie Italian dressing and sprinkled with 1 tablespoon Parmesan cheese; cantaloupe.

◆ 1 cup each canned, drained mandarin oranges and pineapple chunks mixed with 1 cup low-fat yogurt and garnished with a maraschino cherry.

◆ 1 cup steamed artichokes drizzled with lemon juice.

◆ Caesar salad: 1 cup romaine lettuce, ½ cup herbed croutons, 1 chopped hard-cooked egg tossed with 1 teaspoon olive oil, 2 teaspoons lemon juice, dash of garlic, and 1 tablespoon Parmesan cheese; 1 cup raspberries with a dollop of low-fat lemon vanilla yogurt.

◆ Carrot salad: 1 cup shredded carrots, 1 tablespoon each raisins and diet mayonnaise; 1 poppyseed roll.

◆ 1 cup each steamed zucchini and cauliflower seasoned with a squirt of lemon juice and sprinkled with dill; 2"-long slice Italian bread.

◆ 1 cup low-fat cottage cheese spooned over 2 water-packed peach halves and garnished with chopped walnuts.

◆ 2 tomato halves broiled with 1 ounce part-skim mozzarella cheese and seasoned with a dash of garlic and oregano.

◆ Oriental salad: 1 cup each shredded Bibb lettuce and fresh spinach leaves, 1 cup drained mandarin oranges, ½ cup herbed croutons, 1 teaspoon each vinegar and olive oil.

◆ 1 cup cantaloupe balls in 1 cup low-fat vanilla yogurt, spiced with a dash of cinnamon and nutmeg.

◆ 1 cucumber, 1 tomato, red onion, sliced and marinated in low-calorie dressing and seasoned with fresh ground pepper; 1 nectarine.

◆ Fruit kabob: 4 strawberries, 1 cup honeydew chunks, 1 cup pineapple chunks skewered and dipped in 1 cup low-fat vanilla yogurt mixed with 1 tablespoon slivered almonds and a taste of honey.

◆ Spinach and basil salad: 1 cup fresh spinach leaves, ½ cup fresh basil leaves tossed with 2 teaspoons olive oil, 1 tablespoon pine nuts, and garlic powder to taste; 1 plum.

◆ Waldorf salad: 1 chopped apple, 1 tablespoon each raisins, chopped celery, and chopped walnuts moistened with 1 tablespoon diet mayonnaise.

◆ 1 cup steamed broccoli with 1 ounce low-fat cheese melted on top; 3 medium apricots.

◆ 1 cup each steamed carrots and zucchini seasoned with dill; 1 cup red grapes.

◆ 1 cup iceberg lettuce with cup each shredded red cabbage and carrots tossed with wine vinegar and tarragon.

◆ 1 cup raw cauliflowerettes and ½ cup grated carrots with 1 cup plain low-fat yogurt seasoned with dill.

◆ 1 cup cooked green beans sprinkled with sesame seeds and a shake of soy sauce; cup fresh strawberries with a dollop of lemon or vanilla yogurt.

◆ 1 cup cooked brussels sprouts stir fried with 1 cup water chestnuts in 1 teaspoon of vegetable oil; Blueberry parfait: alternate layers of ½ cup each fresh blueberries and low-fat vanilla yogurt and top with a dash of cinnamon and 2 crumbled vanilla wafers.

◆ 1 cup cooked spinach with a zest of lemon juice and dash of nutmeg; 1 cup peach slices sprinkled with ginger.

◆ 1 cup shredded cabbage mixed with caraway seeds and 1 tablespoon diet mayonnaise; small poppyseed roll.

◆ cucumber, 1 tomato sliced into cup low-fat plain yogurt with chives and lemon juice; 1 nectarine.

◆ 1 cup cooked cauliflower with 1 cup each sliced mushrooms and red pepper strips; 1 small whole wheat roll.

◆ 1 cup okra marinated in vinegar seasoned with dry mustard, thyme, and a few drops of olive oil; 2" by 7" wedge honeydew melon.

◆ iceberg lettuce wedge with low-calorie dressing; medium-sized acorn squash baked with 1 teaspoon each margarine and brown sugar.

◆ 1 cup shredded red cabbage cooked with ½ cup each chopped apple and diced onion, as well as wine vinegar and sugar to taste; 1 small hard roll.

◆ ½ cup each carrot, green pepper, and onion strips sautéed in a teaspoon of vegetable oil and a dash of basil; 1 pear.

◆ 2 stalks steamed broccoli sprinkled with pimento; apple baked with cinnamon and a dash of brown sugar.

◆ 1 celery stalk stuffed with low-fat cottage cheese and garnished with pimento; 3 prunes.

◆ Fruit bowl: 1 cup each cantaloupe and honeydew, 1 sliced kiwifruit and 1 cup raspberries with a sprinkle of lemon; 2 gingersnap cookies.

◆ 1 cup cooked collard greens with 1 tablespoon Parmesan cheese; 1 slice pumpernickel bread.

◆ 1 peach and 1 cup sliced strawberries in 1 cup water-packed fruit cocktail; small whole wheat roll.

◆ Chinese salad: 1 cup romaine lettuce, ½ cup canned and drained mandarin oranges, and

2 tablespoons slivered toasted almonds with poppyseed dressing.

◆ 1 banana sliced with 1 orange (and its juice) and sprinkled with 1 tablespoon raisins.

◆ 1 cup steamed cauliflower topped with 1 ounce melted low-fat cheese and 1 tablespoon bread crumbs; 2 apricots.

◆ 3 stalks steamed asparagus; 1 persimmon.

◆ Baked potato covered with spinach and 1 tablespoon Parmesan cheese.

◆ 1 cup corn with chopped red and green peppers seasoned with chili powder; 1 cup red grapes.

◆ Garden salad: 1 cup red leaf lettuce, sliced cucumber, wedged tomato, and ½ cup grated carrot with 1 tablespoon low-calorie dressing (optional: 2 chopped, marinated artichoke hearts).

◆ 1 apple baked with margarine, dash of brown sugar, raisins, walnuts, and 1 cup orange juice.

◆ Raw julienne carrots, yellow and green zucchini, red pepper, dipped in plain, low-fat yogurt with scallions.

◆ Fresh fruit mix: 1 sliced peach, 1 cup each strawberries and blueberries, 1 cup honeydew melon balls.

Make Your Own Frozen Meals

If you enjoy the convenience of heating up a frozen dinner in the oven or microwave but are not satisfied with commercial products, you can make your own nutritious frozen dinners. Homemade frozen dinners give you the advantage of controlling the ingredients used. By choosing fresh and low-fat foods, the home cook can eliminate the extra fat content of many commercial dinners. And if you use lively herbs and spices instead of extra salt, the amount of sodium normally found in these dinners can be cut substantially.

People who prepare frozen dinners in their own kitchens also have the option of increasing the fiber content by choosing whole grains as well as including vegetables rich in vitamins A and C, nutrients that are sometimes lacking in commercial dinners. Making your own frozen dinners brings substantial benefits to your pocketbook, too. Although commercial dinners may be affordable for a single person or a couple, the cost of feeding a larger family this way could become prohibitive.

In addition to being relatively inexpensive to prepare, frozen dinners don't require much in the way of special equipment. All you need to buy are some freezer bags and/or freezer wrap, wire twisters, small aluminum tins, microwave containers (if you'll be cooking with a microwave), strong tape, and a marking pencil to label each package with the name of the food, the portion size, and the date it was frozen. With these items on hand, and after a well-planned shopping trip, you will be ready to put together, with very little effort, dinners that you and your family or friends can enjoy later with a minimum of preparation.

The following suggestions will guide you in preparing and storing your own nutritious frozen dinners:

◆ Set your freezer at 0°F to ensure optimal quality of frozen foods. Freezer thermometers are sold in housewares and hardware stores.

◆ Avoid putting too many hot dinners into your freezer at once. Cool them for five to ten minutes first at room temperature so the freezer temperature will not rise.

◆ Before freezing vegetables, blanch them (placing them for one minute in water that has come to a rolling boil and then plunging them into cold water) to destroy enzymes that can interfere with their texture, color, and flavor. With the exception of salad greens (tomatoes, celery, cucumbers, radishes, and potatoes, which lose their texture during freezing), most vegetables freeze well.

◆ Slightly undercooking dishes before freezing will prevent overcooking when you reheat.

◆ To slash fat from stews and soups, refrigerate them after cooking, skim the fat, then freeze.

◆ Use arrowroot or cornstarch rather than flour to thicken sauces. They'll be less likely to separate when frozen.

◆ Be creative with your use of freezer containers. For example, aluminum tart shells can be used for individual pot pies, and muffin tins can hold mini-meatloaves and vegetable purees.

◆ Do not place aluminum foil directly over dinners that contain tomatoes and fruit juices. The acidity can eat through the foil, causing pits in the wrapping and eventual "freezer burn." Instead, use plastic containers or wrap.

◆ Because liquids expand when frozen, make sure to allow about a half inch or more of head space to prevent containers that have sauces or other liquids from bulging or bursting.

◆ If you prepare food in a casserole dish that you don't want to keep in the freezer, line the dish with freezer foil that covers the bottom and sides and also expands outside of the casserole. When the dinner has finished cooking, take the foil ends, lift the food out, and wrap it separately or place it in a different container.

◆ Stock your freezer with a few frozen dinner "staples." Homemade chicken stock stored in ice cube trays, for example, is an invaluable ingredient to have on hand. Fresh herbs, whole-grain bread crumbs, and grated cheese can be frozen and sprinkled directly onto dinners as they finish reheating.

◆ For extra convenience in preparing quick side dishes, you can freeze fresh-sliced or chopped vegetables in such products as Baggies Extra Protection Freezer Bags, which can go straight from the freezer into boiling water. Fill each bag with a single serving. When you're ready to use one, just take it from the freezer and cook it right in the bag. As an alternative, prepare chopped vegetables as side dishes to go with your homemade frozen entrees.

◆ To freeze fresh fruits, simply place whole fruits, such as berries, in a single layer on a cookie sheet and freeze. Once fully frozen, the fruits can be placed in a container without sticking together. Fruits that are susceptible to browning, such as sliced apples, pears, and peaches, should be sprinkled with lemon juice and ascorbic acid powder (vitamin C) before freezing to prevent discoloration.

◆ Because certain spices, including oregano, thyme, and parsley, often intensify in flavor during freezing, you might choose to slightly underseason dishes in which you use them. You can always add more seasoning later if it's needed.

◆ For dinners that will be reheated by microwaving, cover containers with plastic wrap rather than foil before freezing so the dish can be placed directly into the microwave.

To assure that the dinners are properly stored, defrosted, and reheated, follow these guidelines:

◆ Store your meals in aluminum foil or in plastic containers that specify "freezer-proof" or "freezer safe" on the label. These products are specially designed to prevent moisture loss. You can also reuse containers and microwave trays saved from store-bought frozen dinners as long as you clean them thoroughly.

◆ Try to get rid of as much air as possible from plastic freezer bags by pressing it out with your palms before sealing. This will help foods stay fresh.

◆ Never thaw frozen dinners on the kitchen counter. The longer food sits at room temperature, the greater the chance it will become a breeding ground for bacteria. It's best to thaw foods in the refrigerator overnight.

Make the Most of Microwave Magic

With the advent of the microwave oven, the true promise of convenience cooking has been realized. Now the most complex dishes can be served in minutes, and the tedium of pot scrubbing is virtually eliminated. Even children can use the microwave to fix quick snacks. Still, consumers have some lingering questions about the safety of microwave ovens, the quality and taste of foods cooked in them, and the nutritional benefits of microwaving.

Setting Fears to Rest

Safety concerns occasionally nag even the most knowledgeable microwave owners. People have sometimes associated microwaves with nuclear radiation, but the two are vastly different. Microwaves are just that: waves. They are similar to radio waves that are in the air at all times, the difference being that radio waves are broadcast over a distance, whereas the microwave "broadcasting" is self-contained, inside the oven. The electromagnetic rays in ovens cause the molecules in food to vibrate, and this vibration creates the heat necessary to turn an item from cold to hot or from raw to ready-to-eat. The microwaves do not actually touch most of the food they cook. They penetrate only its surface and three-quarters of an inch to an inch and a half deep. As the vibrating molecules near the surface agitate the deeper molecules, they create the friction required to heat the food all the way through.

Although it's true that too much exposure to any kind of radiation can be dangerous (the way an overdose of ultraviolet light causes sunburn), the safeguards built into microwave ovens make it virtually impossible for any harm

to come from them as long as they are in good working order. The leakage limits set by the Food and Drug Administration (FDA) are substantially below acknowledged danger levels. Even if the leakage were to reach the maximum level set by the FDA, moving only a couple of inches back from the oven dramatically decreases one's risk of radiation exposure. Indeed, a person standing 20 inches away from a microwave that has any leakage will receive just one one-hundredth the exposure of someone standing two inches away.

The construction of microwave oven doors provides another safeguard. No microwaves can be generated while the door is open: By law, two interlock switches must be activated for operation. The door is sealed to keep the microwaves inside the oven, and the viewing window contains a metallic screen that reflects microwaves back into the appliance and prevents their escape into the kitchen. Once the food is cooked, it is not "full of microwaves." They dissipate once they've completed their job.

Attention to these safety basics will virtually eliminate any risk:

◆ Never tamper with the safety interlocks or allow residue to collect on the sealing surfaces of the doors.

◆ Do not operate the oven if the door or viewing window is bent, cracked, loose, or damaged in any way.

◆ Don't operate the oven without food or liquid in it, as this could result in damage to the magnetron tube or energy-absorbing glass tray. Leave a small cup of water in the oven to absorb energy in case the oven is turned on accidentally.

◆ Avoid using metallic materials in your oven unless they're specifically noted to be safe. Metal reflects microwave energy away from the food and can disrupt the operation and damage the oven. Read the owner's manual to find out which materials are safe.

Try These Healthful Homemade Frozen Meals

Parmesan Chicken with Herbed Barley

10 servings. Nutrition information per serving: cholesterol, 81 mg; sodium, 172 mg; protein, 35 g; calories, 287; calories from fat, 19 percent

For the Chicken
1 cup finely ground whole-wheat bread crumbs
1 cup grated Parmesan cheese
1 tbsp dried basil
1 cup skim or low-fat (1%) milk
2 lb. boneless, skinless chicken breasts

For the Herbed Barley
1 8-oz. can low-sodium chicken broth
½ cup chopped onion
2 tbsp safflower oil
½ cup chopped green pepper
3 cups pearl barley
1 tsp each: salt and black pepper
pinch of tumeric (optional)

Instructions: To prepare chicken, combine bread crumbs, Parmesan cheese, and basil in a bowl. Dip chicken breasts one at a time into milk and then roll in Parmesan mixture, shaking off excess. Cook on foil-covered baking sheet coated with nonstick spray at 350° F for 10 minutes. Wrap each breast in heavy-duty freezer foil. Label and freeze.

To make herbed barley, sauté onion in oil in a medium-sized saucepan for about 3 minutes or until translucent. Add green pepper and cook for an additional 3 minutes. Add chicken broth and bring to a boil. Add barley and spices. Lower heat and simmer, covered, for about 45 minutes. Divide the mixture into 10 individual freezer containers.

To prepare from frozen, place foil-covered breast(s) on a baking sheet and heat in the oven at 375° F for 30 minutes or until heated thoroughly. To heat barley, bake at 375° F for 45 minutes. Serve with shredded raw cabbage and carrots, along with steamed asparagus.

Cincinnati Chili

12 servings. Nutrition information per serving: cholesterol, 53 mg; sodium, 356 mg; protein, 21 g; calories, 240; calories from fat, 30 percent
2 lb. lean ground beef
4 bay leaves
1 cup chopped onion
3 finely chopped medium garlic cloves
1 tsp cinnamon
1 tbsp allspice
4 tbsp vinegar

Try These Healthful Homemade Frozen Meals *(cont.)*

1 tsp crushed red pepper
1 tbsp chili powder
2 tsp cumin
1 tsp oregano
2 tsp sugar
1 6-oz. can tomato paste
5 cups water
2 15-oz. cans kidney beans, drained
4 cups cooked vermicelli

Instructions: Place a nonstick skillet over medium heat and add ground beef when skillet is hot. Cook over low heat until the beef is brown. Drain fat from pan.

Add remaining ingredients, except kidney beans, and bring them to a boil.

Simmer, uncovered, for about 1 hour, skimming fat from the surface as necessary. Remove bay leaves. Add kidney beans. Simmer 30 minutes more.

Divide chili into 12 individual freezer containers. Cover and label.

To heat from frozen, bake at 375° F for 40 minutes or until thoroughly heated.

Serve with slice of whole-grain bread and a spinach-mushroom salad.

◆ Fires can start when food is overcooked. Be sure to experiment with cooking times in advance.

◆ Care should be used with combustible products. Eggs cooked in the shell may burst; popcorn cooked without a microwave popping accessory can explode.

◆ Airtight bags should be punctured before heating.

◆ If materials inside the oven catch fire, don't open the door. Turn the oven off and disconnect the power.

◆ Always read the owner's manual thoroughly before using the microwave oven for the first time.

Microwave Cautions

If you cook an egg sunny-side up in your microwave oven but don't pierce the yolk before turning on the power, you're in danger of getting egg on your face—literally! Staffers from a hospital in Birmingham, England, reported two incidents in which women burned their eyes because they waited until after their eggs were heated to pierce them. The first stuck her fork into the yolk of an egg she had microwaved at full power for one minute, whereupon it exploded in her face and caused severe pain around her eye socket as well as burning her eyelids and causing enough other damage to reduce her vision from 20/20 to 20/200. It took six days of treatment with an antibiotic ointment along with double padding for her vision to return to normal. The second woman, who pierced her microwaved egg with a knife, also suffered eye pain along with excess secretion of tears and abnormal sensitivity to light. Her vision went from 20/20 to 20/200, and it took eight days for a full recovery.

What happened? An egg yolk has an outer membrane that puts pressure on its contents during heating. The sudden release of this pressure with the prick of a fork or knife after cooking can cause those contents to spray into the air and onto the face.

Eggs microwaved with their shells on can also be dangerous. A young Ohio man suffered severe burns to his eyes, nose, and forehead when his microwaved eggs exploded in his face. The solution is to remove eggs from their shells before microwaving, and to pierce the yolks.

Also use caution when you open freshly microwaved popcorn. The intense burst of steam can injure hands, face and eyes. Open the bag carefully, directing the steam away from you.

Nutritional Bonuses

Not only are microwave ovens perfectly safe, they also offer nutritional benefits that cannot be attained by traditional means. The fast-heating feature prevents the loss of nutrients that can be caused by overcooking. And because microwaves require little or no water to cook foods, vitamins are not lost into the water.

A number of vitamins, including vitamin C, rapidly break down when they're exposed to heat, dissolving in the cooking water. With shorter cooking times, more vitamin C is retained. To demonstrate the point, Gertrude Armbruster, Ph.D., a professor in the Division of Nutritional Sciences at Cornell University, tested fruits and vegetables cooked both in the microwave and by traditional means of boiling and baking. She found that 23 of 24 varieties of produce—ranging from apples to turnips—came out of the microwave with more vitamin C. For example, an apple baked in a conventional oven for 30 minutes is left with only 7 of its original 15 milligrams of vitamin C; microwaving the apple takes less than 4 minutes and preserves all 15.

Other water-soluble and heat-sensitive vitamins are "saved" by the microwave. The B vitamins thiamin, riboflavin, folic acid, and B-6 are preserved in foods at full strength.

The microwave can be a big help in cutting back on salt and sugar, too. Because it enhances the natural flavors in food, there's less temptation to reach for the salt shaker or the sugar bowl.

The microwave is literally a "lean machine." Because foods cook in their own moisture, no additional fats or oils are needed for cooking. Vegetable, fish, and poultry dishes steamed or poached in the microwave are light and healthful.

Some people might consider the effect on bacon safety as another nutritional bonus of microwaves. Conventional high-temperature frying converts nitrates used for curing bacon into nitrosamines, which have caused cancer in laboratory animals. But in the microwave, the equivalent frying temperatures are reached only in the last seconds of cooking, not enough time to trigger the reaction.

Still Working on Taste and Texture

If there are limitations to the wonders of microwave technology, they exist in the way food tastes, how it looks, and its texture. The fast-cooking feature of the microwave oven renders it less effective for foods that require gradual cooking or dry heat. The microwave's moist heat steams rather than bakes food; it can't crisp a pot roast, fry meats, or get a rise out of bread dough.

Technology will rise to the demands of tradition. Food engineers are working hard to develop taste- and texture-enhancing methods that will combat many of the microwave's limitations. Precooked, presealed meats—already browned and ready to reheat—might provide one solution. And although most of the dough-based items now prepared for microwaves—like pizza, waffles, and sandwiches—lack a flakey, home-baked texture, the invention of new cooking ingredients and utensils could change that. Multipurpose equipment is being introduced that takes the full range of cooking needs into consideration.

The two-in-one microwave convection combination is a single unit that can be used as both a microwave and a regular convection oven, coordinating cooking between the two. For example, with a roast baking in a conventional oven, the microwave element can be programmed to switch on when it's time to steam the vegetables.

For the most part, it's best to use the microwave for cooking tasks it does best: producing rich, moist casserole dishes; steaming fresh, crisp vegetables; making creamy thick soups and puddings; defrosting foods; and reheating leftovers quickly.

Ten Tips for Microwaving

New owners find that there's an adjustment period involved in learning to make the most of a microwave oven. Individual microwaves differ in small ways. For example, finding the precise cooking time for various dishes is a trial-and-error process. Once mastered, a microwave has great versatility, and it can't be beat for convenience. The following tips will help make microwave cooking simpler and more nutritious.

◆ Remove food from the oven a little before it is done: Even after the oven has shut off, food keeps cooking for a while because the molecules near the food's surface continue to agitate those deeper down. If you fail to account for this, food will overcook and you'll lose some of the nutritional benefits. For example, a frozen dish may not look ready when it first comes out, but let it stand for five minutes and you'll see a difference. It can always go back into the oven if it needs more cooking after that.

◆ Cover dishes to promote steaming: A cover will shorten the cooking time by sealing in the heat. Any food you would cook covered in a conventional oven—casseroles, vegetable dishes—should be covered in the microwave.

◆ Don't cook large items: The microwave is probably not the best vehicle for your Thanksgiving turkey. Large items don't work well because the microwave energy is too close to the item to cook it evenly. If possible, cut up pieces of meat before cooking—cubes of beef will work better than a whole roast.

◆ Use dishes that promote evenness in cooking: Wide, shallow dishes work better than deep and narrow ones. Uniformity of shape is also enhanced by the use of a round dish rather than a rectangular or square one. If you must use a dish with corners, cover them with aluminum foil at first because food cooks faster at corners, and foil will keep out the microwaves. (It's okay to use a little aluminum foil in the microwave, but be sure to keep it away from the oven walls.)

◆ Microwaves make great baking aids: Even if you're baking in a conventional oven, the microwave can cut the preparation time substantially. Butter, margarine, and chocolate melt quickly and more evenly than on a stove top; milk heats up and water boils within seconds.

◆ Check the liquid level of leftovers before reheating: Some dishes may absorb all the liquid the first time around, and a dab of butter or a couple of tablespoons of water should be added before reheating.

◆ Heat baby bottles on the stove: Don't use the microwave for heating up bottles of baby's milk. Because the exterior of the bottle remains cool, it is harder to judge the heat of the milk, and infants have been scalded as a result of its being too hot.

◆ Experiment with cooking levels: Practice cooking or reheating foods at various levels to find what works best. Try not to reheat foods at 100 percent heating capacity. Turn your microwave to 50 percent for the first few minutes, and up to 100 percent only during the last minute or two.

◆ Cook foods in advance and freeze: Save time by preparing and freezing favorite dishes in advance. You might slightly undercook them the first time around, but reheating will take nothing away from the flavor or texture.

◆ Learn the secrets of browning: Contrary to popular belief, there are ways meat can be browned in the microwave. Trim as much fat off as possible, because fat attracts and absorbs the microwave energy. (Remember, oil isn't needed for cooking in the microwave the way it is in a conventional oven.) The absence of excess fat allows more heat to get to the meat, and any fat in the meat will then begin to brown. There are also a number of commercial products that enhance the flavor and add the rich brown coloring we're used to in meat.

13

Ensure Your Food's Safety

As many as 80 million Americans suffer from some form of food poisoning each year, experiencing problems that range from mild cramps and diarrhea to severe nausea, diarrhea, and dehydration. Although few die as a result, small children and the elderly are particularly vulnerable.

The growing problem of food contamination is an issue that industry and government must reckon with. Most of our food supply, including meat, poultry, fish, dairy products, fruits, and vegetables, is capable of being contaminated with one of several bacteria. However, in spite of this seemingly grim picture, control over microbiological risk is mostly in the hands of individual homemakers and consumers. According to the Centers for Disease Control and Prevention, up to 85 percent of the incidences of food poisoning could be avoided if people followed basic health and safety guidelines in the preparation, storage, and serving of foods.

The bacteria that cause food poisoning are invisible. You cannot see, taste, or smell them. They attach themselves to dust particles, cling to the skins of fruits and vegetables, linger on peoples' hands and in their noses, and reside in the intestines of animals.

Although there are many varieties of bacteria, five are most familiar to Americans: salmonella, Staphyloccus aureus (S. aureus), Clostridium perfringens (C. perfringens) and Clostridium botulinum (botulism), and E. coli 0157:H7 (E. coli).

Salmonella

Salmonella is the most common bacteria, responsible for about half of all food poisoning. It is generally found in raw animal foods, such as meat, eggs, and poultry. The symptoms of salmonella poisoning, which include nausea, diarrhea, and fever, occur within 12 to 48 hours of ingesting the contaminated food. Not everyone who eats contaminated food gets sick—the problem seems to occur most frequently in young children, the elderly, and the infirm—but, even in mildly infected people, the unpleasant symptoms can linger for a few days.

The federal government and the food industry are engaged in efforts to reduce the incidence of salmonella poisoning. In the meantime, you can avoid it by following these guidelines:

◆ Rinse poultry with cold water before cooking to wash away some of the bacteria.

◆ Cook poultry until there is no pink meat and the juice runs clear. If you use a meat thermometer, check to see that the meat reaches an internal temperature of 180° to 185° F. Make sure to insert the thermometer into the thickest part of the chicken—the thigh, away from the bone—to get the most accurate reading.

◆ Keep utensils and cutting boards used to prepare meat and poultry separate from those used to prepare fruit and vegetables. For example, if you prepare a mixed chicken and vegetable dish, use a separate knife and cutting board for the chicken and for the vegetables.

◆ Be sure to wash thoroughly all the utensils you use to prepare raw meat and poultry with hot, soapy water (dishwasher water is hot enough). For extra protection, keep wood cutting boards clean by washing them every few days with a diluted bleach-and-water solution (about two teaspoons of bleach per quart of water). The bleach should kill any bacteria. Also, try to use a different cutting board for meat, poultry and fish than you use for raw vegetables and salad.

S. aureus

The microorganism S. aureus is responsible for a little more than 25 percent of all food-borne illnesses. It is carried in the noses and throats of most people. That's why sneezing or coughing on food—especially a protein-containing food like meat, or pudding—can contaminate it. Symptoms include mild diarrhea, sometimes accompanied by nausea and vomiting.

It is not the bacterium itself that brings on the symptoms, but the toxins (poisons) it produces. Even though cooking kills the bacteria, it does not destroy the toxins. You can cut down on the effects of S. aureus by following these guidelines:

◆ Never leave yet-to-be-cooked or already cooked foods at room temperature for long periods of time. A lukewarm temperature of 40° to 140° F (not piping hot but not as cold as a refrigerator) allows bacteria to grow rapidly and thereby produce more toxins.

◆ Thaw frozen foods in the refrigerator, not on the counter, to prevent them from getting too warm.

◆ Keep foods hot on the stove or in the oven until you are ready to serve them. Even a dish as seemingly harmless as a rice casserole can produce enough toxins to be potentially dangerous if it is left at room temperature for more than two hours.

◆ Refrigerate leftovers as soon as possible.

C. perfringens

Sometimes called the "cafeteria germ," C. perfringens accounts for about 1 in 10 reported cases of food poisoning. It usually occurs in settings where large batches of meat, turkey, and other foods are cooked. Like S. aureus, it produces toxins, or spores, that are resistant to the heat of cooking. It causes a mild illness of short duration (12 to 24 hours) and is rarely serious enough to warrant medical treatment.

Precautions to be taken are similar to those listed for S. aureus:

◆ Don't leave food out at room temperature for longer than two hours.

◆ When cooking large amounts of food, such as stew, divide the leftovers into small batches so that, once in the refrigerator, they will quickly cool to temperatures that limit the growth of bacteria.

Botulism

Botulism is a most severe food-borne illness, but it is also the most rare; there are fewer than

100 cases reported during a year in the entire country. One familiar telltale sign of the presence of bacteria that leads to botulism is a bulging can. The toxin responsible for the bulging is produced by the bacterium Clostridium botulinum, commonly found in soil, water, and manure. Besides bulging, also watch out for cracked jars and loose lids.

Occasionally, isolated incidents of botulism have been attributed to foods that are not in damaged containers. In one such case, a restaurant allowed a batch of sautéed onions to be kept throughout the day at temperatures slightly lower than 140° F, within the range at which bacteria thrive. Over the course of several hours, large enough quantities of the toxin were produced to make several people very ill. If the onions had been refrigerated and reheated in small batches as needed, the incident could have been prevented.

Symptoms of botulism can range from double vision and difficulty in breathing to, in the most severe cases, death.

E. coli

In 1993, meat served by the fast-food chain Jack-in-the-Box resulted in at least 3 deaths and more than 100 hospitalizations in Tacoma, Washington. The meat was found to harbor the E. coli bacterium, which attaches itself to the intestinal wall and then releases a toxin that causes severe abdominal cramps and bloody diarrhea. In extreme cases, a severe urinary tract infection known as hemolytic uremic syndrome sets in, causing kidney failure and sometimes proving fatal.

Public health officials traced the E. coli responsible for the Jack-in-the-Box outbreak to beef patties the chain bought from their meat supplier, the Von Companies. However, the E. coli would not have caused a problem had the burgers been broiled hot enough. It appears that many of the burgers in question may have been heated to only 120 degrees F. or less, in spite of the fact that the Washington State Health Department had recently upgraded its temperature regulations from 140 to 155 degrees F. (Some health experts suggest cooking meat until the center registers a heat of 160 degrees F.)

Was the Jack-in-the-Box outbreak a fluke, or does our meat supply in general harbor potentially deadly contaminants? The federal government says that E. coli is rarely found in meat sold in this country. And it points out that in the rare instances when the bacterium is present in unhealthfully large amounts in raw meat, thorough cooking completely kills it. That isn't to say that the government doesn't need to update its system for inspecting meat. Meat carcasses at processing plants are examined largely by smell, touch, and sight, but such examinations don't reveal the presence of E. coli, which are odorless and invisible to the naked eye. For that, laboratory testing is needed, and only samples of the larger meat supply are sent for testing. Furthermore, by the time public officials might detect bacteria, the meat is already on the market.

The government is currently developing an in-plant test for microscopic organisms. And stronger meat inspection guidelines are being studied. In the meantime, protect yourself by cooking or ordering ground beef well done, as cooking destroys any bacteria that might be present. Avoid eating ground beef that shows any pink color.

Researchers have also discovered that less fatty meats are safer. In testing ground beef, ground chicken, ground turkey, and pork sausages, researchers at Auburn University in Alabama found that the less fatty the meat, the faster E. coli died at any given cooking temperature. That's because fat is a poor conductor of heat compared with water. And the more fat in meat, the less water to "spread" the heat.

Other Bacteria

Thanks to improved detection methods, food safety experts are now able to identify other microorganisms in our food supply. One, Campylobacter (C. jejuni), is widely recognized as a source of illness in cattle but has rarely been identified as harmful to humans. C. jejuni is present in the intestinal tract of healthy cattle and can taint meat and poultry during the slaughtering process. However, heat destroys this bacterium, so you can easily eliminate the danger by thoroughly cooking raw meat and poultry.

Another cause of human illness is Listeria monocytogenes. In the past identified only with animal disease, it is now known to bring on flu-like symptoms in people. In severe cases, it can cause meningitis, a life-threatening inflammation of the membranes that encircle the brain and spinal cord. Pregnant women, infants, and the elderly seem to be at the greatest risk.

Proper cooking can also destroy Listeria. But in some cases it is present in foods that do not require cooking, such as some dairy products. At present, the best defense, in addition to cooking foods properly, is to avoid raw or unpasteurized milk products.

Cook Your Meat for Safety

Proper handling of meat will go a long way toward protecting you. Here are some tips:

◆ Put meat in the refrigerator or freezer as soon as possible after buying it. Cold temperatures halt the growth of bacteria.

◆ Place raw meat on the lowest refrigerator shelf to prevent its juices from dripping onto other foods, thereby contaminating them. Put the meat on a platter, even if it's wrapped, to prevent juices from running onto the refrigerator surface.

◆ Thaw meat in the refrigerator, not on the kitchen counter where it is warm enough for bacteria to multiply.

◆ Wash hands before touching raw meat, particularly after a trip to the bathroom or dia-

pering an infant, as E. coli and other bacteria reside in fecal matter.

◆ Use hot, soapy water to wash hands, utensils, cutting boards, and work areas that have come into contact with raw meat.

◆ Cook burgers until the center is gray or brown and the juices run clear, without a trace of pink. With whole beef, E. coli resides only on the meat's surface, so a steak grilled on both sides generally becomes hot enough to destroy any E. coli present. But chopped beef is another matter. It may harbor bacteria in the center because when the meat is ground, any organisms on the surface are mixed throughout.

◆ Microwave meat carefully. If your oven has a lower wattage than what is recommended in cooking instructions, heat the patty longer or at a higher setting than is advised. In addition, cover food and rotate it periodically while cooking to help ensure even heating.

◆ Don't partially cook meat ahead of time. Partially cooking burgers and then refrigerating them for tomorrow's barbecue can be dangerous if the raw meat does not become hot enough to kill bacteria. Bacteria can grow in partially cooked meat as it cools.

◆ Don't use the color of the meat as a guide to doneness. Brown meat may still not be cooked enough. Rather, use the color of the juices. They should run yellow, not red.

For answers to your questions about safe food handling, call the USDA's Meat and Poultry Hotline at 1-800-535-4555 (202-720-3333 in Washington, D.C.).

Is Your Milk Really Safe?

There is great concern about the new trend in which dairy farmers inject cows with bovine somatotropin (BST), a growth hormone, in order to produce more milk. Hormones, after all, are automatically associated with steroids. And *growth* hormones sound like substances that might dangerously affect people, especially young boys and girls, who drink lots of milk. BST is produced through genetic engineering, a type of technology by which genes are altered in a laboratory. It sounds worrisome, yet the FDA has recently approved BST for sale, and most health professionals are not concerned that it will cause milk to be tainted. The FDA's assurances of safety are shared by the National Institutes of Health, the Department of Agriculture, the American Dietetic Association, the American Medical Association, the American Academy of Family Physicians Foundation, and the American Academy of Pediatrics, among several other organizations, both national and international.

One reason is that cows produce the hormone naturally, and it has always been present in the milk we drink. BST is secreted by cows during lactation in order to stimulate milk production.

When BST is produced in the lab and then injected into cows, it increases milk production by anywhere from 10 to 25 percent. The milk is identical in taste, appearance, and nutritional value to milk made without BST—so close in resemblance that scientists cannot tell the difference between the two.

Still, despite the proven safety of milk from cows treated with genetically engineered BST, not all experts are sanguine about its introduction into the food supply. The greatest concern stems from the fact that cows treated with genetically engineered BST tend to have a somewhat increased occurrence of mastitis, an inflammation of the udder (the mammary glands) that farmers often treat with antibiotics. The problem is, residues of those antibiotics can potentially make their way into cow's milk. Although cows treated with antibiotics are temporarily taken out of production, if a cow is not out of production long enough to let the residue pass from its system, the antibiotic can get into the milk and therefore into humans.

Why is that a problem? The more often a population is exposed to a particular antibiotic, the more "resistant" it becomes to the bacteria that cause infections. Some doctors are worried that this could occur, although there are certain safeguards in place to assure that it doesn't.

One safeguard is that some types of mastitis are not treated with antibiotics. And when antibiotics are used, cows are taken out of production long enough to flush the residue from their bodies. There are disincentives in place for farmers that discourage attempts to pass along antibiotic-laced milk. Tracking systems that detect antibiotic residues in milk are in place at milk-packaging plants, and if farmers are caught they have to dump the milk without being paid for it and may also have to pay a fine.

Even if all the safeguards fail, experts assure that milk's contribution to antibiotic residues in humans is relatively small. The industry has been aggressive in developing a better screening program, and farmers themselves are cooperating in systems to screen more milk at the farm itself.

The bottom line is that BST does not make milk unsafe. However, there are other issues of social responsibility. For one thing, the trend might put small dairy farmers who cannot afford the hormone out of business. Another issue is the added discomfort and stress to cows who are subject to increasing incidences of mastitis. These issues must be considered in light of the fact that genetically engineered BST does not enhance the quality or nutritional value of milk, nor does it make milk less expensive, more widely available, or more conveniently packaged. Rather, it simply profits the manufacturers who sell it to dairy farmers. Indeed, the United States already has a surplus of milk that the government buys from farmers with our tax dollars in the form of price supports. This raises a serious question about the value of BST engineering in the first place.

Raw Fish Alert

Americans have always eaten certain seafoods raw, but in recent years sporadic reports of ill-

◆ NUTRITION QUIZ ◆
Can You Pick a Good Egg?

Salmonella poisoning has occurred from eating eggs. Do you know a good egg from a bad egg? Do you know the best way to store your eggs before and after cooking? Can you tell if an egg is fresh and safe to eat? Take this quiz and find out.

1. How many minutes does it take to be certain an egg is hard-cooked? (a) 7 (b) 15 (c) 20

2. Dyeing Easter eggs (a) makes them spoil more quickly (b) poses a risk because of hazardous food dyes (c) is a harmless tradition

3. A raw egg is "bad" if it has (a) a blood spot (b) a dark ring around the yolk after it is cooked (c) a cracked shell

4. Which type of egg keeps longest? (a) fertilized (b) unfertilized (c) whether or not an egg is fertilized has nothing to do with how long it will keep

5. Raw eggs will remain fresh in the refrigerator (a) in a paper bag (b) in the box they came in (c) in the refrigerator's built-in egg tray

6. A sure sign that an egg has lost some of its freshness is that (a) the white is thick and cloudy (b) the white is runny and clear (c) the white separates easily from the yolk

ANSWERS

1. (a) Seven minutes is the recommended time to be sure the egg is cooked but not over-cooked. To prevent cracking and toughness, place uncooked eggs in a pan of cold water, then bring them to a boil over high heat. After cooking, remove eggs from the burner and let them sit, covered, for 15 minutes, then rinse them in cold water.

2. (c) There is no reason to worry about the safety of packaged dyes used to color eggs. However, you do have to be careful not to leave the eggs at room temperature for too long. Easter egg hunts are fun, but be sure to hide the eggs right before the hunt and refrigerate them immediately after.

3. (c) If a shell cracks in the supermarket or on the way home, it is best to throw the egg away because it may become contaminated with salmonella or other bacteria before it is refrigerated. If you crack an egg in your kitchen and immediately refrigerate it, it should be safe.
   Blood spots and dark rings are harmless. A blood spot is simply the result of a blood vessel rupture on the egg's surface. The ring results from an interaction between the iron and sulfur naturally present in eggs.

4. (b) The unfertilized eggs typically sold in the supermarket are likely to keep longer than the fertilized eggs sold in certain health food stores. Once an egg is fertilized, the yolk can start to develop, leading to quicker deterioration. Contrary to what health food proponents claim, fertilized eggs offer no additional health benefits.

> # Can You Pick a Good Egg? *(cont.)*
>
> 5. (b) It's best to store eggs in the covered containers in which they are bought because they readily lose moisture and absorb odor from other foods.
>   For best taste and freshness, eggs should be used within two to three weeks after you bring them home.
>
> 6. (b) As an egg ages, it gives off carbon dioxide, causing the white to spread and turn clear.

ness associated with raw clams and oysters have given rise to concerns. Health hazards, although not common, do exist from parasites that imbed themselves in fish. Never eat raw fish or seafood unless it's prepared by a sushi chef.

Anisaki is a tightly coiled, clear, wormlike parasite (about one-half to three-quarters of an inch in length) that imbeds itself in salmon, herring, and other fish. Symptoms of illness caused by ingestion of the worm are a combination of intestinal problems that include diarrhea and abdominal pain. However, incidents of illness are rare in the United States.

If you are concerned about eating raw fish, you might want to substitute vegetable sushi for the kind that contains raw fish, although a well-trained sushi chef can spot the translucent worm, as can most other people once they know what to look for. It might be more risky to eat raw clams and oysters. (To make sure clams are bacteria free, steam them from four to six minutes. The one minute of cooking needed to open the shell is not enough to kill bacteria.)

Tropical Fish Can Be Hazardous

Imagine taking a wonderful vacation in a tropical or subtropical paradise like Hawaii, southern Florida, or St. Thomas, only to come home with symptoms such as diarrhea, itching, headache, weakness, and muscle and joint pain. Worse still, imagine going from doctor to doctor and still being unable to find the source of your illness.

This scenario occurs most often in Hawaii and southern Florida—one reason why many doctors across the country are unfamiliar with it. The cause of the problem is ciguatera fish poisoning.

Ciguatera poisoning comes from a species of fish—frequently, grouper, snapper, amberjack, and barricuda—that lives in warm waters near coral reefs. The poison doesn't actually start out in the fish. It is produced by tiny, one-celled plants that live on the reefs. Those plants are eaten by small fish that in turn are eaten by the larger fish that humans consume. The illness-causing fish are not only served in restaurants but also cooked by vacationers who catch them during recreational fishing. And, unfortunately, you don't have to take a holiday in a sunny coastal setting to be stricken, because tropical species of fish are being shipped for consumption all over the United States.

How can you tell if you have ciguatera? The symptoms tend to start in the gastrointestinal tract within six hours after consumption of contaminated fish. They include a bout of diarrhea, abdominal pain, nausea, and perhaps vomiting. Then, neurologic problems begin: tingling in the mouth, palms, and soles of the feet; aches throughout the body; and quite often the sensation that hot items are cold and cold items are hot. (This last symptom is considered quite definitive.) The trouble can last anywhere from several weeks to several months—longer, in severe cases.

Apart from recognizing its symptoms, there is currently no test for detecting ciguatera poisoning. There is also no way to tell if a fish is contaminated, nor is there a way to kill the toxin before a fish is eaten. And there is no cure for the poisoning—only a relief of symptoms.

For now, food safety experts advise staying away from potentially contaminated fish. That means avoiding certain tropical species such as grouper, snapper, amberjack, moray eel, and barracuda. Those are the species with the worst reputations, although hogfish, tropical mackerels, and certain trigger fish are suspected as well. If you must eat one of the potentially dangerous fish, make sure the entire fish fits on your plate. A fillet that might have come from a large fish is more likely to be contaminated. Another precaution you can take if you are traveling to the Miami-Caribbean area is to call the University of Miami's Ciguatera Hotline (305-361-4619) before going on vacation to find out the current data on dangerous fish in that area.

In the event that you take a vacation and do come down with the telltale symptoms, call a doctor immediately. Although no medication can rid the body of ciguatera poisoning, certain drugs can help mitigate the symptoms, especially if they are administered within 24 to 48 hours.

Grains Are Not Risk Free

Many people believe that the incidence of harmful bacteria is limited to meat, poultry, fish, and dairy products. But that's not true. The bacterium Bacillus cereus is present in starchy items like noodles, as well as in meat and poultry. In fact, fried rice has been identified as a leading cause in the United States of vomiting-accompanied food-borne illness from that particular microorganism. This usually happens when leftover fried rice is not promptly refrigerated and is then reheated too briefly to kill bacteria.

The solution is to refrigerate leftover rice wihin two hours, using the same care you

would give to meat or poultry. If there is a large quantity, break it up into two or more smaller containers to facilitate cooling. To be on the safe side, remember that all cooked leftovers should be refrigerated within two hours of serving, even seemingly innocuous items like pasta and vegetables.

Dining Out Defensively

When you're away from home, what can you do to protect yourself from food poisoning? Evaluate a restaurant's overall health by checking these details: Are the dishes and utensils clean? Is food (for example, desserts) displayed uncovered? Are the hot foods served to you really hot? How are the tables cleaned? Are fresh rags used for each table? Do employees appear clean and neatly dressed? Do you notice that they smoke in the kitchen or nibble at food while they're cooking? Are the bathrooms clean? Do they have sanitary soap and towel dispensers? Of course you can never be 100 percent certain of food that you eat in a restaurant. But if you're concerned about food safety, you should never eat in an establishment that doesn't make cleanliness a priority.

Guidelines for Globetrotters

For people traveling overseas, bacterial infections are one of the greatest nutritional impediments. Unfortunately, there's no surefire way to prevent traveler's diarrhea, which infects an estimated 3 million Americans a year with symptoms that include abdominal cramps, nausea, bloating, fever, and malaise. But the risks can be substantially decreased by paying attention to what you eat and where you eat it.

First of all, use common sense. In most industrialized countries you need only to use the same precautions that you use when dining out at home. No matter where you are, if you have any questions about the food or water, do not consume it. In those instances, your health and comfort take precedence over everything— including the sensitivities of your host.

In locations where you have reason to believe that sanitation is a problem, completely avoid eating raw or undercooked meat and seafood. Raw vegetables and fruit should also be avoided, unless they can be peeled first. Tap water, ice made from tap water, and unpasteurized dairy products should also be avoided. All of these have a comparatively high chance of being infected with diarrhea-causing bacteria. In addition, it is best not to drink more coffee, tea, or alcohol than usual, because large amounts of these can bring on diarrhea. Safe, bottled water is almost universally available.

Food safety is also influenced by how clean food is kept during preparation and the way it is cooked. Dishes bought from street vendors are the most likely to be contaminated. Restaurants vary in their sanitary conditions. The finer ones that have good reputations and are listed in travel guides are most likely to be careful about using high standards of food safety. But it is best to be on guard. Consider also the way food is prepared. Some chefs season foods with spices or other ingredients that may cause severe, though short-lived, reactions. Others do not regularly change oil used for deep-fat frying, so that foods are cooked in rancid fat, which is very irritating to the intestines. The taste of rancidity is sometimes masked by the spices.

If traveler's diarrhea does strike, it's usually within a week of arrival in a foreign country, and it rarely lasts longer than three or four days. Many travelers wait it out without taking any special measures other than increasing fluid intake to avoid becoming dehydrated. However, before leaving the United States, you can obtain from your physician a prescription drug (Lomotil or Imodium) that will slow down intestinal motility and cut down on the number of trips you make to the bathroom. But avoid taking antimicrobial drugs to *prevent* diarrhea, because these medications can bring on side effects such as allergic reactions, skin rashes, and blood disorders.

If you come down with the "runs," it is important to maintain your body's fluid and electrolyte needs by consuming caffeine-free soft drinks, salted crackers, and fruit juices that come in cans or that you know have been made with clean water and peeled fruits. Stay away from dairy products, alcohol, and beverages with caffeine. Although some people think the bacteria in yogurt can help treat this condition, there is no evidence that it works.

Because the water in the United States is treated with chlorine, we rarely encounter many of the microorganisms found in the water of some foreign countries. For this reason, many Americans suffer intestinal problems from drinking the water. Locations that are of particular concern include South and Central America, Asia, the Middle East, Africa, and some parts of the Caribbean. In developing countries, travelers should use caution when drinking the tap water in large hotels. Wherever you are, be sure to ask if the hotel has a water purification system.

Bottled water can be used for drinking and for brushing your teeth. Carbonated water may be the safest, because carbonation appears to kill some of the microorganisms. Be sure that the bottles have been properly sealed.

When dining out, it is safe to drink liquids that require boiling water—such as coffee and tea—because boiling kills bacteria. Bottled drinks such as beer, soda, and juices are also safe. But avoid mixed drinks or drinks served with ice cubes.

In developing countries and rural areas where milk is not pasteurized, all noncanned and dehydrated milk and dairy products should be avoided. Contaminated milk products can cause severe intestinal ailments. If necessary, unpasteurized milk can be made safe by boiling, but this is impractical for most travelers.

If you're "roughing it"—hiking or backpacking through undeveloped areas—note that water-purifying tablets are available (Halzone or

Potable-Aqua) in sporting goods stores and pharmacies. If electricity is available, you can purify your water by boiling it on an electric hot plate—if you have one. Remember that outside the United States almost all countries use equipment that takes 220 volts.

Storing Foods for Taste and Safety

Although no rigid standards have been established as a result of scientific tests, we recommend that you follow these guidelines for food storage to promote safety and maintain quality. To help yourself keep track, date all packages before storing them.

In the freezer at 0°, these foods will last:

◆ Fresh chickens (whole or in parts): 10 months

◆ Beef roasts: 6–12 months (the larger the roast, the longer it will store)

◆ Lamb and veal: 6–9 months

◆ Pork: 3–6 months

◆ Lean fish: 6 months (examples: sole, haddock, and flounder)

◆ Fatty fish: 2–3 months (examples: salmon, mackerel, and bluefish)

◆ Baked bread and rolls: 3–6 months (frosted: 2 months)

◆ Frozen juice: 12 months

◆ Frozen vegetables: 8 months (unless otherwise dated)

◆ Hard cheese: 6–8 weeks

◆ Soft cheese: 3 months

◆ Main-dish casseroles or other precooked dishes: 3 months

◆ Butter: 6–9 months

In the refrigerator at 40°, these foods will last:

◆ Ground meat: 2–3 days

◆ Steaks and chops: 2–3 days

◆ Opened baby food: 2 days

◆ Eggs: 2–3 weeks

◆ Margarine: 4–6 months

◆ Butter (sweet): 2 weeks (a little longer if lightly salted)

On the shelf at 70°, these foods will last:

◆ Salad oils (opened): 1 year (longer in the refrigerator)

◆ Flour: 6–8 months (if kept in a dry container)

◆ Dry cereals (opened): 2–3 months

◆ Dry cereals (unopened): 12 months

Polluted Fishing: Is There Cause for Alarm?

There has been concern among environmentalists for some time about pollution in the bodies of water that give us our fish supply. But when beaches up and down the east coast were closed because of medical waste washing up on shore, the scare hit home for many people. To what extent can we trust that the fish we eat are safe from the effects of industrial pollution and other human-made pollutants? And how can our waters be better protected from indiscriminate illegal dumping of dangerous substances? It is true that the fish and shellfish we eat have been somewhat compromised by the dumping of industrial and sewage waste into harbors, lakes, and rivers, and by such problems as "red tide," which results in a poison's getting into the shellfish we eat.

However, most of the fish we buy is caught offshore or deep at sea where the waters are significantly cleaner. Fish contamination is much more likely to be a problem in sheltered bays, harbors, and recreational freshwater lakes and streams that are near industrial sources of pollution. In addition, most of the problems connected with bacterial contamination are limited to mollusks and shellfish, and these problems can be avoided with adequate cooking.

Even the industrial waste chemicals polychlorinated biphenyls (PCBs), which are most likely to be concentrated in large, fatty fish, may not be as great a problem as some people think. In an analysis of 1,200 bluefish (considered to be one of the fish most susceptible to contamination because it is fatty) caught off the coast from Massachusetts to North Carolina, all samples under 20 inches in length were within the 2-parts-per-million limit set for PCBs by the federal government. Although some of the larger fish exceeded the limit, the National Oceanic Atmospheric Administration, which conducted the study, believes that this excess may pose a problem only for recreational fishermen and their families who eat the fish day after day, year after year.

There are no mandatory federal inspection programs for fish, but the government does watch the fish supply. For example, the FDA monitors swordfish because it is one of the species that are most likely to be contaminated with mercury. If the mercury level is found to be above acceptable limits, regulatory action is taken to prevent the fish from reaching your table. More recent studies have focused on the potential danger of airborne pollutants, which sometimes travel great distances before falling into the water. Congress is currently reviewing legislation that would require the EPA to study the effects of airborne toxic chemicals on the Great Lakes.

You can exercise appropriate caution by taking the following measures: Buy your fish at reputable outlets. Even though the "catch of the day" a local fisherman may be selling off the back of his truck might seem appealing, it's best to avoid fish whose origin is uncertain. You might pay more at the fish store or supermarket, but the extra protection is probably worth it. Once it's in your home, keep fish chilled in the refrigerator prior to cooking in order to retard the growth of bacteria.

When preparing fish for cooking, cut away the skin and dark-colored flesh of fatty fish to eliminate the chance of contamination from PCBs. Grill or broil fatty fish in ways that allow the drippings to run off.

Can We Safely Drink the Water?

Some experts believe that the safety of our drinking water may be the most important public health issue of the next decade—especially the safety of our groundwater, which is the large reservoir lying beneath the earth's surface that supplies half the drinking water flowing through our faucets. One reason for the heightened concern is that industrial chemicals have been discovered in about 20 percent of the country's public water systems, and many of these chemicals have not been rigorously tested to see if they are reaching homes in levels that may be toxic.

Aside from industrial pollutants, environmentalists are concerned about the levels of lead in our water supplies. Indeed, the EPA has recently estimated that 42 million Americans may be drinking water that exceeds a proposed safe level (20 parts per billion) of lead, a metal that can damage the nervous system in infants and children and worsen high blood pressure in adults.

Fortunately, lead in drinking water is a problem you can do something about without waiting for someone to take action from the outside. Here are the practical ways you can act to protect your own water.

◆ First, check your plumbing. Copper pipes may contain some lead solder at their joints. Older homes sometimes have lead pipes.

To find out whether any lead is actually leaching into the water that runs through the

◆ NUTRITION QUIZ ◆
How Safe Is Your Kitchen?

You may know that raw pork is not safe, or that a bulging can spell trouble. But how aware are you of the safety of other items in your kitchen? Take this quiz to find out; circle the correct answer.

IS IT SAFE OR RISKY TO EAT ...

1. Hot dogs that have been stored in an unopened package in the refrigerator for 10 days?

2. A bruised or moldy piece of fruit?

3. Frozen ham that was thawed on the counter?

4. An opened jar of mayonnaise that has been in the refrigerator for six months?

5. A baked potato left out on the counter from the night before?

6. Meatloaf that's pink in the middle after cooking?

7. Raw ground beef that turns brown after a day or two of refrigeration?

8. An uncooked potato with a greenish cast?

9. Lettuce or other produce moistened by poultry drippings in a grocery bag?

10. Steak that was thawed in the refrigerator and then refrozen?

11. Cooked shrimp that was never "deveined"?

12. Mustard or ketchup with a black, crusty ring around the rim of the jar?

13. Moldy or shriveled peanuts?

ANSWERS

1. Safe. Hot dogs that come in vacuum-sealed packages can be kept in the refrigerator for up to two weeks. Once they are opened, you can keep them for about seven days, carefully wrapped in plastic.

2. Safe—if it's just bruised; but possibly risky if the bruised portion has become moldy. Some molds can produce harmful toxins, and it's not yet clear whether fruit molds are among them. The best bet is to cut away the moldy section, which should also remove any toxins that might be present.

3. Risky. Many people think that they can take chances with ham because it has been smoked and salted. But these processes don't make the meat immune to bacterial contamination, especially given that a number of manufacturers are lowering the salt content of cured meats. As with any meat, the safest way to thaw ham is in the refrigerator.

How Safe Is Your Kitchen? *(cont.)*

4. Safe. It's a misconception that foods prepared with mayonnaise may go bad sooner. In fact, such foods' high acid and salt content may actually inhibit bacterial growth somewhat. You can keep an opened jar of mayonnaise in the refrigerator for up to a year, provided you don't let it sit at room temperature for extended periods.

5. Risky. We usually don't think of potatoes as a likely source of food poisoning, but there have been reports of deadly botulism in people who ate foil-wrapped baked potatoes left at room temperature for a day or more, even when they were reheated. Leftovers of most foods should be promptly refrigerated.

6. Risky. Ground meat undergoes a great deal of handling, compared with other forms. This increases the likelihood of bacterial contamination. For this reason, the USDA suggests cooking meatloaf until it is brown or at least brownish-pink in the center. An even better guide is to cook it to an internal temperature of 170° F, checking with a thermometer, particularly if the meatloaf contains pork.

7. Safe. Whether it's brown or pink has to do with the amount of oxygen with which it has come into contact. As a general rule, however, don't keep raw ground beef in the refrigerator longer than two days, and don't use it under any circumstances if it doesn't smell right or was left unrefrigerated for any length of time.

8. Risky. Green-skinned potatoes contain a chemical called solanine, which can cause gastrointestinal illness. You can use green potatoes if you peel them well and remove a layer of flesh underneath the skin.

9. Risky. Uncooked poultry juices may contain harmful bacteria that could lead to trouble when they get into foods that are eaten raw. If the produce is really saturated, you'd better not use it. But if contact was minimal, you can remove outer sections or rinse and peel.

10. Safe—especially if some ice crystals remain. Make sure to thaw the frozen meat in the refrigerator the second time around. Be aware, too, that refreezing might cause flavor and texture deterioration. You might get better flavor and texture if you cook the meat the first time it is thawed, then refreeze it.

11. Safe. You can eat shrimp that hasn't been deveined as long as you cook it. The black line running down the back is actually the intestines of the shrimp, which are susceptible to contamination.

12. Safe. The ring is the result of an interaction of the contents with air, not a sign of spoilage. Simply wipe it off and use the remaining contents.

13. Risky. When you crack open peanut shells only to find sickly-looking nuts, don't eat them. The types of mold that grow on nuts (as well as on grains) can produce aflatoxins, some of which are very potent carcinogens.

pipes, have your water tested, either by the local water utility or by a private laboratory. If the lab determines that a significant amount of lead is getting into your drinking water, consider installing a water purification system.

In the interim, use the cold-water tap for making coffee and for cooking, because lead leaches more easily into hot water than cold. You can also let your water run for a few minutes before using it, because water that has been sitting still in pipes will contain more lead.

◆ Buying bottled water is an expensive alternative—more than 625 times the cost of tap water!—and it isn't necessarily the answer to all the problems associated with tap water. Legally, bottled water does not have to be any freer from contaminants than water from a faucet, aside from meeting regulations that apply to the sanitary bottling of a beverage. And because some bottled water comes from municipal water supplies rather than from privately owned and protected springs and wells, do not assume that it is any cleaner than the water from your kitchen sink. A better option might be a Brita water filter, which removes any lead present in tap water and also improves its taste.

If you want your tap water analyzed, the EPA will refer you to the certified laboratories in your area. Call toll-free: 1-800-426-4791. If you decide to install a water filter but aren't sure how to choose one that is reliable, the EPA recommends that you contact the National Sanitation Foundation at P.O. Box 1468, Ann Arbor, Michigan, 48106.

Are Water Coolers Safe?

The more than 400 million gallons of water flowing through American water coolers every year is testimony to Americans' concerns about the safety of tap water. Ironically, many water coolers may be harboring unhealthfully high levels of bacteria that can cause nausea and diarrhea in some people.

When scientists checked the bacterial content of water from 10 coolers on the campus of Boston's Northeastern University, they found that in each case the count reached at least 2,000 potentially harmful organisms for every thousandth of a liter of water, or four times the 500-organism limit the government recommends. In some cases, particularly when coolers were used frequently, the organism count exceeded one million. Why so high?

The reason, according to scientists, appears to be that organisms from each new bottle of water adhere to a cooler's reservoir—the "well" in which the bottle sits—and also to its hot and cold water spigots, accumulating over time and thereby boosting the bacterial count of the water as it passes through those areas.

Although most healthy people are unlikely to become ill from drinking such water, it can be hazardous to infants, the elderly, and people who suffer from conditions that compromise their immune systems. The solution is to clean water coolers once a month by combining one teaspoon of bleach in one cup of water and running it through the reservoir and spigots. Then remove any bleach residue by rinsing the cooler thoroughly with four or more gallons of tap water.

Avoid Water Purifier Scams

Americans are purchasing home water purifier systems at rapidly rising rates, making it a $3 billion-plus business. But thousands of consumers are reporting to the Better Business Bureaus that they have been victims of fraud. A recent study of the home water treatment business by the U.S. General Accounting Office concluded that regulation of home water purifiers is inadequate, largely because it is fragmented among several different federal and independent agencies. This is bad news for consumers who are left carrying extravagant bills for systems that may not even be necessary.

While regulatory agencies sort out their bureaucracies, what can consumers do to guard against fraud? Here are some practical suggestions:

◆ Be sure you *need* a water filter system. Most companies will use scare tactics to convince people that their tap water is loaded with deadly toxins. Remember, though, that the major portion of our drinking water comes from public water supplies that comply with safety standards set by the EPA.

◆ Be wary of "free" home water tests conducted by the company trying to sell you a purification system. This obviously isn't the best source for objective information; free home tests are usually part of the marketing gimmick. If you want to find out about your water quality, ask your local water utility to send you the latest computer printout of test results on the local water supply. Or, if your water is from a private well, you can have it tested independently.

◆ Do not believe sellers who claim that their water treatment units are government approved. The government does not endorse or approve water treatment companies or units.

If you are interested in a water treatment system, the best place to start your investigation is by contacting the two independent not-for-profit organizations, NSF International and the Water Quality Association, that supply advice and literature about the industry and particular units. Write or call NSF International, 3475 Plymouth Road, P.O. Box 1468, Ann Arbor, MI 48105, 1-313-769-8010; or Water Quality Association, Consumer Affairs Department, 4151 Naperville Road, Lisle, IL 60532, 1-708-505-0160.

The Pesticide Problem

In the early 1980s, the federal government stepped up its efforts to control the levels of harmful pesticides used to protect our fruit, vegetable, and grain supply from insects. One, ethylene dibromide (EDB), a highly effective insect killer, was taken off the market in 1984 after many studies showed that it caused cancer and genetic mutations in animals.

But a public outcry accompanied evidence that the Environmental Protection Agency (EPA) moved far too slowly in its review of pesticides. In response to the outcry, the House of Representatives passed legislation in 1988 that set a nine-year deadline for retesting 600 active ingredients that are used in nearly 50,000 commercial pesticides.

To keep the pesticide issue in perspective, it must be noted that the overall cancer death rate during the 1950s through the 1970s, the decades during which the use of pesticides increased dramatically, rose only slightly. Although the use of pesticides must be monitored carefully, in some respects the public outcry has distracted us from the more significant and personally controllable factors related to cancer, such as cigarette smoking and a diet high in saturated fat and low in fiber.

Keep Up to Date About Lead

Are you thinking of planting a garden but don't know if you should be concerned about lead in your soil? Or are you wondering if it's safe to serve food on old china which may contain that toxic mineral? There is some reason for concern, because ingesting lead can cause reproductive system disorders, learning disabilities, and impaired hearing.

Your questions can be addressed if you call the government's National Lead Information Center clearinghouse toll-free at 1-800-424-LEAD. Or, if you don't have specific questions but would like to receive general information free of charge, call the Center's toll-free hotline at 1-800-LEAD-FYI.

WHICH FOODS ARE ALLOWED TO BE ZAPPED?

While the irradiation controversy did not reach a fever pitch until 1986, when the Food and Drug Administration began allowing the treatment to be applied to fresh fruits and vegetables, the process actually started to be approved for use on foods in 1963.

Here's a look at when various foods were approved for irradiation in the United States and why. (Bear in mind that just because a category of food may, by law, be irradiated, that doesn't necessarily mean it is. Most companies, largely because of consumer fears, elect to forego the process.)

Product	Purpose of irradiation	Date of rule
Wheat and wheat powder	Kills insects	August 21, 1963
White potatoes	Extend shelf life	November 1, 1965
Spices and dry vegetable seasonings	Kill insects; destroy potential contaminants	July 5, 1983
Pork carcasses or fresh noncut processed pork	Control *Trichinella spiralis*, the parasite that causes trichinosis	July 22, 1985
Fresh fruits and vegetables	Delay ripening and prevent spoilage; kill insects	April 18, 1986
Dry or dehydrated aromatic vegetable substances, such as herbs, seeds, and spices.	Destroy potential contaminants	April 18, 1986
Poultry	Control illness-causing microorganisms, including Salmonella	May 2, 1990

14

Winning at Restaurant Roulette

Today, dining out has become commonplace, with more than 66 million Americans consuming at least one meal outside the home every day.

According to the National Restaurant Association (NRA), restaurant traffic has more than doubled since the 1950s, when restaurant meals were reserved for special occasions.

Dietary control is harder to manage when someone else is doing the cooking, but eating out doesn't have to mean sacrificing nutrition. In fact, evidence points to a trend toward more healthful dining. A study conducted by Gallup for the NRA showed that 23 percent of customers use less salt or no salt when dining out, 15 percent avoid fried foods, and 20 percent avoid fats. Four out of ten reported altering their dining out habits in one of these ways. When consumers were asked which of a list of various foods they were likely to try at a restaurant, their responses included lean meat (64 percent), broiled/baked fish or seafood (63 percent), poultry without skin (47 percent), and food cooked without salt (36 percent). Restaurant managers questioned by Gallup mentioned more requests for lean meats, foods prepared without sauces and butter, and foods cooked without salt.

Furthermore, Consumer Reports on Eating Share Trends (CREST) Household Reports shows that changes in menus during the past five years have shifted in the direction of nonfried fish, main-dish salads, rice, fruit, chicken, and low-fat Asian foods.

About two-thirds of restaurants today will serve salad dressing on the side, cook with unsaturated fat, broil or bake instead of fry, and alter foods upon customer request. Food service establishments are making more of an effort than ever to meet the demand for more healthful restaurant fare. But the consumer still must be knowledgeable.

Become a Healthy Gourmet

Even when your restaurant choice is a last-minute impulse and you can't check the menu in advance, it's possible to make nutritional decisions in most restaurants, if you know what to look for.

The cardinal rule of dining out is: Ask questions. Keep a written or mental list of queries and don't be timid about getting the information you need from your waiter before you order. Some of the primary questions nutrition-conscious diners might ask include:

◆ What type of fat is used in preparation? Saturated fats, such as butter, cream, and beef fats, are often used in cooking. These can increase blood cholesterol levels. Better choices are foods prepared with unsaturated fats derived from plant sources like canola, corn, safflower, and sesame. And the best choices are foods made with little or no fat.

◆ Are high-sodium ingredients used? Ask if salt is added in preparation. Smoked, cured, or canned meats and fish tend to be high in sodium, as do canned, powdered, and dried stocks often used in preparation and for sauces and gravies.

◆ Which cuts of meat are used? Lean cuts of meat (with a minimum amount of marbling) contain the least fat. The best cuts are loin, round, flank, shoulder, and leg. Also, when you order ground beef, ask for extra-lean hamburger or ground round. The light meat on poultry has less fat.

◆ What types of liquids, fats, and thickening agents are used in sauces? Some sauces are reduced from vegetable or chicken broth by cooking the broth long enough for the water to evaporate. These are preferable to sauces made from cream or fat, but they may contain more sodium.

◆ What cooking methods are used? The best preparation methods for meat, fish, and poultry are baking, broiling, grilling, poaching, roasting, and boiling. For vegetables, the best methods are microwaving, steaming, and stir-frying.

Make Wise Selections from the Menu

Learn to find the healthiest options on the menu. And don't hestitate to ask for substitutions. Three out of five restaurant managers surveyed by the NRA have expressed a willingness to make substitutions in ingredients and prepa-

ration when they are requested by customers. This new flexibility can make dining out a more pleasurable experience.

Use the guidelines on page 174 when you order.

Recognize "Light" Foods

Many restaurants, conscious of consumers' interest in eating lighter, serve smaller portions or main course salads which supply much less fat and fewer calories. However, don't assume that ordering "just an appetizer" will yield fewer calories and less fat than a main course. Chicken wings, potato skins, fried calamari, and Mozzarella sticks, for example, can add up to the equivalent of a high-fat meal.

Main-course salads represent a health-related trend, although there are plenty of nutritional land mines hidden in the average salad bar. Diners who head for the salad bar instead of ordering a hamburger or meat dish might be surprised if they added up the calorie toll. A Mississippi State University study that compared salad bar meals with regular cafeteria hot meals found that the average salad contained 1,000 calories, compared with only 900 for the hot meal.

Today's salad bars are soup-to-nuts affairs. Many offer cheeses, breads, soups, desserts, and side dishes of macaroni, potato, and pasta salads—not to mention bacon bits, croutons, olives, and heavy cream dressings. If you pay attention to what you're putting on your plate at the salad bar, you can have a satisfying meal without adding extra calories and fat.

The samples on page 173 show two salads built from the same salad bar. Salad Plate 1 has 880 calories and is high in saturated fat contributed by the coleslaw, cheese, macaroni salad, and dressing. These ingredients plus the egg also make it high in cholesterol. More than one-half of the calories are accounted for by nonvegetable items. Plate 2 has only 300 calories and very little fat, contributed by the grated cheese. The reduction in calories was achieved by eliminating bacon bits, croutons, egg, coleslaw, macaroni salad, and potato salad and by substituting a low-calorie, low-fat dressing.

Other variations of Salad Plate 2 could be put together by making the following choices:

◆ Substitute low-fat cottage cheese for grated cheese

◆ Top the salad with bean sprouts

◆ Add kidney beans in moderation (go easy on three-bean salad, which is high in fat and sodium)

◆ Add plain, water-packed tuna

◆ Add two whole-wheat crackers or bread-sticks

◆ Add a fresh fruit salad or an apple, orange, banana, or half of a melon

◆ Use a dressing of vinegar and a little olive or vegetable oil

Delight in the Ethnic Cornucopia

One of the great pleasures of dining out is the chance to sample a wide variety of the world's best cuisines. Ethnic dining has gained in popularity in recent years. According to an NRA study of consumer preferences, Americans patronize Italian, Chinese, and Mexican restaurants regularly, although they sample an even wider variety of ethnic cuisines.

From the standpoint of healthful eating, dining in ethnic restaurants can be confusing, especially if you're testing a new cuisine. Lack of familiarity with language, terminology, and the ingredients of dishes can leave you guessing. Happily, you can enjoy healthful and delicious meals no matter which type of cuisine you are eating, if you know what to look for. The following guidelines for seven popular ethnic cuisines demonstrate that a variety of good choices is available. Keep in mind that a lot depends on how the foods are prepared. Don't hesitate to ask about what goes into the cooking, or request substitutes.

SALAD BAR COMPARISONS

Salad Plate 1: 1 cup sliced beets, 1 cup broccoli, ½ cup shredded carrots, ¼ cup grated cheese, 1 cup Chinese noodles, 1 cup coleslaw, 2 tbsp diced egg, 2 tbsp potato salad, 2 tbsp macaroni salad, 3 slices tomato, 5 slices cucumber, cup mushrooms, 1 cup green peas, 2 tbsp chopped green pepper, 1 cup lettuce, 1 tsp bacon bits, 1 tsp sunflower seeds, 2 tbsp croutons, 2 tbsp Thousand Island dressing.
Total Calories: 880

Salad Plate 2: 1 cup sliced beets, 1 cup broccoli, 1 cup shredded carrot, 2 tbsp grated cheese, 3 slices tomato, 5 slices cucumber, 1 cup sliced mushrooms, 1 cup green peas, 1 cup sliced green pepper, 1 cup lettuce, 2 tbsp low-calorie Italian dressing.
Total Calories: 300

ITALIAN

Southern Italian dishes, cooked with olive oil instead of butter, are better choices than northern Italian. And there is a rich variety of hearty vegetable and bean dishes. Pay attention to the descriptions: Crema or Fritto-style is heavy cuisine, usually cooked with butter or lard; Pomodora indicates a light preparation.

Better
  Pasta with meatless marinara or pesto
  Boneless chicken breast with tomato-mushroom sauce
  Sautéed shrimp in white wine sauce
  Pizza with low-fat cheese and vegetable toppings
  Eggplant Pomodora style
  Green salad with oil and vinegar dressing
  Fresh fruit dessert
  Italian ice

Avoid
  Veal in cream sauce
  Fettuccine Alfredo
  Meatballs
  Gnocchi
  Lasagna
  Cannelloni

DINING OUT NUTRITIONALLY

Choose These Foods. . .	Instead of These. . .
Appetizers	
Fruits and juices, vegetables and juices, low-fat dip made from yogurt or cottage cheese	Hard cheeses, cheese dips, chips, nachos
Relish trays with raw vegetables such as carrot and celery sticks, cherry tomatoes, and cauliflower florets	Breaded or fried vegetables
Broth and vegetable-based soups, and consommé with the fat removed	Traditional cream soups, chowders, soups with cheese
Steamed shrimp and scallops; skewered grilled chicken	Breaded or fried fish, shellfish, or chicken; pâté; mousse
Salads	
Vegetable, fruit, or gelatin salads	Salads with bacon, eggs, cheeses, cold cuts, sour cream, or nuts
Dressings (request that it be served on the reduced-calorie, oil and vinegar side)	Roquefort, blue cheese, and other creamy dressings
Entrees	
Beef: "Select" cuts: flank steak. Loin: tenderloin and sirloin steaks, sirloin tips. Round: top and bottom round steaks, eye of round roasts and steaks, rump roast, round tip roast and steak, ground round; lean veal	"Prime" cuts: marbled, fatty meats such as corned beef, ground beef, brisket, ground chuck; rib roasts and steaks, porterhouse and T-bone, organ meats
Pork: shoulder steak, blade chops, loin roast and chops, tenderloin leg (fresh ham)	Ribs, sausage, bacon, salt pork, ground pork
Poultry (with skin removed): chicken, all cuts; turkey, all cuts; cornish game hen; capon; pheasant	Goose, duck
Fish: all types of plain, fresh, or frozen; canned fish packed in water	Breaded or fried fish, canned fish in oil, caviar
Eggs: whites only	Whole eggs or egg yolks
Pastas with low-fat sauce (like vegetable sauces or those made with skim milk and thickened with arrrowroot or cornstarch)	Traditional sauces made with cream, butter, or eggs (such as velout, hollandaise, and white sauces
Vegetables and Grains	
All (except avocado) fresh, frozen, or canned; seasoned with herbs, spices, or citrus fruits	Vegetables covered with sauces or butter; avocado (except sparingly)
Brown, white, or wild rice; noodles, bulgur; couscous; buckwheat; macaroni	Fried rice; egg noodles
Breads: brown, white, wheat, rye, pumpernickel, French, pita, Italian, and raisin; dinner and hard rolls	Biscuits, cheese breads, croissants, popovers, brioche, fried bread, egg bread
Desserts	
Fresh, frozen, canned, or dried fruit; sherbet, fruit ice, sorbet, ice milk, fruit whip, pudding made with skim milk, angel food cake, frozen yogurt	Ice cream, pies, pastries, frosted cakes, whipped cream, custard, flan

DINING OUT NUTRITIONALLY *(cont.)*

If you're particularly concerned about reducing sodium, follow these guidelines:

Fresh or frozen meats, fish, poultry, and shellfish	Cured, salted, or smoked meats (corned beef, ham, bacon, sausage, cold cuts, frankfurters); canned meats or fish
Fresh, frozen, or low-sodium vegetables	Canned vegetables, sauerkraut, pickles, olives, vegetables in brine
Whole-grain or white breads, rolls, unsalted crackers, biscuits, muffins, and pastry	Saltines, salted snacks (pretzels, chips)
Unsalted homemade soups and stocks, and low-sodium canned soups and bases	Canned or dried soups and stocks
Seasonings: fresh or dried spices and herbs, horseradish, aromatic bitters, extracts, Tabasco, vinegar, dried mustard	Salt, seasoned or flavored salt, MSG, chili sauce, soy sauce, meat tenderizers, capers

Garlic bread
Pizza with sausage and pepperoni toppings
Crema or Fritto style
Cannoli or other cream pastries

MEXICAN

Mexican cuisine offers many dishes that are high in complex carbohydrates. If you limit grated cheese and try to avoid Americanized fare such as tortilla chips fried in lard, and heavy sour cream, you can make a healthful feast of Mexican food. Guacamole, a favorite topping made from avocado, is high in fat, although it's unsaturated. Eat it sparingly. Take advantage of the many seasonings that give Mexican food its special flavor: salsa, made of chopped tomato, onion, and chile, and spices, is a favorite. If you like to make your own fajitas, choose chicken instead of beef, and keep them light by avoiding sour cream, grated cheese, and guacamole toppings.

Better
Chicken taco or tostada
Corn tortilla
Chicken or bean burrito
Fish or chicken marinated in lime juice
Chicken fajitas
Shredded lettuce and tomatoes
Rice
Soft shell taco
Salsa

Avoid
Sour cream burrito
Beef and bean burrito with cheese
Nachos
Refried beans
Beef and cheese enchilada
Guacamole
Tortilla chips
Chimichangas
Frozen margaritas and piña coladas

FRENCH

Like Italian food, French cuisine varies in style depending on the region. Provençale and Riviera-style cooking favor olive oil rather than butter or lard, and they feature fish and vegetable dishes. If you choose your restaurant correctly, you won't be tempted by heavy pork and goose dishes or elaborate cream sauces. Haute cuisine and cuisine bourgeoise both indicate the use of butter, cream, pork lard, goose fat, and eggs. If you order salad nicoise, you might request the dressing on the side and avoid eating the olives when calories are a consideration. Cuisine minceur literally means "cuisine of slimness."

Better
Poached fish
Salad nicoise
Bouillabaisse
Chicken in wine sauce
French bread
Endive and watercress salad
Fresh or poached fruit

Avoid
- Quiche
- Duck or goose
- Meat or fish in béarnaise or hollandaise sauce
- Pâté
- Fondue or crepes
- Brioche, croissants, eclairs, and other pastry

CHINESE

Chinese cooking's reliance on vegetables, rice, and noodles makes it a naturally healthful cuisine. Pork is the primary meat used in Chinese dishes, followed by poultry and duck. Many vegetables and meat dishes are stir-fried or steamed; avoid those that are deep fried. Also stay away from heavy sauces like lobster sauce or sweet and sour sauce. Sodium can be a problem if monosodium glutamate (MSG) is added in the cooking; you might want to request that food be prepared without it. Soy sauce is also sodium-heavy, with 800 milligrams of sodium in a tablespoon.

Better
- Stir-fried vegetables
- Stir-fried fish or chicken
- Broccoli chicken
- Vegetable dishes with mushrooms, broccoli, water chestnuts, bamboo shoots, bok choy, squash, snow peas, lotus root, and mushrooms

Avoid
- Sweet and sour pork
- Fried rice
- Spareribs
- Egg rolls
- Egg Fu Yung
- Pork or beef dumplings
- Seafood with lobster sauce
- Pressed duck

INDIAN

Indian cuisine employs a creative use of unusual spices and seasonings to produce wonderful flavors without paying nutritional costs. Perhaps the most problematic aspect of Indian cooking is the use of highly saturated ghee (clarified butter) and coconut oil in food preparation. Shredded coconut and coconut milk are also added to some dishes. Stick with the non-fried foods and abundant vegetable and bean dishes.

Better
- Tandoori chicken
- Chicken marinated in yogurt
- Vegetable or fish curry
- Vegetables or salad with yogurt dressing
- Lentil beans, chick peas, tomatoes, onions, cucumbers

Avoid
- Deep-fried meat, fish, or vegetable pastries
- Fried breads
- Coconut soup or dressing
- Lamb dishes
- Rice or cheese pudding
- Honeyed pastries

JAPANESE

Japanese cuisine is basically low in fat, stressing soybean-based foods, small quantities of fish and meat, and rice and noodles. Traditional sauces contain no oil: Teriyaki sauce is a mixture of soy sauce, sake, and sugar; miso is a paste made of fermented soy beans, rice mold, and salt. Strong spices—green mustard and ginger—heighten the flavors. The primary foods to avoid are pickled, smoked, and salted dishes and sauces that have a high sodium content. Surimi (fake crab) is also high in sodium.

Better
- Sushi (except surimi and salmon caviar)
- Sashimi
- Chicken teriyaki
- Broiled fish or chicken over rice
- Sukiyaki
- Japanese vegetables
- Tofu and other soybean dishes
- Rice and noodles

Miso soup
Rice crackers

Avoid

Tempura and other deep-fried dishes
Smoked or pickled fish
Pan-fried pork
Fried dumplings
Breaded meat, fish, and chicken
Surimi (white fish with crab) and ikura
   (salmon caviar)
Salted fish
Soy sauce

SOUTHERN AND CAJUN-STYLE

Southern and Cajun-style dining has increased in popularity. There are many good dishes available, but watch for the preponderance of fried and richly sauced dishes. Sample the tasty and nutritious vegetables—like okra, black-eyed peas, sweet potatoes, and greens—but be alert to the cooking oils used, which are often grease, lard, and fatback. Replace traditional Southern fried chicken with a Cajun dish: Blackened fish is usually cooked with less oil.

Better

Seafood gumbo
Blackened fish and chicken
Grilled seafood
Rice and pinto beans
Vegetables: okra, greens, black-eyed peas,
   sweet potatoes
Corn bread
Shrimp or crab boil

Avoid

Fried fish and chicken
Crab cakes
Hush puppies
Gravy
Jambalaya
Honeyed dressings
Corn or fish chowder
"Mudpies" and other rich desserts

Health Tips for Diners

Make your restaurant meal a healthful pleasure by following these basic guidelines:

◆ Contact the restaurant in advance to find out if it offers entrees that are steamed, broiled, baked, or poached without sauces. Ask if special requests are honored, such as serving sauces on the side or not adding salt in the preparation of dishes.

◆ Cut down on or avoid rich cream sauces, condiments, butter on bread, and cheese sauces.

◆ Learn to recognize the language of menus. Descriptions like "garden fresh," "broiled," "steamed," and "cooked in its own juices" indicate low-fat preparation; "pickled," "smoked," and "cured" indicate high sodium content; "butter sauce," "pan fried," "sautéed," "rich," and "crispy" indicate high fat content.

◆ Don't hesitate to consult with the waiter on preparation methods and ingredients used in the dishes.

◆ Trim the visible fat off meat or ask for "lean" cuts, if they're available.

◆ Request dishes cooked in vegetable oils, such as canola, corn, soybean, or safflower, instead of butter. These oils contain no cholesterol. Better still, request dishes made with a minumum of *all* fat.

◆ Select vegetable dishes that have been minimally cooked. Overcooking depletes them of vitamins.

◆ If you have an appetizer, choose raw vegetables, melon, a seafood cocktail with sauce on the side, a small green or endive salad, or fresh cold or hot asparagus with vinaigrette dressing.

◆ At dessert time, look for fruit, fruit ices, or sherbets. If you opt for a rich dessert, consider ordering one serving to share between two people.

◆ Alcoholic beverages add empty calories to your total. Stick to a glass of wine with dinner, a wine spritzer (half wine and half sparkling water), or a nonalcoholic glass of soda water with a twist of lime. Avoid after-dinner liqueurs and drinks that use high-calorie mixers.

If you would like to find restaurants in your area that serve low-fat meals, contact your local chapter of the American Heart Association.

Find the Fast-Food Balance

Of the 66 million Americans who consume at least one meal a day away from home, 33 percent choose fast-food restaurants. Today more than 55,000 fast-food restaurants service a demanding public with an expanding range of selections. But these meals are not always nutritious. According to the *New England Journal of Medicine*, the typical fast-food meal derives between 40 and 55 percent of its calories from fat. Sometimes diversification makes a direct appeal to nutrition-conscious customers, as in the addition of salad bars and the inclusion of baked potatoes and broiled entrees. Unfortunately, many of the intended benefits are compromised by calorie- and fat-laden extras. For example, a plain baked potato is an excellent nutritional choice; even the addition of a pat of margarine won't hurt. But potatoes are often topped with bacon and cheese, a Stroganoff mixture, sour cream, and chili and cheese, along with other high-fat and high-calorie foods. For example, the Wendy's Baked Potato with Bacon and Cheese has 570 calories (more than the Double Hamburger), and 47 percent of the calories come from fat.

Many fast-food chains include breakfast. Consumer purchases of takeout breakfast items like McDonald's Egg McMuffin or Biscuit with Sausage, Burger King's Croissan'wich, Wendy's omelets, and Carl Jr.'s Sunrise Sandwich are on the rise. Some choices are better than others; the worst are usually the combination sandwiches. For example, the McDonald's meal of an English muffin with butter, scrambled eggs, and six ounces of orange juice has 40 percent less fat and fewer calories than the Sausage Egg McMuffin.

Because fast-food restaurants appeal to the lifestyle requirements of so many consumers, the question becomes how to make more healthful choices. Indeed, there are a number of ways to find a balanced, reasonably nutritious meal in a fast-food restaurant. Follow these guidelines when you dine:

Entrees

◆ Choose plain hamburgers or cheeseburgers instead of those that contain a "special sauce."

◆ "Junior" burgers and sandwiches are smaller and contain fewer calories.

◆ Don't be misled into thinking that fish or chicken sandwiches are better than burgers. The fish and chicken are often breaded and then fried in fat. For example, the McDonald's Filet-O-Fish has 435 calories, and 53 percent of them are from fat. Some restaurants, like Arthur Treacher's, offer broiled fish and shrimp, which are good choices, but diners should go easy on the tartar sauce.

◆ Pizza is one of the best fast-food nutrition values, if you use the right toppings. Choose vegetable toppings like mushrooms, onions, and green peppers. Avoid extra cheese, olives, pepperoni, sausage, and anchovies.

◆ McDonald's, Burger King, and Wendy's all offer grilled chicken sandwiches—a more healthful choice than fried.

Breakfast

◆ Avoid sandwiches that combine a cheese, egg, and/or meat filling with a muffin, croissant, or biscuit; it's hard to find one that doesn't top the fat chart.

◆ Hotcakes and French toast with syrup are reasonable choices if you don't use butter.

◆ Some chains offer cereal with milk and low-fat muffins.

Side Dishes

◆ Many fast-food restaurants have salad bars. Use the suggestions cited earlier in this chapter to keep your salad low in fat and calories.

◆ A plain, baked potato is a good choice, even with a pat of butter or margarine. These are available at Arby's, Roy Rogers, and Wendy's. Avoid the elaborate toppings. Kentucky Fried Chicken also serves mashed potatoes and corn on the cob.

Drinks

◆ A typical 10-ounce frozen dessert drink milkshake has between 300 and 400 calories,

and about as much sugar as a can of soda. A shake isn't bad (especially as a combination drink/dessert), but be on the alert for chains that offer larger shakes or malts. For example, Dairy Queen's chocolate shake is 20 fluid ounces and nearly 1,000 calories.

◆ Most fast-food restaurants carry low-fat or skim milk.

◆ To round out your fast-food meal, add low-fat or skim milk or orange juice.

Other Suggestions

◆ If you visit the salad bar, avoid bacon bits, cheddar cheese, olives, croutons, coleslaw, macaroni salad, potato salad, and high-fat dressing.

◆ For dessert, take fresh fruit from home.

◆ Take out your fast-food meal and serve it at home with salad, vegetables, and fruit.

NOT-SO-FAST FOODS

Menu	Calories	Fat(g)[1]	Sodium(mg)[2]
Appetizers			
Denny's Chicken Strips (4 oz)	240	10	600
Denny's Mozzarella Sticks (1 stick)	88	7	206
Ponderosa's Breaded Zucchini (4 oz)	102	1	584
Ponderosa's Chicken Wings (2 pieces)	213	9	610
Red Lobster's Bayou-Style Seafood Gumbo (6 oz)	180	5	800
Red Lobster's Shrimp Cocktail (6 large shrimp with shrimp sauce)	120	2	460
Soups			
Big Boy's Cabbage Soup (cup)[3]	37	0	623
Country Kitchen's Old-Fashioned Calico Bean Soup	<400	NA	>1000
Denny's Cheese Soup (1 bowl)	309	22	898
Denny's Split Pea Soup (1 bowl)	231	5	1519
Shoney's Clam Chowder (6 fl oz)	94	5	66
Shoney's Vegetable Beef Soup (6 fl oz)	82	2	1254
The Olive Garden's Minestrone (6 fl oz)	45	<1	220
Side Dishes			
Ponderosa's Potato Wedges (3.5 oz)	130	6	171
Ponderosa's Stuffing (4 oz)	230	11	800
Red Lobster's Rice Pilaf (4 oz)	140	3	390
The Olive Garden's Breadsticks (1)	70	2	365
Salads			
Big Boy's Chicken Breast Salad with Dijon	391	11	415
Chili's Caribbean Chicken Salad	374	7	NA
Country Kitchen's Grilled Chicken Breast Salad	<400	NA	>1000
Denny's Chef Salad	492	20	1370
Denny's Taco Salad (includes fried tortilla shell)	953	50	2628
Perkin's Mini Chef Salad	238	11	1883
T.G.I. Friday's Garden Cobb Salad	320	10	NA
T.G.I. Friday's Salad & Baked Potato	400	5	NA
The Olive Garden's Garden Salad	230	15	560
Sandwiches (Values are for sandwiches only unless otherwise indicated; no fries, coleslaw, etc. are included.)			
Big Boy's Breast of Chicken with Mozzarella Sandwich	404	13	421
Big Boy's Turkey Pita Sandwich	224	5	833
Country Kitchen's Barbecued Pork Sandwich	<400	NA	>1000
Denny's Club Sandwich	590	20	582

Special Report

	Calories	Fat(g)[1]	Sodium(mg)[2]
Sandwiches			
Perkin's Cajun Chicken Pita Sandwich (includes fruit cup)	429	12	432
Red Lobster's Broiled Fish Fillet Sandwich	300	10	450
Ruby Tuesday's Open-Faced Chicken Breast Sandwich	458	16	616
Shoney's Reuben Sandwich	596	35	3873
Shoney's Shoney Burger	498	36	782

NOT-SO-FAST FOODS (cont.)

T.G.I. Friday's Fresh Vegetable Baguette	290	11	NA
T.G.I. Friday's Gardenburger	390	8	NA

Entrees

Big Boy's Cajun Cod[a]	364	12	461
Big Boy's Chicken 'n Vegetable Stir Fry[a]	562	14	750
Big Boy's Spaghetti Marinara[a]	450	6	761
Big Boy's Vegetable Stir Fry[a]	408	10	703
Chili's Chicken Fajitas	557	9	NA
Chili's Grilled Chicken Platter	742	21	NA
Denny's Catfish (2–4 oz)[b]	576	0	460
Denny's Chicken Fried Steak (2 pieces, without gravy)[b]	252	15	422
Denny's Liver with Bacon and Onions (2 slices)[b]	334	15	516
Perkin's Cajun Chicken Dinner[c]	516	10	867
Perkin's Lemon Chicken Dinner[c]	517	10	868
Perkin's Orange Roughy[c]	364	6	891
Ponderosa's Chopped Steak (4 oz)[b]	225	16	150
Ponderosa's New York Strip (10 oz)[b]	314	15	1420
Ponderosa's Sirloin Tips (5 oz)[b]	473	8	280
Ponderosa's Steak Kabobs (3 oz meat only)[b]	153	5	280
Red Lobster's Bay Platter (shrimp, scallops, pollock, and rice)	500	20	1820
Red Lobster's Seafood Lover's Sampler (crab, shrimp, scallops, pollock, and crab legs)	650	27	1800
Red Lobster's Shrimp Scampi	310	23	250
Ruby Tuesday's Steamed Vegetable Plate	404	2	138
Shoney's Baked Fish[b]	170	1	1641
Shoney's Country Fried Steak[b]	449	27	1177
Shoney's Hawaiian Chicken[b]	262	7	593
Shoney's Italian Feast[b]	500	20	369
T.G.I. Friday's Pacific Coast Chicken	320	13	NA
The Olive Garden's Baked Lasagna (lunch item)	330	18	1030
The Olive Garden's Eggplant Parmigiana (lunch item)	220	14	720
The Olive Garden's Veal Parmigiana	590	40	1120
The Olive Garden's Veal Piccata	230	16	150

Desserts

Big Boy's Frozen Yogurt Shake	184	0	127
Big Boy's No-No Frozen Dessert	75	0	36
Ponderosa's Chocolate Mousse (1 oz)	78	4	18
Ponderosa's Spiced Apple Rings (4 oz)	100	0	20
Shoney's Apple Pie A La Mode	492	23	574
Shoney's Carrot Cake	500	26	476
Shoney's Hot Fudge Sundae	451	22	226
Shoney's Strawberry Pie	332	17	247

[a] Includes dinner salad (no dressing), bread, and margarine.

[b] Entree only

[c] Salad, salad dressing, and bread not included; values based on accompaniments of 4 oz steamed broccoli and 6 oz rice.

All calorie and fat figures have been rounded to the nearest whole number. Consumers should be aware that the figures are not "engraved in stone." The calorie and fat content of a steak, for instance, will vary depending on a particular piece's proportions of protein, fat, and water and whether it's cooked rare or well-done.

NOT-SO-FAST FOODS *(cont.)*

Breakfast Items

Denny's Cinnamon Roll	450	14	750
Denny's Eggs Benedict (1)	658	36	2197
Denny's French Toast (2 slices with butter and powdered sugar)	729	56	275
Denny's Waffle (1 waffle)	261	10	62
Perkin's Denver Omelette (with muffin & fruit cup)	511	17	1125
Perkin's Harvest 'Cakes with Reduced Calorie Syrup (stack of 5)	533	10	2300
Perkin's Seafood Omelette (with muffin & fruit cup)	549	16	925
Shoney's Country Gravy (¼ cup)	82	7	255
Shoney's Grits (¼ cup)	57	3	62
Shoney's Home Fries (¼ cup)	53	2	24
Village Inn's Fresh Veggie Omelette	413	17	1367
Village Inn's Granola & Fruit with Yogurt and Blueberry Muffin	860	27	758
Village Inn's Low Cholesterol Fruit & Nut Pancakes	332	10	1287

[1]Someone following an 1,800-calorie diet should average a maximum of 60 grams of fat a day.
[2]The National Academy of Sciences recommends a sodium limit of 2,400 milligrams a day.
[3]All Big Boy dishes are Big Boy Health Smart menu items.

PART THREE

Nutritional Life-Cycles

Every human being travels a cycle in life, from birth to growth to maturity to death. Each stage of the cycle is unique, marked by a new series of physiological changes, some of them dramatic.

This section addresses three specific populations whose nutritional concerns can be considered "special." Much of the advice in this book easily applies to most people, but children, women of all ages, and the elderly face unique circumstances and needs. Some of the issues addressed in this section include: What should new parents know about starting their baby off on the right foot nutritionally? Is breast-feeding substantially preferable to bottle feeding? When a baby is ready for solid foods, how can parents avoid nutrient deficiencies and make the best choices from among commercial baby products? What are the special nutritional issues for children during the first two years of life? Certain nutritional practices for infants present a clear example of how "common wisdom" for older children and adults can actually endanger a baby's health. In this section you'll see, for example, how well-meaning parents who put their infants on low-fat diets may be creating serious health problems for them.

As they grow, children need a good balance of nutrients for the development of bone, muscle, and tissue. But as they pass into the toddler stage and beyond, children become conscious of their autonomy, and they can be very stubborn about their likes and dislikes when it comes to food. What are parents to do when faced with finicky eaters? How important is it that children eat certain foods? What can be done to neutralize the "sugar monster"? How can you avoid daily battles over food and still be sure your child gets the nutrients that he or she needs? Many parents throw up their hands in despair over the eating habits of their teenagers. They can seem like bottomless pits of hunger, and they often rely on fast foods and snacks to fill the pit. During these years, parents exert less daily control over diet. How can a little nutritional know-how and planning help you create better nutritional options for your teenagers? Sometimes parents are confronted with "weighty issues" when it comes to their child's diet and health. How do you know if your child's weight should be of concern, or if he or she is just going through normal hormonal changes? Many parents overreact to a child's weight gain and try to force rigid restrictions. There is hard evidence that this approach almost always backfires. So what do you do if your child's doctor agrees that there's an obesity problem? And what if the reverse is true? How can you recognize the beginnings of a severe eating disorder like anorexia nervosa before it has progressed to the danger point? What are the steps you can take to get proper care for a child who is "starving"?

Adult women have special nutritional needs, particularly as they apply to pregnancy and lactation. As the RDAs stipulate, pregnant and lactating women need more of most essential nutrients. But what does this mean in terms of the nuts and bolts of daily eating? How can the mother-to-be and the breast-feeding mother plan diets that enhance health for both woman and child? Women also need special consideration during their menstruating years. Iron may become depleted during menstruation and need to be replaced. In addition, many women suffer a condition known as Premenstrual Syndrome (PMS) that involves symptoms ranging from mild to severe. Can nutrition make a difference? We'll look at the current expert wisdom on this subject.

Finally, menopause marks a point in a woman's life when new nutritional issues arise. We will explore these, too.

Tufts University has devoted much attention to issues related to diet and aging. Since 1982 it has operated the Jean Mayer USDA Human Nutritional Research Center on Aging. The center has led the field in research related to the nutrient needs during the aging process. Although the RDAs list general guidelines for adult men and women 51 years and older, we have learned that special considerations must be applied to senior citizens. Tufts has led the way in encouraging the RDA committee to establish a new category for adults who are 69 years of age or older.

Lifestyle changes common among seniors can influence diet. Older people may lack the physical stamina to prepare balanced meals or the information or money to purchase the right foods. Widowed seniors, unaccustomed to cooking for one, often ignore their nutritional needs.

We believe that once people begin to consider good nutrition a part of their lifestyle in every stage of life, many of the nutritional problems that plague various populations will be diminished.

15

The Well-Nourished Child

Today's parents have access to more nutrition information than the parents of any other generation. But this knowledge can seem like a mixed blessing as they struggle to understand the complex and often conflicting advice they hear from dozens of sources. Parents also have to confront new dilemmas that have emerged out of the times we live in, such as worries over the safety of our nation's food supply, the growing crisis of obesity in children, and the changes in family styles that have led to fewer meals' being prepared at home and less control over what their children eat.

Nutrition is a factor in many of the decisions parents make in raising their children, from the moment of birth to the time they leave home.

A Healthy Beginning for Baby

All new parents are intensely interested in making decisions that will start their baby off on a long and healthy life. The first nutritional question, usually raised before the baby is born, is whether or not to breast-feed. For many people, it seems perfectly logical that a mother's breast milk, the "natural" form of nutrition for a baby, would be the best possible choice. Is this true? In the mid-1970s, the American Academy of Pediatrics described mother's milk as "the best food for every newborn infant." That endorsement has received the support of the U.S. surgeon general and of the vast majority of nutritionists.

Fortunately, for mothers who are unable to breast-feed, the formulas on the market duplicate breast milk to the extent that your child won't suffer ill health. But breast milk is considered the food of choice for infants.

The most important benefit of breast milk is that it is believed to carry, from mother to infant, immunity against several kinds of infection. In addition, colostrum, the premilk substance secreted during the first few days of breast-feeding, supplies even higher levels of antibodies. Research conducted over a period of 30 years provides evidence that mother's milk is a prime infection fighter.

New research shows that breast-fed babies have a dramatic decrease in the incidence of ear infections. After reviewing the medical records of more than 1,000 infants, pediatricians at the University of Arizona Health Sciences Center in Tuscon found that those who were fed solely by breast-feeding for at least the first four months had an average of half the number of ear infections as those who were not breast-fed at all, and 40 percent fewer than babies who were given a combination of breast milk and other foods. Furthermore, only 10 percent of infants who were breast-fed exclusively suffered recurrences of ear infections, whereas 20 percent of babies who were breast-fed for less than four months came down with several infections. There are a number of reasons for this apparent protection. One is that breast-fed infants are held in a more or less upright position during nursing, allowing the fluid to flow directly to the stomach. By contrast, bottle-fed babies often drink their formula while reclining, a position that may allow small amounts of formula to make their way from the back of the throat to the tubes connecting the nose and ears. The liquid could then collect in the inner ear, where bacteria may multiply and cause an infection. Another possibility is that the antibodies naturally present in breast milk defend the baby's body against the bacteria responsible for ear infections. It is also possible that high levels of substances found in breast milk, called prostaglandins, stymie the body's reaction to bacteria—specifically, the swelling and inflammation of the inner ear.

An additional benefit of breast-feeding is that it may offer protection for the mother. Research indicates that a woman who breast-feeds her child, even for only a few months, may be protecting herself against breast cancer. Scientists at the Fred Hutchinson Cancer Research Center in Seattle, Washington, found that women who breast-feed have as little as half the risk of developing breast cancer as those who have never breast-fed. The protective effect seems to extend from the time a woman starts breastfeeding until menopause. The reason behind this phenomenon is not fully understood, but it could be related to hormonal changes that occur during nursing. Another possibility is that breast-feeding might bring about some (as yet undiscovered) positive changes in the breast tissue.

If You're Nursing, Don't Drink

As far back as the first century A.D., medical annals advised new mothers to drink a glass of wine or beer before breast-feeding to boost the amount of milk they produced. Alcohol has also been recommended to help relax breast-feeding women and their babies, presumably increasing infants' milk consumption. Newer research calls this "old mother's tale" into question.

Scientists at the Monell Chemical Senses Center in Philadelphia found that breast-fed infants drank an average of 22 percent less milk after their mothers consumed orange juice mixed with the amount of alcohol in a can of beer than when the women drank the same amount of juice with no alcohol. Granted, the researchers tracked the infants' feeding patterns for only three hours after their mothers drank the alcohol concoctions, so they did not examine whether babies made up for the drops in consumption by drinking more later in the day. Still, the study did suggest that contrary to long-held beliefs, alcohol does not boost breast-milk consumption.

There are several reasons why a mother's alcohol consumption might reduce the amount of milk her baby takes in. One is that alcohol may affect a nursing mother's ability to produce as well as eject milk. A second theory has to do with alcohol's direct effect on the baby. Although the amount of alcohol transmitted through the breast may be small, an infant's tiny body makes the dose more potent. In addition, babies are not as efficient as adults in breaking down alcohol, so any dose consumed is much stronger. A third possible explanation for the affects of alcohol is that it changes the odor and flavor of breast milk, perhaps making it less desirable. A panel of adults recruited by the Monell researchers sniffed samples of the mothers' breast milk and concluded that those taken from women after they had consumed alcohol had a distinctly different odor from those taken from women who consumed no alcohol.

The likelihood that infants are adversely

affected by alcohol is supported by the Monell researchers' observation that they sleep for shorter, more frequent periods after breast-feeding from mothers who have imbibed.

Delay the Start of Cow's Milk

Rapid growth during the first two years of life makes very young children particularly dependent on nutrient-dense foods, which contribute to the growth of cells and development of muscle and tissue.

Perhaps the most common mistake parents make is to replace vitamin- and mineral-rich breast milk or iron-fortified formula with regular cow's milk too soon. Although cow's milk is a good source of nutrients that children need as they grow, it is a relatively poor source of iron, copper, and vitamin C. It contains less than a milligram of iron per quart, and, of that, only about 2 to 10 percent is absorbed. Even if a 6- to 12-month-old drinks the typical amount of one quart a day, he or she is still at least 14 milligrams shy of the RDA's 15 milligrams.

Delay the use of cow's milk until your baby is at least six months old, and when you do use it, supplement it with iron-rich solid foods. The best source is iron-fortified infant cereal that you mix with a liquid.

Picking the Best Baby Food

Baby food manufacturers have gone to a great deal of trouble in recent years to send a nutrition-conscious message to consumers. In the past, baby food was criticized for containing too much salt and sugar. Manufacturers tended to make it taste the way Mom would like it, so that when she sampled it, she would think it tasted good. But babies don't need strong flavors because their taste buds are more acute, and many of today's baby food selections reflect this understanding. It is possible, for example, to find many simple foods in jars,

such as peas that have been pureed with water and don't contain a lot of "extras." The key to finding the best baby food is to look beyond labels that read "no added salt, no artificial flavors or preservatives" to find out what else is inside the jar. To be sure, many parents prefer that their babies' food contain no added sugar, salt, or starch fillers whatsoever. If that's your concern, give labels a closer examination to ensure that you're getting what you really want.

In most cases, the less sugar, corn syrup, starch, modified food starch, and added flour, the more nutrients you get for the calories. The problem isn't that these ingredients are harmful to your baby; it's more a matter of not "spending" calories on extra ingredients that are not nourishing.

Consider baby fruits, which can be good sources of vitamin C or A. The fine print on the ingredients label will show that plain fruits, such as baby pears, applesauce, or strained bananas, have no sweeteners added. However, fruits thickened with tapioca invariably have added sugar or corn syrup. Although there is no evidence that small amounts of these sweeteners are harmful as long as a baby's teeth are kept clean, the sugary thickener takes up space in the jar that could be given to the fruits themselves. Also, be aware that the presence of fillers may dilute a food's vitamin and mineral value. In general, we recommend that you limit the use of fruit "cobblers," "desserts," and "supremes" because they are typically high in sugar and therefore contain more empty calories.

Check for the protein content of baby meats. The highest-protein baby foods are strained and junior meats and poultry that list broth or water as the only added ingredient. A three-and-a-half-ounce jar may provide up to 80 percent of the RDA for protein. On the other hand, meat and vegetable combination dinners are not necessarily a high source of protein. A seven-and-a-half-ounce jar of a vegetable-beef combination may have more vegetables than beef and contain only 20 percent of the RDA for protein.

Few babies have a hearty enough appetite to eat the whole jar, in any case. Also be aware that the heavier, stew-type dinners for toddlers tend to be low in protein and very high in salt. You may rely upon the popular instant baby cereals for their fortified iron content, particularly desirable if your baby is not on iron-fortified formula.

And this might surprise you: Although foods that are low in fat and cholesterol are often recommended as wise choices for older children and adults, this advice does not hold true for children under the age of two years old. For them, limiting foods that contain fat and cholesterol could spell trouble. Skimming the fat (and therefore calories) from a baby's diet could stunt his or her growth. Severely limiting an infant's dietary cholesterol could deprive the baby of the calories he or she needs to develop.

Doctors at North Shore Hospital in Manhasset, New York, have seen first-hand what diets low in fat, cholesterol, and calories can do to infants. Children were admitted to the hospital's research center with severe growth problems that, according to doctors, were related to their having been fed overly strict diets. Well-meaning mothers and fathers, concerned that their babies would become overweight, deliberately watered down their formula. In several cases, parents also cut back on snacks or fat in meals eaten by babies on solid foods. The result was that babies were short-changed on calories, and their growth was poor.

Sugar Helps the Medicine Go Down

A little bit of sugar might be helpful when it comes to unpleasant but necessary procedures. When researchers at Brown University placed a small amount of sugary fluid on the tongue tips of two- and four-month-old infants just before they were about to receive routine vaccinations, the babies cried and fussed less than those who were given a dab of plain water. Furthermore, after the shots the sugar-treated babies' cries weren't as loud and didn't last as long. And their heart rates returned to normal more quickly than the heart rates of water-treated babies.

The findings lend weight to earlier research that infants, even newborns, can benefit from a bit of the sweet stuff. Investigators at Johns Hopkins University made the discovery a few years ago when they gave a bit of sugar water to newborn infants about to have their heels lanced for blood collection. They cried only about half as much as newborns who received plain water. The Johns Hopkins scientists also studied newborn boys undergoing circumcision and learned that those who sucked on pacifiers dipped in sugar cried during just 30 percent of the procedure, whereas those who sucked on pacifiers dipped in plain water cried 50 percent of the time and those with no pacifier cried 70 percent of the time. The researchers suspect that sugar activates the pathways of the body's natural opiates, which have a pain-reducing effect.

This news is a potential godsend for infants, who must endure a number of painful and stressful medical procedures. Even within the first few days of birth, babies have to go through several unpleasant episodes of prodding and poking—including circumcision for most American males, a shot of vitamin K to promote blood clotting, and a skin prick to collect blood for testing for the presence of the metabolic disorder phenylketonuria. Parents who worry that infants given a small drop of sugar might develop a taste for it too early needn't worry. The truth is that we are *born* with a preference for sugar. It's not something that develops with exposure.

Limit Juice Intake

Children under age five drink more juice than any other age group, mostly in the form of apple juice. It's easy to understand why. Even picky eaters tend to like its sweet taste, and parents perceive it to be a healthful beverage. Indeed, parents who worry about the high-fat content of whole milk may think that juice is the beverage of choice.

But too much juice can spell trouble for some children. As a case in point, a group of 1- and 2-year-olds in Brooklyn, New York, whose growth and development were not keeping pace with those of others in their age group turned out to be drinking too much apple juice. In some instances, they were consuming 30 ounces a day—between 25 and 60 percent of their total calories. The pediatricians and dietician caring for the youngsters noted that filling up on juice left little or no room for other high-calorie foods kids need, such as milk and solid foods. What's more, high levels of the sugars in apple juice—fructose and sorbitol—might cause diarrhea in children, making it hard for them to put on weight. When the Brooklyn children's juice allotment was dropped to 4 ounces daily, all of them began putting on weight within a month.

Pediatric experts caution that parents should not put children under the age of two on low-fat, high-juice diets. Whole milk and other dairy foods are a concentrated source of calories and nutrients kids need to ensure proper growth and development. Consider that a cup of whole milk contains not only 150 calories but also protein, vitamins A and D, calcium, and a number of other vitamins and minerals. The same amount of apple juice, on the other hand, supplies only about 120 calories and little else.

None of this is to say that parents should not give juice to children at all. Fruit juices can be gradually introduced to children when they are able to drink from a cup—at about nine months for most kids. Avoid feeding juice in bottles, and serve only two to four ounces at a time. Over the course of a day, feed no more than four to eight ounces of fruit juice—and never as a replacement for milk or other foods.

Get Your Kids to Eat Right

If you're a parent, you may wonder why it's such a struggle to get your kids to eat a nutritious variety of foods. One good reason, of course, is that kids have minds of their own, and sometimes it takes Herculean strength to change those minds.

Most people become overly obsessed with their young children's eating habits. It's a rare parent who hasn't called the pediatrician to complain that "Billy won't eat anything but bread and jam" or "I'm worried about Susan— she eats like a bird." These small battles of will are usually short-lived, and your child's temporary eating quirks are unlikely to cause permanent harm. Cajoling, threatening, or bribing will only make things worse. In truth, American children, even when they're being finicky, have sufficient variety in their diets that they get enough of the nutrients they need.

The best way to teach your child to eat well is to maintain a relaxed attitude about food, avoiding fanaticism. Stay informed about the range of nutrients your growing child needs, and incorporate these foods into your family's daily diet, without making an issue of it.

It's a good idea to involve children in their own nutrition. Most respond better when they are included in the planning. They don't respond to abstract concepts such as "This is good for you" or "Eat your beans so you can grow up healthy and strong." Children will respond better if you take a more relaxed approach and don't try to make every meal a life-and-death nutritional battle.

Let them help design the weekly menu and shopping list, gently educating them about simple nutrition concepts as you go along.

Children are creatures of habit, and the best way to guarantee that their habits are healthful is to keep eating periods structured. Mealtimes should be set for regular hours so you can keep track of what your child is eating. Be sure to schedule snack times throughout the day, especially for small children.

If your child refuses to eat a certain food, don't force the issue. Simply try again a few days later, serving a small portion of it. Studies show that the more a child is exposed to a food, the more likely it is that he or she will eventually try it, and maybe even enjoy it. You may have to try as many as 10 or 15 times, but your child should eventually come around. Even if it doesn't work, it's not the end of the world. Essential nutrients are available in enough foods that a child's refusal to eat one or two of them won't cause a nutritional deficit.

Which Foods Do Children Need?

A growing child's body demands lots of nutrients to support the creation of new tissue. Basically, that means eating a variety from the Food Guide Pyramid. Parents often worry that their children are not eating enough, but a young child does not require much quantity. While children are growing, their appetites may be unpredictable. On some days thay may be ravenous, especially if they've been very active. On other days, they may seem to pick at their food.

As a general rule, consider an average child's serving to be one tablespoon for each year. For example, the average adult serving of a cooked vegetable is around one-half cup. For a three-year-old, it's three tablespoons or slightly less than one-fourth cup. A five-year-old would eat a little more than one-fourth cup.

Because children need to pack more nutrients into fewer daily calories, there isn't much room in their diets for empty calories. Sugary snacks and drinks take away from the foods they need and should be limited to small "treats" two or three times a week.

Pack a Healthy Bag Lunch

Once your child walks out the door in the morning, nutrition control is out of your hands.

Although you may send your child off with a nutrient-packed lunch, once he or she is away from you those nutrients might end up any number of places other than your child's body: Lunch items might get traded with a friend, the bag might be forgotten on the bus, or the most nutritious items might be dumped into the garbage.

The best way to ensure that your child eats the lunch you prepare is to make it taste good. This is another place it might help to involve your child in the planning and shopping. Start with lists of foods in the basic food groups, including as many different choices as possible. Then use your imagination to make the bag lunch fun to open.

Happy, Healthful Lunch Tips

◆ Many kids like peanut butter sandwiches, but you can jazz up the old standby with different toppings besides jellies. To a peanut butter sandwich on whole-grain bread, add sliced banana, raisins, dates, or apple butter.

◆ Pep up chicken and tuna salad by adding almond slivers, sesame seeds, raisins, apple pieces, or seasonings such as curry powder.

◆ Make your own healthful, low-sodium lunch meats by cooking lean roast beef and chicken or turkey breast and slicing them thinly.

◆ If you do purchase lunch meats, choose the lean brands of roast beef, ham, turkey, and chicken. Unfortunately, most packaged lunch meats are high in sodium, but you can cut fat substantially by choosing one of the leaner, low-fat brands.

◆ Pack snack-size applesauce or raisins. Or supply a tasty homemade side dish in a serving-size plastic container. Mix plain yogurt with raisins, apples, or berries and add a dash of sugar and cinnamon. Or make your own trail mix with cereal, pretzels, seeds, and raisins.

Keep Lunches Safe

◆ Freeze or refrigerate sandwiches the night before and pack them frozen so they won't be warm and soggy by lunchtime. Wrap tomato and lettuce separately so your child can add them right before eating. (You might also want to use frozen gel packs to keep foods cold.) Don't save paper bags for packing lunches. Used bags can pass insects or bacteria from other foods. Never use a bag that's wet or stained.

◆ Wash lunch boxes daily, and once a week scrub them with baking soda.

◆ Be sure that everything that touches food is kept clean. Wash all utensils, cutting boards, and counter tops thoroughly before preparing each portion of the meal.

◆ If you send soup or drinks in a thermos, keep in mind that the kind that comes with most lunch kits, plastic and insulated with foam, does a better job of keeping cold liquids cold than hot liquids hot. If you're sending a hot food that could go "bad" if it cools down, use a vacuum-insulated thermos, which is constructed with stainless steel or glass inside another bottle, with a vacuum between the inside and outside layers. This prevents heat from escaping. It is also helpful to preheat the thermos before using it by filling it with hot tap water and letting it stand for a minute or two. Then, empty the water and fill the thermos with food that has been brought to a boil. Using this method with a thermos in good condition will assure that food is kept at a safe temperature for hours.

Improve Your School's Lunch Program

Government-sponsored school lunch programs still have a way to go to be acceptable. Although the U.S. Department of Agriculture (USDA) has started supplying schools with more nutritious foods (adding fish, pasta, and fresh produce; packing fruits in natural juice or light syrup; limiting fats and oils used in processing to vegetable oils), there are still plenty of high-fat government surplus foods of lesser nutritional value on the average school lunch menu.

Indeed, cost-cutting maneuvers may be undercutting your child's nutrition. Although it has been more than 20 years since the senate, USDA and Department of Health and Human Services—along with many health organizations—recommended that Americans limit their fat consumption to 30 percent of calories, a 1992 survey found that less than one percent of school lunch programs met this goal. Furthermore, as of this edition, the entire future of school lunch programs is at stake, with many elected officials lobbying to limit or eliminate them altogether.

Parental pressure and community action have worked in some parts of the country to get schools to improve the nutritional quality of lunches. If you are concerned about this issue, you should contact your local board of education, parent groups, and elected officials.

Is Your Child a Cookie Monster Captive?

The cookie jar has been the bane of many a mother's existence. Many children consider cookies a favorite snack, dessert, and comfort food. In fact, Americans love cookies, consuming more than 2 billion pounds of them each year. Supermarkets devote entire aisles to an increasing number of hard-to-resist cookies. Should they be resisted? Should you simply ban the "monster" from your home? Probably not. A better alternative is to know how to choose the cookies that are lowest in sugar and calories and then limit their consumption. And, as we have stated before, indulging in a small treat two or three times a week will do your child little harm.

Most cookies are made from three primary ingredients: sugar, flour, and shortening (in effect, fat). The differences among cookies result from differences in the ratios of these three components to one another, and whether other ingredients, such as chocolate chips or fillings, have been added. There is also a larger variety of low-fat and fat-free cookies available in supermarkets.

As a general rule, the softer the cookie, the higher the fat content; it's extra fat that helps soften the texture of baked goods. Also, try some of the reduced fat and fat-free cookies on the market—such as reduced fat Oreos and fat-free Fig Newtons.

Does Sugar Affect Behavior?

It's a fact that your child might become particularly high-spirited after eating a sugary candy bar or an ice cream cone. After all, eating food provides energy. Furthermore, many children become excited simply as a result of being given permission to eat a sweet treat that is generally off limits. But a number of parents believe that sugar (as well as the artificial sweetener aspartame) keeps kids "wired" in general—that is, impulsive, unable to concentrate in school, restless, and disruptive. Does this belief have validity?

According to an investigation into the matter by researchers at Vanderbilt University in Nashville, Tennessee, and the University of Iowa College of Medicine, sugar and asparatame are not the behavioral villains they're often purported to be. The research involved three- to five-year-old preschoolers described by their parents as "sugar-sensitive." All of them followed three different diets for three weeks each. One was high in sugar, one was high in aspartame, and one was high in saccharin. Neither the children nor their parents nor the researchers knew which child was eating which diet at any given time, because the sweet items looked and tasted identical regardless of which

sweetener was used. To make the study even more valid, all foods were cleared out of the children's homes before the research began, and the foods to be eaten by the children—*and* their families—were delivered each week.

The result was this. Frequent assessment of the children's conduct by their parents, teachers, and members of the research team never showed any significant differences in 30 to 40 behavior-related factors, including attention span, academic performance, noisiness, memory, coordination, and mood. This held true for all the children, including those who had been described by their parents as sugar-sensitive and a few who had also been diagnosed with psychiatric disorders such as attention deficit disorder. The only two differences noted on the high-sugar regimen were that the preschoolers did a little better in learning tasks and were a little slower working with pegboards. However, the children's responses were well within the normal range and did not negate the basic findings.

Even though a carefully controlled study such as this one would seem to validate previous studies that reached the same conclusion, many parents are still convinced that sugar makes their kids go wild. Marcel Kinsbourne, M.D., a pediatric neurologist at Tufts University, explains that when a child actually has a neurological disorder but its origin is unclear, there is a tendency to find a simple external factor like sugar rather than to look at more complex socio-psychological or genetic factors. That's one reason why sugar has become the scapegoat in childhood behavioral issues.

But, although there are plenty of nutritional reasons to limit sugar intake, depriving kids of sweet foods won't necessarily improve their behavior.

Nutrition Aid for Parents

You can help your child eat well by following these simple, no-stress guidelines:

FOR FAT-CONSCIOUS COOKIE MONSTERS

	Calories	Fat(g)[1]
Archway		
Frosty Lemon, 0.9 oz	130	5
Gingersnaps, 0.2 oz	25	1
Oatmeal Raisin, 0.9 oz	100	3
Rocky Road, 1 oz	130	6
Entenmann's		
Chocolate Chip, 0.3 oz	47	2.3
Oatmeal Chocolatey Chip, 0.4 oz	40	0
Health Valley		
Fat-Free Raisin Oatmeal, 0.4 oz	25	0
Fat-Free Raspberry Jumbo Fruit, 0.9 oz	80	0
Oat Bran Honey Jumbos, 0.6 oz	60	1.5
Keebler		
Chips Deluxe, 0.5 oz	80	5
Deluxe Grahams, 0.3 oz	45	2.5
Pecan Sandies, 0.5 oz	80	5
Soft Batch Chocolate Chip, 0.5 oz	80	4
Sweet Spots, 0.3 oz	25	1.5
Nabisco		
Chips Ahoy! (Pure Chocolate Chip) 0.5 oz	50	2
Fat Free Fig Newtons, 0.8 oz	70	0
Fig Newtons, 0.5 oz	60	1
Lorna Doone Shortbread, 0.3 oz	35	2
Nilla Wafers, 0.1 oz	17	0.6
Nutter Butter Peanut Butter Sandwich, 0.5 oz	70	3
Oreo Chocolate Sandwich, 0.5 oz	50	2

	Calories	Fat(g)[1]
Nabisco Snack Well's		
Chocolate Chip, 0.1 oz	10	0.2
Oatmeal Raisin, 0.5 oz	60	1
Pepperidge Farm		
Chessmen, 0.3 oz	**45**	**2**
Chocolate Chip, 0.3 oz	50	2.5
Chocolate Chunk Pecan, 0.4 oz	70	4
Milano, 0.4 oz	60	3
Sausalito Milk Chocolate Macadamia, 0.8 oz	120	7
Pepperidge Farm Wholesome Choice		
Apple Oatmeal Tart, 0.6 oz.	70	2
Cranberry Honey, 0.5 oz	60	2
Oatmeal Raisin, 0.5 oz	60	1
Raspberry Tart, 0.5 oz	60	1
R. W. Frookie		
Fat Free Oatmeal Raisin Cookies, 0.5 oz	50	0
Fat Free Raspberry Fruitins, 0.5 oz	45	0
Frookwich, 0.4 oz	50	2
Sunshine		
Chip-A-Roos, 0.5 oz	60	3
Lemon Coolers, 0.3 oz	30	1
Mallopuffs, 0.5 oz	70	2
Sugar Wafers, 0.3 oz	45	2

[1]Someone following an 1,800-calorie diet should average a maximum of 60 grams of fat a day. Values for weights and fat content are per cookie and have been rounded. Note weights when making nutritional comparisons.

◆ Establish set meal and snack times. Children who are allowed to help themselves to snacks when they feel like it may not have enough appetite to eat the nutritious foods that are served at the table.

◆ Make meals tantalizing by serving a variety of foods with different colors and textures. If children refuse to eat certain foods, look for others that offer the same nutrients. For example, the vitamin A precursor beta-carotene in dark-

CANDY COUNTER COUNT-UP

	Weight(oz)[1]	Calories	Fat(g)[2]
Almond Joy	1.76	250	14
Baby Ruth	2.1	290	14
Butterfinger	2.1	280	12
Good & Plenty	1.8	191	0
Hershey's Milk Chocolate	1.55	240	14
Junior Mints	1.6	192	5
KitKat	1.5	230	12
LifeSavers, 11 candies	0.9	88	0
m & m's (plain)	1.69	230	10
m & m's (peanut)	1.74	250	13
Milky Way	2.15	280	11
Mr. Goodbar	1.65	240	15
Nestle Crunch	1.55	220	11
PayDay	1.85	250	12
Raisinets	1.58	190	8
Reese's Peanut Butter Cups, 2 cups	1.6	250	15
Rolo, 10 candies	1.93	270	12
Snickers	2.07	280	13
Sno-Caps	2.3	322	12
Sugar Daddy	2.0	218	1
3 Musketeers	2.13	260	9
Tootsie Roll	2.25	252	6
Twix Caramel Cookie Bars	2.0	280	14
Whoppers	1.75	238	10
York Peppermint Pattie	1.5	180	4

[1]Package sizes here are those typically found at the "corner" store.

[2]One gram of fat contains nine calories. Someone following a 1,800-calorie diet should average a maximum of 60 grams of fat a day.

green, leafy vegetables can also be found in cantaloupe, apricots, and sweet potatoes.

◆ Include children in food choices. If you have served something several times that they won't eat, ask what they don't like about it. You might find that it's a simple thing to change. Children who turn up their noses at cooked carrots may be perfectly happy to crunch away on the raw variety.

◆ Allow for childrens' idiosyncrasies. For instance, children may refuse to eat if foods on the plate touch one another. Or they may dislike foods that are certain colors. Don't force the issue. Serve meals on a plate that has dividers.

◆ Try to mix new or objectionable foods with favorite foods to make them seem different.

◆ Give lots of time at meals. Children need more time to eat than adults. Never criticize children for dawdling over their food. Let them eat at their own pace.

◆ Keep meal times free of disruption. Meals are not the time to scold children or give them the third degree about school performance. It is impossible to enjoy food and digest it properly when one is in a harsh and stressful setting.

◆ Invite your children to participate in meal preparation. If they are involved in the process, they are likely to become more interested in the foods themselves. For example, if you let children create their own salads or "build" their own tacos, they'll feel that the food "belongs" to them, that it wasn't forced on them.

◆ Avoid creating the impression that there are "good" foods and "bad" foods. Rather, concentrate on communicating positive messages about food. For example, instead of saying, "Cookies are bad for you," tell your children, "Cookies are fun to have for a Saturday treat, but they're not for every day."

Keep Your Child Heart-Healthy

High blood cholesterol and the risk for heart disease have usually been associated with the adult population. But studies show that heart disease may begin early in life. Indeed, current statistics show that an estimated 30 to 40 percent of children in families with a history of heart disease have high blood cholesterol, and up to 80 percent of them will carry it into adulthood.

In one study, researchers observed the children of the Louisiana city Bogalusa, using techniques similar to those that are used with adults. The researchers interviewed thousands of children about their parents' habits and health, analyzed their blood, measured their blood pressure, and assessed their diets. Tests showed high cholesterol levels in the blood of many of the children. In addition, autopsies performed on 88 children who had died in accidents or from illnesses showed that almost 40 percent of them had the first signs of heart disease—fibrous plaque or fatty deposits in the walls of blood vessels. The American Academy of Pediatrics has issued a statement recommending routine cholesterol screening for all children in families that have a history of heart disease.

The first step in lowering the risk of heart disease is to reduce the intake of dietary fat. But pediatric health professionals have traditionally been reluctant to impose strict guidelines on children, because they are growing rapidly and need vast nutritional resources to lay the foundation for brain, bone, and muscle.

Health experts unanimously agree that no dietary restrictions related to heart disease should be imposed on children younger than age two. But older children can benefit from a reduction in dietary fat, especially considering that American children consume an average of 37 percent of their diets as fat.

The changes do not have to be dramatic; small adjustments in the way food is prepared can make a big difference. For example, begin trimming all visible fat from meats, avoid processed luncheon meats, and serve skinless broiled rather than fried chicken.

Physical activity is also an important way to keep cholesterol levels in check. That means more exercise and less TV watching. In fact, researchers at the University of California, Irvine, matched the cholesterol measurements of more than 1,000 young children and adolescents with their TV-viewing habits. They found that those who reported watching at least two hours of television a day were twice as likely to have high blood cholesterol as those who tuned in for less than two hours a day. Children who watched four or more hours of TV a day were nearly four times as likely to end up with high cholesterol levels.

Keep Your Teens on Track

If your child has not developed sensible eating habits by the time he or she reaches the teen years, you may feel that it's useless even to try. Your teenager's diet is more or less out of your control, and it may seem that a typical menu for your teen is made up of hamburgers, French fries, sodas, ice cream, and other fatty or high-calorie foods.

Teenagers, especially boys, can appear to be bottomless pits of hunger. Unfortunately, they're not always very concerned about what they're eating.

As a recent Gallup Poll demonstrated, today's teens are aware of the fundamentals of good eating and are especially conscious of highly publicized issues like the dangers of cholesterol and the need for adequate amounts of calcium. But their actual eating behavior seems at odds with their nutritional knowledge. For example, although 87 percent of those surveyed said they put a lot of effort into a good diet, 79 percent listed hamburgers, cheeseburgers, pizza, and luncheon meats as preferred foods.

You can't completely control your teenager's diet, and badgering certainly won't help. What you can do is encourage good eating at home. Schedule regular family meals and let your teens know that you expect them to be present. Keep healthful snack foods handy—such as fruit, raw vegetables, and yogurt—so that refrigerator raids are good for them. Healthful snacks can also include moderate amounts of dried fruit and nuts, popcorn, and even oatmeal and raisin cookies and milk, or a slice of plain pizza. Instead of store-bought sodas, make your own fruit drinks, combining real fruit juices with seltzer. If you suspect that your teenager is indulging in sugar- and salt-laden snacks outside the home (and he or she probably is), there's no need to keep those items in your home. It won't hurt your teen to indulge occasionally in fast-food meals, but if you provide a balance at home, you can better assure that the full range of nutrients is being consumed.

It helps to know which nutrients are particularly important for teens and to recognize the key distinctions between male and female dietary needs. For example, even though your teenage boy may consume many "junk" foods, that doesn't necessarily mean he isn't getting enough of the nutrients he needs.

Indeed, teenage boys eat so much of all kinds of food that their diets usually end up meeting their needs. Boys continue to grow until about age 19, so an active boy of 15, at the peak of his growth period, may need as many as 4,000 calories a day to maintain body weight.

It's different with girls, who stop growing at around age 15. A sedentary 16-year-old girl who has stopped growing may have to consume fewer than 2,000 calories per day to avoid being overweight. She has less leeway in eating empty calories. Calories she consumes from "junk" become calories taken away from the foods that supply the nutrients she needs.

Be aware of the special needs of teenagers: Teenagers need calcium in large quantities. In fact, during the teen years (11 through 18) the RDA for this nutrient increases by 50 percent, from 800 to 1,200 milligrams per day, a rise that is not hard to understand when you consider that a full 45 percent of the adult skeletal mass is formed during the teen years. Because of this increased need, teenagers should consume at least four servings of milk or milk products each day. Researchers have found that teenage girls and young women who drink milk with their meals have significantly denser bones when they reach middle age and are therefore resistant to osteoporosis. Low-fat or skim milk are the best choices.

Teens need plenty of iron, found in red meats, poultry, and fish, as well as in nuts and seeds. The RDA for iron increases by 80 percent from the elementary school years to the teenage years, rising from 10 milligrams to 15. Girls need extra iron to replace the iron they lose during the menstrual flow. Boys need more iron because the large increase in their tissue mass is accompanied by a rise in their levels of iron-containing hemoglobin.

Keep in mind that at the start of the teen years, the RDAs for all nutrients rise to at least adult levels. To meet their dietary needs, teenagers are advised to consume a variety of foods from the Food Guide Pyramid.

Every parent of teenagers knows that you have less control over their diets than when they were younger. But, in addition to having healthful foods around the house, you can be an educational force in your teen's life. Once again, if you avoid the "good/bad" distinctions about food and stress the point that there are more nutritional alternatives for every low-nutrient food, you'll be contributing practical data that will help your teen make better choices on his or her own.

Weighty Issues

The two most common dietary problems that afflict youth are obesity among children of all ages and anorexia nervosa (a syndrome of self-imposed starvation), the latter usually seen in girls after the onset of puberty.

If you are concerned that your child's eating habits and weight gain or loss are causing problems, your first step is to get him or her a thorough health examination. There are any number of factors that might cause changes in appetite and weight, and the doctor should rule these out before you look for nutritional solutions.

You should also be aware that psychological factors can contribute to extreme eating behaviors, and your child's medical treatment may need to be supplemented by some form of psychological counseling. Most important, remember that if your child has an eating disorder, criticism will not help. To constantly nag a child about eating, in an effort to convince him or her to "shape up," is rarely, if ever, effective.

Obesity: A Crisis for Our Youth

American children are getting too big for their britches—literally. According to the U.S. Department of Ariculture's Human Nutrition Center on Aging at Tufts University, 1 in 4 teens carries enough excess weight to put him or her at risk for suffering fatal heart attacks, strokes, colon cancer, gout, and other health problems later in life—whether or not the weight comes off in adulthood.

Our researchers studied the school health records of young children, tracked their weights and health through adolescence, and then continued to study them for another 55 years.

Specifically, teen boys about 20 pounds too heavy for their height were found to be twice as likely as their slimmer counterparts to have died or fallen victim to heart disease by age 70. The heavier boys also appeared more likely to suffer colon and rectal cancer as adults and were more likely to develop gout.

The overall risk for heavy adolescent girls was lower; they were no more likely to have died by age 70 than their thinner counterparts. Nevertheless, the researchers found a striking difference in overweight teenage girls' ability to function from day to day in old age. They became eight times more likely to have trouble walking a quarter of a mile, climbing stairs, and lifting heavy objects. In addition, their risk of developing arthritis later in life rose nearly twofold. This research concludes that being overweight in youth can be a serious lifetime risk factor for many ailments and should be treated as such.

Along with this increase in fat has come a rise in the number of children with high blood pressure, one of the major risk factors for heart disease. Obesity also puts children at greater risk for respiratory disease, diabetes, and a number of orthopedic disorders, as well as psychological and social problems.

How to Help an Overweight Child

If you think your child has a weight problem, have him or her checked by a doctor before trying to devise a weight-loss diet of your own. Many health professionals question the wisdom of weight-loss diets for children. It has been suggested that creating an obsessive atmosphere of denial might backfire later by leading to eating disorders. And not all apparent weight problems are what they seem to be. For example, it is normal for children's weight to fluctuate as they grow; don't overreact to a little plumpness, especially during puberty.

Also, before deciding that your child is overweight, examine your own attitudes about weight and diet. Americans have a thin-body bias that is at times unhealthy. When you communicate the thinness obsession to your children, you may be setting them up for a lifetime of dieting problems and even more severe eating disorders.

A case in point is a study reported by investigators at the University of California, San Francisco, which revealed that 81 percent of the nine-year-old girls surveyed were already dissatisfied with their weight and were dieting. This extreme reaction on the part of such young children is almost certainly due to the reinforcement of the American ideal that one cannot be too thin. It's a sad testimony to our values that we would set our children up in such a way.

Many of these girls will, no doubt, have eating problems all of their lives; some may develop severe eating disorders such as anorexia nervosa and bulimia (a disorder characterized by frequent binging and purging).

In light of these cautions, if you and your doctor agree that your child needs to get fit, design a regimen that is practical and nonrigid, and one that stresses increased activity over decreased food. Here are some guidelines:

◆ Gradually incorporate good nutritional techniques into your cooking. Making moderate changes will benefit the entire family while it teaches your child good eating habits in a flexible, nonmoralistic way.

◆ Treat your overweight child just like everyone else in the family with respect to food. For example, if you want to serve him or her fruit for dessert, don't serve cake to the other family members.

◆ Encourage your child to be active. Current figures issued by the President's Council of Physical Fitness and Sports show that two-thirds of our youth between the ages of 6 and 17 couldn't pass a basic fitness test. Regular exercise is the best way to promote fitness, and some studies indicate that it can be a more significant factor in preventing obesity than diet. Once again, get the entire family involved in active sports, walking, swimming, and other forms of exercise. You will all benefit.

◆ Serve occasional treats at the family meal; don't ban high-calorie foods altogether. If your child feels deprived, he or she will want to eat more. Place the emphasis on controlling portions, rather than on avoiding favorite foods.

◆ Look for ways you can send positive messages of support and encouragement to your child. Nagging, even with subtle looks and comments, won't motivate a child to eat more wisely. If you let your child know that your love for him or her is not tied to weight, your child will be more relaxed and open to making changes.

◆ Emphasize fitness over weight. Don't be "pound foolish." People tend to put too much value on what the scale says and not enough value on how they look and feel.

Encourage Exercise!

A contributing factor to obesity is the overall decline in physical exercise among American youth. Regular physical exercise not only increases your child's strength and coordination, it also boosts self-confidence and provides a release from stress. Studies even show that, on average, fit students do better in school than their comparatively sedentary peers. How do you best encourage your child to engage in physical activity? The American Academy of Pediatrics has set forth some practical guidelines, which vary according to age.

When it comes to infants, the academy points out that organized exercise programs do not confer any advantages. A baby's instinctive curiosity, along with opportunities to interact with other children and adults, will result in enough movement to achieve the necessary development and motor skills. The academy also points out that children younger than three or four years of age should not be enrolled in swimming programs, even those designed specifically for babies. Infants usually hold their breath instinctively if they are immersed accidentally, but they keep swallowing water, which in turn can be absorbed into the bloodstream in quantities sufficient to dilute the blood. The result is hyponatremia, a dangerously low concentration of sodium in the blood that can bring about seizures within a few hours of the time the baby leaves the pool. Parents who want to help a child get used to splashing in water should stay with him or her at all times and be sure to keep the child's head above the surface.

Once a child reaches the age of three or four, he or she should have regular opportunities to interact with other childen in neighborhood groups, preschool centers, or day care. Young children should be allowed to play freely and creatively rather than be expected to engage in organized activities designed by adults. Parents can, however, play with youngsters in active games like "hide and seek." Parents can also encourage their children to be active from early on by limiting television time to less than two hours a day.

After a child's sixth birthday, swimming lessons are an excellent type of exercise. Children of school age might want to get involved in team sports as well. However, the decision to participate in a certain sport or activity should be determined by a child's preference, not by an adult's. If a youngster is pressured to join a team or engage in a sport, he or she may resist and be less likely to succeed.

As for teenagers, they should understand that regular exercise can help them look and feel better, as well as stay healthier. But weight training and power lifting, usually engaged in by boys who have become body conscious and want to be bigger and stronger, should be discouraged until the child's body reaches full adult development (between ages 15 and 18). And all youth should be encouraged to take safety precautions, such as wearing helmets on bike rides and donning protective knee and elbow pads when using roller or in-line skates.

In 1995, former Surgeon General C. Everett Koop introduced Shape Up America! through his C. Everett Koop Foundation. The program is designed to teach Americans how to eat sensibly and exercise effectively. It's a program the whole family can try. The Shape Up America Guide, "On Your Way to Fitness," is free. Write to: Shape Up America, P.O. Box 9713, Bridgeport, CT 06699-9713. Enclose $1 for shipping and handling.

Teens Who Starve

You also have reason to be concerned if your child is not eating enough. Here, we do not refer to the occasional bouts of finicky eating that all children go through, but to young people (often preteen or teenage girls, but increasingly boys) who are suffering from the disease of anorexia nervosa.

Anorexia frequently starts near the time of puberty, when a young woman is undergoing a great many physical and psychological changes. As her body becomes more "womanly," she may experience embarrassment or fear and try to downplay the changes by staying thin. Or she may simply believe that she is getting fat. She becomes obsessed with diet and exercise in an effort to reach a thin ideal. (Another disease, bulimia, which involves a binge–purge response to eating, is also frequently the result of a weight obsession. However, bulimia occurs more often in young adult women than in young girls.)

Anorexia nervosa is a serious disease. Anorectics lose the ability to view themselves objectively. A girl who has reduced her weight to as little as 70 pounds might still regard herself as fat, even though she is literally starving herself to death. And a lengthy period of severe nutrient deficiency can have irreversible effects.

The muscle waste eventually affects the heart, and even some girls who have been treated and started eating again have died from the disease. One of the most famous cases is that of the singer Karen Carpenter, who suffered heart failure several months after she had started eating normally. If you suspect that your child might be suffering from anorexia, do not try to reason with her or force her to eat. She'll find ways to thwart your efforts. She needs immediate attention.

What are the early signs that your child may have a problem? These are the most common:

◆ Changes in eating behavior, such as alternating between binging and starving, obsession with dieting, frequent loss of appetite.

◆ Frequent weighing, inappropriate concern about losing weight, overexercising, use of diuretics or laxatives.

◆ Constipation, dry skin and hair, skin rashes, and sluggishness.

◆ Gradual but constant weight loss or the appearance of weight loss. (Anorectics can be wily; they may carry heavy objects in their pockets when being weighed, or drink large amounts of water to convince others that they've gained weight.)

◆ Depressed behavior, withdrawal or extreme sullenness, accompanied by any of the above symptoms.

If your teenager shows these signs, do not take a wait-and-see attitude. The consequences of anorexia nervosa are so severe that it's better to overreact than to underreact. Take your child to a medical doctor, as well as a psychologist. The physical disease must be treated first. Your doctor can recommend therapists who specialize in counseling anorectics. (For more details about anorexia nervosa and bulimia, contact one of the organizations that address these conditions listed in The Nutrition Hotline at the back of this book.)

Parents' attitudes matter, too. Studies show that teenage girls who feel that their parents always lecture them about eating and weight, rather than talking to them sensitively, are more prone to have problems with body image. For example, researchers at Concordia College in Moorhead, Minnesota, found when they asked 454 high school girls about their relationships with their parents that those who perceived their parents as critical were more inclined to have extreme desires for thinness, feelings of ineffectiveness, body dissatisfaction, fears of maturity, perfectionism, and interpersonal distrust—all traits associated with eating disorders.

Given the sensitivity of teenagers, parents can do well to monitor their own reactions and to encourage positive self-esteem in their youngsters.

Teens and Alcohol: A Worrisome Trend

Most of today's parents have some fears when it comes to their teenagers' experimenting with illegal drugs. They know that drugs are available in their communities, and there is plenty of peer pressure to experiment. But in their worry about drugs, parents may not be aware that alcohol is a drug, and that the potential for abuse runs extremely high. Although only about one in ten high school seniors has tried cocaine, nine out of ten have experimented with alcohol. And every two weeks, an estimated 40 percent of them consume five or more drinks in one sitting. Although teens receive consistent messages about the hazards of illegal drugs, they are given mixed messages about alcohol—most notably, that it's okay to use it as long as they aren't using other drugs or driving.

Adding to the confusion are liquor advertisements that highlight bikini-clad women, professional sports stars, surfers, and mountain climbers who make drinking look like the key to health, beauty, popularity, and happiness.

These ads are allowed to proliferate because

Diagnostic Criteria for Anorexia and Bulimia[1]

Anorexia Nervosa

a. Refusal to maintain body weight over a minimal normal weight for age and height—for example, weight loss leading to maintenance of body weight 15 percent below that expected; or failure to make expected weight gain during period of growth, leading to body weight 15 percent below that expected.

b. Intense fear of gaining weight or becoming fat, even though underweight.

c. Disturbance in the way in which one's body weight, size, or shape is experienced—for example, the person claims to "feel fat" even when emaciated or believes that one area of the body is "too fat" even when obviously underweight.

d. In females, absence of at least three consecutive menstrual cycles when these would otherwise be expected to occur (primary or secondary amenorrhea). A woman is considered to have amenorrhea if her periods occur only following administration of a hormone, such as estrogen.

Bulimia

a. Recurrent episodes of binge eating (rapid consumption of a large amount of food in a discrete period of time).

b. A feeling of lack of control over eating behavior during the eating binges.

c. Regular occurrence of self-induced vomiting, use of laxatives or diuretics, strict dieting or fasting, or vigorous exercise to prevent weight gain.

d. A minimum average of two binge eating episodes a week for at least 3 months.

e. Persistent overconcern with body shape and weight.

[1]Source: *Diagnostic and Statistical Manual of Mental Disorders,* 3rd edition, revised. American Psychiatric Association, 1987.

government regulation of alcohol advertising is fragmented, involving three different agencies—none of which has clear-cut authority to regulate advertising aimed at youth.

Until that day comes, parents of teenagers can make it a point to talk to their kids about alcohol and treat it with the same degree of seriousness with which they treat other drugs.

16

Women and Nutrition: Their Special Needs

Whether a woman bears children or not, from the time she reaches puberty until the onset of menopause, her body is constantly preparing to do so. The role women play in the propagation (and therefore survival) of the human race makes them very special in their nutritional needs. Indeed, even after menopause, a woman's health is affected by her previous childbearing potential. For example, osteoporosis, which becomes a problem for many women when they have passed the childbearing years, is associated with a decreased production of the hormone estrogen, which aids the metabolism of calcium. And there is strong evidence that estrogen protects women from heart disease, changing their nutritional imperatives after menopause when estrogen is depleted.

Here, we focus specifically on several key nutritional issues that women have during their childbearing years and beyond: the influence of a woman's general, prepregnancy health on her ability to conceive and bear a healthy child; the management of a successful pregnancy; the avoidance of ongoing problems, specifically premenstrual syndrome, that can plague her throughout her childbearing years; and the special nutritional issues that arise after menopause.

The Nutritional Key to Childbearing

It was not until the 1930s that serious research was started on maternal and child nutrition, with practitioners voicing the view that the mother's diet could substantially influence the birth weight and health of her baby. In 1946, the National Academy of Sciences appointed a Committee on Maternal Nutrition and Child Feeding. The committee's 1950 report, "Maternal Nutrition as It Relates to Child Health—An Interpretive Review," served as the basic guideline on the subject for many years. Maternal and infant nutrition was a major focus of the 1969 White House Conference on Food, Nutrition, and Health, directed by the late Dr. Jean Mayer, noted nutrition expert and former president of Tufts University. The conference panel on Pregnant and Nursing Women and Young Infants clearly identified a sound diet as a necessary factor in the birth of healthy infants. The panel concluded that good nutrition throughout the mother's life was the best way to promote infant health. During the following years, more specific guidelines were developed for the nutritional needs of pregnant women and infants.

In 1979, The Surgeon General's Report on

Health Promotion and Disease Prevention defined some broad goals for pregnancy and infant health to be achieved by 1990. These goals included a reduction in infant mortality, education of pregnant women about nutritional requirements and the dangers of alcohol, and an increase in the number of mothers choosing to breast-feed their babies. The 1988 Surgeon General's Report on Nutrition and Health included a chapter updating nutritional recommendations for mothers and children. Its guidelines have been adopted by the National Institutes of Health, medical scientists, and nutrition experts. A woman can manage her own and her child's health by paying attention to healthful eating, starting with the period before she becomes pregnant.

Getting Ready for Pregnancy

If you are a healthy woman of average weight with no preexisting medical condition, the best way to prepare for pregnancy is to eat a balanced diet, using the RDA guidelines and the Food Guide Pyramid. However, if you are either dramatically underweight or obese, you should address this condition before becoming pregnant.

When it comes to pregnancy, it is possible to be too thin, because the fat stores in the hips and thighs are needed to nourish the fetus in the later months of pregnancy and for breast milk. It is ironic that the American ideal, which during the past twenty years has increasingly moved away from the "womanly" figure, is really at odds with the biological wisdom of giving women more generous hips and thighs. A woman with too little body fat—for example, an anorectic or, in some cases, an athlete—would have a difficult time bearing a healthy child of normal birth weight. For this reason, women's bodies sometimes intervene to make it more unlikely that they will become pregnant. That is why menstrual periods sometimes cease in anorectic women or in women who diet and exercise too

heavily. The same phenomenon occurs in conditions of famine, when women become less likely to conceive. Their bodies "recognize" that the famine condition makes it impossible to support the growth of a normal fetus, or to produce the milk a newborn baby needs to survive.

Obesity can also lead to problems in pregnancy. It is linked with an increased risk of complications to the mother, including hypertensive disorders, gestational diabetes, toxemia, urinary tract infections, and the need for cesarean deliveries. An obese woman—that is, one who is 30 percent or more above her recommended healthy weight—should plan to reduce her weight gradually *before* becoming pregnant, because weight loss during pregnancy has been associated with low birth weight. Studies have shown that when weight is not gained during pregnancy, even in obese women, infants suffer low birth weight. For example, one study showed that out of a group of pregnant, overweight women, infants born to those who gained the least weight had double the infant mortality rate of babies born to mothers who had higher gain.

Adolescent pregnancies pose greater risks for both the mothers and their infants. According to the American Academy of Pediatrics' Committee on Nutrition, mothers who are 15 years old or younger (approximately 60,000 every year in the United States) have increased rates of pregnancy-induced hypertension and premature delivery. They are also more likely to deliver infants with low birth weights and have higher rates of fetal loss and infant mortality.

Weight Gain During Pregnancy

In recent years, nutrition and medical experts have revised their estimates of how much weight a woman should gain during pregnancy. Once, it was believed that weight gain should not exceed 18 pounds and was better if kept between 10 and 15 pounds. Today, most obstetricians believe that a weight gain of between

22 and 27 pounds is acceptable.

Further, most experts believe that the pattern of weight gain during pregnancy is as important as the total amount. Although each woman will have her own pattern, the goal should be a slow, steady gain. So, for instance, if you gain a large amount one month, you should not panic and start to cut back on your intake. The main thing to watch out for is sudden, unexplained jump in weight, which could be the result of fluid retention—a sign of toxemia and a serious problem if not treated promptly.

Should a woman who is carrying twins eat (and gain) twice as much? Although very little research has been conducted on the needs of a mother carrying twins, a study done at Grady Memorial Hospital in Atlanta showed that out of 137 twin pregnancies, the healthiest babies were born to mothers who gained about 41 pounds during the typical 36-week pregnancy term. Sherri Carlton, M.Sc., R.D., who led the study team, believes that tall or thin women who are expecting twins should gain somewhat more than that. She also says that the need for folic acid and protein appears to be greater for twin pregnancies, although the exact increment is not yet known.

Where does the additional weight go? Many women are surprised after delivery to discover how little of their added weight actually is accounted for by the weight of the baby. For example, a woman who gains 27 pounds during pregnancy will usually find that the added weight breaks down this way: 7 pounds is baby; 3 pounds is the increase in the size of the breasts and uterus; 9 pounds is contributed by a combination of the placenta, amniotic fluid, extra blood volume, and other fluids; and 7 pounds is body fat, usually in the hips and thighs, as a reserve for the mother who breast-feeds.

Keeping Fit During Pregnancy

It is best to consult with your physician before planning an exercise regimen for your preg-

nancy because women with certain health risks or medical conditions may be advised not to exercise. However, the American College of Obstetricians and Gynecologists has recommended a number of exercises suitable for pregnant women, including walking, swimming, stationary cycling, and modified forms of low-impact aerobic exercises, dancing, and calisthenics. When exercising, be sure that your heart rate does not exceed 140 beats a minute, and do not engage in strenuous activity for more than 15 minutes at a time.

It is also recommended that pregnant women practice deep-breathing exercises and gentle stretching; these will help during the delivery process.

Avoid Dangerous Substances

Health researchers are in agreement that alcohol consumption during pregnancy might adversely affect fetal development. The condition, called Fetal Alcohol Syndrome, was first discovered in the early 1970s among infants whose mothers were chronic alcoholics. The effects of the syndrome were severe, including abnormalities of the eyes, nose, heart, and central nervous system. Further, these infants suffered the pains of alcohol withdrawal and normally showed impaired mental and physical development, even after rehabilitation.

The lack of awareness about Fetal Alcohol Syndrome is troubling. Although many adults know the dangers of drinking alcohol during the first trimester of pregnancy, a national survey suggests that few know that pregnant women should also abstain from alcohol during the second and third trimesters. According to the ARC, the country's largest volunteer organization devoted to improving the lives of mentally retarded people, drinking during the later stages of pregnancy can cause brain damage to the baby. In fact, the organization found that Fetal Alcohol Syndrome is the leading cause of preventable mental retardation, which affects more than 5,000 babies born each year. Although the minimum level of alcohol that can lead to Fetal Alcohol Syndrome is not yet known, some studies have shown that as little as a drink or two a day might lead to spontaneous abortion, premature detachment of the placenta, or infants born with low birth weights. Although other studies contradict these claims, the Surgeon General has recommended in his 1988 report that, to be on the safe side, pregnant women avoid alcohol completely.

As we noted earlier, caffeine is another substance that pregnant women should view with caution. Although the National Institutes of Health has reported that there is no firm link between caffeine consumption and impaired fetal development, the recent study by Montreal University–affiliated Sainte-Justine Hospital suggested that drinking as little as a cup and a half to two cups of coffee a day could double the risk of miscarriage. And three to four daily cups could triple the risk. This study supported earlier results of a study conducted with pregnant rats who, when given large amounts of caffeine, showed impaired development of fetuses. However, the study has been criticized because the amounts of caffeine fed to the rats were considered to be unnaturally high.

It's true that studies on humans have not proved conclusive. One study of 20,000 pregnant women showed that coffee drinking has little or no effect on fetal health. However, another study of 5,200 women reported lower birth weights in babies born to women who consumed five or more cups of coffee a day.

Even though researchers have not yet reached a firm understanding of the effects of caffeine on pregnancy, it can be argued that, because the caffeine does pass on to the fetus through the placenta, limiting your consumption is probably a good idea during pregnancy. In fact, the Food and Drug Administration has advised cutting back on caffeine as a precautionary measure.

Gestational Diabetes: A Special Concern

Gestational diabetes, a special form of the disease, occurs in between 1 and 2 percent of all pregnancies. It appears between the sixth and seventh months, when the mother's pancreas cannot meet the demands of the pregnancy. The condition is most common among women who have family histories of diabetes, who have previously given birth to babies weighing more than 10 pounds, or who have a condition of "sugar in the urine" during pregnancy. Insulin resistance (a drop in the efficiency with which insulin is utilized) is linked both to the rising levels of several hormones and to increased weight.

Gestational diabetes can cause health problems both for the mother and the baby. The pregnant woman suffers an increased risk of hypertension. And, because infants of mothers with gestational diabetes tend to be large, they are more likely to be delivered by cesarean section. Such infants suffer an increased chance of respiratory-distress syndrome, and they are more likely to be hypoglycemic.

Even if no risk factors exist, the American Diabetes Association recommends that all women be checked for abnormal glucose tolerance between the sixth and seventh months of pregnancy. The test involves drinking a single dose of a glucose solution, after which blood sugar levels are measured. If the levels remain abnormally high, further testing is required.

Often gestational diabetes can be successfully treated by making changes in the diet. The goal is to normalize blood sugar, and, for some women, this can be accomplished by controlling food intake.

Gestational diabetes usually disappears after pregnancy, although women who have had the condition are at a higher risk for developing Type II diabetes, particularly if they are obese.

Cravings and Morning Sickness

Most people take it for granted that pregnant women will have strange cravings, although they probably think these cravings are "all in the head." In fact, there are two common types of cravings that affect pregnant women.

The first and most common craving is the proverbial "ice cream and pickles" syndrome, wherein women desire unusual amounts of certain foods, or offbeat combinations of foods, such as salty foods along with sweets. These women commonly feel an aversion to some foods: in particular, coffee, tea, alcohol, and meat. Usually these cravings seem to have nothing to do with nutritional needs.

A second type of craving is more rare. Known as "pica," this craving involves a strong desire to eat nonfood items such as cornstarch, laundry starch, or clay. Although such cravings have been described since biblical times, they remain a tantalizing mystery. We do know that pica is most common among pregnant women who suffer from iron-deficiency anemia. How this craving might be linked to the need for the mineral is not fully understood.

Another factor of concern for pregnant women who are interested in meeting their nutritional needs is the onset of "morning sickness," or bouts of nausea, which can occur at any time during the day. Half of all pregnant women are afflicted by this ailment, usually between the second and fourth months of pregnancy. For as many as 10 to 20 percent of pregnant women, symptoms of morning sickness persist for the entire pregnancy.

Morning sickness is a real physiological ailment, but, disturbingly, as many as half of all obstetricians believe it to be psychosomatic. As recently as 1988, a U.S. government publication said, "It is thought that emotional factors, such as ambivalence about pregnancy, may play a role if vomiting persists into the second trimester." But science suggests otherwise, linking morning sickness with a positive pregnancy outcome rather than ambivalance about having a baby. Consider that after looking at the records of some 9,000 mothers-to-be, researchers at the National Institutes of Health found that those who reported throwing up during their pregnancies were a little less likely to suffer miscarriages or stillbirths than women who said they didn't vomit.

Although it is not known exactly what causes the nausea, some scientists speculate it is the body's reaction to the surge of hormones, including estrogen, that accompanies a healthy pregnancy. One theory is that this hormone surge enhances the sense of smell to the point that background odors in the environment become particularly potent, making women queasy. These women may find relief by ventilating their living spaces well.

Another theory is that morning sickness is linked with a drop in blood sugar. Many women experience it most intensely upon waking; for them, it helps to eat a couple of dry crackers right away. It also helps to eat small meals throughout the day and never allow oneself to get too hungry, and to drink liquids separately instead of with meals.

Pregnant women also complain of other digestive maladies, such as heartburn and constipation. It is best to take care of these problems by concentrating on a high-fiber diet and by eliminating spicy, greasy, or rich foods.

Growing a Healthy Child

During pregnancy, it is most important to be sure that you are eating a well-balanced diet, in accordance with the Recommended Dietary Allowances for pregnant women. Even if you are consuming adequate calories, your diet must reflect the proper nutrient balance or it could severely affect the health of your baby. Consider that during the approximately nine months of pregnancy, a baby's bone structure and tissue development are taking place.

Although there are difficulties in quantifying

the effects of pregnancy and lactation on nutritional requirements for calories and individual nutrients, it is accepted by all knowledgeable people that pregnant and breast-feeding women have additional nutritional needs. Not only must the women meet their own needs, they also must meet those of their infants during fetal growth and early infancy. Pregnancy and lactation may affect the nutrient requirements of women by altering their physiological and metabolic states.

To ensure that pregnant and lactating women receive sufficient nutrients, the RDA values have been increased for them (see Chapter 7). For example, the RDA for protein is increased 65 percent, and those for vitamin D and folacin are 100 percent higher.

Dietary Guidelines: Getting Enough Nutrients

Protein

Protein needs during pregnancy and breast-feeding (lactation) are substantially higher than normal. To supply enough protein, eat an additional 1 to 2 ounces of any of these foods three or four times each day: meat, poultry, fish, or cheese.

Vitamin C

One cup of orange juice, broccoli, red or green pepper, grapefruit juice, strawberries, brussels sprouts, cauliflower, dark greens, or one orange will each come close to meeting the RDA for pregnancy.

Thiamin, Niacin, and Riboflavin

Six to eleven daily servings or enriched or whole-grain breads, cereals, rice, crackers, or pasta will meet the requirement for pregnant women. Lactating women should add one serving.

Vitamin B-6

Good sources include liver, light-meat chicken, bananas, and navy beans. A three-ounce serving of each provides close to 20 percent of the RDA for pregnant and lactating women. Other good sources include tuna, halibut, avocados, peanuts, beef, and salmon.

Folic Acid (Folacin)

To help meet the doubled RDA for pregnancy, eat at least one to two cups a day of these folacin-rich vegetables: spinach, turnip greens, endive, dark-green lettuce, asparagus, okra, broccoli, parsnips, cauliflower, peas, brussels sprouts, or cabbage. Lactating women's needs are closer to the average for nonpregnant women—only 100 mg more per day. But it is a good idea to include one of these foods in the diet each day while breast-feeding.

Calcium

About four servings of milk products are recommended for each day. A serving is an 8-ounce glass of low-fat or whole milk or buttermilk, 1 cup of yogurt, 1 ounce of hard or American cheese, 2 cups of cottage cheese, or 1 cup of ice cream or ice milk. You can also substitute 8 ounces of tofu made from a calcium coagulant such as calcium sulfate, 2 cups of broccoli, or 4 ounces of salmon (with soft bones).

Zinc and Iron

Even if you're taking an iron supplement, you should not ignore good sources in food, in part because most are also high in zinc. Both iron and zinc are available in animal foods, including red meats, organ meats, seafood (especially shellfish), and poultry. Fortified breads and cereals, as well as nuts and legumes, may carry extra iron, but rarely zinc. Milk is a good source of zinc, but not of iron.

Are Dietary Supplements Needed?

Many obstetricians routinely recommend prenatal multivitamin/mineral supplements to their pregnant patients as a safety precaution, just in case they're not getting adequate nutrients in their diets. But other physicians disagree, feeling that multivitamin/mineral supplements are unnecessary.

One nutrient that virtually all physicians think is necessary as a supplement during pregnancy is iron. Because a large percentage of what is ingested isn't absorbed, anywhere from 30 to 60 milligrams of iron are suggested to assure that women absorb the 3.5 milligrams they need. Until recently, there was little information on the availability of iron to the body when it was given in the form of prenatal multivitamin/mineral supplements, which typically contain about 60 milligrams of iron, along with many other vitamins and minerals. But when a number of their pregnant patients developed iron deficiency even though they were taking daily prenatal supplements, Paul Seligman, M.D., and his colleagues at the University of Colorado Health Sciences Center became suspicious and decided to research the matter. They gave nonpregnant healthy women either iron supplements alone or iron in the form of prenatal multivitamin/mineral supplements. Of the four different brands of vitamin/mineral supplements tested, fewer than the needed 3.5 milligrams of iron were absorbed in each case. When 65 milligrams of supplemental iron alone were given, 8.1 milligrams were absorbed. Further examination showed that the reason so little iron was absorbed in the multivitamin/mineral preparations was largely that the calcium carbonate and magnesium oxide in some of them interfered with iron absorption. When the researchers reformulated the supplements to contain less calcium and magnesium, 4.5 milligrams of iron were absorbed. But the calcium carbonate and magnesium oxide did

not account for all of the decrease in iron absorption. The researchers believe that additional factors, such as fillers, other vitamins and minerals, or the coating and compressing of the nutrients might also have played a role.

Dr. Seligman and his colleagues also had their subjects take the supplements on empty stomachs, because iron absorption may be as much as 75 percent less when the supplements are taken with meals.

Nutrition During the Menstruating Years

It has been known since ancient times that in the days preceding menstruation each month, some women experience a variety of symptoms ranging in intensity from unpleasant to debilitating. But the medical community did not seriously begin to consider Premenstrual Syndrome (PMS) a clinical disorder until 1931, when a physician named Robert T. Frank called it a syndrome of "indescribable tension and irritability." The symptoms, said Dr. Frank, were relieved with the onset of menstruation.

Although the definition of PMS has grown more sophisticated since 1931, much remains unknown about the syndrome. It is generally recognized as a set of physical and/or emotional symptoms that begin every month after ovulation and end abruptly with the start of the menstrual flow. For some women, the syndrome lasts for the entire two weeks or so from ovulation to menstruation. For others, it appears for only a few days, or even for just one day, before the period begins. But it is this cyclical pattern—the timing of the symptoms—that defines PMS, more than the nature of the symptoms themselves, which range considerably in nature and severity from woman to woman. More than 150 PMS symptoms have been described. The most common include tension, depression, irritability, inability to concentrate, crying spells, headaches, breast tenderness, bloating, weight gain, acne, clumsiness, and cravings for chocolate or other sweet or salty foods.

Unfortunately, some physicians still consider PMS a neurotic condition rather than a clinical syndrome caused by an altered endocrinologic state. As more information becomes available on PMS, physicians may reach a consensus on its treatment as a medical condition.

The Misleading Nutrition-PMS Connection

At this time, no well-conducted clinical trials establish a direct relationship between nutrition and PMS. An added difficulty is the fact that the symptoms of PMS cannot be objectively viewed on X-rays or in lab tests. Only the woman herself can say whether she feels better.

Of special concern to physicians and nutritionists is the proliferation of expensive and potentially harmful supplements and other "remedies" that have flooded the marketplace. We know that these remedies are not based on scientific studies. So how do the proponents reach their conclusions? Usually, an isolated nutritional factor is used as the basis for conclusions that, in a scientific setting, would not be acceptable. In other cases, the conclusions are simply quackery. There is no evidence to support them—only questionable anecdotal references and hefty marketing budgets.

It is important that consumers understand the truth behind these claims. Not only are some of the remedies expensive, but they can also cause severe problems, ranging from stomach irritation to calcium deficiency to nerve damage. These are the most popular theories:

THEORY 1: VITAMIN B-6 DEFICIENCY

The vitamin B-6 deficiency theory is perhaps the most widely held theory and has been making the rounds since the 1940s. Proponents claim that a deficiency of B-6 is somehow related to hormonal imbalance, in particular an imbalance of estrogen, which leads to depression or dramatic mood swings. In spite of there being no evidence that women with PMS have estrogen imbalances or B-6 deficiencies, practitioners prescribe megadoses of the vitamin. In some instances, the recommended levels have been as high as 2,000 milligrams a day, 1,000 times the RDA of 2 milligrams.

Because B-6 is a water-soluble vitamin, it is believed that any excess amounts in the system will simply be excreted in urine and therefore cause no harm to the body. But research has shown that even doses much lower than 2,000 milligrams a day can cause damage to the nervous system, resulting in numbness, tingling, difficulty in walking, and spinal cord problems. These symptoms have developed in women who have taken as little as 500 milligrams a day. Indeed, one woman suffered symptoms after taking only 200 milligrams a day over the course of three years. From a scientific point of view, supplements of vitamin B-6 have never proven to be more effective than a placebo, in spite of their popularity.

THEORY 2: A NEED FOR EVENING PRIMROSE OIL

Some people believe that victims of PMS do not have enough of the enzyme needed to produce a fatty acid called gamma linolenic acid, leading to a deficiency in a very active biochemical called prostaglandin E-1. This deficiency, they think, may be involved in PMS symptoms such as breast tenderness. Their solution is oral ingestion of evening primrose oil, sometimes sold as Efamol, which they say contains the missing fatty acid and allows the balance to be restored.

Besides the fact that evening primrose oil, widely sold in health food stores, is expensive, it has never been demonstrated that a prostaglandin deficiency is what causes PMS symptoms or that any oil given in supplement form will correct such a deficiency. And evening primrose oil has never been shown to relieve any of the discomfort, physical or emotional, of PMS. It can, however, cause gastric irritation if taken on an empty stomach.

THEORY 3: TOO MUCH CALCIUM, TOO LITTLE MAGNESIUM

Some experts have observed that some women with Premenstrual Syndrome have lower levels of the mineral magnesium than women who do not suffer from PMS. Therefore, the possibility exists that the condition may have something to do with a magnesium deficiency. According to the theory, the deficiency develops in part because of too much calcium consumption in the form of dairy products. Calcium is transported through part of the gastrointestinal tract via the same carrier that transports magnesium. Thus, calcium competes with magnesium for absorption and leaves a woman with a magnesium shortfall. The supposed solution is to take a magnesium supplement.

The hitch is that although some women with PMS were found to have lower levels of magnesium in their blood cells than symptom-free women, their levels were still within normal range. The fact is that other than in cases of alcoholism or a malabsorption disorder, women of childbearing age in the United States generally have no trouble getting enough magnesium from the animal foods, nuts, seeds, legumes, green vegetables, whole-grain products, and milk they consume.

The real problem in taking megadoses of magnesium is that a woman can, in fact, impair her absorption of calcium by consuming too much magnesium. Furthermore, in very high doses, magnesium can be toxic. And magnesium salts like those in Milk of Magnesia will act as laxatives—even if you're not looking for that effect.

The bottom line is that the "miracle" remedies won't cure PMS and might lead to serious problems. But a well-balanced, healthful diet will at least ensure that PMS sufferers are getting all the nutrients they need.

The Yogurt–Yeast Infection Connection

At least once in their lifetimes, more than half of all women suffer the itching, burning irritation, and white cheesy discharge characteristic of a vaginal yeast infection. For one in ten women, the problem becomes chronic, occurring on the order of five or more times a year. Doctors usually recommend treatment with antifungal medications such as Gyne-Lotrimin or Monistat 7 (sold over the counter), but folklore has long held that simply eating yogurt can prevent the problem from occurring in the first place.

To put that folklore to the test, researchers at New York's Long Island Jewish Medical Center monitored a group of women with chronic yeast infections for a year. For six months, the women followed a yogurt-free diet, and the second six months they included 8 ounces of yogurt daily. The result: While consuming yogurt every day, the women experienced a threefold decrease in the number of infections.

The researchers believed that the improvement may be traced to live bacterium present in yogurt. Called Lactobacillus acidophilus, this "good" bacterium is believed to survive the passage from the mouth through the gastrointestinal tract and eventually to the vagina, where it helps by "crowding out" the yeast fungus responsible for the infection.

Although the results are promising, yogurt has not yet been identified as a proven treatment for yeast infections. Women should also keep in mind that most commercial yogurts do not contain the good bacteria because they are killed during the pasteurization process; it's important to read the labels. Women should also be cautious about self-diagnosis and self-treatment. The fact is, unless a doctor examines a woman and analyzes a sample of her vaginal discharge, there is no way to know for certain whether she is suffering from a yeast infection or from something else. A condition that resembles a yeast infection may actually be caused by certain strains of "bad" bacteria rather than yeast and therefore require a different treatment. In some cases, recurrent yeast infections may signal a more serious problem, such as a disorder of the immune system that would go undetected—and untreated—without a medical examination.

Cranberry Juice May Prevent Urinary Tract Infections

A new report by a group of Boston scientists provides evidence that the folk wisdom about cranberry juice's ability to prevent infections of the urinary tract may actually be grounded in scientific fact.

Researchers looked at two groups of elderly women whose urine commonly contains bacteria and white blood cells—signs that an infection may be taking hold even if there are no symptoms. One group drank 10 ounces of cranberry juice a day while the other consumed the same amount of a "placebo" beverage that looked and tasted the same but contained no cranberry juice. After about six weeks, the percentage of juice drinkers with bacteria and white blood cells in their urine dropped and remained low for the duration of the six-month study. The placebo group showed no change.

The popular presumption about cranberry juice's role in fighting urinary tract infections is that it makes urine more acidic. The theory goes that because the bacteria that cause the infections are unlikely to flourish in an acid environment, drinking the acid-producing juice helps prevent the problem. But studies have failed to prove that theory. In fact, in the new study, cranberry juice drinkers' urine was actually less acidic than the urine of their placebo-drinking counterparts.

The latest theory is that a substance in cranberry juice keeps the problem bacteria from clinging to the wall of the urinary tract, where they can multiply and cause such symptoms as painful urination. A few years ago, a group of Israeli researchers tested seven juices and found that blueberry and cranberry juice contained a substance that seems to interfere with bacteria's ability to "stick." This is not to say that people with urinary tract infections should self-prescribe cranberry juice instead of seeing a doctor for treatment with antibiotics. However, it is possible that cranberry juice may become a useful secondary treatment in conjunction with antibiotics.

Good Nutrition for Menopausal Women

Menopause is not actually an "event" in a woman's life. Rather, it is a period of time, typically between the mid-forties and mid-fifties, that marks the end of a woman's childbearing years. With the onset of menopause, a woman's production of estrogen declines, and this changes her nutritional needs. In particular, women at menopause and beyond are at a greatly increased risk of heart disease and osteoporosis, two conditions affected by estrogen loss.

Estrogen levels affect more than just fertility. There is an important effect on other tissues. Indeed, there are estrogen receptors in nearly every tissue in the body. That means that a woman's ovaries are not a separate entity; rather, they are related to every other organ system—the cardiovascular system, the skeletal system, the urogenital tissue, the brain, the colon, and the immune system.

A growing body of scientific evidence supports a link between estrogen and protection against heart disease—one reason why women typically do not get the diease before menopause. There is also strong evidence that estrogen replacement therapy (ERT) results in a highly significant decline in the risk for heart disease in postmenopausal women. Studies have shown that estrogen inhibits the incorporation of cholesterol into the vessel wall of the heart, raising HDL and lowering LDL blood cholesterol. Estrogen also increases the dilation of the blood vessels and makes them less spasticky.

The decision to take hormone replacement therapy at menopause must be made in conjunction with a medical professional. Some women, particularly those with family histories of breast or endometrial cancer, may be poor candidates for this treatment.

If you're concerned about the potential health risks of estrogen replacement therapy, consider new research into plant substances. Plant foods also have hormones, called phytoestrogens, which are a weaker version of human estrogen. Current research suggests that if phytoestrogens are consumed in large enough amounts, they might have a profound effect on certain cancers, as well as menopausal symptoms. Phytoestrogens may ultimately prove to be an effective alternative to estrogen replacement therapy, particularly for women with a high risk of breast or uterine cancer.

In the meantime, there is convincing evidence that phytoestrogens—found most potently in soy products—may help alleviate some of the symptoms such as hot flashes, night sweats, mood swings, and vaginal dryness that often accompany menopause.

In addition to hormone replacement therapy, women can protect themselves from heart disease by following the guidelines in Chapter 18. And they can avoid the frailty that afflicts so many older women by considering the factors described in the following section.

Preventing Osteoporosis in Later Life

Osteoporosis, or loss of bone mass, is universal in all people as they age. It is estimated that 15 to 20 million Americans currently suffer from the problem. Osteoporosis is a particularly severe condition that leaves the skeleton abnormally fragile. Each year the condition is responsible for about 1.3 million fractures of the vertebrae, hips, forearms, and other bones of people who are 45 years old or older. All people lose bone mass as they age. Bones reach their peak density about the age of 30, then begin to decline. At maturity, men have more bone density than women, and blacks more than whites.

Postmenopausal women are at greatest risk for developing the disease because their protective levels of the hormone estrogen have declined. Following the onset of menopause, declining estrogen levels can lead to a rapid loss of bone mass.

The development of osteoporosis is hard to track because there are usually no symptoms of bone loss until the condition actually becomes a problem. Once it becomes detectable on X-rays, as much as 50 percent of bone loss may have occurred already. And once bone is lost, it cannot be replenished. In that respect, osteoporosis cannot be "cured." The focus of action must be on prevention.

Intense public attention has been devoted to the calcium–osteoporosis connection in recent years. Few scientists believe that the disease is simply a case of calcium deficiency that can be halted by consuming large quantities of calcium-rich foods and/or supplements. Osteoporosis is far more complex than that. Calcium deficiency is only one of several factors, including genetics, hormone levels, exercise, lifestyle, and general nutrition, that may lead to the condition. The casual assumption that calcium alone can eliminate the risk for osteoporosis has proved to be lucrative for many food manufacturers who have added the mineral to their products, and for the producers of nutrient supplements. (Sales of calcium supplements total more than $200 million a year.) But a serious review of the causes and preventions of osteoporosis must include a comprehensive analysis of all the factors. For example, certain other nutrients are needed to assure proper absorption of calcium; without these, even large quantities of calcium may be ineffective.

Further, there is evidence that exercise may play an important role in osteoporosis prevention. There are also genetic factors that place certain individuals and populations at greater risk for developing the disease. For example, thin women and women with small bone structures seem to be at greater risk than larger, big-boned women. Also, Caucasian and Asian women appear to be at greater risk than blacks. There's also a family connection. Women who have a history of osteoporosis in their families suffer a greater risk.

A Complex Nutritional Picture

Calcium is the key player in the formation and maintenance of the body's bones and teeth, which contain 99 percent of the body's calcium. It stands to reason that a sufficient supply of calcium is needed for building and maintaining the skeleton. But studies of the effects of dietary calcium on osteoporosis are relatively new, and they are complicated by the need to evaluate not just the amount of calcium consumed but how much of that calcium is absorbed and retained by the body.

The factors that influence calcium absorption and utilization include the physical and chemical form of the calcium that is consumed, the way that calcium interacts with other nutrients, the way that calcium is transported through and maintained in the body, and the way it is excreted by the kidneys.

Our body's ability to absorb calcium is influenced by the interaction of a variety of nutrients. The most important of these is vitamin D, which is converted to a hormone called calcitriol, which regulates the transport of calcium from the digestive tract to the bloodstream and its deposition into bone. However, this does not mean that large amounts of vitamin D will make a difference. Scientists have found that calcium absorption is enhanced by a "normal" intake of the vitamin. Patients who were given supplement doses of vitamin D in quantities of 50,000 to 150,000 IU (international units) per week showed no measurable improvement. Furthermore, vitamin D is potentially toxic in megadoses; it can lead to calcium deposits in the kidneys, blood vessels, heart, and lungs. Toxicity has been reported at dosages ranging from 10,000 IU per day taken for four months, to 200,000 IU per day taken over a period of two weeks. New research shows, however, that women who live in areas with less sunlight should eat more vitamin D-rich foods and consume more than the RDA of 200 International Units.

Next to calcium, phosphorus is the most abundant mineral in our bodies. Bone consists of salts of calcium and phosphorus. Too much or too little dietary phosphorus may have a harmful effect on bone formation.

Another critical dietary factor is protein. Because much of the protein we consume is channeled into tissue (including bone) growth and maintenance, an adequate intake of protein is essential for prevention of bone loss. However, too much protein might be a contributing factor in the development of osteoporosis because it increases the amount of calcium excreted in the urine.

High sodium intakes can also increase the amount of calcium lost in the urine, and massive fiber intakes can interfere with calcium absorption. Also, because bone is made up of many elements, they all contribute to the way calcium is utilized in the body. Among these, fluoride has attracted the most attention, because some data indicate that the bones of people raised on fluoridated water may be denser than those whose access to fluroide has been limited.

The Best Way to Meet Calcium Needs

The current RDA for calcium is 1,200 milligrams for persons 11 to 24 years old, who need larger amounts during the period of growth and bone development, and 800 milligrams for other adults.

Heightened interest in the osteoporosis–calcium connection has led to heavy marketing of calcium supplements, as well as to the frequent fortification of foods that do not naturally contain the mineral. The supermarket shelves are filled with calcium-fortified foods, including orange juice, flour, bread, cereal, and even milk. Many people are convinced that it is a good idea to buy calcium-fortified products whenever they can, as well as to take calcium supplements, just to be sure they're getting what they need.

Scientists are not certain to what extent calcium-fortified foods protect against osteoporosis or how effectively the calcium is absorbed and used by the body. Nor are they certain how added calcium affects other nutrients. Some tests have shown that postmenopausal women who take calcium supplements but do not also have hormone replacement therapy receive little or no benefit from calcium alone.

There are also a number of problems with the calcium supplements on the market today. As discussed in Chapter 6, many calcium supplements contain very little calcium. The best source, calcium carbonate, is only 40 percent calcium. Some people may need to take a calcium carbonate supplement if they are unable to reach the RDA level with diet alone. However, it also appears that consuming too much calcium carbonate can have the opposite-than-intended effect. Researchers at the Vitamin D and Bone Metabolism Laboratory at the Tufts USDA Center on Aging have found that, in high doses, calcium carbonate may actually lower the levels of calcitriol, leading to incomplete absorption of the calcium consumed.

To place the issue in context, it must be understood that the reason the medical and health communities have been talking up calcium is not that they have seen the need for people to consume it in larger quantities in supplement form. The emphasis is placed on encouraging people regularly to include high calcium sources in their diets. The average calcium consumption of women over age 50 in the United States is only about one-half the requirement. Calcium-rich foods are readily available in the American diet. For example, the following foods each contain between 300 and 350 milligrams, or slightly more than one-third the RDA:

8 oz. skim, low-fat, or whole milk
8 oz. buttermilk
1 cup non-fat or low-fat or whole-milk yogurt
2 cups non-fat or low-fat or whole-milk cottage cheese
1 cup part-skim ricotta cheese
1 cup ice milk or ice cream
1 oz. cheddar cheese
1 slice American cheese
2 oz. sardines with bones
4 oz. salmon with bones

Calcium is also found in a number of vegetables, but in much smaller amounts. It would be hard to meet the daily requirement for calcium with vegetables alone. For example, one-half cup of cooked mustard greens supplies only about 100 milligrams of calcium, and one-half cup of cooked broccoli supplies only 68 milligrams.

Further, there is some evidence that the calcium in certain foods may be poorly absorbed by the body. For example, studies now show that spinach, once thought to be an excellent source of the mineral (139 milligrams in one-half cup, cooked), may not be absorbed at a great enough level to be of much benefit. A group of scientists at Creighton University's Hard Tissue Research Center in Nebraska and at the Department of Foods and Nutrition at Purdue University in Indiana gave a group of men and women spinach and then traced the route its calcium took inside their bodies. They found that only about 5 percent of the mineral was absorbed. The rest was tied up by the oxalic acid contained in spinach and was excreted.

COUNTING CALCIUM

Even those who are not dairy lovers have a variety of foods to choose from in order to take in adequate amounts of calcium. Check out the calcium sources below to determine for yourself how to make bone building taste good.

	Calcium (mg)
low-fat fruit flavored yogurt, 1 cup	314
skim (non-fat) milk, 1 cup	302
Swiss cheese, 1 oz	205
canned salmon with the bones, 3 oz	203
canned sardines in tomato sauce, 3	273
cooked, chopped broccoli, 1 cup	94
boiled kale, ½ cup	90
boiled navy beans, ½ cup	64
dried figs, 3	81
medium orange, 1	50
ice cream, ½ cup	
Borden	80
Breyer	100
Sealtest	100
frozen yogurt, ½ cup	
Ben & Jerry's, low fat	135
Columbo non-fat Slender Scoops	100
raw tofu (firm) with calcium sulfate or calcium lactate, ½ cup	258[1]
Sunny Delight Plus Calcium Florida Citrus Punch, ½ cup	125

[1]Calcium content varies widely by brand. Check labels.

Preventing Osteoporosis: Start Young

Even though postmenopausal women are at greatest risk for developing the disease, it does not necessarily stand to reason that women should start taking larger amounts of calcium as they get older. For older women with osteoporosis, estrogen replacement therapy might be of greater benefit than calcium supplements.

Estrogen is important to the normal utilization of calcium in women. Some researchers believe that adding estrogen, not calcium, is the best way to halt the disease.

In one study, reported in the *New England Journal of Medicine*, researchers in Denmark divided women into three groups. The first group was composed of women who received estrogen replacement therapy for osteoporosis; the second group was composed of women who received 2,000 milligrams of supplemental calcium each day; and the third group was composed of women taking placebos. Researchers studied the changes in calcium metabolism among the three groups over a two-year period. They found that, whereas those on estrogen did not lose calcium, the high-dosage supplements did not seem to slow the loss of calcium markedly.

To be effective, estrogen therapy must be started in the first few years after menopause, when the rate of bone loss is accelerated. It can't restore bone mass once it's lost. The necessity and implications of this treatment should also be discussed carefully with a physician, because estrogen therapy may increase the risk of other diseases for some women.

Most important, women need to pay attention to their calcium intake long before menopause occurs. Women who consume the recommended levels of calcium in the time between puberty and menopause are less likely to suffer from the disease.

The same holds true when describing the merits of exercise for reducing the risk of osteoporosis. Physical activity plays an important role in preserving bone. In particular, "weight bearing" activities such as walking, jogging, and aerobics help maintain bone mass. But these activities may do little to halt bone loss in postmenopausal women. Researchers have found that premenopausal women who exercised regularly had a higher calcium content in their bones than those who did not. However, it is not clear whether exercise by postmenopausal women will protect against bone loss.

The National Osteoporosis Foundation has a new toll-free number women can call to learn of the bone testing facility nearest them. Call 1-800-464-6700 Monday through Friday, 8:00 A.M. to 9:00 P.M. EST; weekends, 9:00 A.M. to 5:00 P.M. EST.

17

Growing Old with Grace

From the moment of birth, every human being starts on the process of growing older. We don't just wake up one day to find that our bones are brittle, our skin has wrinkled, and our bodies don't function as well as they once did. There is no cutoff point at which we stop being "young" and start being "old." Yet that is exactly the way most of us have learned to view growing older—as a point in time when the good days are gone forever. Gerontophobia, or fear of aging, has infected our society for so long that it comes as no surprise that we have avoided investigating so many issues involving the elderly.

The study of nutrition and its relationship to the aging process is a new field, but as the life expectancy of Americans grows it is taking on great significance. Today, people are living some 30 years longer than they were at the turn of the century, and the number of elderly people is increasing at a rapid pace: By the year 2030, it is estimated, the number of Americans over the age of 65 will be double what it is today and twice the number of teenagers. And because people are living longer, they want to live those years more fully.

Today the average, healthy 50-year-old woman has a life expectancy of 80 years; it's absurd to think that she should spend those 30 years "winding down." Since 1982, Tufts has been involved in the study of aging at its federally sponsored Jean Mayer USDA Human Nutrition Research Center on Aging. Research at the center focuses on how nutrition during the entire life cycle influences the way people age. The center has a staff of more than 200, including 50 research scientists with Ph.D. or M.D. degrees. During the years since its inception, the center's researchers have already uncovered a number of critical connections between nutrition and aging, including:

◆ Protein requirements for physically active older men are higher than the current RDA.

◆ Physical exercise markedly increases muscle size and strength in men and women, even at 90 years of age.

◆ Certain identifiable genetic factors might predict the risk of early heart disease and may be used to recommend diet therapy for high-risk individuals.

◆ A hormonal form of vitamin D might be related to skin aging and conditions such as psoriasis.

◆ Weight-bearing exercise increases bone density in post-menopausal women.

◆ B vitamin status may influence cognitive functioning in older adults.

◆ High blood levels of the amino acid homocysteine are associated with increased risk of heart disease. These may be caused by B vitamin deficiencies.

◆ The ability of the skin to synthesize vitamin D from sunlight decreases markedly with age, supporting the need for the elderly to be more dependent on dietary vitamin D than younger people.

◆ A decreased ability to produce stomach acid occurs in 20 percent of the elderly population and interferes with the absorption of several vitamins and minerals.

◆ Elderly women who ingest low levels of calcium lose that mineral from the spine at a significantly greater rate than those whose intakes exceed the RDA.

◆ Calcium supplements, when taken with a meal, impair the absorption of iron from that meal.

◆ Under experimental conditions, vitamin E has been shown to play an important role in the immune system and may act partially to reverse some age-related declines in immune response.

◆ There seems to be a dietary relationship between the delay of cataract or cataract-like changes in the eye lens and nutrients that act as antioxidants, such as vitamins C and E.

◆ Vitamins A and D may be involved in important skin protection functions.

These and many other studies at Tufts provide new information that may have important effects on the health and vitality of the elderly. Unfortunately, nutrition research on the elderly shows that, for the most part, diet cannot miraculously reverse the health status of the current generation of elderly. Rather, it suggests that the sooner healthful patterns of nutritional behavior are practiced, the greater will be the effects of good nutrition on the vitality level and longevity of the older population. That is, a man or woman can begin good nutritional practices at age 40 or before that will make a significant difference in later life.

For today's seniors, the health and nutrition picture is complex. Although life expectancy continues to increase, 80 percent of today's elderly have at least one chronic condition; among the most prevalent are osteoporosis, arthritis, hypertension, hearing and visual impairments, and cardiac conditions. Yet nutrition remains one of the controllable factors that can influence the overall health of the elderly, even those who already have one or more chronic conditions. For example, as discussed in other chapters, cardiac conditions, hypertension, and osteoporosis can all be controlled, at least in part, with diet. In addition, an understanding of the physiological changes that occur with aging can help to prevent many diet-related health problems that commonly plague the elderly population.

To help turn things around, the American Academy of Family Physicians, the American Dietetic Association, and the National Council on Aging have spearheaded what is known as the Nutrition Screening Initiative, designed to identify people at nutritional risk *before* their health has deteriorated as a result. The centerpiece of this initiative is a checklist based on background work by Dr. Johanna Dwyer, director of the Frances Stern Nutrition Center at the New England Medical Center and a professor at both the Tufts University School of Nutrition and the School of Medicine. The checklist (see page 213) is designed to make people aware of nine key risk factors for poor nutritional status among older Americans, and if enough of those factors apply to someone over 65, to help determine whether a professional should be seen.

NUTRITION EVALUATION CHECKLIST[1]

The warning signs of poor nutritional health are often overlooked. Use this checklist to find out if you or someone you know is at nutritional risk.

Read the statements below. Circle the number in the yes column for those that apply to you (or someone you
know.) Add the points for all the yes answers and put the score on the Total line.

	Yes
I have an illness or condition that made me change the kind and/or amount of food I eat.	2
I eat fewer than two meals per day.	3
I eat few fruits or veqetables, or milk products.	2
I have three or more drinks of beer, liquor, or wine almost every day.	2
I have tooth or mouth problems that make it hard for me to eat.	2
I don't always have enough money to buy the food I need.	4
I eat alone most of the time.	1
I take three or more different prescribed or over-the-counter drugs a day.	1
Without wanting to, I have lost or gained 10 pounds in the last six months.	2
I am not always physically able to shop, cook, and/or feed myself.	2

Total

If your nutritional score is:

0-2   Good! Recheck your score in six months.

3-5   You are at moderate nutritional risk. See what can be done to improve your eating habits and
lifestyle. Your local office on aging, senior nutrition program, senior citizens center, or health
department can help. Recheck your nutritional score in three months.

6 or more   You are at high nutritional risk. Bring this checklist the next time you see your doctor, dietitian,
or other qualified health or social service professional. Talk with them about any problems you
may have. Ask for help to improve your nutritional health.

A reminder: warning signs suggest risk, but do not represent diagnosis of any condition.

[1]Developed and distributed by the Nutrition Screening Initiative, a project of the American Academy of Family Physicians,
The American Dietetic Association, and the National Council on Aging.

Biological Changes That Affect Nutrition

Many of the natural physiological changes that
occur with age alter food preferences and nutritional requirements. They affect the way our
bodies metabolize food, as well as the types of
foods we are comfortably able to eat. Lean
body mass decreases as our bodies lose muscle
and our systems slow down. It is estimated that
a 70-year-old man requires about 30 percent
fewer calories than a 30-year-old man of the
same size. With a decline in metabolism and

physical exercise, calorie needs are less, and
diets must become more nutrient-dense to
assure that the proper intakes of nutrients are
being maintained on the lower-calorie diets.

Aging is also associated with alterations in
smell, taste, and texture preferences in foods.
Diets designed for young people are not as
appetizing to people as they grow older, in part
because many elderly people have teeth missing or dentures that fit poorly and cover taste
receptors. Such people can find it hard to chew
foods like crunchy vegetables and fruits, or
meat.

As we grow older, the small intestine loses some of its ability to make lactase, the enzyme that digests milk sugar (lactose). Because the undigested lactose sits in the intestines and ferments, a number of elderly people are troubled by gas, bloating, and sometimes diarrhea after eating certain dairy products.

The intestines are affected in another way. Basically, with age everything slows down, so there is a tendency toward constipation, especially on diets low in fiber. Another change in the gastrointestinal tract is that the stomach produces less acid, which is needed to absorb some vitamins and minerals. A decrease in acid alters the normal bacterial flora found in the intestines, with a variety of nutritional ramifications.

There are also hormonal changes; for example, a decrease in estrogen production in women causes calcium to be withdrawn from the bones and makes postmenopausal women more susceptible to osteoporosis (see Chapter 21).

Getting Enough Fluids

Dehydration is not often thought of as a major health issue, but according to the Health Care Financing Administration, it ranks as one of the 10 most frequent diagnoses among hospitalized patients on Medicare, costing some $450 million annually. And about half of the people over age 65 who are hospitalized with illnesses accompanied by dehydration die within a year of admission. Why is this such a big problem for the elderly?

Under normal conditions, the average adult loses roughly 2 quarts of water a day, mostly in urine but also in sweat, in feces, and through breathing. This loss must be replaced or we become dehydrated and die. One way our bodies protect us is through the signal that we're thirsty. We are also protected by a mechanism that causes the kidneys to begin conserving water—reabsorbing it back into the blood instead of excreting it—when there is deprivation.

It has been found that, as people age, thirst signals become less strong. Studies conducted at Oxford and Johns Hopkins universities suggest that many elderly people fail to drink enough fluids, even when their bodies need it. To make matters worse, the kidneys do not act as efficiently to conserve water when it is needed. As a result, elderly people are more prone than others to dehydration.

Because it is impossible to rely on thirst as a sole indicator of need, the elderly should create a regular regimen of fluid intake. Although approximately half the body's water stock is supplied by food, the remaining requirement should be consumed by drinking six to eight cups of fluid each day. For hydration, the best choice is water, but milk and juices can supply valuable nutrients as well. It is especially important to increase water intake during hot weather, because, in addition to replacing fluids lost through sweat, it acts as a body coolant, reducing the effects of body heat production and loss.

Also, be aware that the peak dehydration season is not summer, as many people assume, but winter. That's because 25 to 30 percent of all cases of serious dehydration result from pneumonia and flu, which peak during the winter months.

Seniors Need to Watch Their B-12

For a significant number of people over age 60, a lack of vitamin B-12 may be responsible for neurologic symptoms, including tingling sensations, inability to coordinate muscular movements, weakened limbs, lack of balance, memory loss, mood changes, disorientation, and psychiatric disorders. It's not necessarily that some senior citizens aren't eating enough foods rich in B-12. Indeed, it would be difficult for anyone other than a strict vegetarian to develop a serious vitamin B-12 deficiency based on food choices alone, as B-12 is abundantly present in meat, poultry, fish, milk, cheese, and fortified cereal products.

The problem is that some 20 percent of people in their sixties and 40 percent of people in their eighties develop a condition of aging known as atrophic gastritis, which generally means that their stomachs no longer produce enough hydrochloric acid for the body to utilize the B-12 taken in. Without the acid, the digestive enzyme that separates B-12 from the protein to which it is attached when food is swallowed does not function properly. So, the vitamin is unable to travel from the stomach to the rest of the body tissues.

Furthermore, according to experiments conducted at the USDA Human Nutrition Research Center at Tufts, the lack of sufficient acid in the stomach provides a perfect environment for overgrowth of certain bacteria that utilize whatever B-12 *has* been cleaved from protein.

Tufts scientists have found that the best way to treat the problem is to take a vitamin B-12 supplement. They're not sure why, but it seems that supplemental B-12, as opposed to the B-12 bound to protein in food, prevents the bacteria from devouring the vitamin.

Unfortunately, although the treatment for B-12 deficiency resulting from atrophic gastritis is simple and inexpensive, the diagnosis is not. It is a "silent" condition that is not readily picked up on a visit to the doctor. Even more problematic, it doesn't take a severe B-12 deficiency— the kind that shows up on routine blood work—to cause problems. Even a mild deficiency, discernible only with the most sophisticated laboratory tests, can result in neurologic abnormalities.

The best approach is to work backward, eliminating other causes for problems before screening for B-12 deficiency. What people should *not* do is to self-prescribe vitamin B-12 supplements to treat neurologic problems. If B-12 deficiency is not the cause, they are wasting valuable time on a false solution. Furthermore,

some seniors have a type of atrophic gastritis that is so severe that they are unable to utilize B-12 in pill form. These people need to have vitamin B-12 injected into the tissues.

Socioeconomic Factors That Affect Nutrition

In the United States, aging is normally accompanied by a variety of psychologic, economic, and social changes that may affect the nutritional status of individuals. It is impossible to separate the socioeconomic and psychological issues from the biological realities when we evaluate the risk factors for the elderly in our society.

As a group, older Americans have a lower economic status than other adults in the United States. According to recent U.S. Senate studies, the decline in income most often results from retirement from the work force, the effects of inflation on fixed income, death of a wage-earning spouse, or failing health. Low income is clearly a major risk factor for inadequate nutrition in the elderly.

The process of evaluating nutrition and health factors for older people is complicated, and there are currently no firm guidelines for their nutritional requirements. The RDAs, for example, were developed largely from research on the nutrient needs of young, healthy people. The present standards for adults over 50 are almost identical to those for other adults because they were extrapolated from this research.

In studying the elderly population, researchers have been stymied by the lack of correlation between certain nutrition-related findings. For example, over the past 20 years, several comprehensive nutritional surveys have been conducted that identified a substantial proportion of older men and women who fell below the RDA for calories, protein, vitamins, calcium, and iron. At the same time, studies have found that obesity is a real problem in the aged, especially in women.

The two conflicting points are not hard to reconcile. It is clear that many elderly do not engage in work or exercise that uses many calories. Several credible studies have established the decline in physical activity as people age. One study of male executives in the Baltimore Longitudinal Study of Aging found a steady decline in average energy expenditure; other studies have supported this evidence. This decline is particularly unfortunate because recent studies at Tufts clearly demonstrate that even the very old may respond positively to exercise (see Chapter 25).

Alcohol and the Elderly: A Hidden Crisis

Alcohol dependency among people over 60 is far more common than most people suppose. According to a study from the Medical College of Wisconsin, more elderly people are hospitalized for alcohol-related problems than for heart attacks.

Although many older people with alcohol problems have been drinking for decades, an estimated one out of three does not start drinking to excess *until* the "golden" years. People who have recently lost a spouse are thought to make up the largest percentage of the late-onset drinkers, but new retirees, who may experience boredom, loneliness, and reduced income, are susceptible as well. And they can become hooked in a very short time—sometimes within months. The reason, in part, is that it takes much less alcohol to affect someone at 65 than it does at 45, because of age-related changes in metabolism and body composition. Furthermore, the medications that many older people take may increase the effects of alcohol.

Unfortunately, it's often hard to spot alcohol dependency in an older person. One reason is that it's frequently easier for an elderly person to keep others from seeing the problem. In addition to living alone, many elderly people don't have anyone else depending on them, so they can't get "caught" by neglecting responsibilities. They may also not drive, or not drive much, so their alcohol problems are less likely to get them into trouble with the law. Furthermore, many of the symptoms of alcohol problems—depression, memory loss, confusion, unsteady gait, and reduced physical capabilities—can be confused with other signs of advanced age.

However, there are some signals that might help tip off concerned family members and friends: a change in appearance and grooming; a significant personality shift, perhaps toward becoming more aggressive and argumentative, or toward an overall "slowing down"; excessive sleepiness or insomnia; a flushed face or bloated appearance; an excessive desire to be alone; and a need to explain away memory lapses by making up stories. There are, of course, also the telltale signs of alcohol on a person's breath and hidden or empty bottles.

Older alcoholics, especially those who started drinking later in life, tend to respond better than younger ones to treatment programs and other support systems designed to help people stay sober. For access to help, call the National Council on Alcholism's Help Line (1-800-NCA-CALL) to be referred to a local association or a state agency.

People who make a call for someone other than themselves should be aware that a person with alcohol dependency, whether old or young, cannot be forced into treatment. However, some families and friends of alcohol-dependent individuals have found success in setting up what is known as an intervention. In an intervention, family members and other concerned individuals, usually with the help of a professional, confront a person with his or her drinking problem and break through the denial.

If you are concerned about an elderly person's drinking habits, there are certain things you should *not* do. Don't pretend that the drinking doesn't bother you, or make things seem all right by compromising your own life in an effort to handle the alcoholic's responsibilities. And do not try to convince yourself that an elderly person should be left to drink as

AN EATING GUIDE FOR SENIORS

The elderly need to take special care to maintain a varied diet that is rich in all the nutrients they need. The following are some suggestions for nutrients that are sometimes a problem for the elderly.

Suggested Foods and Servings

Protein
2 scrambled or poached eggs
1 cup low-fat cottage cheese
3-½ oz. tuna
3-½ oz. broiled or baked chicken breast
1 cup low-fat milk
3-½ oz. broiled lean ground beef or round steak
1 cup plain low-fat yogurt

Vitamin C
1 4-oz. glass orange juice
½ sliced tomato
1 cup sliced strawberries
½ cup cooked spinach
1 baked or mashed potato
½ honeydew melon
1 medium orange
1 4-oz. glass grapefruit juice

Vitamin A
1 cup low-fat fortified milk
1 cup cooked broccoli
½ cantaloupe
½ cup cooked carrots or 1 raw carrot
1 medium baked sweet potato

Vitamin E
1 slice whole-wheat or enriched bread with 1 tbsp margarine
1 cup wheat flakes, bran cereal, or hot oatmeal, whole-grain or enriched
1 cup cooked whole-grain or enriched pasta
1 tbsp vegetable oil–and–vinegar salad dressing on a green salad

Vitamin D
1 cup fortified low-fat milk

Calcium
1 cup low-fat milk
½ cup low-fat cottage cheese
3-½ oz. canned salmon (with soft bones)
1 cup plain low-fat yogurt cup
½ cup ice milk

Niacin
1 slice whole-grain or enriched bread or 1 muffin or 4 wheat or rye crackers
½ cup (cooked) brown or enriched rice
3-½ oz. lean ground beef
1 cup lima bean soup or ½ cup cooked lima beans
½ cup cooked peas

Folacin
3-½ oz. broiled or baked beef liver
1 cup shredded cabbage coleslaw
1 cup cooked broccoli or cauliflower
1 cup cooked brussels sprouts
1 orange

Vitamin B-6
1 cup cooked corn or 1 piece of corn on the cob
½ cup low-fat cottage cheese
1 medium banana
1 3–4 oz. lamb chop
3-½ oz. broiled halibut

Iron
3-½–4 oz. shrimp or tuna
3-½ oz. steamed clams
3-½ oz. lean roast beef, broiled
3-½ oz. broiled beef liver
3-½ oz. broiled chicken breast
1 slice whole-grain or enriched bread or 1 medium enriched roll
1 cup lentil bean soup

much as he or she wants in the mistaken belief that this remaining "pleasure" should be allowed. Excessive drinking causes pain, not pleasure. It can damage the quality of life of an elderly person and reduce his or her active years.

Practical Vulnerabilities

Even when detrimental socioeconomic factors do not exist, many older people are vulnerable nutritionally simply because they lack the capacity to buy or prepare nutritional meals. Or they may be unable to shop for food, particularly if the weather is bad or they live far from the supermarket.

An elderly man or woman is far more susceptible to food poisoning than the average person, for two reasons. First, a declining power in the senses of taste, smell, and vision weakens the ability of elderly persons to recognize easily when a food has gone bad, when fresh foods are damaged, moldy, or off-color, when packaging is broken, or when dishes and utensils are not clean. They are less facile in identifying flavors and odors. A test conducted by Duke University demonstrated this. When asked to identify common odors such as those of chocolate, cinnamon, coffee, grape, onion, pepper, root beer, soy sauce, and tea, college students named the odors correctly 86 percent of the time. When the same test was administered to elderly subjects, they identified the odors correctly only 34 percent of the time.

Second, Tufts researchers have found that in at least 20 percent of the elderly, less stomach acid is being produced. Because stomach acid helps to digest food and kill microbes, an elderly person might become ill after eating food that would not cause a problem for a younger person.

Further, because the immune system appears to weaken with age, even a mild case of food poisoning can be a severe health problem for an older person. Add to that the fact that many older people suffer additional health complications, such as heart disease or diabetes, and it becomes easy to see why their bodies are less able to fight off infections.

Physical handling and ease of food preparation are other factors that influence health in seniors. Many rely heavily on canned or processed foods because they are easier to prepare. Or they may be limited in their ability to shop for a wide range of fresh fruits and vegetables. Additionally, package expiration dates may go unnoticed, or food may be saved beyond its safe consumption date out of frugality.

The Food and Drug Administration offers the following tips for people who want to help their older relatives and friends avoid trouble in the kitchen:

◆ Be observant: Note any marked change in habits which might indicate that an elderly person needs more help in the kitchen.

◆ Watch nutrition: Check to see that older people are eating a variety of animal and dairy foods, cereals, grains, fruits, and vegetables.

◆ Shop weekly: Either shop for elderly people or encourage them to shop every week and purchase perishable foods in small quantities. Suggest that they look for single serving–sized prepared foods and not allow leftovers to linger in the refrigerator.

◆ Help in cooking: Prepare batches of favorite foods and pack the portions in TV-dinner-size containers. Mark the containers clearly and store them in the freezer for easy preparation.

◆ Ensure freezer safety: Date all packages to be stored in the freezer, using a dark felt-tip pen. Suggest that older packages be moved forward as new items are added.

◆ Provide easy snacking: Suggest that people with dentures keep a basket of soft fruit handy for snacks. Good fruits include bananas, grapes, and ripe pears.

◆ Allow proper timing: Purchase a brightly colored, sufficiently loud timer for the elderly person who is becoming forgetful but who still likes to cook.

◆ Use package aids: If hand strength and dexterity are a problem, note that there are special devices available to help. Your local Arthritis Foundation can supply information on locating gripper pads, can poppers, and other package-opening aids.

◆ Check equipment: Make sure that your elderly relative or friend's refrigerator (safe at 40°F) and freezer (safe at 0°F) are running properly and that the freezer is defrosted when necessary.

Mixing Food and Medication

Because many elderly people take regular medication, it is important to know that some drugs may affect appetite and the metabolism of nutrients. One person out of two in the over-65 population takes two to five medications a day, and approximately one out of four takes at least five. For those who live in nursing homes, the numbers are even higher. That's significant because drugs, especially two or more drugs interacting inside the body, can hurt nutritional well-being by decreasing appetite as well as by causing poor absorption and metabolism of certain nutrients. Even simple aspirin by itself can result in painless and therefore unnoticed bleeding from the stomach, which when heavy enough can result in iron-deficiency anemia.

When medication is prescribed, a person should discuss with the doctor when it should be taken and whether it may affect nutritional needs. The mere presence of food can change the chemical environment of the intestinal tract in such a way that the effects of certain drugs can be profoundly altered.

Drugs and nutrients, when consumed together, may interact by binding tightly to each other and passing through the intestinal tract at the same time. The result is that the body is unable to utilize properly either the drug or the nutrient.

Another possible undesirable reaction can occur with drugs that alter the metabolic environment of the body significantly enough for the nutrients or other substances in foods to behave quite differently in the blood and tissues from the way they would without drugs.

Those who are taking certain prescribed medications should be aware of the effects they may have on dietary needs and discuss these factors with their physician:

ANTIBIOTICS

In addition to killing harmful bacteria, antibiotics destroy beneficial bacteria in the intestines that synthesize nutrients such as vitamin K and folacin. Those taking antibiotics should be sure to include adequate amounts of these nutrients in the diet by eating green leafy vegetables. Also, certain foods may influence the effectiveness of antibiotics. For example, acidic beverages such as fruit juices destroy penicillin G and "uncoated" erythromycin, when consumed at the same time. And because calcium binds tightly with tetracycline, making it unabsorbable, dairy foods should not be consumed within several hours of taking this drug.

DIURETICS

Diuretics are often used to treat high blood pressure and water retention due to liver, kidney, or heart disease. They function by increasing the rate of urine formation. But in washing out excess fluid, some diuretics, such as Hydrodiuril and Furosemide, may wash out potassium as well. People taking diuretics should take care to eat plenty of potassium-rich foods, such as fruit juices and bananas.

ANTICOAGULANTS

People with cardiovascular diseases are often treated with anticoagulants, which reduce the risk of blood platelets' sticking together and forming artery blockages. Certain foods can influence the effectiveness of these drugs. In large amounts, vitamin K, which helps blood clot, may reduce the effects of anticoagulants. And omega-3 fatty acids may increase their effectiveness.

CHOLESTEROL-LOWERING DRUGS

One strategy for lowering cholesterol levels is to remove bile acids from the intestinal tract, as the body must resort to its store of cholesterol to replace them. But because bile acids are necessary to absorb the fat-soluble vitamins (A, D, E, and K), these vitamins may be poorly assimilated when a drug known as cholestyramine is taken. In these cases, increased dietary intake may be advised.

Caution is needed, not only with prescription drugs, but with over-the-counter drugs as well. Many commonly used medicines can influence nutritional health:

ASPIRIN

Many arthritis sufferers tend to overuse aspirin. Although some doctors are now encouraging regular use of aspirin (based on the hypothesis that it helps slow blood-clot formation), consuming large amounts of aspirin over a long period of time can cause painless internal bleeding from the stomach that could ultimately lead to iron-deficiency anemia. Taking 12 to 15 aspirins a day—not an unusual dose for some arthritis sufferers—increases normal loss of blood from the stomach by 5 to 13 times.

LAXATIVES

Persistent use of laxatives can result in the loss of vitamins and minerals because laxatives speed foods through the system before some of their nutrients can be adequately absorbed. Mineral oil, for example, can prevent the absorption of vitamins A, D, E, and K. Regular use of saline-type laxatives, such as Epsom salts and Milk of Magnesia, can deplete the body of fluid and mineral nutrients such as potassium.

ANTACIDS

Continued use of large quantities of antacids that contain the ingredient aluminum hydroxide, such as Rolaids or Maalox, may result in a phosphorus deficiency and thereby lead to osteomalacia, or "soft bones." Elderly people must be sure to be honest with their doctors about their eating habits, alcohol consumption, and all of the medications they are taking. They should discuss potential side effects of drugs and never self-medicate or take more than the prescribed dosage.

Straight Talk About Nutrition and Dementia

More Americans than ever are faced with the difficult task of caring for elderly parents or relatives who suffer from age-related dementia or Alzheimer's disease, characterized by deteriorating mental facilities.

The Food and Nutrition Department of the Hebrew Home for the Aged in Riverdale, New York, has pioneered a program to help those with dementia eat more healthfully and gain back a measure of control over their lives. The program has succeeded in enabling undernourished dementia sufferers to gain weight—and also to approach life in a less angry and agitated way. Among the various strategies is the Finger Foods Menu Program, including this advice:

◆ Prepare bite-sized portions of items such as fruits, vegetables, cheese, and sandwiches that can be picked up by hand rather than with knives and forks—utensils whose uses may not be remembered or understood anymore. Bite-sized portions are also helpful because people with dementia often wander about and can eat as they walk.

◆ Puree soups so that nutritious ingredients won't settle at the bottom. Serve pureed soup in a mug rather than in a bowl.

◆ Don't rush meals or insist on "normal" mealtimes. People with dementia eat slowly. In addition, they eat better when they're hungry, not when it's "time" to eat.

For people caring for loved ones with dementia at home, Riverdale's Hebrew Home for the Aged has put many of its tips into a brochure entitled "Finger Foods Make Mealtimes Easier." Sample menus and recipes are also included. To order a free copy, send a self-addressed, stamped business-size envelope to The Hebrew Home for the Aged at Riverdale, 5901 Palisade Avenue, Riverdale, NY 10471, Attention: Finger Foods Program.

Can We Slow Down the Aging Process?

Our search for the Fountain of Youth goes on. No doubt we humans will always be interested in finding ways to expand our lives and maintain a young look and vitality. We know that certain health and nutrition habits, carried over a lifetime, can dramatically improve health into the older years for many people. We also know that genetic factors play an important role in longevity. But a point of real controversy exists concerning the extent to which certain supplements might influence the aging process. Some manufacturers have aggressively promoted the idea that the aging process might be reversed or forestalled with supplement use.

There is interesting research taking place to see if nutrition is related to conditions such as Alzheimer's disease, cardiovascular disease, cancer, and cataracts—specifically, whether certain nutrients can protect against these and other degenerative diseases. But it can be dangerous for consumers to jump the gun on research and become involved with unproved nutrient and nonnutrient therapies.

High doses of many minerals, such as selenium, and vitamins A, D, and B-6 can be harmful and may interfere with the metabolism of other nutrients. For example, high doses of vitamin E can interfere with the absorption of vitamin A. And large amounts of some nutrients can interfere with the action of certain drugs.

Furthermore, despite claims to the contrary, there is no evidence that nutrients or special foods will help slow down the cosmetic changes that accompany aging, such as hair loss, graying hair, or wrinkles. Most of these changes are genetically programmed, and you can't do anything about them.

However, considering the fixation Americans have developed about aging skin, it's surprising that so many people continue to bake in the sun year after year. But then, think how many of us continue to smoke or develop chemical dependencies.

Our quest for health and long lives will not be satisfied by a magical antidote to aging. Rather, we must commit ourselves to a steady, commonsense approach to nutrition and health during every stage of our lives.

PART FOUR

Making the
Diet–Health Connection

Diet management is a major factor in treating certain health problems. Although it is always recommended that you consult with your physician about medical issues, experts have reached some basic conclusions about diet and health, and this knowledge can work in tandem with medical and other therapies.

Unfortunately, those who are most physically needy often become the easiest victims of dietary misinformation. But the rules of common sense continue to apply. In fact, if common nutrition sense were used in this country, we could substantially cut down on incidences of our number-one killer, heart disease.

Most primary risk factors for heart disease—high blood cholesterol, high blood pressure, obesity, smoking, and a lack of exercise—are controllable factors. Even those people who, because of family history, are naturally at greater risk can minimize their chances of suffering from this disease if they take the appropriate dietary measures. The Tufts Low Cholesterol Diet may provide the first step in the process of improving cardiovascular health. Contrary to what many people fear, a heart-smart diet doesn't have to be dull and tasteless.

Much has been written about the diet–cancer connection, but it's not so easy to tell what's fact and what's fiction. On one hand, there's plenty of promise in the research linking certain types of cancer to nutritional factors. On the other hand, there is a good deal of misinformation and "magic" promises. Here, we'll separate fact from fiction and supply the latest information on the diet–cancer connection.

Other major health concerns, such as diabetes, kidney disease, arthritis, and AIDS, also have nutritional connections. All of these are the subject of intense study in the Tufts laboratories and elsewhere. But it is important not to think of diet and disease as a simple cause-and-effect proposition. Nutrition is just one factor in the diagnosis and treatment of many diseases. We also want consumers to be aware that research into the nutrition–disease connection is in its infancy. Many things remain unknown about the specific dietary practices that might decrease the risk of certain cancers and other diseases. But doors have been opened and directions have been shown.

For us, this knowledge represents an exciting new field of study. We believe that nutrition science will someday be able to uncover the links between nutrition and many diseases. But, for now, we suggest that people focus on those things that we do know and avoid participating in scientifically unproven practices.

18

Challenging Heart Disease

Coronary heart disease (CHD) is our nation's number-one killer. Every year, almost 1 million Americans suffer heart attacks, and more than half of them die as a result. CHD has typically been a "silent" killer. There are few warning signals: The first "symptom" a victim might have is a massive heart attack.

A substantial amount of clinical and epidemiologic evidence has identified risk factors that are statistically associated with CHD. Many scientific studies have been conducted in a variety of circumstances and types of populations. Although experts acknowledge that some contradictions exist and that they do not yet know all there is to know about CHD, there has been enough consistency in study results to establish certain risks, including high cholesterol, high blood pressure, diabetes, obesity, cigarette smoking, and a family history of CHD.

The leading cause of CHD is generally believed to be atherosclerosis, commonly known as hardening of the arteries, which involves the accumulation of fatty substances (primarily cholesterol) and fibrous tissues along the inner lining of medium and large arteries. Atherosclerosis starts with damage to the layer of cells lining an artery, caused by one or more of several irritants: the turbulent flow of blood, the impact

of blood under excessive pressure (high blood pressure), possibly toxic chemicals, a high concentration of blood fats, or a bacterial or viral infection. If damage to the artery wall occurs repeatedly because of untreated high blood pressure or other factors, it is believed, the body's normal repair processes are overwhelmed. Blood fats and platelets are attracted to the site of the injury, leading to an accumulation of cell debris and cholesterol. If the damage persists, smooth muscle cells migrate from adjacent areas and multiply, forming a mat of scar-like tissue. The resulting accumulation is called plaque. Plaque subsequently hardens with deposits of calcium. With continued insult to the artery, plaque grows larger, protruding into the interior of the artery and progressively narrowing the vessel. Plaque is particularly dangerous when it forms in the coronary arteries, which deliver oxygen and nutrients to the heart muscle. If the narrowing becomes severe enough to impair the flow of oxygen, the result is a heart attack.

Heart attacks often occur without warning, but they are usually the result of the slow buildup of atherosclerotic plaques in the coronary arteries over a period of many years. A plaque rarely grows large enough to occlude a coronary artery completely by itself, but it can combine with a blood clot to shut off abruptly the flow of blood to the heart. When this happens, the result is a heart attack, or myocardial infarction. Blockage of an artery can also be caused by spasm of the vessels around the plaque, bleeding into a plaque, or dislodgment of a plaque from the artery wall, creating an obstruction downstream. Whatever the cause of the blockage, because of it the portion of the heart muscle that is nourished by the occluded artery becomes oxygen-starved and dies. If the damage occurs in a particularly vital spot, sudden death may result. Indeed, for about 25 percent of heart attack victims, sudden death is the first sign of the disease.

Less severe damage to the heart muscle may disrupt the electrical impulses emanating from the heart's internal pacemaker, causing abnormal heart rhythms. These "arrhythmias" are dangerous because they can lead to rapid, uncoordinated contractions (fibrillations) of the ventricles, the large chambers of the heart. Unless these ventricular fibrillations are corrected, they can lead to death within minutes.

The Cholesterol Connection

Scientists have been studying the relationship of diet to CHD since the turn of the century, when researchers noticed that rabbits fed diets high in cholesterol developed arterial lesions resembling atherosclerosis in humans. But it wasn't until the 1950s, when CHD had already reached epidemic proportions, that saturated dietary fats were considered to be primary culprits in the development of the disease. In recent decades, many studies have deepened our understanding of the relationship between high blood cholesterol and CHD (see also Chapter 5).

One of the most famous of these investigations is the long-running Framingham, Massachusetts, Heart Study, which has tracked incidents of CHD in men and later, entire families, since 1948. The study has found that men with average blood cholesterol levels of 260 have had three times the number of heart attacks as men with blood cholesterol levels that averaged 195. In 1988, the Surgeon General's report concluded that high blood cholesterol is one of the major modifiable risk factors for CHD. Although there may be other factors that contribute to CHD, such as smoking and hypertension, the role of cholesterol is clearly a primary one.

Our bodies produce all the cholesterol they need, and we increase our blood cholesterol levels in two main ways: (1) by eating foods that contain dietary cholesterol, and (2) by eating foods that are high in saturated fats, which result in a series of events causing a buildup of cholesterol in the blood.

Many studies back up our current understanding of the relationship between levels of cholesterol in the blood and risk for CHD. A landmark study published in 1984 showed convincingly for the first time that reducing cholesterol led to fewer heart attacks. The Lipid Research Clinics Coronary Primary Prevention Trial showed, in a study of 3,806 men, that a 9 percent reduction of blood cholesterol in the treatment group led to a 19 percent reduction in fatal and nonfatal heart attacks. But, as discussed in Chapter 5, it is not simply a matter of how much cholesterol is present in the blood; the method of transport must be considered.

Cholesterol travels back and forth between the liver and the cells through the bloodstream, carried by lipoproteins. High-density lipoproteins (HDLs) are strong carriers that remove cholesterol from the cells and deliver it safely to the liver for processing. Low-density lipoproteins (LDLs) are more fragile, and they tend to leave deposits of cholesterol behind in the arteries, leading to plaque buildup. It is possible to reduce coronary risk either by lowering LDL levels or by increasing HDL levels.

Testing Your Cholesterol Level

How do you know if your blood cholesterol level is too high? It is currently believed that the highest risk is present when blood cholesterol levels are greater than 240 milligrams per deciliter (mg/dl) of blood. Moderate risk exists when levels are between 200 and 239 mg/dl, and low risk exists when levels are below 200 mg/dl. It is estimated that 40 million Americans between the ages of 40 and 70 have blood cholesterol levels above 200 mg/dl.

However, the real issue with cholesterol measurements is ratio. For example, a person with a total cholesterol measurement of 200 whose HDL is less than 35, is considered to be at high risk for heart disease.

Government guidelines suggest that all Americans over the age of 20 have their blood cholesterol levels tested to determine their degree of risk. This test is conducted by having blood samples analyzed in a laboratory, or by using the home test now available. There are a number of points you should bear in mind when you have a cholesterol test:

◆   Sit down for at least five to ten minutes before you take the test. Standing can cause test results to be skewed by about 5 percent.

◆   Be aware that viral infections, certain medications, pregnancy, and recent surgical procedures may interfere with accurate test results. For example, it takes about two months after a heart attack, stroke, or cardiac surgery for the test to reflect an accurate picture of blood cholesterol level.

◆   Make sure you've had at least two tests taken before beginning (or forgoing) dietary and/or medical treatment based on your blood cholesterol level. The tests should be spaced a month or two apart. If the results are within 30 points of each other, the average of the two is probably a safe estimate of your true blood cholesterol, because cholesterol totals vary somewhat from day to day and week to week. If the discrepancy between the two tests is more than 30 points, a third test is in order.

◆   Make sure that your doctor also measures cholesterol "fractions"—HDL cholesterol, LDL cholesterol, and triglyceride levels.

◆   When considering the results of any cholesterol test, remember that a number of factors, including diet, genetics, lack of exercise, and obesity, can influence cholesterol levels and the likelihood of heart disease.

NEW: A HOME TEST FOR BLOOD CHOLESTEROL

In 1994, the Food and Drug Administration gave the go-ahead to the AccuMeter Cholesterol Self Test, a product that was previously available only to medical professionals. Priced at under $20, AccuMeter comes in a kit that includes everything you need to check your cholesterol at home.

To perform the test, simply prick a finger and drip blood into a plastic cassette that fits into the palm of your hand. The cassette contains a "test strip" that resembles a thermometer and changes color as the cholesterol rises on it. After 10 to 15 minutes, you can compare the color shown on the test strip with a chart that equates the color to the amount of cholesterol in your blood. The results, says the FDA, are as accurate as those obtained with cholesterol tests conducted by medical laboratories.

However, you must be careful to perform the test correctly. For instance, if you are not seated for at least five minutes before pricking a finger, as the instructions advise, test results may be off by about 5 percent. You should also be aware that this is not a test for people who are squeamish about pricking themselves and collecting blood.

Most important, you should not expect this test to replace the care of a doctor. A single reading from a cholesterol test is not a sufficient basis for making changes without the advice of a doctor. Furthermore, the home test measures total cholesterol but does not measure the HDL and LDL ratio. So, the home test should be used only as a supportive tool to medical professionals, especially for people who are trying to lower their blood cholesterol and want to keep track on a frequent basis.

◆ NUTRITION QUIZ ◆
A Heart Disease Checkup

Only about one in three adults knows his or her blood cholesterol level, an unfortunate fact since high cholesterol is one of a handful of major heart disease risk factors that people can take into their own hands by making changes in their diets. People are not only unaware of their blood cholesterol concentrations but also are often not as knowledgeable as they may think about the dietary steps it takes to keep cholesterol down—as well as lessen other heart disease risks. Have you had your cholesterol checked yet? And, just as important, do you know everything you need to know about how the foods you eat affect the health of your heart? Take this quiz to see if you're as equipped as possible to stave off coronary heart disease through the dietary and other lifestyle choices you make daily.

1. *True or false?* Saturated fat—the kind found in beef and dairy products, for instance—has more calories than the mono- and polyunsaturated fats contained in high proportions in olive oil and safflower oil, respectively.

2. The single most important thing you can do to stave off as well as reduce high blood pressure—one of the major risk factors for the development of heart disease—is (a) reduce salt, or sodium, intake (b) maintain or get down to healthy weight (c) limit alcohol consumption to no more than two drinks a day.

3. *True or false?* Heart disease rates are consistently lower in populations of people who drink up to two glasses of wine a day than in groups who drink little or no wine at all.

4. The kind of fiber that helps lower blood cholesterol is (a) the soluble kind, found in relatively large proportions in fruits and vegetables (b) the insoluble kind, found in the largest amounts in whole-wheat products (c) neither of the above—fiber helps keep you regular and may help keep certain types of cancer at bay, but it cannot, as some hypothesize, reduce blood cholesterol levels.

5. *True or false?* It doesn't matter whether you eat margarine or butter. From your heart's point of view it's six of one and half a dozen of another.

6. *True or false?* Cholesterol is found only in foods that come from animals.

7. The best way to raise the blood level of HDL-cholesterol, otherwise known as the "good" cholesterol that actually helps keep arteries clear, is to (a) reduce total fat consumption as much as possible (b) eat more fish, which contain what are known as omega-3 fatty acids that help "thin" the blood and therefore play a role in preventin clots that could lead to a heart attack or stroke (c) lose excess weight and/or engage in more exercise.

ANSWERS

1. *False.* All fats have the same number of calories, on the order of 120 per tablespoon (which comes to about 14 grams.) That doesn't mean all fats have the same effect on the arteries, however. Saturated fats are the ones most responsible for raising blood cholesterol levels and therefore clogging the pathways to the heart. Currently, Americans eat about 13 percent

A Heart Disease Checkup (cont.)

of their calories as saturated fat. If we reduced that to, say, 8 percent of our calories (health experts recommend we at least bring the intake below 10 percent,) the average *total* fat intake of Americans—saturated, monounsaturated, and polyunsaturated fat combined—would be about 32 percent, much closer to the advised maximum of 30 percent rather than the 37 percent we currently average.

2. (b) All three strategies—keeping off excess pounds, limiting sodium intake to 2,400 milligrams a day (check food labels), and having no more than two drinks a day—are effective for controlling blood pressure, which is known in scientific circles as hypertension and afflicts as many as one in every four Americans. But staying or getting slim appears to be the most effective. Consider that when a team of researchers known as the Hypertension Prevention Collaborative Research Group put more than 2,000 men and women on a weight-reduction sodium-reduction regimen, or other types of eating plans, those following the weight-loss program experienced the largest drops in blood pressure.

   Other research has indicated that as little as a 5 percent reduction in extra pounds can be associated with a lowering of blood pressure so significant that some patients are able to stop taking blood pressure medication.

3. *False.* It most assuredly is true that in countries where something on the order of two daily glasses of wine is a national "habit"—France and Italy, for instance—heart disease rates are lower than they are in more teetotaling nations such as the United States and Britain. But there are several groups of people who drink little or no wine and suffer very low mortality from heart disease as well: the Japanese, the Chinese, and American Seventh Day Adventists, for example. In other words, wine by itself does not make or break heart disease risk.

4. (a) It appears that soluble fiber helps lower total blood cholesterol even when the diet is already low in fat and cholesterol. Researchers at the University of Toronto found that out when they took two groups of adults following low-fat, low-cholesterol diets and placed them on a regimen either relatively high in soluble fiber—contained in large proportions in foods such as barley, dried lentils, peas, and oat bran along with fruits and vegetables like apricots, grapefruit, oranges, peaches, plums, Brussels sprouts, and onions—or on a meal plan particularly abundant in items rich in insoluble fiber—wheat-bran cereal, high-fiber crackers, and high-fiber wheat-bran bread.

   After four weeks, the group on the soluble-fiber plan ended up with blood cholesterol levels that averaged almost 5 percent lower than in the other group. This is not to say that people should forget about eating whole-wheat foods high in insoluble fiber. That's the kind of fiber that helps keep people regular and has been implicated as well in warding off various types of cancer, including colon cancer.

5. *False.* Butter is harder on the heart. An accumulating body of research does suggest that margarine can raise blood cholesterol, to be sure. The "guilty" ingredients in margarine are called trans fatty acids, which are formed when manufacturers harden vegetable oils from liquids into tub spreads or margarine sticks via a process called hydrogenation. Other products that contain trans fatty acids include many brands of cookies and crackers and fried dishes served at fast food chains. Still, if you replace a saturated fat like butter with a less

A Heart Disease Checkup (cont.)

saturated one such as margarine, your blood cholesterol will drop. Saturated fat, incidentally, makes up fully a third to a half of the fat in our diets, while trans fatty acids comprise less than a tenth—another reason to concentrate more on reducing saturated fat consumption rather than trans fatty acid consumption. Of course, the best bet is to cook with liquid cooking oils such as safflower, canola, or olive oil whenever taste and texture considerations permit, since they have little saturated fat and no trans fatty acids whatsoever.

6. *True.* While a plant-based food may contain a lot of fat, it will never contain any cholesterol. It should be mentioned that although cholesterol in the diet has the capacity to raise cholesterol in the blood, fat in the diet, particularly saturated fat, can raise blood cholesterol much more significantly.

7. (c) While "bad," artery-clogging LDL-cholesterol is most affected by the foods we eat, particularly the amount and types of fat we eat, HDL-cholesterol levels change most dramatically in response to changes in the number of calories we consume (which can have an impact on weight loss or weight gain) as well as in the number of calories we burn (which is influenced largely by the amount of exercise we do.) Another way of putting it: thinness and large amounts of physical activity, or burning plenty of calories and not taking in too many, help keep HDL-cholesterol levels up.

   An HDL level of 60 (milligrams per deciliter of blood) or greater is considered particularly protective; an HDL level under 35 is considered low and therefore a risk factor for heart disease. (LDL-cholesterol is considered to be at a desirable level if it stays below 130 and is viewed as a heart disease risk factor at or above 160.)

What About High Triglycerides?

Triglycerides are your body's fat store. The bloodstream always contains some of them, and their levels are higher right after you've eaten. Elevated triglycerides, by themselves, are not thought to be a risk factor for CHD. However, several studies have shown that people who have high triglycerides also tend to have high cholesterol and low HDL levels and to be obese. This is in part due to the fact that many of the same factors that contribute to high blood cholesterol, such as diets high in calories and saturated fats, also cause high triglycerides.

The American Heart Association has set standards for triglycerides based on age and sex. The chart indicates the levels at which triglycerides are determined to be high.

Severe elevations of triglycerides—500 to 1,500 mg/dl—occur in only a very small number of people, and they're rarely caused by diet alone. But diets high in saturated fat, cholesterol, and alcohol, accompanied by lack of exercise and obesity, appear to be major contributors to less extreme elevations. Whether or not these less extreme levels present a health risk is open to debate, but certainly any of the factors mentioned would independently contribute to CHD.

Can Niacin Make a Difference?

The question of whether supplemental niacin should be used to help lower blood cholesterol is one that must be weighed carefully. On one hand, niacin is known to help reduce blood cholesterol. On the other hand, niacin can cause side effects ranging from itching to nausea to wartlike growths in the groin and armpits to liver damage.

HIGH BLOOD TRIGLYCERIDE LEVELS
Blood Plasma Total Triglycerides (mg/dl)

Age	Male	Female
5–9	85	126
10–14	111	120
15–19	143	126
20–24	165	168
25–29	204	159
30–34	253	163
35–39	316	205
40–44	318	191
45–49	318	223
50–54	313	223
55–59	261	279
60–64	240	256
65–69	256	260
70+	239	289

Researchers who gave supplemental niacin to a group of men and women with high levels of LDL cholesterol had mixed resuts. When over the course of about eight months the researchers gradually worked the group up to 3,000 milligrams of niacin a day (150 times the USRDA), blood cholesterol levels dropped dramatically. In the men and women given what is known as the sustained-release form of niacin (meaning it is released into the bloodstream slowly), LDL cholesterol went down by an average of 50 percent. And in those on what is called immediate-release niacin, LDL cholesterol fell by 22 percent. Even at levels as low as 1,500 milligrams a day, both forms of niacin cut LDL cholesterol considerably and raised HDL cholesterol as well.

The hitch is that even when the group had worked up to just 1,000 milligrams of niacin a day after about two months, some had to stop taking it because of side effects such as nausea, flushing of the face, itching, rash, and fatigue. Worse still, some had laboratory tests that suggested liver abnormalities. By the time the researchers had upped the dosage to 3,000 milligrams a day several months later, almost four out of five people taking the sustained-release form had quit. Almost one in two taking the immediate-release niacin had also quit, some because they developed warty growths and skin discoloration.

The conclusion of researchers is that although supplemental niacin may be a useful tool in lowering cholesterol, it should never be self-prescribed. High-dose niacin preparations are comparable to drugs. As such, they should be viewed with the same kind of caution.

Control Cholesterol with Diet

The leading factor in controlling cholesterol levels is diet. According to doctors at the Lipid Metabolism Laboratory of the Jean Mayer USDA Human Nutrition Research Center at Tufts University, diet can lower blood cholesterol by as much as 30 percent. The Tufts Low Cholesterol Diet, outlined in the next chapter, eliminates about one-fourth of the fat calories in the 38- to 40-percent-fat diet that is typical for most adult Americans. Because, ounce for ounce, carbohydrates have less than half the calories of fat, a high-carbohydrate, low-fat diet also tends to cause weight loss, which can lower LDL levels. In fact, for some people, slimming down to a healthy body weight will completely correct elevated LDL concentrations.

The fat that needs to be restricted most is saturated fat, the kind that raises the LDLs and presently makes up about 15 percent of the calories in the American diet. If saturated fat were reduced from 15 percent of total calories to less than 10 percent, the goal of eating less than 30 percent fat calories would be achieved by most Americans. It's easy to see why. If a person who gets 38 percent of his or her calories as fat were to reduce the saturated fat intake from 15 percent to 8 percent of total calories (a drop of 7 percent), the net result would be 31 percent fat, close to the guideline of 30 percent.

Heavy sources of saturated fat include the marbleized fat you can see on beef, processed meats such as sausages and hot dogs, hard cheeses, butter, whole-milk dairy products, and snacks containing coconut, palm, and palm kernel oil, as well as cocoa butter. Healthful substitutions for these foods are lean cuts of meat in smaller portion sizes; beans (a low-fat source of protein); fruits and vegetables; margarine made with safflower, sunflower, or other polyunsaturated oils; skim milk; low-fat yogurt; and low-fat cottage cheese.

Because the soluble fiber in oats, fruits, and beans has been shown to reduce LDL levels, they are good foods to include in a low-cholesterol diet. Similarly, many types of coldwater fish, which contain omega-3 fatty acids, may also bring down cholesterol levels. Although the value of omega-3 fatty acids is questionable, fish certainly contains less fat, particularly less saturated fat, than meat and is a good choice for a cholesterol-lowering diet.

The Hypertension Factor

One out of four Americans, or approximately 50 to 60 million people, are victims of hypertension, commonly referred to as high blood pressure. Sustained high blood pressure is a silent disease that can go unnoticed for years until it is picked up during a medical exam or suddenly results in a stroke, heart attack, or kidney failure.

In a small percentage of cases, the cause for the disease can be traced to some physiological malfunction, such as a kidney problem, a narrowing of the aorta (from which blood leaves the heart on its journey to the rest of the body), or a tumor in the adrenal glands. In these instances, the hypertension is called secondary hypertension and can often be cured by medical treatment. However, about 95 percent of the people who have high blood pressure have primary, or idiopathic, hypertension, which means that the cause of the disease cannot be determined, and it is a lifetime ailment.

This type of hypertension can be controlled with relative ease by medication and/or diet, and the chances for illness can be reduced. Although some high-risk groups have been identified—among them, blacks, the elderly, and people with a family history of hypertension—it is still not possible to predict with a degree of certainty who will end up with elevated blood pressure. That's why it is important for everyone to take precautions against the disease, particularly modifications in eating habits.

What the Readings Mean

Hypertension literally refers to a condition in which too much pressure is placed on the walls of the arteries. To understand how this happens, imagine that your arteries are so many garden hoses, and your blood is the water pumped through them. If you turn the water higher, more is pushed through in less time, increasing the pressure on the walls of the hoses. Or, if you pinch the hoses, the same amount of water is forced to circulate through narrower spaces, again increasing the pressure on the walls of the hoses. That's the basic mechanism of high blood pressure. It's a condition in which either the blood volume is increased or the arteries constrict. The extra pressure weakens the artery walls and thereby accelerates the wear and tear they undergo.

What does a blood pressure reading signify? Physicians consider approximately 120/80 (120 over 80) to 140/85 the normal range. The first, or upper, number represents the systolic pressure—that is, the pressure that is exerted when the heart contracts to pump out blood to all the arteries of the body. (A reading of 120 means that the heart is pumping hard enough to be able to drive a column of mercury up a tube to a height of 120 millimeters.) The second, or lower, number is the diastolic pressure—that is, the pressure exerted by the blood on the walls of the arteries between heartbeats.

Both numbers are important, although traditionally physicians have been more concerned with diastolic pressure because, if the diastolic pressure is high, it means that the arteries are under great pressure even when the heart is relaxed and simply filling with blood in preparation for its next beat. However, there is evidence that elevated systolic pressure may be equally cause for concern, even if it is the only one of the numbers that runs high. Researchers with the Framingham Heart Study found that those who had normal diastolic pressure but high systolic readings were at greater risk of suffering the consequences of heart disease than those with normal systolic readings. Dubbed borderline isolated systolic hypertension, the condition affected nearly one in five people over the age of 65 and ranked as the most common type of high blood pressure that was left untreated. Compared with people with normal blood pressure, those with the borderline condition were more likely to end up with high blood pressure in which one or both numbers were severely elevated, putting them at even greater risk of ill health and early death.

Obesity and Hypertension

It is believed that one of the best defenses against hypertension is to maintain a healthy weight. The incidence of hypertension among obese adults—that is, those people whose body weight is 30 percent or more above average—is estimated to be double that of nonobese people. And studies of large population groups have revealed that, in countries in which weight does not increase with age, neither does blood pressure. In the United States, where people tend to gain weight as they grow older, about half the population has hypertension by age 74.

Overweight people who already have high blood pressure can often reduce it dramatically by getting rid of their excess pounds, even if they do not manage to lose them all. As little as a 5 percent reduction in weight has been associated with a reduction in blood pressure so significant that some patients are able to stop taking antihypertensive medication.

Furthermore, it is now accepted that some obese hypertensives are able to reduce their

blood pressure to normal even when they lose only half of their excess weight. Why this happens is not fully understood, but it is known that the heart has to pump harder in overweight people, in part because the amount of tissue the blood has to reach is greater than in thin individuals.

Obesity isn't always a factor in hypertension. Being overweight doesn't always lead to the disease. Nor does becoming or staying thin necessarily ward off high blood pressure. But in the absence of a clear understanding of how weight and blood pressure are related, it is wise to keep your weight close to the recommended level.

Dietary Risk Factors

It appears that only some people are what is called "salt sensitive." For these people, too much sodium in the diet can lead to a marked rise in blood pressure. Such individuals apparently have an altered ability to excrete excess sodium in their urine. The extra sodium remains in the blood, making it "thirsty"—not unlike the way in which salty foods bring on thirst—and thereby drawing water to the blood, increasing blood volume, which creates greater pressure as the blood is pumped through the arteries.

The trouble is that it is hard to pinpoint who is salt sensitive and who is not. Researchers at the Indiana University School of Medicine have gone so far as to discover a particular gene that predisposes people to sodium sensitivity under certain laboratory conditions. But there is still no way to say whether the carriers of that gene will benefit by restricting sodium in their day-to-day diets. So, how should you act, in light of these uncertainties? Perhaps the following figures will help answer that question.

Our bodies need only about 200 milligrams of sodium a day (equivalent to a tenth of a teaspoon of salt) to regulate the amount of fluid that passes in and out of the cells and to maintain the acid–alkali balance; these are functions necessary for life. The National Academy of Sciences advised that people consume no more than 2,400 milligrams daily.

There are many sources of sodium in our diets, the greatest being processed foods. Sodium deficiency is not a concern in this country. Rather, it would seem that most Americans could stand to cut back on their sodium intake. According to the Food and Drug Administration, even if only 10 to 15 percent of the population were potential candidates for hypertension because of salt sensitivity, a nationwide reduction in salt intake could still help protect as many as 23 to 35 million Americans against the risk of stroke, heart attack, and kidney failure.

Like salt, alcohol appears to increase the risk for high blood pressure. Statistically, between 5 and 11 percent of the cases of hypertension in men are attributed to alcohol consumption. The evidence linking alcohol to increased blood pressure is strong. In one study, 20,000 people in Australia were observed, and it was found that the more they drank, the higher their blood pressure became. The association between drinking and blood pressure grows even stronger after adjusting for age, obesity, and smoking.

In another study of patients entering a hospital, it was shown that more than half of those who drank more than three ounces of alcohol a day were hypertensive. However, by the time their hospital stays were over and the drinking had stopped, fewer than 10 percent of the patients still had high blood pressure. When they were on their own again, just about all of those who remained abstinent continued to have normal blood pressure readings, whereas most of those who resumed drinking became hypertensive again.

Caffeine has been studied as to its possible contribution to hypertension, and there does not appear to be an important relationship between reasonable caffeine consumption and hypertension.

Potentially Helpful Dietary Practices

The medical literature contains many studies which suggest that nutrients such as potassium, calcium, and some forms of fiber may help protect against hypertension. The data in these studies vary in quality and, in some cases, are almost anecdotal. For example, studies in Japan showed that the amount of salt eaten by the residents of two villages was very high, yet one village had a much lower incidence of hypertension than the other. Closer examination of the villagers' habits revealed that those with the lower blood pressure ate diets high in soluble fiber and with a moderately good source of potassium.

It should not be too surprising that potassium might play a role in the regulation of high blood pressure, as it is a close relative of sodium. Like sodium, potassium is an electrolyte, a substance that helps regulate the water balance between the body cells and the blood. And, like sodium, it is essential for life. In fact, many people whose hypertension is so severe that they must take diuretics to rid their bodies of excess fluid must also take supplements to replace the potassium that is excreted along with the fluid. When the potassium level in the body falls too low, it can result in hypokalemia, a condition characterized by general weakness, an unexplained tingling sensation, cramps, an irregular heartbeat, and excessive thirst and urination.

Some scientists have suggested that it is not potassium per se that influences blood pressure but the ratio between dietary sodium and potassium. It is an idea worth considering. Often, when people eat fewer of those highly processed, prepackaged foods that are high in sodium, they tend to increase their consumption of fresh items such as fruits and vegetables, which are low in sodium and high in potassium.

Some researchers have tried to link calcium intake and a lowered risk of hypertension. A number of studies, some quite controversial, point to a possible connection. Observation of participants in the Puerto Rico Heart Health Program found that individuals who drank no milk (which is high in calcium and potassium) had twice the incidences of hypertension compared with those who were heavy milk drinkers. In another study, more than 5,000 adults in southern California were surveyed for heart disease risk factors as part of a Lipid Research Clinics population study. Hypertensive men (but not women) had a significantly lower calcium intake from milk than those who did not have the disease. With an increase in milk consumption, diastolic blood pressure decreased significantly.

Calcium might even help control blood pressure when negative factors are present. In a study of hypertensive blacks conducted at Wayne State University in Detroit, it was found that those on high-salt diets who were given supplemental calcium experienced reductions in blood pressure that were sometimes dramatic enough to produce normal blood pressure readings.

Despite all the promising clues concerning calcium's effect on blood pressure, the evidence is still much too sketchy to warrant increasing calcium for the purpose of controlling hypertension, especially if it's done in lieu of controlling dietary factors like sodium. Although epidemiological evidence suggests that high calcium intake leads to lower blood pressure, it does not prove it. Lifestyle patterns or other nutrients that have not yet been accounted for may be the factors making the difference.

Several other dietary variables may be involved in controlling high blood pressure. One may be a higher ratio of polyunsaturated to saturated fat. In Finland, where the amount of fat consumed, particularly saturated fat, tends to be quite high, blood pressure fell when the total fat intake was decreased and the ratio of polyunsaturated to saturated fat was increased. This result was seen both in those with hypertension and in those with normal blood pres-

sure. A single study such as this one does not prove that eating more polyunsaturates than saturates will keep your blood pressure down, but doing so won't hurt, and the practice would be consistent with dietary guidelines for reducing the risk of heart disease.

Dietary fiber has also been said to reduce blood pressure. A number of experiments have lent some support to the theory that the higher the fiber content of the diet, the lower the chance of developing hypertension. The evidence to support this conclusion is still incomplete.

Interestingly, all the measures mentioned—increasing polyunsaturated versus saturated fats; eating more fiber; keeping weight down; cutting back on alcohol; eating more fresh, low-sodium foods such as fruits and vegetables; eating low-fat, calcium-rich foods—are good ideas for a healthful diet in general. So, even though all the facts are not known about the relationship between diet and high blood pressure, following these guidelines will certainly help maintain overall health.

Exercise Aids Cardiovascular Fitness

According to the Centers for Disease Control and Prevention, the sedentary lifestyle of many Americans is a CHD risk factor—possibly as great as high cholesterol or high blood pressure. The CDC made this claim after evaluating more than 40 studies that demonstrated the heart-beneficial effects of certain kinds of exercise programs.

One long-term study conducted by the Stanford University School of Medicine and Harvard's School of Public Health tested the relationship between health and exercise in 17,000 Harvard graduates. Researchers began the study in the mid-1960s, recruiting subjects from among alumni aged 37 to 74. The subjects were followed until 1978. By the conclusion of the

Evaluate Your CHD Risk

A variety of factors contribute to the risk of developing coronary heart disease. Your answers to the following points will help you become aware of the ways heredity and lifestyle might influence your CHD risk.

This test is not designed to replace physical examinations or clinical tests. Rather, our intention is to call attention, in a personal way, to the wide variety of factors that might increase or reduce your risk of CHD. If you have reason to be concerned about your risk, consult your doctor.

Add the points to the right of your answers, and compare your total with the scores at the bottom.

AGE

20–40 (1)
40–55 (2)
over 55 (3)

SEX

male, over 45 (1)
female, postmenopause (1)

FAMILY HISTORY

no family history of heart disease (0)
1 relative¹ who had a heart attack after age 60 (1)
2 relatives who had heart attacks after age 60 (2)
1 relative who had a heart attack before age 60 (3)
more than 2 relatives who had heart attacks before age 50 (6)

BLOOD PRESSURE (SYSTOLIC, OR UPPER NUMBER)

101–120 (0)
121–140 (1)
141–160 (2)
161–180 (4)
181–208 (6)

BLOOD CHOLESTEROL

below 180 (0)
180–200 (1)
201–240 (2)
241–260 (3)
over 260 (5)

Evaluate Your CHD Risk *(cont.)*

DIET

consume less than 30 percent calories as fat, 15–25 percent as protein, and 40–55 percent as complex carbohydrates, in a varied diet (0)

consume 31–35 percent of daily calories as fat (1)

consume 36–40 percent of daily calories as fat (2)

consume 300 or fewer milligrams of cholesterol per day (0)

consume 301–400 milligrams of cholesterol per day (1)

consume 401–500 milligrams of cholesterol per day (2)

consume 2,001–3,500 milligrams of sodium per day (1)

consume more than 3,500 milligrams of sodium per day (2)

SMOKING

nonsmoker (0)

½ pack or less per day (1)

½ to 1 pack per day (2)

more than one pack per day (3)

2 or more packs per day (5)

WEIGHT

within 10 percent of ideal weight (0)

10–20 percent overweight (1)

21–35 percent overweight (3)

36–50 percent overweight (5)

more than 50 percent overweight (8)

EXERCISE

3–5 times a week for at least 20 minutes (0)

1–2 times a week for at least 20 minutes (1)

occasionally (3)

rarely or never (5)

OTHER FACTORS

history of diabetes (6)

female taking oral contraceptives (1)

alcohol consumption of more than 3 oz. per day (2)

SCORE

10 points or less = low risk

11–20 points = moderate risk

21–30 points = high risk

over 30 points = dangerously high risk

¹Parent, grandparent, or sibling

study, 1,413 of the subjects had died, 45 percent of them from heart disease. In evaluating the risk factors, the researchers found that lack of exercise was of greater consequence than obesity, cigarette smoking, or a family history of heart disease. Exercise also appeared to lower the risk of high blood pressure and cut the risk of smoking by as much as one-third. It also seemed to reduce some of the risks from genetic predisposition to heart disease.

The type of exercise that seems to do the most good is aerobic—sustained exercise that increases the strength of the heart. Aerobic exercise appears to raise HDL cholesterol, increase muscle mass to alleviate stress on the heart, strengthen the heart, and stabilize the heart rate. See Chapter 25 for advice on improving cardiovascular fitness with exercise.

Incidentally, you might be confused by some reports that very heavy exercise can actually trigger heart attacks. Two recent studies in Boston and Germany show that heavy physical exertion can block the flow of blood to the heart and bring on a heart attack. But that's true only for out-of-shape individuals who exert themselves suddenly—for example, by jogging or playing ball for the first time in months or years. If you're even just moderately active, on the other hand, the increased risk of suffering a heart attack during exercise is little to none. That's because regular exercise strengthens the heart muscle. (Of course, older, sedentary people should see a doctor before beginning any exercise regimen.)

So, the advice remains the same: Exercise regularly and eat a well-balanced low-fat, low-cholesterol diet to protect you against heart disease. The Tufts Low-Cholesterol Diet, outlined in the next chapter, is the first step to addressing the CHD danger in your own life. By reducing saturated fat, dietary cholesterol, and sodium and increasing the percentage of high-carbohydrate, high-fiber foods, you can make a substantial dent in the risk factors for CHD. And you will no doubt be pleasantly surprised when you see how appealing and full of variety this diet is.

19

The Tufts Low-Cholesterol Diet

The Tufts Low-cholesterol Diet is a 21-day meal plan designed to introduce you to low-cholesterol eating—the fun way. Each of the menus has been carefully planned to be consistent with the way people really eat and to incorporate the kinds of foods many people enjoy.

Each day's menu gets 50 to 60 percent of its calories from complex carbohydrates, with a minimum of 15 to 20 grams of fiber. Fewer than 30 percent of the calories come from fat, with only 10 percent of the total from saturated fat. In all, the daily menus fall well below the 300 milligrams of cholesterol that most experts consider the healthful limit.

The daily calorie total is approximately 1,800 calories. If you want to shave calories, it's easy to do so by eliminating the snacks (100 to 200 calories), having three ounces of meat instead of four, eliminating margarine, or having one slice of bread where two are called for. Men whose calorie needs are more than 1,800 should add calories to the complex carbohydrates—for example, having one to one-and-one-half cups of cereal instead of three-fourths cup, two muffins instead of one, or an extra baked potato or piece of corn on the cob.

We have tried to make the menus interesting by varying the types of breads, juices, and cereals. But you should feel free to switch them around as you please.

Following the menus are a few delicious recipes that taste as rich as the fattiest foods you've ever eaten. The asterisk (*) next to a menu item indicates that a recipe for it is given.

21-Day Menus

Day 1

BREAKFAST
Apple juice, ½ cup
Crushed pineapple, cup
*Cinnamon French Toast, 2 slices
Maple syrup, 2 tbsp
1% milk, 1 cup
Freshly brewed coffee or tea

LUNCH
Cream of tomato soup (made with 1% milk)

Submarine sandwich
deli-sliced turkey, 1 oz.

deli-sliced roast beef, 1 oz.

deli-sliced mozzarella cheese, 1 oz.

lettuce, tomato, as desired

mayonnaise, 1 tsp

mustard, as desired

Fresh, sliced nectarine, 1 medium

DINNER

Broiled center cut pork chop, sprinkled with
    rosemary, 4 oz.

Applesauce, ½ cup

Sauerkraut, ½ cup

Mashed potatoes

1 medium potato mashed with 1% milk and 1
    tsp tub margarine

Steamed medley of zucchini and carrots, cup,
    with 2 tsp tub margarine

SNACK

Berries and yogurt
low-fat French Vanilla yogurt, ½ cup

mixed fresh berries (raspberries, strawberries,
    blueberries), ½ cup

Day 2

BREAKFAST
Orange-pineapple juice, ½ cup

Bran flakes, ¾ cup, with 1 cup 1% milk and ½
    sliced banana

Marbled rye-pumpernickel toast, 1 slice, with 1
    tsp tub margarine

Freshly brewed coffee or tea

LUNCH
Charbroiled hamburger: lean ground beef, 3 oz.

tomato, onion, lettuce, as desired

ketchup, 1 tbsp

mustard, as desired

sesame-seed bun

Fruit and cheese salad: 1%-fat cottage cheese,
¼ cup fresh melon, medium pineapple, 1 slice
(ring) bed of leaf lettuce

DINNER
Chicken Oriental stir-fry: boneless chicken
    breast (cut into thin strips), 4 oz.

Oriental vegetables (snow peas, bamboo
    shoots, mushrooms), ¾ cup

Green pepper and carrot strips, 1 cup

Vegetable oil (for stir-frying), 1 tbsp

Soy sauce, 2 tsp

Steamed rice, 1 cup

Lemon-lime sorbet, ½ cup

Fortune cookie

SNACK
1% milk, 1 cup

Graham crackers, 4 squares

Day 3

BREAKFAST
Toasted English muffin, with 2 tsp tub mar-
    garine

Yogurt-Berry Swirl: low-fat lemon yogurt, 1 cup
    fresh blueberries, ¾ cup

Freshly brewed coffee or tea

LUNCH
*Curried chicken salad

Whole-wheat pita pocket, 1 medium

lettuce, tomato, as desired

Watermelon, 2" x 4" wedge

Grape Fizz: grape juice ½ cup, club soda ½ cup

DINNER
Poached haddock with dill, 5 oz. (use 1 cup 1%
    milk as poaching liquid)

*Parmesan noodles

Steamed zucchini and summer squash, cup, with 1 tsp tub margarine

White Zinfandel wine, 4 oz.

SNACK

Orange freeze: orange sherbet, ½ cup, blended with 1 cup 1% milk

Day 4

BREAKFAST

Scrambled eggs: 1 egg plus 1 egg white, cooked in 1 tsp tub margarine

Whole-wheat toast, 2 slices, with 1 tsp strawberry jam, 2 tsp tub margarine

Cantaloupe wedge, ⅓ medium

Freshly brewed coffee or tea

LUNCH

Roast beef sandwich: lean roast beef, 3 oz.

lettuce, tomato, as desired

mustard, as desired

mayonnaise, 1-½ tsp

roll

Fresh peach, 1 medium

1% milk, 1 cup

DINNER

Roasted light-meat turkey, 5 oz., with 2 tbsp meat juices (skim fat from drippings)

Stove-top stuffing, made with tub margarine, ⅓ cup

Cranberry sauce

Green beans, ½ cup, with 1 tsp tub margarine

Whole-grain dinner roll, with 1 tsp tub margarine

SNACK

Fresh, sliced strawberries, 1 cup

Day 5

BREAKFAST

orange juice, ½ cup

Raisin bran, ¾ cup, with 1 cup 1% milk

Cracked-wheat toast, 2 slices, with 2 tsp tub margarine

Freshly brewed coffee or tea

LUNCH

*Cashew turkey salad, served on a bed of lettuce

Crusty pumpernickel roll

Celery sticks

Fresh pineapple, ¾ cup

Mandarin orange sparkling water

DINNER

*Mom's meatloaf, 1 serving

Corn on the cob, 1 medium, with 2 tsp tub margarine

Steamed English peas, ⅔ cup, with 1 tsp tub margarine

Italian-style broiled tomato
tomato

1 tbsp Parmesan cheese

sprinkling of basil

Fresh fruit salad (diner's choice), ½ cup

SNACK

Angel food cake, 1/12 cake (cut cake in 12 slices and eat 1 slice)

1% milk, 1 cup

Day 6

BREAKFAST

Pineapple-grapefruit juice, ½ cup

Italian vegetable omelette
1 egg plus 2 egg whites

diced tomato, zucchini, mushrooms, ½ cup

1 tbsp Parmesan cheese

2 tsp tub margarine

Toasted Italian bread, 2 slices

Freshly brewed coffee or tea

LUNCH

Chicken with rice soup, 1 cup

French vegetable salad
leafy greens

1 cup diced red and green pepper

¼ cup sliced cucumber

¼ cup garbanzo beans

French dressing, 1 tbsp

Crusty French roll, with 1 tsp tub margarine

Red Delicious apple, 1 medium

1% milk, 1 cup

DINNER

Parsley halibut bake: halibut steak, 5 oz.

bread crumbs, 2 tbsp

crumbled fresh parsley

tub margarine, 2 tsp

lemon juice, 1 tbsp

Butternut squash with nutmeg, ¾ cup

Fresh asparagus, 5 spears

Oven-crisped potatoes: sliced potato, ½ cup, with 2 tsp hot margarine

Citrus sections, ½ cup

SNACK

Low-fat apple fruit yogurt, ½ cup

Ginger snaps, 3

Day 7

BREAKFAST

Cranberry juice cocktail, ½ cup

Low-fat peach or tropical fruit yogurt, 1 cup

Raisin toast, 2 slices, with 2 tsp tub margarine

Freshly brewed coffee or tea

LUNCH

Tarragon chicken salad sandwich: diced chicken, ½ cup chopped celery, 1 large stalk; mix 1 tbsp. each mayonnaise and low-fat, plain yogurt; add tarragon

Small French roll

Marinated raw vegetables: carrots, broccoli florets, red pepper, with 1 tbsp Italian dressing

Lemon spritzer

DINNER

Spicy taco salad: lean ground beef, browned and drained, 3 oz.

shredded cheddar cheese, 1 tbsp

lettuce, diced tomato, as desired

salsa, taco sauce, as desired

Soft flour tortilla, 1

Steamed Mexican corn: corn, ¾ cup chopped red and green pepper, ¼ cup

Poached pear with cinnamon

SNACK

Blueberry cheese crumble: fresh blueberries, ¼ cup layered with 1%-fat cottage cheese, ½ cup sprinkled with 4 crumbled ginger snaps

Day 8

BREAKFAST

White grape juice, ½ cup

Bran flakes, ¾ cup, with 1 cup 1% milk

Toasted oatmeal bread, 1 slice, with 1 tsp tub margarine

Freshly brewed coffee or tea

LUNCH

*Two-alarm chili

Saltines, 6

Side salad: red leaf lettuce tomato wedges oil and vinegar, 1 tbsp, basil to taste

Watermelon, 2" x 4" wedge

DINNER

Broiled salmon à l'orange: 4 oz. salmon, cooked with 1 tsp tub margarine, 2 tbsp orange juice

Baked potato, 1 medium, with 2 tbsp low-fat yogurt and 1 tbsp chives

Steamed green beans, 1 cup, with 1 tsp tub margarine

Red seedless grapes, 1 cup

Sparkling water with lemon slice

SNACK

Graham crackers, 4 squares, with 1 tbsp peanut butter

1% milk, 1 cup

Day 9

BREAKFAST

Orange-grapefruit juice, ½ cup

Toasted poppy-seed bagel, with 2 tsp tub margarine

1% cottage cheese, cup, served in cantaloupe

Freshly brewed coffee or tea

LUNCH

Ham sandwich on rye: deli-sliced ham, 3 oz.

lettuce, tomato, as desired

rye bread, 2 slices

mayonnaise, 1 tsp

mustard, as desired

Marinated cucumbers, ½ cup, soaked in 1 tbsp Italian dressing

Fresh bing cherries, ½ cup

1% milk, 1 cup

DINNER

Charbroiled porterhouse or sirloin steak (trimmed of fat), 4-½ oz.

Baked potato, 1 medium, with 2 tsp tub margarine

Fresh broccoli, 2 stalks, with 2 tsp Parmesan cheese

Sourdough dinner roll, with 1 tsp tub margarine

Boysenberry or pineapple sorbet, ½ cup

SNACK

1% milk, 1 cup

2 vanilla wafers

Day 10

BREAKFAST

Sparkling apple juice: ½ cup of apple juice, ½ cup of club soda

Bran flakes, ¾ cup, with ½ sliced banana

1% milk, 1 cup

Toasted whole-grain bread, 1 slice, with 1 tsp. tub margarine

Freshly brewed coffee or tea

LUNCH

*Italian tuna pasta salad, served on a bed of leaf lettuce

Cherry tomatoes, 4

Crusty French roll, with 1 tsp tub margarine

Red Delicious or Granny Smith apple, 1 medium

1% milk, 1 cup

DINNER

*Mexi-stuffed green pepper

Mixed green salad: leaf and red-leaf lettuce, 1 cup raw scallion, ¼ cup cucumber, French dressing, 1 tbsp

Medley of sliced peach and pear, ½ cup each

SNACK

French vanilla ice milk, ½ cup

Ginger snaps, 2

Day 11

BREAKFAST
Pineapple juice, ½ cup

Wheat or corn flakes, ¾ cup, with 1 cup 1% milk

Whole-wheat toast, 1 slice, with 1 tsp tub margarine

Fresh strawberries, ½ cup

Freshly brewed coffee or tea

LUNCH
*Chef Salad, with 1 tbsp oil, 1 tbsp balsamic vinegar

Pumpernickel roll

Fresh pineapple, 1/2 cup

Lemon spritzer

DINNER
Spaghetti and meat sauce: spaghetti, 2 cups, cooked tomato sauce, ⅔ cup lean ground beef, 3 oz., cooked Italian seasonings, as desired

Parmesan cheese, 1 tbsp

Italian bread, 1 slice

Romaine lettuce, with 1 tbsp Italian dressing

Italian ice, ½ cup

SNACK
Mixed fresh fruit salad, ½ cup

Day 12

BREAKFAST
Fresh grapefruit, ½

Scrambled eggs: 1 egg plus 1 egg white, cooked in 1 tsp tub margarine

Whole-grain toast, 2 slices, with 1 tsp tub margarine, 1 tsp strawberry jam

Freshly brewed coffee or tea

LUNCH
Tuna salad sandwich: tuna, 3 oz., water-packed; chopped celery, 1 tbsp

mayonnaise, 1-½ tsp, mixed with 1-½ tsp plain yogurt

Sesame-seed bun, 1

Carrot sticks

Fresh plums, 2 small

1% milk, 1 cup

DINNER
*Chicken Parmesan, served over 1 cup of fettuccine

Spinach salad: fresh, chopped spinach, 1 cup grated carrots, ¼ cup chopped red pepper, 1 tbsp oil and vinegar

Toasted garlic bread: 1 Italian roll, spread with 1 tsp tub margarine, garlic powder

SNACK
Peach milk shake: 1% milk, 1 cup, blended with ½ cup sliced peaches, 1 tbsp sugar

Day 13

BREAKFAST
Grapefruit juice, ½ cup

Corn or bran flakes, ¾ cup, with ½ cup sliced peaches

1 cup 1% milk

Freshly brewed coffee or tea

LUNCH
Cream of tomato soup, made with 1 cup 1% milk

Club sandwich: deli-sliced turkey and ham, 1 oz. each; low-fat cheese, ½ oz.

lettuce, tomato, as desired

mayonnaise, 1 tsp

mustard, as desired

whole-grain bread, 2 slices

Carrot and celery sticks

DINNER
Chicken in wine: skinless chicken breast, 5 oz., poached in ½ cup of red wine

Steamed wild rice, 1 cup, with 1 tsp tub margarine

Fresh asparagus, 5 spears, with 1 tsp tub margarine

Honeydew melon, ¼ medium

SNACK

Fig Newtons, 3

1% milk, 1 cup

Day 14

BREAKFAST

Orange juice, ½ cup

*Cinnamon French toast, with 2 tbsp maple syrup

Blueberries, ¾ cup

Freshly brewed coffee or tea

LUNCH

Corned-beef sandwich: deli-sliced lean corned beef, 3 oz.

rye bread, 2 slices

spicy or regular mustard

Coleslaw: ½ cup shredded cabbage, 2 tbsp shredded carrots, 1-½ tsp mayonnaise, mixed with 1-½ tsp plain, low-fat yogurt sprinkling of caraway seeds

1% milk, 1 cup

DINNER

Broiled rainbow trout: 5 oz. trout, broiled with 1 tbsp lemon juice, 1 tsp tub margarine

Spinach and orange salad: 1 cup leaf spinach, ¼ cup mandarin orange sections, 1 tbsp toasted almond slivers

French dressing, 1 tbsp

Steamed yellow and zucchini squash, ¼ cup each, with 1 tsp tub margarine

Boiled red potatoes, 2 small, with 1 tsp tub margarine, parsley

White-wine spritzer: ½ cup white wine, ½ cup club soda

SNACK

Peach crumble: ½ cup fresh sliced peaches, sprinkled with 3 crushed graham cracker squares

1% milk, 1 cup

Day 15

BREAKFAST

Raisin bran cereal, ¾ cup, with 1 cup 1% milk

Whole-wheat toast, 2 slices, with 1 tsp tub margarine, 1 tsp orange marmalade

Banana and kiwifruit salad: ½ medium banana, 1 sliced kiwifruit

Freshly brewed coffee or tea

LUNCH

Ham sandwich: deli-sliced ham, 2 oz.

lettuce, tomato, as desired

mayonnaise, 1 tsp

mustard, as desired

pumpernickel bread, 2 slices

Fresh orange or tangerine

1% milk, 1 cup

DINNER

*Spinach-chicken calzone

Broiled Italian tomatoes: 2 tomato halves, broiled with 1 oz. shredded part-skim mozzarella cheese, dash of oregano

Raspberry sorbet

Ginger snaps, 3

SNACK

1% milk, 1 cup

Day 16

BREAKFAST

Grapefruit, ½ medium

Spanish omelette: 1 egg plus 2 egg whites, ¼ cup chopped red and green pepper, 1-½ tbsp hot sauce, sauté in 1 tsp tub margarine

Toasted oatmeal bread, 2 slices, with 1 tsp tub margarine, 1 tsp grape jam

Freshly brewed coffee or tea

LUNCH

Stuffed pita bread sandwich: salad stuffing: 1 cup assorted vegetables (shredded carrots, chopped mushrooms, tomato, green pepper, shredded lettuce) 1 oz. shredded part-skim mozzarella cheese

pita pocket, 1, medium, drizzle with 1 tsp Italian dressing, 1 tsp flavored vinegar

Apple, 1 medium

1% milk, 1 cup

DINNER

Scallop scampi: sea scallops, 6 oz., broiled with 2 tbsp tub margarine, garlic

Baked potato, 1 medium with low-fat yogurt, 2 tbsp, chives

Steamed broccoli, ½ cup

Carrots with ginger, ½ cup, with 1 tsp tub margarine

Lime sherbet, ½ cup, with ½ cup sliced strawberries

SNACK

Seedless green grapes, 12

Vanilla wafers, 3

1% milk, 1 cup

Day 17

BREAKFAST

Apple-cranberry juice, ½ cup

Fruit yogurt, 1 cup, low-fat

*Three-grain muffin, 1

Melon balls, ½ made with cup each cantaloupe, honeydew

Freshly brewed coffee or tea

LUNCH

Tuna Nicoise: 3-½ oz. water-packed tuna, ½ cup

steamed green beans, 3 tbsp chopped pimento

chopped onion, 1 tbsp

celery sticks

vinegar and olive oil with basil, 1 tbsp

Crusty hard roll, 1

Red seedless grapes, 12

Fresh whole strawberries, 4

Lemon water

DINNER

Broiled tenderloin steak, 4 oz.

Corn on the cob, 1 ear, with 1 tsp tub margarine

Steamed carrots with mushrooms, ½ cup

Linguini noodles, ½ cup, with 1 tsp tub margarine, fresh parsley

Coffee ice-milk, ½ cup, with 1 tbsp slivered almonds

SNACK

Angel food cake, ¹⁄₁₂ cake (cut cake into 12 slices and eat 1 slice)

1% milk, 1 cup

Day 18

BREAKFAST

Fresh-squeezed grapefruit juice, ½ cup

*Cinnamon French toast, with 2 tbsp maple syrup

Berries and oranges: blueberries, ¼ cup; mandarin orange sections, ¼ cup

Freshly brewed coffee or tea

LUNCH

Roast beef sandwich: deli-sliced roast beef, 2 oz.

lettuce, tomato, as desired

mayonnaise, 1 tsp

bulky roll, 1

fresh plums, 2 small

1% milk, 1 cup

DINNER

Grilled chicken kabobs: cubed chicken breast, 4 oz.

cherry tomatoes, 3; pearl onions, 2; green pepper, ½ medium

Steamed brown rice, ⅔ cup, with 1 tsp tub margarine

Bibb lettuce, 1 cup, with ¼ cup herbed croutons, 1 tbsp vinegar and oil

SNACK

Lemon-berry parfait: ½ cup low-fat lemon yogurt, layered, with ¼ cup blueberries and 2 crushed graham cracker squares

Day 19

BREAKFAST

Pineapple-grapefruit juice, ½ cup

Oatmeal, ½ cup, with 2 tbsp raisins and cinnamon

1% milk, 1 cup

Whole-wheat toast, 1 slice, with 1 tsp strawberry jam

Freshly brewed coffee or tea

LUNCH

*Lentil-pasta soup, 1 cup

Spinach salad: chopped spinach, 1-½ cups; sliced mushrooms, ½ cup; tomato wedges, ½ cup; hard-boiled egg, 1; low-calorie French dressing, 1 tbsp

Fresh nectarine

DINNER

*Oriental beef stir-fry

Steamed rice, ⅔ cup

Fresh fruit salad: sliced strawberries, ½ cup; pineapple chunks, ¼ cup; chopped walnuts, 1 tbsp

Fortune cookie

Sparkling water with lime

SNACK

Three-grain muffin, 1

1% milk, 1 cup

Day 20

BREAKFAST

Apple juice, ½ cup

Low-fat vanilla yogurt, 1 cup, with fresh peach slices, nutmeg

*Three-grain muffin, 1

Freshly brewed coffee or tea

LUNCH

*Curried Chicken and Rice Salad, served on a bed of lettuce

Crusty rye roll, 1 small

*Low-fat lemon cheesecake, 1 slice

Iced tea with lemon

DINNER

Broiled lemon cod: 4 oz. cod, broiled with 1 tsp tub margarine, 2 tbsp of lemon juice; sprinkle with basil

*Parmesan Noodles, ½ serving

Steamed broccoli, 3 stalks, with 1 tsp tub margarine

Side salad: romaine lettuce, 1 cup; sliced mushrooms, ¼ cup; shredded part-skim mozzarella cheese, 1 oz.

low-calorie Russian dressing, 1 tbsp

1% milk, 1 cup

SNACK

Gingersnaps, 3

1% milk, 1 cup

Day 21

BREAKFAST

Fresh grapefruit, ½ medium

Bran flakes, ¾ cup, with 1 cup 1% milk

Cinnamon-raisin toast, 1 slice with 1 tsp tub margarine, 1 tsp apple jelly

Freshly brewed coffee or tea

LUNCH

*Lentil and pasta soup, 1 cup

Tuna salad sandwich: tuna, 3 oz., water-packed; chopped celery, 2 tbsp; mayonnaise, 1-½ tsp plus 1-½ tsp plain yogurt; lettuce, tomato

Marbled rye bread, 2 slices

Fresh pear

1% milk, 1 cup

DINNER

Glazed Cornish hen: ½ of a 1-lb. hen, skinned, roasted, and glazed with 1 tbsp apricot jam during last few minutes of cooking; sprinkle with tarragon

Baked sweet potato, 1 medium, with 1 tsp tub margarine

Steamed zucchini, 1 cup, sprinkled with lemon juice, dill

Pumpernickel dinner roll, 1 small with 1 tsp tub margarine

Raspberry sorbet, ½ cup, with ½ cup of fresh blackberries

SNACK

Blueberry cheesecake crumble: ½ cup blueberries, topped with ½ cup low-fat vanilla yogurt, 4 crumbled vanilla wafers

Kitchen-Tested Recipes

Lentil and Pasta Soup

4 cups low-sodium chicken broth
4 cups water

1 cup dried lentils, rinsed
28-oz. can whole tomatoes, chopped with their juice
6 oz. tomato paste
1 tbsp brown sugar
1 cup each sliced carrots and chopped celery
9-oz. package frozen Italian green beans
1 large onion
3 garlic cloves, minced
1 cup dry (uncooked) tubettini pasta
1 bay leaf
1 tsp each basil, oregano, thyme, black pepper, marjoram
1 cup wine vinegar

In large pot, combine broth, water, lentils, tomatoes, tomato paste, brown sugar, vegetables, and garlic. Bring to a boil, lower heat, cover pot, and simmer for 30 to 45 minutes. Add about 2 more cups of water, pasta, spices, and vinegar and simmer for about 30 minutes more. Remove bay leaf before serving.

Yield: 14 cups

Spinach-Chicken Calzone

10-oz. homemade or ready-to-bake pizza crust
1 pound chicken, skinned, cooked, and shredded
10-oz. frozen chopped spinach, thawed and drained
1 cup fresh mushrooms, chopped
1 cup grated Parmesan cheese
1 cup 1%-fat cottage cheese
1 cup parsley flakes
1 tsp oregano
1 tsp garlic powder
1 tsp onion powder
pepper to taste

Preheat oven to 375°F. On a lightly floured surface, roll dough to a 12" x 14" piece. Cut into six equal squares and place on a cookie sheet coated with vegetable oil spray. Combine remaining ingredients to make filling. Divide filling equally among the six squares by spooning it into the middle of each.

Fold squares in half diagonally. Firmly press edges together and crimp with a fork to make a tight seal. Lightly prick the top of each calzone with the fork and bake for 20 to 25 minutes or until crust is golden brown.

Yield: 6 calzones

Three-Grain Muffins

1 cup bran flakes cereal
1 cup dry (uncooked) oatmeal
1 cup whole-wheat flour
1 tbsp baking powder
1 tsp cinnamon
1 tsp nutmeg
1 cup skim milk
1 cup egg substitute
3 tbsp molasses
1 tbsp corn or safflower oil
1 medium apple, chopped

Preheat oven to 400°F. Combine bran flakes, oatmeal, flour, baking powder, and spices in a large bowl. In a separate bowl, mix the remaining ingredients and add to the dry cereal mixture. Stir contents until just moist. Coat 12 muffin tins with vegetable oil and divide batter equally among them. Bake 20 to 25 minutes until lightly browned.

Yield: 12 muffins

Low-Fat Lemon Cheesecake

Crust
1 cup graham crackers, crushed
1 tbsp margarine, melted
1 tsp cinnamon

Filling
4 cups low-fat lemon yogurt, drained
1 cup 1%-fat cottage cheese
1 cup all-purpose flour
1 egg

1 cup egg substitute
1 cup sugar
2 tsp vanilla

Line a colander with cheesecloth and place in dish deep enough to collect liquid that drains from yogurt. Pour yogurt into lined colander to drain. Cover and refrigerate overnight.

Preheat oven to 300°F. Combine crust ingredients and press into bottom of a 9" springform pan coated with nonstick vegetable oil spray. Combine filling ingredients and blend thoroughly with a hand mixer or food processor. Pour filling over prepared crust. Bake in preheated oven for approximately 1 hour (the edges will pull away from the pan when the filling is set). Set pan on rack and cool completely. Loosen edges with a knife before removing the pan sides. Chill and cut into 12 slices.

Yield: 12 slices

Cashew Turkey Salad

2 oz. turkey breast, cooked and chopped
7 cashews, broken into pieces
1 cup green pepper, chopped
1 medium carrot, grated
1 tbsp mayonnaise
1 tbsp low-fat plain yogurt

Mix ingredients and chill.

Yield: 1 serving

Mom's Meatloaf

1 lb. lean ground beef
2 eggs
8 tbsp tomato sauce
2 tbsp chopped onion
Italian seasoning

Mix meat, onion, Italian seasoning, and ½ of tomato sauce and place mixture in a small loaf pan. Bake at 350°F for 30 to 40 minutes. Drain fat and top with remaining tomato sauce.

Yield: 4 servings

Parmesan Noodles

1 cup noodles, cooked
2 tsp tub margarine
2 tbsp Parmesan cheese
fresh ground pepper

Mix thoroughly and serve hot.

Yield: 1 serving

Curried Chicken Salad

3 oz. chicken breast, cooked and diced
2 tsp mayonnaise
2 tsp low-fat plain yogurt
2 tbsp raisins
2 tsp chopped walnuts
curry powder to taste

Mix thoroughly and chill.

Yield: 1 serving

Curried Chicken and Rice Salad

2 oz. chicken, cooked and cubed
1 cup rice, steamed
1 cup grapes, sliced
1 tbsp walnuts

Dressing

2 tsp mayonnaise mixed with
3 tsp. low-fat plain yogurt
Curry powder to taste

Mix chicken and rice in a bowl, cover, and set in refrigerator to chill. Before serving, mix in thoroughly grapes, walnuts, dressing, and curry powder.

Yield: 1 serving

Two-Alarm Chili

3 oz. lean ground beef, cooked and drained
1 cup canned kidney beans
1 cup chopped onion

2 tbsp medium-hot salsa
3 tbsp water

Mix together all ingredients and slowly cook over low to medium heat. Add more water, if necessary.

Yield: 1 serving

Chicken Parmesan

4 oz. boneless chicken breast
1 oz. part-skim mozzarella cheese
1 tsp tub margarine
1 tbsp Parmesan cheese
1 cup spaghetti sauce

Remove skin from chicken and sauté in margarine until cooked. Place chicken in oil-sprayed pan and cover with spaghetti sauce. Top with cheese. Bake at 350°F until cheese melts. Serve over linguine.

Yield: 1 serving

Cinnamon French Toast

2 slices wheat or raisin bread
1 egg plus 1 egg white
1 tbsp 1% milk
cinnamon to taste
2 tsp tub margarine

Mix egg, egg white, and milk. Add cinnamon and dip bread into egg mixture to coat. Sauté in oil-sprayed pan using tub margarine.

Yield: 1 serving

Chef Salad

2 cups assorted leafy greens (spinach, leaf lettuce, iceberg lettuce)
1 oz. each of lean ham and turkey, cut in strips
1 oz. part-skim mozzarella cheese, cut in strips
1 cup grated carrots
1 tomato, cut in wedges

Layer ingredients onto lettuce bed and top with 1 tbsp vinegar and oil dressing.

Yield: 1 serving

Italian Tuna Pasta Salad

3 oz. water-packed tuna
1 cup cooked pasta, any kind
1 cup shredded raw carrots
1 cup shredded raw zucchini
2 tbsp Italian dressing

Lightly mix all ingredients. Top with fresh ground pepper, if desired.

Yield: 1 serving

Oriental Beef Stir-Fry

4 oz. flank steak or other lean cut of beef
1 medium carrot
1 cup snow peas
1 cup water chestnuts
1 cup bean sprouts
2 tbsp dry-roasted cashews
1 tbsp sesame oil
1 tbsp soy sauce

Cut beef into strips and carrots into thin slices. Sauté beef in wok or skillet until cooked. Add vegetables and stir-fry until tender crisp. Remove from heat and sprinkle with soy sauce.

Yield: 1 serving

Mexi-Stuffed Green Pepper

4 oz. lean ground round
1 cup boiled rice
1 cup tomato sauce
1 tbsp salsa
1 green pepper

Brown ground round in a skillet and drain off excess fat. Mix meat, cooked rice, tomato sauce, and salsa and stuff into pepper. Bake at 350°F for 30 minutes.

Yield: 1 serving

20

The Diet—Cancer Connection

Cancer is the second leading cause of death in the United States. Not a single condition but rather a group of conditions, cancer results from the uncontrolled growth of cells originating from almost any tissue in the body. Many factors appear to influence the onset of these conditions, including the environment, heredity, and smoking. However, the most current data suggest that diet may play an important role as well.

A great deal of research is going on worldwide about cancer and diet. And although there is gathering evidence that there are links between what we eat day-to-day and the long-term development of many types of cancer, there is also a growing body of conflicting evidence that these links may not be as specific as was once believed. This disagreement is fueling a behind-the-scenes debate within the scientific community over whether the public is being misled with statements that may not be quite true. A host of practical questions are being raised: Will a high-fiber, low-fat diet prevent cancer? Can antioxidants (so-called "protector nutrients") guard the body against cancer? Can supplements fight cancer? What are the real cancer-causing dangers of carcinogens in our food supply? There are no final resolutions to most of these questions. However, an examination of what is currently being seen in research should help put the issues in perspective.

Can Antioxidants Prevent Cancer?

The debate rages on as to whether antioxidant supplements (pills containing vitamins C and E and beta-carotene) play a preventive role in cancer, or whether it's the effect of whole foods containing these and other nutrients that has value.

To see just how well single antioxidant nutrients stack up next to whole fruits and vegetables, researchers at Cornell University compared vitamin C supplements with various fruits and vegetables in a head-to-head test to determine which might be better at warding off cancer. In the first of two studies, they compared taking a vitamin C supplement with drinking the same amount of the vitamin in different juices, including tomato, pineapple, strawberry, carrot, and green pepper juice. The result favored the juice drinkers. They were found to have significantly lower levels than the supplement takers of substances in their bodies called nitrosamines, which can work to turn normal cells cancerous.

The researchers then set out to determine which other components of fruits and vegetables besides vitamin C are involved in this protective effect. Specifically, they compared the vitamin C in tomatoes with a large group of non-nutrient chemicals in tomatoes known as phenolics. Both the vitamin C and the phenolics were found to help keep nitrosamines in check. Although the researchers examined only tomatoes, their findings could have much broader implications, because phenolics are ubiquitous throughout the plant world.

Other non-nutrient substances in plant foods have also been coming to light as possible protectors against cancer. For example, scientists have identified a component of broccoli and other cruciferous vegetables such as cauliflower and brussels sprouts that appears to ward off cancer-causing agents, thereby blocking tumor formation.

The bottom line is that it may be the foods themselves, not the isolated vitamins in antioxidant supplements, that protect against cancer.

Lung Cancer

Lung cancer is the number-one cause of cancer deaths for both men and women. The medical community is in agreement that cigarette smoking is the leading causal factor; smokers have a 20 to 30 times greater risk of contracting the disease than nonsmokers.

The research on the link between diet and lung cancer has been mixed. Some research does suggest that beta-carotene, the vitamin A precursor, may help protect people against a common form of lung cancer called squamous cell carcinoma. Other research indicates that vitamin E may help reduce the risk for developing any type of lung cancer. Research at Johns Hopkins University in Baltimore suggested that people with relatively low levels of beta-carotene in their blood might be at least four times as likely to fall victim to lung cancer as others; the risk for those who had low blood levels of vitamin E were as much as two-and-a-half times greater.

Scientists reporting in the *New England Journal of Medicine* found that the blood of 99 people who eventually developed lung cancer (most, but not all, were smokers) contained almost 14 percent less beta-carotene and 12 percent less vitamin E than the blood of 200 people who had similar smoking habits but remained free of lung disease. The mechanism by which beta-carotene and vitamin E might work to inhibit the development of lung cancer was not certain. It is known, however, that beta-carotene and vitamin E "trap" and "deactivate" free radicals, chemical components in the body that can harm cell structure and, in the process, presumably predispose tissues to cancerous growths.

Another study of 25,000 people over the course of a decade in Japan uncovered what appeared to be a link between daily consumption of vegetables high in beta-carotene and a decreased risk of cancer of the lung, colon, stomach, prostate, and cervix.

The early euphoria about the role of antioxidants in protecting against the development of lung cancer was challenged in 1994 by the results of the Finnish study referred to earlier. In that study, some 29,000 male smokers were given either beta carotene or vitamin E, alone or combined, or a placebo, for five to eight years. There was no reduction in the incidence of lung cancer among the antioxidant takers. In fact, there was actually more lung cancer among the beta-carotene takers.

To find out more about whether beta-carotene and vitamin E play a role in preventing cancer—and if they do, how so—scientists are conducting studies known as chemoprevention trials, in which large numbers of people are given supplemental doses of one or more substances and are then observed over a period of several years to see if they are less likely to contract cancer than others.

Currently, some 25,000 male physicians

throughout the United States are participating in a trial funded by the National Cancer Institute to determine if beta-carotene supplements will decrease the overall incidences of cancer. Other groups are being given vitamin E.

Even if the connection between these two nutrients and the avoidance of lung cancer were valid, there is some concern that people might use the information to begin or continue practices that are harmful. For example, smokers should not take this information to mean that it's okay to smoke as long as they increase their intake of these two nutrients. According to Dr. Charles H. Hennekens of the Harvard Medical School, even if beta-carotene were effective in reducing lung cancer deaths by half, lifelong smokers would still have a 10 to 15 times greater risk than nonsmokers of contracting the disease. Cigarettes are associated with a much greater risk of lung cancer than low levels of beta-carotene and vitamin E. Furthermore, these two nutrients may be only indirectly associated with a decreased risk of lung cancer. It may be that other, as yet undiscovered, substances in foods with beta-carotene and vitamin E are responsible for the protection against cancer that the researchers observed.

For this reason, it is not recommended that people take vitamin supplements of these nutrients, either in lieu of foods or in addition to foods. Rather, it is advised that people include in their diets the orange- and yellow-colored produce and the leafy green vegetables that contain beta-carotene, as well as the whole grains that contain vitamin E. Those who might take the early results of ongoing research to mean they should start taking large doses of certain nutrients in supplement form should be aware that this could be a dangerous practice. Although large doses of beta-carotene are relatively harmless, too much vitamin A can cause permanent liver damage. Selenium, a mineral that is currently being tested in anti-cancer studies, can be toxic in amounts easily obtainable from supplements. Even vitamin C, which, like vitamin E and beta-carotene, is being tested for its possible

properties in warding off cancer, may cause problems when it is consumed in megadoses. Furthermore, nutrient tests being conducted are related to people's patterns of food intake, and there are currently no data that might justify self-treatment with nutrient supplements.

Second-Hand Vitamin Loss

Current research shows that it is not only smokers who lose vitamin C. Even breathing other people's smoke can deplete your body of the nutrient.

Scientists at the Stanford Center for Research in Disease Prevention found that nonsmokers exposed to cigarette smoke at work or at home for more than 20 hours a week had lower blood levels of vitamin C than nonsmokers who didn't have to inhale secondhand smoke—even though the vitamin C content of their diets was similar. Twelve percent of the "passive" smokers had vitamin C levels that were alarmingly low.

Here's how it works. Burning tobacco spews forth pollutants that, once inhaled by smokers and nonsmokers alike, lead to the body's production of free radicals—highly toxic compounds that can damage cells and promote cancer. Vitamin C then acts as a scavenger and destroyer of those free radicals. But the more smoke a person breathes, the more free radicals are produced, and the more vitamin C is used up to fight them. Over time, too little vitamin C is on hand to fight free radicals, and this can pave the way for cancer and other ills.

Colon Cancer

Colon cancer is second only to lung cancer as the leading cause of cancer deaths among men in the United States, and it is the third leading cause of cancer deaths among women. An estimated 107,000 Americans will be diagnosed this year with cancer of the colon, and almost 50,000 people will die of it. Another 7,000 will die of rectal cancer.

A high-fiber, low-fat diet can be a preventive factor. Research demonstrates that a high intake of fat causes greater secretion of bile acids. And while bile acids are necessary to help the body digest fats, they or their breakdown products have also been shown to promote tumors in the colon (or large bowel) in laboratory animals.

Dietary fiber may minimize the harmful affects of bile acids and thereby inhibit tumor development. But, even if it has a positive effect, it has not yet been determined whether an increased fiber intake works independently of decreased fat intake or whether the two must operate in tandem for an optimal anti-cancer effect. In either case, fiber may help to decrease risk in one or more ways. It increases the bulk of the stool, which may dilute the concentration of cancer-causing agents. This increased bulk speeds the passage of stool through the colon and lessens the time carcinogens or carcinogenic substances in waste can do damage. It also may bind carcinogens that might otherwise remain free to work on producing a tumor.

One of the problems in assessing the precise relationship between fiber and colon cancer is that there are many different types of fiber, and not all of them appear to be protective. Although the insoluble fiber present in whole-wheat products has held up relatively consistently as a cancer inhibitor in research on rats, in some studies the soluble fiber found in oat bran and fruits has been shown to stimulate tumor production in laboratory experiments, possibly by increasing the concentration of bile acids. Of course, one problem with animal studies is that they often use potent carcinogens or unrealistically high levels of fiber. To make matters even more confusing, Greenland Eskimos, who eat no fiber to speak of but whose diets are extremely high in fat, have a low rate of colon cancer.

These seeming inconsistencies might lead you to conclude that "you're damned if you do, and damned if you don't." But closer examination reveals that the type of fat Greenland Eskimos eat consists largely of the omega-3 fatty acids found in fish, which may not have the same effect on the secretion of bile acids as the typical saturated and polyunsaturated fats of the American diet.

According to experts, in addition to diet and lifestyle, one of the keys to prevention and survival is early detection. With early detection, mortality can be reduced 30 to 50 percent. For this reason, the American Cancer Society recommends an annual digital rectal examination by a physician after age 40. Yearly tests to determine if there is blood in the stool should be done after age 50. And screening sigmoidoscopies, in which a physician uses special instruments to inspect the rectum and lower colon, are recommended every three to five years after age 50.

Warning signs that should also precipitate a visit to the doctor include rectal bleeding, blood in the stool, or changes in bowel habits. These symptoms can also indicate other conditions that are less serious than cancer, but it is better to be safe than sorry.

Little Help from Antioxidants

Early reports that antioxidants might protect against colon cancer appear to be in question. The results of a four-year experiment showed that hundreds of people who swallowed high doses of beta-carotene, vitamin E, and vitamin C did not end up with fewer precancerous growths in their colons and rectums than non-supplement takers. All had been treated for at least one of these growths before entering the study. Called colorectal adenomas, they can turn into colon or rectal cancers.

One reason researchers investigated the possibility that antioxidant vitamins could help stave off colon and rectal cancers is that populations which consume a lot of foods containing those nutrients (that is, diets rich in fruits and vegetables) typically have low rates of these cancers. Although more studies need to be done, scientists suspect there may be compounds in fruits and vegetables other than antioxidants that exert the protective effect, or that people who eat relatively large amounts of plant food avoid excesses of meat and fat.

Breast Cancer

Breast cancer is the second leading cancer killer of women after lung cancer. It is estimated that a 50-year-old woman has a one-in-fifty chance of developing the disease, and the risk continues to rise with age. Against the backdrop of this distressing statistic, scientists are now debating whether women can reverse the trend by cutting back on the percentage of fat in their diets.

Several convincing studies back up the contention that there is a relationship. In fact, according to Leonard A. Cohen, Ph.D., of the American Health Foundation in Valhalla, New York, "The association between dietary fat and breast cancer comes closest to fulfilling the criteria epidemiologists look for when they make inferences about what causes disease."

One recent study, led by Dr. Paolo Toniolo of the New York University Medical Center, studied 750 Italian women. Those who ate the most fats, saturated fats, and animal protein had a three times greater chance of getting breast cancer than those who had the lowest intake of these foods. The study also showed that a high-calorie diet seemed to increase the risk of cancer; women who consumed more than 2,700 calories a day had almost twice the risk of breast cancer as those who ate fewer than 1,900 calories. (It is not certain whether the high-calorie diets were culpable because they were also high in fat.)

Studies of Japanese women who eat a traditional diet that is only about 20 percent fat have shown that these women are less likely to contract breast cancer than women in countries, such as the United States, in which the diet is higher in fat. In fact, breast cancer has been estimated to be four to five times as common in the United States as it is in Japan. Particularly telling is the evidence gathered on the granddaughters and great-granddaughters of Japanese families who migrated to Hawaii and the mainland of the United States and adopted diets higher in fat. The breast cancer rate among these Americanized women approaches that of other women in this country. The same has proved true for American-born women of Polish descent, who have a higher rate of breast cancer than their ancestors who ate a lower-fat diet. Furthermore, in Japan today, where the diet has become more Westernized, the incidence of breast cancer is on the rise. These studies indicate that genetic factors are not the sole determinants in assessing breast cancer risk.

Despite this evidence, there are those who cautiously point out that none of these studies linking high-fat diets to breast cancer have proved a specific cause-and-effect relationship between the two. It is true that even the most carefully constructed epidemiological studies cannot rule out the possibility that other environmental influences or genetic variations account for some of the differences. Studies on laboratory animals cannot provide an absolute link either, because they cannot automatically be extrapolated to humans.

Skeptics of the dietary fat–breast cancer link also point to a Harvard study of almost 90,000 women, which revealed that those who took in 44 percent of their calories from fat were no more likely to develop breast cancer than those who consumed only 32 percent of their calories from fat. But is 32 percent fat low enough to draw the comparison?

Not according to scientists whose research suggests that the risk of breast cancer does not decrease little by little as fat is cut out of the diet; instead, they believe there may be a cutoff point below which women are not at high risk for breast cancer and above which they are. In effect, there may be a "threshold point." If that is true, where is the threshold? Not all scientists agree on the exact number, but most believe it is below 30 percent. Sherwood L. Gorbach,

M.D., a professor of medicine at Tufts who has conducted numerous studies on the link between diet and breast cancer, recommends a diet consisting of 20 to 25 percent of fat calories. There is new evidence that part of the health effect might be caused not so much by lower fat but by a higher intake of phytoestrogens, the plant hormones present in soy products and other plant foods. Researchers suspect that the phytoestrogens in soy may help reduce cancerous tumors in the breast by providing an antiestrogenic effect—blocking the cancer-promoting action that estrogen is capable of having.

Breast tissue cells contain what are known as estrogen receptors, which enable them to "recognize" estrogen. Think of the receptors as key holes and the body's chemical compounds as keys with estrogen-shaped compounds being the only keys that will fit. Some researchers speculate that because the weak plant estrogens have structures very similar to the estrogen of mammals, they are able to insert themselves into the locks and "jam" them. That, in turn, could keep out some of the naturally produced estrogen and reduce its ability to cause the production of cancer cells. While this research is in the early stages, it might ultimately be an important breakthrough in the prevention of breast cancer.

The Role of Vitamin A/ Beta-carotene

When researchers at Harvard University looked at the eating habits of almost 90,000 women and followed their health for eight years, they found that those who ate just a little bit of vitamin A–rich foods every day (in many cases, only about a serving's worth) were more apt than others to stave off malignant breast tumors. Large amounts, however, did not reduce the breast cancer risk any further.

Good dietary sources of beta-carotene include deep orange and yellow, as well as dark, leafy, vegetables—for example, sweet potatoes, cantaloupe, kale, apricots, and broccoli. Vitamin A is found in large amounts in beef liver, as well as in eggs and full-fat dairy products. But because these foods are also high in fat and cholesterol, it's wiser to use fat-free or low-fat items that are supplemented with vitamin A.

Exercise Offers Protection

In addition to nutritional benefits, there is evidence that exercise can make a big difference in a woman's breast cancer risk. In a study of more than 1,000 women, scientists found that those who exercised at least four hours a week from the time they started menstruating were 60 percent less likely than nonexercisers to fall victim to breast cancer by age 40. Those who exercised one to three hours a week reduced their risk by 30 percent.

The researchers theorize that exercise diminishes the chance of suffering breast cancer by lowering levels of two hormones produced by the ovaries—estradiol and progesterone. Both have been linked with breast tumor production.

How does physical activity reduce a woman's ovarian hormones? One way is by suppressing ovulation during adolescence. Teenage girls who engage in regular exercise are more likely not to ovulate, even if they get their periods. Without ovulation, less estradiol and progesterone are produced. Furthermore, habitual exercise makes a woman ovulate later in her cycle and thereby shorten her luteal phase—the number of days between ovulation and the time she menstruates. That's important because it is during the luteal phase that exposure to ovarian hormones is greatest.

It's the hormone–breast cancer link that many believe explains a woman's relative protection from the disease if she begins menstruating relatively late and starts having babies early. The later in life a woman begins menstruating, the less time her ovaries spend producing estradiol and progesterone every month. And the sooner she stops menstruating because of pregnancy, the sooner the monthly cycle of progesterone and estradiol production is interrupted. Breast-feeding tends to halt menstruation and its attendant hormone production, too, which is why some researchers believe that new mothers who breast feed are less likely to fall victim to breast cancer than mothers who bottle feed.

Whatever the hormone connection, it should be remembered that the exercise study is only one piece of research. And it failed to address whether physical activity reduces breast cancer risk *after* age 40, when most cases of the disease occur. Still, its conclusions indicate that teenage girls and young women can give themselves a big protective bonus by starting to exercise regularly.

Prostate Cancer

The cause of prostate cancer, which affects 20 to 30 percent of all men in their lifetimes, is still a mystery. However, at least one study suggests that obesity and heavy consumption of meat and dairy products may play a role in the development of the disease. David A. Snowden, Ph.D., and his colleagues at the University of California, Loma Linda, examined the 1960 diet and weight records of more than 6,700 men over the age of 60 and focused their attention on those who died during the following 20 years because of prostate cancer.

Dr. Snowden's group found that heavy consumers of animal products were more than three-and-a-half times more likely to die of prostate cancer than light consumers of animal products. Heavy consumption was defined as eating cheese, eggs, meat, or poultry three or more times a week and drinking more than two glasses of milk each day. Light consumption entailed eating each of these foods on the average of one day a week and drinking less than a glass of milk every day. The researchers also found obesity to be a significant risk factor. Men who were one-third or more above their

desirable weight in 1960 were two-and-a-half times more likely to succumb to prostate cancer than men of normal weight.

Another study at Harvard University supports this evidence. In studying the health and eating habits of nearly 48,000 men from 1986 to 1990, scientists found that those who consumed the most red meat had the highest risk of ending up with an advanced or fatal case of prostate cancer. The researchers also discovered a link between the disease and a particular type of fat called alpha-linolenic acid, which is present not only in meat but also in foods such as butter, whole-milk-based dairy products, and processed foods made with soybean oil.

Phytoestrogens, thought to show promise in preventing the growth of cancerous tumors in breasts, may also be a factor in preventing or treating prostate cancer. It has long been known that estrogen can retard prostate tumor growth by slowing the production of testosterone. Some scientists think that phytoestrogens, especially those in soy products, may provide the same benefit—without the undesirable side effects of estrogen.

Laboratory research has been encouraging. Scientists in Finland have shown that phytoestrogens inhibit the development of blood capillaries that normally form around prostate tumors to nourish them. In other words, it may be that soy could stop prostate cancer by literally cutting off its blood supply. Researchers at the University of Alabama have found that the phytoestrogen in soy call genistein can inhibit the growth of prostate cancer cells in test tubes. They are now feeding men about two ounces of soy a day to see if early signs of prostate cancer will disappear.

Early Screening Is Key

Doctors say that many of the deaths from prostate cancer could be prevented with early detection. The American Cancer Society, the Prostate Cancer Education Council, and the American Urological Association all recommend that after age 50, men undergo annual check-ups for the disease. Men at high risk for prostate cancer, including African Americans and those with family histories of the disease, should begin getting tested at age 40. A visit to the doctor is also in order for men who have symptoms of prostate problems, including frequent urination, especially at night; difficulty starting urination or holding back urine; weak or interrupted flow of urine; painful or burning urination; blood in the urine; painful ejaculation; and chronic pain in the back, hips, or upper thighs.

Zinc and the Prostate

You may have heard that prostate problems, as well as impotence, can be alleviated with a daily high-dose zinc supplement. Unfortunately, this misconception has led to zinc toxicity in many men who have tried the "cure." One 48-year-old Indiana man who self-prescribed a zinc supplement amounting to 50 times the RDA arrived at an Indiana University hospital complaining of long-standing fatigue. All the excess zinc had caused a severe form of anemia. The extra amounts of metal impair the body's ability to absorb copper, and this can lead not only to anemia but also to other complications such as kidney failure.

The overuse of zinc is particularly unfortunate because no scientific evidence supports its claims to aid prostate problems and correct impotence. Indeed, unless you're suffering from an out-and-out zinc deficiency—an unlikely situation because zinc is supplied in many meats, poultry, and seafood—taking large doses of the mineral will only hurt, not help.

Stomach Cancer

During the past 50 years, there has been a remarkable decline in stomach cancer in the United States and many other industrialized nations. It is believed that at least part of the reason for the decline is that people are eating less smoked and pickled foods. Salt-cured and salt-pickled foods have been linked to gastric cancer, possibly because the nitrates in these foods are converted to nitrosamines in the body. Nitrosamines have been shown to be carcinogenic. There is compelling evidence that vitamin C may inhibit nitrosamine production.

Skin Cancer

There is preliminary new evidence that cutting down on fat in the diet may be one key to protecting yourself against skin cancer. At Houston University, researchers monitored the skin health of some six dozen men and women, all of whom had already suffered at least one episode of skin cancer. Half of them cut their fat intake from 40 percent to roughly 20 percent of their diets. The other half continued to follow their usual diets, which were relatively high in fat. At the end of two years, the higher-fat eaters developed an average of ten new premalignant spots, or lesions, each. Those who adopted the lower-fat regimen, however, averaged only about three new precancerous lesions each.

The lesions, which may be tan or brownish in color, are not the little dots that are commonly referred to as aging or liver spots. Rather, they are rough, dry, scaly bumps that measure anywhere from one-quarter inch to an inch in diameter and may also be red or gray in color. Technically known as solar keratoses, these bumps rank as the most common precancerous skin condition, affecting more than five million Americans—frequently those over age 60, with fair as opposed to dark skin. They appear most often on the face, lower lip, back of the hands, forearms, neck, and on the scalps of bald men. They have anywhere from a 1 to 25 percent chance of developing into a type of skin cancer called a squamous cell carcinoma if they are not removed. Although squamous cell carcinoma is not among the most serious types of skin cancer (the cure rate is about 95 percent when detected and treated early), in some cases it can metastasize to other parts of the body and prove fatal.

So, why might a reduction in dietary fat help protect against skin cancer? The researchers who have studied this aren't sure, but one possibility is that lower levels of dietary fat may lead to lower levels in the body of substances that regulate immune function, such as prostaglandins. In high concentrations, those substances could pave the way for inflammation and possible tumor formation.

Incidentally, while you're watching your diet, also take care to avoid excessive sunlight—or at least wear sunscreen with a high protection factor. Sunlight, after all, is a *known* risk factor for both solar keratoses and skin cancer.

Current Recommendations in a Nutshell

Although questions remain about which dietary components may protect against or contribute to the development of various kinds of cancer, most experts agree that by following a certain dietary pattern, health-conscious eaters can apply the best of what has been gleaned so far about reducing the chance of developing cancer. Even if it turns out that dietary measures do not reduce the risk as much as many scientists hope, this pattern will provide the balance of nutrients that is essential to the maintenance of general health, as well as assist in the fight against obesity and heart disease. Here are the suggested dietary guidelines:

◆ Eat fewer items that are high in fat, especially saturated fat, including heavily marbled meats, fried foods, cold cuts such as bologna and salami, bacon, whole milk and cream, creamed dishes, rich desserts, and meals prepared with lots of oil, butter, or margarine.

◆ Consume more low-fat dairy products, such as low-fat yogurt, cottage cheese, and skim milk; baked or broiled poultry without the skin; fish; and lean cuts of meat with all the fat trimmed away.

◆ Select fiber-rich whole-grain breads, cereals, and pastas (the ingredient list must contain the words "whole-grain" or "whole-wheat"), all types of fruits and vegetables, legumes, oat-based products, and, in moderation, nuts (which are relatively high in fat).

◆ Increase your consumption of soy products to take advantage of the potential cancer fighting effects of phytoestrogens.

◆ Increase your daily intake of fruits and vegetables rich in beta-carotene, such as cantaloupe, apricots, sweet potatoes, spinach, and broccoli.

◆ Eat a variety of produce that contains appreciable amounts of vitamin C, which includes everything from citrus fruits to tomatoes to dark-green leafy vegetables.

◆ Get enough vitamin E by using small amounts of polyunsaturated oils when cooking and by eating a wide variety of vegetables and whole grains.

21

Can Diet Cure What Ails You?

We are reaching a point in our scientific research where certain conclusions can be formulated, based on the data that now exist, regarding many illnesses that afflict Americans today. Again, we caution you that you should not take the results of early research to mean that diet can provide some kind of magic healing function. Instead, consider the dietary factors one piece of the puzzle.

Scientists and health experts have reached preliminary conclusions about dietary factors that influence various types of common ailments, among them diabetes, kidney disease, heartburn, arthritis, Parkinson's disease, seasonal affective disorder, and the most perplexing disease of modern life, AIDS. Let's examine the evidence.

Diabetes Can Be Controlled by Diet

Diabetes mellitus occurs when the pancreas either does not produce enough of the hormone insulin or when the cells of the body are not able to use it properly. In order to understand how diabetes causes problems, it helps to look at how the normal body functions.

When you eat food, your body must process the nutrients, carbohydrate, protein, and fat before the body cells can use them. Carbohydrate, for example, is converted in the process of digestion to a simple sugar, most often glucose. The glucose is then released from the intestines into the bloodstream, where it is transported to the body cells for use as an energy source or converted to fat and stored. Protein and fat are also broken into smaller components to be used by the cells.

When a person eats a meal, the pancreas releases insulin into the bloodstream to assist the cells in absorbing and utilizing the sources of energy glucose, fatty acids, and amino acids. Insulin is also involved in the synthesis of protein and the storage of glucose and fatty acids as glycogen and fat. Without insulin, or without the ability to properly utilize it, your body cannot adequately use the foods you eat. Hence, the glucose that comes from dietary sources accumulates in the blood, and people are said to have "high blood sugar." Further, when blood glucose builds to a certain point, the kidneys, which filter all of the blood, are unable to handle the load, and some glucose quite literally spills into the urine. The appearance of glucose in the urine is the major diagnostic test for diabetes.

Diet is known to be a critical factor in the management of diabetes. There are three different types of diabetes mellitus. One of them, gestational diabetes, is a temporary condition that sometimes afflicts pregnant women (see Chapter 16 for more details). The other two forms are insulin-dependent diabetes (Type I) and noninsulin-dependent diabetes (Type II).

Type I: Diabetes

This form usually occurs in childhood and lasts throughout the person's life. Those afflicted with Type I diabetes make little or no insulin, so they must rely on injected insulin to metabolize food. They also must make an effort to match their food intake to their insulin dose to minimize the fluctuations in their blood sugar levels. Until recently, insulin was derived from animals. Modern molecular biology enables the production of an identical form from bacteria.

With the advent of home blood-glucose monitoring and the practice of taking two or more daily insulin injections, people with Type I diabetes are now able more easily to control their condition, and they have greater freedom in making food choices and timing their meals than they once did.

Type II: Diabetes

This is the most common form of diabetes. It can exist in varying degrees of mildness or severity. Type II diabetes is usually seen in adults over 30 years of age who have problems with obesity. Unlike those with Type I diabetes, who cannot produce enough insulin, Type II sufferers often produce enough but are unable to use it properly, often because they are carrying too much weight. For these people, weight loss often makes it possible for their bodies to begin using insulin in a normal way. Although Type II diabetes is often hereditary, diet, exercise, and weight loss are the most important factors in its control.

Dietary Guidelines for Diabetics

When a person is diagnosed with the disease, the first thing he or she usually hears is "no more sweets." Indeed, for the more than 14 million Americans afflicted with diabetes, one of the most difficult aspects of living with the condition has long been feeling guilty about enjoying a piece of birthday cake or eating a cookie.

But during the past ten years, more and more evidence has come to light indicating that rigid, prohibitive "diabetic diets" are not the way to go. New research challenges conventional wisdom regarding not only the thinking on sweets but also the best approach to weight control, the proportions of fat and carbohydrate in the diet, and the amount of fiber to eat. So much has changed, in fact, that the American Diabetes Association recently revamped its nutritional guidelines, breaking with the past by liberalizing a number of its earlier recommendations.

The old advice specified the exact percentage of calories that were supposed to come from protein, carbohydrate, and fat. But except for recommending 10 to 20 percent of calories from protein, the new guidelines reject the idea of promoting the same proportion of major nutrients for everyone.

One of the main reasons for the shift is that diabetes, particularly Type II, often goes hand in hand with other health problems, such as heart disease, that are equally important to consider when planning the diet.

As a result, many people with diabetes have to plan eating patterns that will not only steady their blood sugar levels but also keep down levels of blood cholesterol and blood triglycerides.

So what's the answer? It appears that the type of low-fat diet used to prevent and treat heart disease isn't always the best for a person with both heart disease *and* diabetes. In some studies of people with Type II diabetes, a low-fat diet that contained 60 percent carbohydrate and only 20 to 25 percent fat calories actually *raised* triglyceride and blood sugar levels as well as reduced "good" HDL cholesterol. But when investigators put people with Type II diabetes on diets containing as much as 40 percent fat (most of it monounsaturated), these adverse effects were avoided. Granted, the studies were short-term, so it's unclear whether a high-monounsaturated fat diet would be appropriate for large numbers of people with the disease. Still, the fat issue underscores the fact that everyone with diabetes should consult with a dietician as well as a physician and come up with a tailor-made eating plan that takes into consideration all the individual factors.

Are Sugary Foods Off-Limits?

The notion that people with diabetes should avoid sugar and sugary foods comes from the belief that during digestion the sugar, or simple carbohydrate, is broken down into molecules of glucose much more rapidly than other foods. The thinking goes that these glucose molecules enter the bloodstream in droves, causing sugar levels to skyrocket. Of course, starches, or complex carbohydrates, found in bread and potatoes are broken down into glucose, too. But they have been assumed to break down more slowly, thereby producing a slower, steadier rise in blood sugar.

It may surprise you to learn that little or no scientific evidence supports this belief. In fact, research conducted over the past decade has shown that bread, potatoes, and rice are just as likely as plain table sugar to prompt a rapid rise in blood sugar. That's because starchy complex carbohydrates are quickly broken down into glucose during digestion, just as sugary foods are. To be sure, carbohydrates from sweets still play a key role in the overall diet. But they don't appear to have any more of an impact on blood sugar than the complex carbohydrates that come from starchy foods. Thus, a person with diabetes should pay attention to the total amount of carbohydrate in the diet, not the simple (sugar) versus complex (starch) carbohydrates.

The new guidelines also call into question the conventional wisdom that people with diabetes should consume more high-fiber foods. Although scientists theorize that soluble fiber (the kind found in oatmeal, legumes, fruits, and vegetables) may combine with other foods to form a thick gel along the wall of the intestine that might prevent that organ from absorbing glucose, it is not known whether this translates to a significant effect on blood sugar. Most of the studies attempting to pinpoint fiber's effect on blood sugar haven't adequately accounted for the many other factors that play a role, such as the amount of total carbohydrate in the diet. The American Diabetes Association has concluded that the overall impact of fiber is "probably insignificant." Nevertheless, highly respected physicians and nutrition researchers have reported considerable success treating Type II diabetes with soluble fiber.

Carefully Planned Exercise Can Help

It was once thought that people with diabetes could not withstand vigorous physical exercise. That is no longer believed to be true. Granted, insulin takers have to carefully plan long bouts of exercise because vigorous physical activity can allow blood sugar to fall dangerously low. For example, if a person takes a dose of insulin at noon and doesn't eat anything for the next couple of hours, going for a run at 2:30 may spell trouble. There are three reasons: The insulin dose had a couple of hours to lower the blood sugar; there's no food in the runner's system to supply more sugar to the blood; and exercise will prompt the blood sugar to drop lower still. If blood sugar falls too low, the result could be dizziness, lightheadedness, fainting, and, in severe cases, coma, also known as "insulin reaction" or "insulin shock."

The way around the problem is to carefully

time exercise, meals, and insulin doses to make sure that the body has enough glucose available in the blood to fuel the entire workout. Insulin takers are advised to check their blood sugar levels with a blood glucose meter before and after a workout. If blood sugar is low, they should eat a snack such as a piece of fruit.

For people with diabetes who are not on insulin, regular exercise does not have to be timed as carefully. Indeed, exercise ranks as one of the most effective ways of normalizing high blood sugar levels. One reason is that exercise can promote weight loss, which in turn boosts the body's ability to make the most efficient use of its insulin.

Even exercisers who don't lose weight often see long-term improvement in blood sugar levels. The reason is that exercise in and of itself improves the body's ability to respond to insulin's attempts to move glucose from the bloodstream into the cells. A recent study carried out at the Jean Mayer USDA Research Center on Aging at Tufts concluded that people who pedaled a stationary bicycle for 55 minutes four days a week improved their body's ability to move glucose from the blood to the cells by about 11 percent—even though they didn't shed any excess pounds. Exercise is so important in keeping blood sugar levels normal that some research has indicated that regular activity helps prevent diabetes from developing in the first place.

Easing Heartburn

Many people suffer heartburn at one time or another. One condition that promotes heartburn is a hiatal hernia.

A hiatal hernia is a condition wherein a portion of the stomach protrudes abnormally. In most people, the entire stomach sits below the diaphragm, a muscular wall that essentially separates the stomach from the esophagus. But when you have a hiatal hernia, part of the stomach pushes upward through the diaphragm via an opening called the esophageal hiatus. When that protrusion occurs, a muscle at the base of the esophagus called the sphincter is less likely to contract (close) sufficiently after food makes its way through it. Then, when the food mixes with digestive acids in the stomach, it has a good chance of backing up into the esophagus. The result is heartburn. Acid going in the wrong direction can also occur in someone with a hiatal hernia because food may become trapped in the herniated part of the stomach, where it can mix with acid and easily travel back up rather than down.

Foods that can potentially aggravate heartburn by making the sphincter even less apt to close tightly are coffee (including decaf), caffeine-containing foods like cola and chocolate, and alcoholic drinks. These items, which also make the stomach contents more acidic, should be limited or avoided, as should fatty foods. Spicy foods and carbonated beverages bother some heartburn sufferers, but not others.

Of course, many people have heartburn who do not also have a hiatal hernia. If you have problems with heartburn, you can minimize the discomfort by following these guidelines:

◆ Eat four or five smallish meals a day rather than two or three big meals, so there is less pressure in the stomach that could send food and acid back into the esophagus.

◆ Eat slowly so that you're less likely to swallow excess air and then belch it up in conjunction with fluid and acid.

◆ Don't lie down for at least two hours after eating. Gravity helps prevent the backward flow of acid.

◆ Don't wear tight clothing.

◆ Lose weight, if necessary.

Some physicians recommend over-the-counter antacids or prescribe acid-reducing drugs such as Zantac, Tagamet, or Prilosec.

ANTACID CHECKLIST

Check to see where the checks are below. That will tell you which antacids contain which ingredients.

	Calcium	Magnesium	Aluminum	Simethicone	Sodium (mg)[1]
Alka-Seltzer (original)					1134
AlternaGEL			x	x	<5
Amphojel		x	x		0
Bromo Seltzer					1522
Di-Gel		x	x	x	0
Maalox Plus		x	x	x	<3
Gaviscon		x	x		78
Mylanta		x	x	x	0
Rolaids (Regular)		x	x		100
Rolaids (Calcium-rich)	x	x			0
Tempo	x	x	x	x	0
Titralac	x	x			<1
Tums	x				<8

[1]Values given are for maximum recommended dosages.

A New Dietary Prescription for Kidney Stones

More than half a million Americans are diagnosed with kidney stones every year. These crystallized masses of particles can cause pain so intense that it has been likened to the pain of labor.

The conventional wisdom has been that the way to prevent kidney stones is virtually to eliminate calcium-rich foods, such as cheese, milk, ice cream, and yogurt, from the diet. This recommendation certainly has its merits, given that the great majority of kidney stones contain calcium and, in many cases, form when there is an excess of calcium in the urine. It's similar to what happens when you add salt to a glass of water. Add just a little and it dissolves easily. Add a lot, however, and it doesn't dissolve; it collects as tiny crystals at the bottom of the glass. The creation of kidney stones often works on the same type of principle. If the urine, which forms in the kidneys, contains too much calcium, the mineral will not stay dissolved but, rather, will combine with other substances to form a crystal that attaches itself to the kidney surface and may eventually grow to stone size. While it is still attached, it may cause blood in the urine but not necessarily pain. Once it breaks loose, however, it can cause pain ranging from mild abdominal discomfort to agony in the lower abdomen, the lower back (on the side, just below the lower ribs), and the groin.

Fully four out of five kidney stones contain calcium, making the recommendation that kidney stone sufferers cut down on calcium-containing foods seem plausible. Yet recently published studies of some 45,000 men participating in Harvard University's Health Professionals Follow-Up Study showed that those who took in the highest amount of calcium were one-third *less* likely to develop a stone over the next four years than those who consumed the smallest amount of calcium. The difference in calcium consumption between the two groups was equivalent to about two glasses of milk a day.

The researchers speculate that calcium in the diet helped prevent the formation of kidney stones because it decreased the presence of a substance in the urine called oxalate.

Oxalate, found in high levels in foods such as chocolate, spinach, tea, and peanuts, can become incorporated into a stone much the way calcium can. Eating plenty of calcium, however, keeps dietary oxalate from becoming a part of the urine by binding with it and eliminating it from the body through feces. This might be an important step in cutting down on the possibility of kidney stone formation because just like calcium, oxalate is a common component of stones. Indeed, three out of four stones contain both calcium and oxalate. Furthermore, it takes much smaller increases in urinary oxalate to promote the formation of stones than it does increases of urinary calcium.

Despite the new findings, people who have already formed stones should take their physician's advice about whether to lower calcium consumption, as there are some stone sufferers for whom decreasing calcium is still the best policy. Like other diet–health issues, it's an individual matter.

Other Dietary Factors

In the Harvard study, fluid intake seemed to play a role in kidney stone development. The men who drank two to three quarts of fluid a day were about 30 percent less likely to end up afflicted than those who drank one quart or less. Potassium seems to have had an impact, too. The men who took in the most potassium—available in fruits and vegetables—had half the risk of stones that low-potassium consumers had, presumably because potassium decreases calcium excretion in the urine. Conversely, the biggest consumers of animal protein had a one-third higher risk of developing stones than those who consumed the least, because animal protein increases calcium secretion through the urine. Perhaps the high fruit and vegetable consumption and low intake of animal protein among vegetarians explains why there is a reportedly lower incidence of kidney stones in this group.

Separating Truth from Fraud in Arthritis Cures

More than 37 million Americans suffer from arthritis, a painful and potentially crippling disease in which the joints become inflamed so that the simplest movements are difficult or next to impossible to perform. Unfortunately, this makes arthritis victims susceptible to a wide variety of supposed cures—among them, copper bracelets, snake venom, and mussel extracts.

According to the FDA, unproven arthritis remedies are among the top ten health frauds in the United States. The Arthritis Foundation has found that more than a billion dollars a year are spent on these frauds; sadly, for every dollar that goes to legitimate arthritis research, 25 dollars go to unproven remedies.

One of the reasons people rely so heavily on unproven, outlandish, and sometimes dangerous "remedies" is that the symptoms of arthritis tend to come and go without warning, so a useless treatment may actually seem to be the source of relief. The unpredictable nature of arthritis flare-ups is also the reason many people think diet is involved. Because symptoms vary from day to day, it's easy to assume that what was or wasn't eaten yesterday might be the cause of pain today. But the link between diet and arthritis has remained tenuous, despite a number of studies conducted to see if any foods or ingredients affected symptoms.

Hope for Rheumatoid Arthritis Sufferers

Although there has been no firm evidence of a dietary link to arthritis in general, those who suffer a form of the disease called rheumatoid arthritis may find some dietary hope, according to a promising study. In the study, a group of people in Norway with rheumatoid arthritis enjoyed significant relief from pain when they followed a modified fast for seven to ten days, followed by a strict vegetarian diet that eliminated dairy products, eggs, refined sugar, citrus fruits, and foods containing gluten (a protein found in any item made with wheat, oats, rye, or barley). Within just a few weeks, they experienced a decrease in the number of tender and swollen joints as well as in morning stiffness. Better still, the improvement in symptoms was maintained after a year's time, even though the patients were gradually allowed to reintroduce dairy items and gluten-containing foods to their diets. The Norwegian researchers speculate that the gains rheumatoid arthritis sufferers made may have been related to the extensive changes in the fatty acids in their systems as a result of cutting out most animal foods. Fatty acids have a hand in how the inflammatory process is regulated.

While scientists are studying the possibility that vegetarian diets that include some dairy foods might prove useful therapy for rheumatoid arthritis sufferers, it must be noted that no diet has alleviated symptoms entirely, and most people probably require a combination of diet and medication. Furthermore, no individual should make such dramatic changes in his or her diet without the advice and supervision of a doctor, as the diet could create nutrient shortfalls in other areas.

The Arthritis Foundation recommends that people with any form of arthritis eat a healthful diet and shed any excess pounds that might be placing added stress on diseased joints. For specific tips, the organization invites people to order its free brochure "Arthritis Diet: Guidelines and Research" by calling toll-free (800)283-7800.

The Facts About Gout

Gout is a form of arthritis characterized by severe pain, tenderness, and swelling of the joints. The culprit is a substance called uric acid. Normally, the body dissolves uric acid into the blood, filters it from the blood in the kidneys, and excretes it in the urine. But in people with gout, the amount of uric acid in the blood rises excessively high, either because the kidneys can't get rid of it quickly enough or because the body produces too much of it. Either way, the excess uric acid forms crystal-like deposits that accumulate in the joints, often in the large joint of the big toe, leading to swelling and pain.

Traditionally, it was believed that certain foods were off-limits to people with gout because they were high in purines, compounds that break down into uric acid. However, dietary measures to control gout have been largely replaced by the use of drugs that reduce uric acid buildup. For example, many of the million or so Americans who suffer from gout take allopurinol (trade names Lopurin, Zurinol, and Zyloprim), a drug that slows the rate at which the body makes uric acid and thereby prevents the accumulation in the blood. Others take one of a category of medicines known as uricosuric drugs (Benemid, Parbenem, and Anturane, to name a few), which reduce blood levels of uric acid by increasing the amount passed out of the body in the urine.

Although these drugs help keep gout in check, people with the condition are advised to control their intake of foods with a high purine content. These include anchovies, brains, kidney, game meats, gravy, herring, liver, mackerel, meat extracts, sardines, scallops, and sweetbreads. Foods moderately high in purines include asparagus, bran, cauliflower, eel, fresh and saltwater fish, legumes, meat, meat soups and broths, mushrooms, oatmeal, poultry, shellfish, spinach, wheat germ, whole-grain breads, and cereals. Medication in conjunction with a reduced-purine diet is more effective than drugs alone.

Gout sufferers should also moderate their alcohol consumption, as excess alcohol can raise blood levels of uric acid. In addition, they should drink 10 to 12 glasses of non-alcoholic liquids each day to help flush uric acid crystals out of the body.

Finally, it should be noted that high blood uric acid levels have been linked with excess weight, so people with gout should take steps to lose weight.

Dietary Help for Parkinson's Disease

There's promising evidence that the food a Parkinson's sufferer eats and when he or she eats it could extend the benefits of a drug commonly used to treat the illness.

When researchers first developed the drug levodopa, in the 1950s, it was considered a major breakthrough for people with Parkinson's—a nervous system disorder characterized by progressively worsening symptoms that include stiff limbs, hand tremors, slow movement, and the inability to manage even simple motions such as lifting an arm.

Often referred to as L-dopa and commonly adminstered in a drug called Sinemet, levodopa works by entering the brain, where it is converted to a chemical called dopamine that is lacking in people with Parkinson's. Dopamine carries messages from the brain that tell the muscles to move, improving muscle movement so dramatically that even Parkinson's victims who are bedridden may regain the ability to walk.

Unfortunately, after approximately five years, about half of L-dopa takers begin to experience the "on–off" syndrome, which may result from an inconsistent flow of L-dopa to the brain. Typically, when people start taking L-dopa, the brain is still making some dopamine, so the rate at which the medication reaches the brain isn't crucial. But as Parkinson's disease progresses and the natural levels of dopamine continue to decline, people must increasingly rely on L-dopa to boost dopamine levels.

As a result, Parkinson's victims often suffer periods of erratic, uncontrollable tremors, rigidity, and loss of movement—known as "off"

periods. These incidents occur suddenly and unpredictably, sometimes several times a day. Fortunately, researchers are now finding that it's possible to prolong L-dopa's positive effects through diet.

One strategy for people who have begun to suffer "off" periods is to start taking their L-dopa 45 minutes to an hour before eating, because food can interfere with the drug's ability to reach the brain. Another, more controversial, dietary recommendation is to keep protein consumption to a minimum. Protein poses a particular problem for Parkinson's sufferers because during digestion, amino acids enter the bloodstream and are taken from the blood to the brain via the same "carrier" that transports L-dopa.

In other words, the more amino acids present at the time a person takes L-dopa, the harder it is for the drug to get a "seat" on the carrier that goes to the brain.

A solution introduced a few years back—avoiding protein during the day and eating a large amount in the evening so that L-dopa can work during waking hours—has been found to do more harm than good by causing severe "off" phases at night. For example, a person who tries this method might wake up in the middle of the night unable to move, a terrifying and dangerous situation, especially for someone who lives alone.

Many experts are now recommending the careful distribution of protein throughout the day. The quantity should be enough for the L-dopa taker to meet his or her nutritional needs, but not too much to interfere with the body's ability to carry the drug to the brain. Some recent research suggests that meals with seven parts carbohydrates to one part protein make a good balance. For example, a breakfast using this ratio might consist of two pancakes with margarine and syrup, a piece of fruit, a small glass of milk, and a cup of coffee or tea.

People with Parkinson's who decide to try this dietary approach can benefit from the help of a doctor and a dietitian. It's a regimen that requires careful planning to assure that adequate quantities of food are eaten and the proper nutrient balance is achieved.

Parkinson's sufferers might also want to contact Elan Pharma (1-800-473-3663), a company that offers a line of foods specifically for Parkinson's patients. Called Hearty Balance, the special entrees, snacks, soups, desserts, and shakes adhere to the seven-to-one carbohydrate-to-protein ratio. A dietitian is on hand to discuss menu planning, label reading, dining out, and other issues.

Nutritional Support for People with AIDS

Those who are involved with the treatment of people with AIDS (PWAs) are aware of the high percentage of cases—between 60 and 80 percent—where death is the result of malnutrition. Malnutrition is the most debilitating and complicated outcome of AIDs, and nutritionists believe that if this side effect could be prevented, the quality and length of PWAs' lives would be improved.

Why do PWAs suffer malnutrition? There are two reasons: malabsorption of calories and difficulty in eating.

People with AIDS often have problems with digestion and absorption that lead to nutritional deficiencies. Chronic diarrhea from bowel disease, protein malnutrition, and problems absorbing essential nutrients can compound the immunodeficiency in PWAs and make them more susceptible to infections.

The most severe nutrient deficiencies found in PWAs are of the amino acids in proteins and certain minerals such as zinc and selenium. The most common cause of the deficiencies is secondary infection or a parasite in the bowel. But even without a secondary infection, it may be that the AIDS virus itself causes malabsorption.

The Key Is High-Calorie, Low-Fat

One of the biggest mistakes PWAs and their caretakers make when trying to reverse the effects of malnutrition is to eat too much of the wrong kinds of foods. It's easy to see why this would occur. The natural tendency when someone is losing large amounts of weight from malnutrition is to encourage that person to eat more calorie-rich foods. Unfortunately, foods high in calories are often high in fat as well, and fat merely exacerbates the problem by causing diarrhea in AIDS sufferers. So, simply loading up with food—any food—is not the solution.

The best solution is a diet that is high in calories and low in fat—that is, consisting of 55 to 60 percent of daily calories in the form of complex carbohydrates. This diet may be supplemented by liquid nutrition drinks such as Ensure, which provide extra calories without the fat.

When It's Hard to Eat

For many people with AIDS, the nutritional barrier is simply having the will, energy, or ability to eat food in the first place. The infections that result from AIDS cause many uncomfortable conditions that interfere with eating. Mouth and esophagus impediments can make eating painful. Loss of appetite, chronic nausea, diarrhea, and being too sick to prepare food are among the problems PWAs face.

The following suggestions will help PWAs and their caregivers maintain a nutrient balance:

For diarrhea:

◆ Reduce the fiber in the diet, along with the fat and lactose. Low-fiber foods include white breads, fruit and vegetable juices, eggs, cottage cheese, rice, noodles, mashed potatoes, and lean cuts of meat.

◆ Drink plenty of liquids, including water, diluted fruit juices, flavored drink mixes, and skim milk with powdered milk added.

◆ Limit fat intake to between 20 and 25 percent of daily calories, with less than 10 percent in saturated fat.

◆ Avoid caffeine.

◆ Eat bananas, mangos, and diluted orange and nectar juices to replace minerals that may have been lost.

For mouth and esophagus pain:

◆ Avoid eating foods at extremely hot or cold temperatures.

◆ Avoid acidic and spicy foods, especially if there are open lesions.

◆ Eat refined and processed foods, which are easier to swallow.

◆ Mix foods with liquids or puree to help swallowing.

◆ Dunk toast, cookies, and crackers in liquid to make them softer.

◆ Avoid coarse foods like corn and nuts, which can get stuck in the throat.

◆ Use a straw to help swallowing.

For nausea:

◆ Eat dry crackers or cereal in the morning.

◆ Drink carbonated beverages or clear liquids between meals.

◆ Eat small, frequent meals.

◆ Avoid foods with strong aromas, which may cause nausea.

◆ Eat Popsicles and ice cubes made from fruit juices.

◆ Eat meals before taking medication that is known to cause nausea.

For further information, *Surviving With AIDS: A Comprehensive Program of Nutritional Co-Therapy*, by C. Wayne Callaway, M.D., with Catherine Whitney (Little, Brown), can be used as a resource for meal plans, recipes, and dietary guidelines for PWAs. You can also contact the AIDS Hotline of the National Public Health Service—1-800-342-AIDS—for information about local support groups.

Seasonal Affective Disorder

Some 10 million Americans suffer during cold weather months from a very real condition called seasonal affective disorder (SAD). The characteristics of this ailment include sadness, fatigue, irritability, difficulty concentrating, increased appetite, and other woes. Scientists believe that SAD is a type of depression distinguished mainly by sensitivity to changes in light. It afflicts primarily women who live in northern climates where a decline in sunlight occurs during winter months.

Fortunately, an estimated 75 percent of people with SAD can find relief through light therapy, which involves getting anywhere from 30 minutes to a few hours a day of extra exposure to natural sunlight, or to artificial light that is five to 20 times brighter than typical indoor lighting.

In the past, researchers were never able to tell which SAD victims would respond to the treatment. Now, a preliminary study from Switzerland suggests that a SAD sufferer's dietary habits may help predict his or her likelihood of feeling relief. They might also provide clues about why some people develop this condition in the first place.

A Sweet Solution?

When scientists at the Psychiatric University Clinic in Basel, Switzerland, scrutinized the dietary habits of a group of people with SAD, they found that those who tended to eat more than one portion of a sweet food like chocolate, cake, or ice cream during the second half of the day were the most likely to experience quick, lasting relief from their depression as a result of light therapy. Better still, people whose moods lifted after light treatment tended subsequently to decrease their sweet intake. The Swiss scientists speculate that in some SAD sufferers, sweets may trigger a release of the same mood-altering substances that light seems to trigger. Thus, once light therapy is used, the craving for sweets may drop.

This is not to say that people who have a sweet tooth and also experience the winter blahs now and then should self-diagnose themselves as suffering from SAD. Unlike the normal moodiness and irritation people often feel as a result of "cabin fever" or the added inconveniences of winter weather, SAD is a psychiatric illness that requires medical attention. It is also important to make sure that some of the hallmark symptoms of SAD—excessive fatigue coupled with increased appetite—are not caused by medical problems such as low blood sugar or a thyroid disorder.

If you suspect that you or someone you know suffers from SAD, keep in mind that the problem is very treatable, if not with light therapy then with some other antidote such as an antidepressant. Proper diagnosis should be made by a professional, who will evaluate a person's history, environment, episodes of stress, and symptoms.

For more information about SAD, contact the National Organization for SAD, a support group for SAD sufferers and their families, at Box 40133, Washington, DC 20016.

22

When You're Oversensitive to Food

Two out of five Americans believe they have adverse reactions or "allergies" to certain foods. Chronic headaches, arthritis, depression, skin rashes (such as hives), fatigue, weight fluctuations, and hyperactivity are just a few of the problems people attribute to food allergies. Some popular practitioners of "allergy cures" would have people believe that nearly everyone suffers them to some extent; they prescribe expensive supplements, injections, and complicated dietary regimens to combat these allergies. In fact, the number of people who suffer from food allergies is probably exaggerated. That's not to say that there's no such thing as a food intolerance, which is a food-related illness. But, unlike allergies, food intolerances have little or nothing to do with the immune system. Much of the mislabeling of problems as food allergies results from a lack of understanding about the difference between allergies and intolerances.

Identifying a True Food Allergy

A food allergy can best be described as an "overreaction" of the body's immune system, which includes the disease-fighting white blood cells, lymph tissues, thymus gland, and bone marrow.

Substances, usually proteins, that are harmless for most people trigger an allergic person's immune system to release antibodies that attack the proteins that are seen as unwelcome. Subsequently, the body releases chemicals, such as histamine, that irritate tissues. The most commonly affected tissues are those of the gastrointestinal tract, skin, and respiratory system. That's why the typical symptoms of food allergies are nausea, vomiting, diarrhea, skin rashes, or difficulty in breathing. In severe cases, fatal shock may occur.

About 90 percent of food allergies are caused by relatively few substances. The most common offenders are proteins in cow's milk, egg whites, shellfish, peanuts, wheat, and soybeans. A number of foods commonly believed to be allergenic are not. Chocolate, for instance, rarely causes an immunologic reaction. And the notion that sugar is allergenic is simply false. Strawberries and tomatoes are often blamed for allergic reactions, but they too are rarely allergenic.

It's often difficult to pinpoint when a physical problem is actually the result of a food allergy, because the typical symptoms—diarrhea, vomiting, rashes—can be caused by any number of medical conditions. Even psychological factors, such as emotional stress, can bring on the same type of symptoms as those triggered by an allergic reaction to food. Indeed, just believing strongly enough that a particular food will make you sick can cause you to become ill. Consider the case of a woman who complained of cramps and nausea after drinking as little as four drops of milk. When she was fed water through an opaque tube inserted into her stomach and was told it was milk, she experienced nausea and abdominal cramps within ten minutes. When she was given milk and was told it was water, no symptoms occurred.

Because symptoms that can be attributed to food allergies are relatively common, laypeople and physicians alike often consider food allergies more prevalent than they are. In fact, it is not uncommon for physicians to label problems as food allergies when they can find no other explanation.

Reputable Allergists and Reliable Tests

If you suspect you have a food allergy, the best way to ensure that the problem is properly diagnosed is to consult a physician who has been certified by the American Board of Allergy and Immunology. Such a qualified allergist will take a detailed history of your family's medical problems, as well as a personal history, and follow it up with a thorough medical examination. Special attention will be paid to the details of your symptoms and when they occur in relation to eating food. You may be sent home with an assignment to keep a diary of everything you eat. You'll also be told to note when you eat it and to record any symptoms you develop. When "suspicious" foods are identified, the allergist will likely advise you to eliminate them for a period of time to see if the adverse symptoms disappear. Then you'll be told to add back

the suspect foods one at a time to see whether the problems recur.

Sometimes it's hard to identify specific foods as the cause of the symptoms. If that's the case, the next step might be to follow a restrictive "elimination" diet in which all but very well-tolerated foods are cut out. Gradually, items will be added back to see whether you develop a reaction in response to eating any of them. These "elimination" and "rechallenge" diets are also useful in identifying food intolerances.

Another method for determining food allergies is to use skin tests. Liquid extracts of single foods are placed either on your arm or back and pricked or scratched into the skin with a needle. If an itchy swelling appears within about 20 minutes, it means you had a "positive" response. One problem with skin tests, however, is that they are not completely reliable in showing a food that is causing a problem. In some cases, people develop skin reactions to foods that do not cause allergic reactions when eaten.

Still another test that is used to diagnose food allergies is called the RAST test, which involves mixing small samples of your blood with food extracts. If you are allergic to a particular food, measurable levels of allergy antibodies to that food will be detected. Because a RAST test is conducted outside the body, it has the advantage of being safer than a skin or challenge test for someone who might react severely to a specific food. But it has the disadvantage of being less accurate than a skin test.

If none of these tests reveals the source of your symptoms, the allergist may resort to a double-blind challenge. This test, usually performed under close supervision in the allergist's office or in a hospital, is one of the best ways of confirming both allergies and intolerances. The "challenge" involves giving the patient capsules of dried food suspected of causing reactions, as well as capsules containing a nonreactive substance. Neither the physician nor the patient knows which type of supplement is being administered at any given time. Thus, both are "blind." If symptoms occur after consumption of any of the food extracts but not after consumption of the nonreactive substance, the symptoms can truly be blamed on food. Double-blind challenges are especially valuable because they can detect, as well as rule out, allergies or intolerances to many foods and other substances, such as additives. They also eliminate nonfood factors that can cause symptoms, including psychological influences.

For all the legitimate ways to determine whether someone has a food allergy, there are at least as many tests and remedies that have never been proved accurate or effective. Nevertheless, quite a few of these approaches have popular followings and are employed by nontraditional physicians. The procedures have been promoted through such channels as books, franchised clinics, and mail-order ads. Following is a review of some of the questionable theories and practices, many of which claim that foods are responsible for conditions ranging from anxiety to arthritis.

Clinical Ecology

Clinical ecology sprang from a 1930s theory that food "allergies" cause a plethora of poorly defined problems, including headaches, itching, dizziness, insomnia, drowsiness, and epilepsy. Modern-day "clinical ecologists" attribute similar ailments to hypersensitivities that certain people supposedly develop because their immune systems are damaged by chemically contaminated air, food, and water. Consequently, clinical ecology patients are often placed on very strict "all natural" diets and may even be told to move to different locations.

An evaluation of clinical ecology methods shows that they do not meet the medically accepted requirements for treating illnesses. In one study, 50 patients who had been treated by clinical ecologists were found to have no food-induced immunologic abnormalities. Ironically, three out of five patients developed one or more new symptoms while undergoing clinical ecology treatment.

Cytotoxic Testing

Also known as Bryan's test, leucocytotoxic testing, and food sensitivity testing, cytotoxic testing involves taking small samples of blood, separating out the white blood cells, and mixing them with dried extracts of specific foods. If, upon examination with a microscope, the white cells change in shape or size in response to a particular food, the patient is said to have a "sensitivity" to that food.

The white blood cells are part of the immune system, and this gives the test its air of legitimacy. However, there is no evidence that the white blood cells of people with food allergies have defects that would cause them to take on a unique change in shape or size when they are exposed to foods outside the body.

There is evidence that cytotoxic testing doesn't pick up food allergies when they really exist. In one study, the white blood cells of people with known food allergies reacted in the same way to allergenic as to non-allergenic foods. Further, test results appeared to be inconsistent, altering a person's cells on one day but not on the next. (Note: Cytotoxic testing should not be confused with the RAST test, which involves a different type of reaction.)

Provocation and Neutralization

Provocation and neutralization is a double-edged procedure. First, people are given doses of suspected allergenic foods—either as drops placed beneath the tongue or as injections—to provoke a reaction that corresponds to their complaints. Immediately following, weaker or stronger doses of the offending foods are introduced to neutralize the reaction.

These tests are not effective and might be dangerous, because when someone has a real food allergy, the more of the offending food eaten, the more severe the reaction. Moreover, the patient's "reaction" in these cases is subjective, and the test is unable to reveal an immunologic cause.

Provocation and neutralization is not the same as the allergy shots or immunotherapy that patients sometimes receive from reputable allergists. These shots can be of value for individuals with allergies to such airborne substances as pollen. But they have not been shown to be effective in treating food allergies.

Yeast Hypersensitivity Treatment

Yeast hypersensitivity treatment is based on the theory that a host of ills, ranging from depression to headaches to schizophrenia to cancer, are caused by a sensitivity to yeast-like fungi called Candida. The belief is that the fungi multiply in the body and weaken the immune system. Treatment includes a diet in which all the yeast and mold-containing foods, as well as fruits and milk, are temporarily avoided. The patient is also told to stay away from refined carbohydrates and processed foods.

It is unreasonable to assume that Candida could cause the wide array of symptoms attributed to them, because they are ubiquitous organisms that inhabit the mouth, skin, and intestines of most healthy people without creating any problems. It's true that for a few people, Candida cause fungal infections on such areas as the skin and nails, but in no way do these individuals manifest the host of problems ascribed to "yeast sensitivity." Further, there is no evidence that the foods to be avoided stimulate yeast growth or weaken the immune system, as proponents of this theory claim.

In light of the proliferation of unscientific allergy theories that attribute all kinds of physical and psychological problems to food allergies or "sensitivities," it is easy to understand why so many individuals conclude that they suffer some sort of adverse reaction to food, even when they have never been tested and shown to have a problem. But there is no sound evidence that allergies and intolerances lead to many of the conditions they are said to bring about, including arthritis, anxiety, and muscle pains.

Many of the popular practitioners of food-allergy theories put the cart before the scientific horse, espousing untested dietary remedies based on little more than anecdotal case histories. A new medical treatment, such as a drug or diet, should not be recommended by physicians unless it has first been tested by researchers in what are known as clinical trials. In these experiments, the new treatment is tested under carefully controlled circumstances to make certain that no outside factors influence the results. To date, no clinical trial has conclusively demonstrated that food allergies or intolerances can bring on fatigue, depression, or other of the many problems ascribed to them. But it is easy to be swayed by the many "success stories" of people who reported dramatic health improvements when certain foods were avoided. Consider, for example, the dramatic turn for the better that is sometimes reported in hyperactive children when they are placed on additive-free diets. When the same children are placed on additive-free diets in a "blind" test, few, if any, show improvement.

Indeed, although many parents of hyperactive children will try just about any dietary technique to tame the unruly behavior, scientific studies have not shown that dietary intervention is of any value in most cases. Perhaps the reason behavior sometimes improves with a special diet is that the new eating regimen requires the parents to devote more attention to their child.

What Are Food Intolerances?

Food intolerances are different from food allergies, either because they are unrelated to the immune system or because the immune system reacts in a different way from the way it does to allergenic proteins in foods. One such condition is lactose intolerance. People with this condition cannot adequately digest lactose, or milk sugar. Consuming products like milk and ice cream may lead to gas, diarrhea, and stomach cramps.

Another food intolerance is "gluten enteropathy," more commonly known as celiac disease. A person who suffers from it cannot eat gluten, a protein in wheat, rye, barley, and, to a lesser extent, oat products without damaging the small intestine. The result is chronic diarrhea and abdominal pain.

Certain additives may cause intolerances, too. Tartrazine, or FD & C Yellow (Dye) 5, for example, may induce asthma attacks in a very small minority of asthmatics.

Sulfites can also bring on attacks in a few people who have asthma. They are used as preservatives in salad bars and in certain processed foods and dried fruits. Although previous estimates were higher, the number of sulfite-sensitive adult asthmatics now appears to be limited to fewer than 100,000 people in the United States.

Understanding Lactose Intolerance

For some people, eating milk products can cause severe abdominal cramps, bloating, and diarrhea. These people are "lactose-intolerant"—that is, they do not have enough lactase, the enzyme needed to digest lactose, the sugar found in milk and milk products. Lactose intolerance can occur in one of three ways: After the age of two, some people gradually stop producing sufficient quantities of lactase, which breaks down lactose into the simple sugars glucose and galactose. The condition, which is usually inherited by non-Caucasians, affects an estimated 70 percent of the world's population to some degree. People of African, Asian, and Mediterranean descent are more prone to lactose intolerance than others. A rare congenital disorder makes some people unable to produce lactase from the time they are born or to produce it only in limited amounts.

Any illness that affects the lactase-producing cells of the small intestine, such as inflammatory bowel disease or even the flu, can induce a temporary lactase deficiency. However, in these cases, the condition is more likely to be temporary; once the damaged cells recover, they begin producing the enzyme again.

Contrary to popular advertisements, which suggest that lactose intolerance is a rapidly growing condition, true lactose intolerance affects relatively few people. One of the biggest misconceptions surrounding lactose intolerance concerns the difference between true lactose intolerance and another condition, called lactose maldigestion. Lactose maldigestion, unlike intolerance, is not necessarily accompanied by unpleasant gastrointestinal symptoms. In fact, only a small fraction of the estimated 50 million lactose maldigesters have an out-and-out intolerance. And for the maldigesters, research suggests that avoiding lactose altogether may not be a good idea. The hypothesis is that the consistent consumption of milk-based foods allows the colonly of friendly, lactose-digesting bacteria in the stomach to stay strong, while causing the gas-producing bacteria to falter.

Sometimes a person perceives he has a lactose intolerance not because of an inability to digest lactose but simply because of a belief that milk products disagree with him—a belief embedded in cultural norms.

The researchers at Meharry Medical College demonstrated this when they checked for lactose maldigestion in more than 150 African Americans who claimed they could not drink a cup of milk without discomfort. Lab tests showed that only 58 percent of them were true lactose maldigestors. And when they further tested some of the maldigesters by giving them both regular and low-lactose milk, not telling them which was which, one in three reported unpleasant reactions no matter which beverage was consumed. In other words, perhaps just the *idea* of milk made them sick.

People who are milk-intolerant are usually lactose-intolerant and experience stomach upset and gas after drinking milk. In rare instances, however, the same symptoms are the result of a different problem, that is, an allergy to the protein in milk. For this reason, some physicians use a hydrogen breath test to diagnose lactose intolerance. When food containing lactose is not digested, hydrogen gas is produced, and its rate of expiration can be measured from the mouth. The more hydrogen gas produced, the more lactose-intolerant the patient is.

Lactose intolerance is not the same as milk intolerance. It is possible for most lactose-intolerant people to handle moderate amounts of milk or milk products over the course of a day without pain. If lactose-containing foods are eaten in conjunction with other foods, the chances of developing the symptoms are decreased. The intensity of symptoms increases as more lactose is consumed. When the concentration of undigested lactose becomes particularly high, the large intestine responds by drawing water from the surrounding tissues, causing watery diarrhea.

Milk is the food with the most lactose. Yogurt is high in lactose, although lactose-intolerant people don't appear to suffer from eating yogurt that has active cultures. That's because the bacteria in yogurt produce lactase that breaks down the milk sugar on its own. The same thing occurs in the production of cheese—generally, hard, aged cheeses, such as Swiss and cheddar, contain less lactose than softer cheeses.

Sweet acidophilus milk is sometimes said to be good for milk-intolerant people, but because it does not have reduced levels of milk sugar they do not tolerate it any better than regular milk. Cultured buttermilk is slightly lower in lactose content than regular milk, but it does not agree with most milk-intolerant people either.

Fortunately, there are a number of dairy products on the market designed for those who are milk-intolerant. These specially treated products make it possible for milk-intolerant people to benefit from the major nutrients found in milk foods, such as calcium, vitamins A and D, riboflavin, and protein. LactAid, a company that caters specifically to people with the problem, adds a lactase solution to milk, ice cream, and cottage cheese. As a result, much of the lactose in these foods is broken down to glucose and galactose before it reaches the body. This gives the products a sweeter taste because each of these sugars is sweeter on its own than in the combined form of lactose. For those who want to add lactase to their own milk, LactAid now supplies lactase in both liquid and tablet form. The liquid version has to be added to milk 24 hours before serving in order for the lactose to be sufficiently broken down. The tablets are swallowed before a meal and go to work almost immediately.

There are also many nondairy products that can be used as alternatives to dairy foods. Ice cream can be replaced by a number of desserts made with tofu or fruit instead of with milk. And soy milk, although not a perfect substitute for cow's milk because it lacks calcium and some vitamins, is widely available in health food stores, including in fortified forms.

Diet-Induced Skin Reactions

A number of well-known vitamin deficiency states are associated with abnormalities of the skin. For example, severe vitamin C deficiency, leading to scurvy, is accompanied by bleeding of the skin and gums. Deficiency of niacin leads to pellagra, which is characterized by a severe skin rash on parts of the body exposed to the sun. Deficiencies of other B vitamins and vitamin A may be associated with dermatitis and mucous-membrane changes such as mouth ulcers and redness and cracking at the corners of the mouth. However, these symptoms appear only with very severe deficiencies.

There's no truth to the assumption that topical application of vitamins or ingesting special vitamin supplements will improve your skin. In some cases, they might even hurt skin. For example, too much vitamin A can make the skin rough and dry. High doses of niacin taken internally cause itching and flushing in some people. And despite vitamin E's wide use as a topical solution, there is no proof that it provides anything more effective than the soothing qualities of the oil in which it is contained. Vitamin E even causes acne and rashes in some people.

There is also no evidence to support the notion that vitamin treatments can slow down or reverse the effects of aging on the skin. One of the causes of wrinkling is exposure to the ultraviolet rays of the sun, and the only known way to prevent the sun's damaging effects is to wear sunscreen and avoid sunbathing.

What about the relationship of the foods we eat to the tendency to get acne? In spite of the wide belief that certain foods, such as sugar, chocolate, and dairy products, cause acne, the relationship has never been proved. Today, most dermatologists minimize the effects of diet on acne, except when patients do not respond to other treatments and the specific food or food group can be identified as causing the problem.

One allergenic skin disease that is clearly associated with food is urticaria, or hives, which afflicts one in five Americans. The most common food offenders are eggs, nuts, beans, tomatoes, fish, pork, corn, citrus fruits, and certain condiments and spices. Some synthetic food additives, such as the dye tartrazine (FD & C yellow dye 5) and the preservative sodium benzoate, can also cause hives, as can the naturally occurring salicylates in almonds, apples, peaches, potatoes, and a number of other foods. In addition, the small amounts of salicylates and benzoates in blueberries, bananas, green peas, lingonberries, and licorice may cause problems for some people. Salicylates are also found in aspirin-containing compounds.

The cause of psoriasis, characterized by red, scaly patches that result from skin cells' being produced at a greater-than-normal rate, is still not known. Research in progress suggests that an abnormality in the production of certain metabolic products of a fatty acid, arachidonic acid, may play an important role. Because body levels of some of these metabolic products may be affected by certain foods, it is conceivable that diet may play a role in its cure. But the matter is still in research, and supposedly effective treatments, such as lecithin and other vitamins, are of no benefit.

Some people develop rashes simply from touching certain foods. For example, mangoes contain an allergen similar to poison ivy allergens and can cause a similar rash. Oils of cinnamon, oranges, and certain preservatives can produce hand dermatitis, especially for people who have repeated exposure, such as bakers and chefs. In certain instances, a chemical, drug, or food that causes a rash upon skin contact can produce a similar result when it's taken orally. Cashew nuts, for example, contain a chemical related to poison ivy allergens, and a generalized rash from eating cashews has been observed in a few exceptionally sensitive people.

Rosacea is a chronic facial eruption in which acne-like blemishes appear along with redness and flushing. A number of foods and drinks have long been recognized as factors that exacerbate the condition. For example, alcoholic beverages and spicy foods are thought to agitate rosacea by causing repeated flushing.

The relationship of diet to skin problems is hard to study because many of the conditions undergo spontaneous remission. Although scientists have not ruled out even some of the most outlandish claims, neither have they found evidence to substantiate them. Caution is in order until proper scientific research confirms courses of treatment.

PART FIVE

Keeping Fit and Trim

Obesity has become a crisis in the United States for young and old alike, increasing the risks for heart disease, hypertension, diabetes, and other health problems. There is evidence that obesity, as we know it today, is a relatively new condition, related to both the increased availability of food and the technology that has made the process of procuring and preparing food less strenuous. In fact, anthropologists and other scientists speculate that the efficiency with which our bodies store calories might have an ancestral basis: The storage mechanism helped prevent starvation during prehistoric times when food was scarce. For this reason, plumpness was often considered a sign of affluence and good health. In women, it was often equated with fertility and maternity, because adequate fat stores are essential for the successful bearing and nurturing of infants. Today, in industrial societies, the emphasis has changed to the point where being lean is associated with health and affluence, and excess weight is considered unhealthy and undesirable.

But the question of healthy weight and desirable body fat is far more complicated than a simple fat-versus-lean evaluation. For, at the same time that we express concern with the growing problem of obesity in the United States, we also observe with concern the intensification of a lean-body bias that has spawned a $32 billion weight-loss industry. All too often, the emphasis of this industry is placed on arbitrary cosmetic standards rather than on true health concerns. While sidestepping the legitimate questions of nutrient sufficiency, many weight-loss programs stress the social advantages of being thin. The thin-body bias of our society has created new issues for nutritionists, including the damaging effects of chronic dieting and how to address a new population of people who engage in forced starvation. Nevertheless, health-damaging obesity grows as a problem in a society where diet and weight loss are obsessional concerns.

It is our intention in this section to examine the fundamental issues regarding nutrition and obesity, and to reframe the dialogue about weight and fat. Specifically, we will focus on:

◆ The distinction between cosmetic and health concerns regarding body fat and weight

◆ The different criteria for determining healthy weight

◆ The genetic factors that influence body shape and size

◆ The research about the health-related dangers of obesity

◆ The ways that our cultural thin-body bias often interferes with achieving healthy weight

◆ The health crisis presented by the large number of people with eating disorders

◆ The criteria for legitimate approaches to weight loss and nutritional well-being

◆ A weight-loss approach that emphasizes nutrition and self-sufficiency

◆ The role of physical exercise in fitness and health, and practical guidelines for exercise programs

We believe that it is time for health professionals in this country to take a stand against the weight-loss/diet charlatans whose scientifically unproven, gimmicky, and often unhealthful approaches to diet have distracted the public from focusing on the true issues of health and fitness. It is our conviction that if people would stop following false promises and, instead, listen to the evidence that scientists now have about how to maintain a healthful body size and weight, the problem of obesity could be successfully addressed in our society.

23

Fight Fat Nutritionally

Nearly 50 percent of all American women and 30 percent of all American men report that they are engaged in the process of losing weight, either by reducing calorie intake, increasing physical exercise, or both. Although this involvement indicates a positive trend of increased interest in health and fitness, it also raises new questions for health and nutrition professionals about how to define healthful versus unhealthful weight, and what are the most appropriate and nutritionally responsible methods for treating obesity.

Defining Healthful Weight

Traditionally, the favored measure of healthful weight has been the Metropolitan Life Insurance Company's height and weight tables. The tables were established based on the evaluation of the weight-for-height ratios of insured persons with the greatest longevity. The tables give a range of weight-for-height, with the midpoint being considered the "ideal" for most people.

However, in recent years, the validity of using these tables as a basis for evaluating healthful weight has been seriously questioned

by a number of health researchers and nutrition experts. Not only do the tables fail to consider the percentage of body fat and fat distribution, but the methodologies used might not have been accurate determinants for judging the overall population. In particular, critics cite the self-selection aspects of the study; although data were collected on nearly 5 million people, they were all purchasers of life insurance and may not be indicative of the general population because, statistically, insured people tend to be generally healthier and have longer life spans than the overall population. The insured population also tends to be predominantly white, middle-class males who are not necessarily representative of other groups. Furthermore, the data were not scientifically gathered or always consistent. Some study subjects answered questions about weight on insurance forms but were not independently weighed; others, who were weighed, sometimes wore shoes and clothing and sometimes did not.

The largest issue, however, relates to the overall criteria for determining healthful weight. Height-to-weight tables are certainly valuable measures that help people determine safe weight ranges. But it is clear that it's not appropriate to think of them as rigid standards; rather, they offer general guidelines. Since the Metropolitan tables were first published, investigators in the field have discovered important new evidence that age, body composition, and body-fat distribution are as important as, and sometimes more important than, overall weight.

Taking Age into Account

There are a number of conflicting views regarding the accuracy of weight-to-height measures. Surveys of health and longevity and average height-to-weight ratios have been hampered by a number of shifting factors, in particular the changes in weight patterns that occur as people age.

Many scientists now believe that height–weight charts must take age into account in order to be accurate. In 1990, the Department of Health and Human Services shifted the emphasis in its weight guidelines to stress *healthful* weights over the previously used *ideal* weights. The focus is on what's healthful, not on arbitrary standards of appearance. The new guidelines are also age-adjusted, taking into account that people gain some weight as they grow older.

In 1995, there was publicity about sudies linking weight gain after age 40 with illness and a shorter life expectancy. While stricter weight guidelines might be in our future, they are probably not relevant for people over 70. Furthermore, you shouldn't take this research as a charge to be obsessed with every pound.

Evaluating Body Composition

Many people believe that excess weight is mostly the result of excess fat. Although this is generally true, it is not always the case. To use one clear example, a boxer might have a weight that is substantially greater than that given for his height, but it is still possible that he has a "healthy" weight, because a high percentage of his weight is accounted for by muscle, not fat. Also, some people have larger body

THE NEW HEALTHY WEIGHTS[1]

Height[2]	Weight (pounds)[3]	
	19 to 34 years	35 years and older
5'0"	97–128	108–138
5'1"	101–132	111–143
5'2"	104–137	115–148
5'3"	107–141	119–152
5'4"	111–146	122–157
5'5"	114–150	126–162
5'6"	118–155	130–167
5'7"	121–160	134–172
5'8"	125–164	138–178
5'9"	129–169	142–183
5'10"	132–174	146–188
5'11"	136–179	151–194
6'0"	140–184	155–199
6'1"	144–189	159–205
6'2"	148–195	164–216
6'3"	152–200	168–216
6'4"	156–205	173–222
6'5"	160–211	177–228

[1]Source: *The Dietary Guidelines for Americans,* U.S. Department of Agriculture, U.S. Department of Health and Human Services.
[2]without shoes
[3]without clothes

frames than those given in traditional height–weight charts; in their cases, weight and height alone would not be a valid measure for determining excess fat.

An accurate measurement of body composition (overall percentage of fat tissue to lean tissue) can be conducted only in a clinical setting. The test most commonly used measures the skin-fold thickness in the shoulder and triceps areas. The amount of adipose (fat) tissue determined by the test is then subtracted from the total body weight to find the percent of fat to total weight.

There are a variety of more accurate (and more complex) ways of measuring body fat, but skin-fold measures are adequate for most people. In fact, the average person doesn't need a scientific method to determine the presence of excess fat. A good home method involves grasping the skin beneath the upper arm between the thumb and forefinger. If more than an inch of skin sticks out, there is probably excess fat in the body.

Body-Fat Distribution

Scientists have learned that excess body fat in some locations is more dangerous than in others. Studies show that people (usually men) who have excess fat in their abdominal areas suffer many health risks, whereas people (usually women) who carry extra fat in their buttocks, hips, and thighs suffer few health risks associated with this fat. This theory, often referred to as "apple versus pear," proposes that, except in cases of overall obesity, having extra padding on the lower part of the body is not necessarily a health risk, although carrying fat in the stomach and upper body may be very risky.

The female hormone estrogen actually encourages fat in the hips, thighs, and buttocks, because the reserve is needed in late pregnancy and during breastfeeding. The often-voiced complaint of many women that "My hips are too fat" seems to be irrelevant from a health standpoint; in fact, anorectics and women who engage in semi-starvation diets or excessive exercising often stop menstruating, the body's signal that they're not carrying enough fat stores to support the reproductive process.

On the other hand, excess fat cells in the abdominal area are more likely to be associated with increased health hazards, including interference with the metabolism of insulin (leading to diabetes) and an increase in the liver's production of triglycerides and cholesterol (leading to heart disease and strokes).

To some extent, fat distribution is observable—you can see that you have broad hips or a potbelly. But clinical tests are available that measure fat distribution with some accuracy. The most common method measures the ratio of the abdominal area to the widest portion of the hips. The waist-to-hip ratio is then measured against criteria, different for men and women, that are used to determine a healthy ratio.

Waist-to-hip ratio can be determined with a tape measure: Measure the circumference of the waist, then the widest part of the hip, and divide the first number by the second. The average healthy ratio is below 0.8 for women and 1.0 for men.

Genetics Makes a Difference

We do not completely understand all the factors that lead to obesity, but we know that it is much more complicated than what you eat and how much you exercise. In addition to overeating and underexercising, there is evidence that heredity and altered metabolic functions also contribute to obesity. Some of the most significant studies relating obesity to heredity versus environment have been conducted by a Canadian researcher, Dr. Claude Bouchard, and his colleagues. In one study, Bouchard fed an additional 1,000 calories a day to six sets of identical twins. When the results were evaluated, it was found that weight gain within the sets of twins was almost identical, whereas weight gain among the different groups differed greatly. The same pattern was observed when exercise was increased by several hours a day. So, although the weight gain varied notably among unrelated individuals who consumed the same number of calories, it tended to be fairly consistent between twins, suggesting that genetics plays a role in the determination of body weight.

Another study, conducted by Albert Stunkard and his colleagues at the University of Pennsylvania, examined the adult heights and weights of more than 4,000 people who were adopted as children and compared them with those of both their adoptive and biological parents. Results indicated that the heights and weights of the adoptees were similar to those of their biological parents and not to those of their adoptive parents, suggesting that environmental factors may have less control over certain aspects of body size than heredity.

New studies are also being conducted that suggest hereditary implications for both metabolic rate (the efficiency with which people use calories) and fat-cell size and number. All of these studies are designed to identify whether some people might have hereditary tendencies toward obesity.

In 1995, researchers at Rockerfeller University in New York City reported finding a gene which, if defective, does lead to obesity—at least in laboratory mice. Using the mouse gene, named obese or ob for short, scientists then scanned DNA to find its human equivalent. It turned out that the mouse and human ob genes were 84 percent identical. In both species, the gene is activated in fat tissues, where it appears to produce a hormone-like protein that is secreted by the fat cells into the bloodstream. Scientists speculate that the blood carries the protein to the brain where it "communicates" how big or small the fat cells are. The brain then regulates the appetite and eating accordingly. But if the gene is defective, the brain does not get the proper signal from the fat cells and fails to regulate long-term appetite and food consumption.

If the ob gene theories hold true, the discovery could eventually lead to the development of a drug that mimics the protein produced by the gene. Another outcome of the discovery might be a test that measures the genetic predisposition to obesity early in life, when the diet might be modified to overcome the effects of the gene.

However, genetic experts warn that obesity in humans is much more complicated than the one-gene mouse phenomenon. Obesity in humans is considered "polygenic"—that is, many factors contribute to it. Even if the obesity gene exists, we cannot discount or minimize the role of diet and exercise on human obesity.

New Data on Yo-yo Dieting

Chronic or "yo-yo" dieting has long been considered the cause of the problem so many people have in permanently controlling their weight. Many studies have supported the claim that chronic dieting may decrease the metabolic rate making it harder to lose the second time around. Chronic dieting has also been viewed as the culprit in binge eating.

There is plenty of evidence to support the idea that chronic dieting is not a healthful pattern. However, newer research suggests that it may not be as harmful as once believed—especially in comparison with the need for overweight people to lose weight.

According to the National Task Force on the Prevention and Treatment of Obesity, there is no conclusive scientific evidence that yo-yo dieting itself is the cause of repeated weight gain. The task force based its statement on a review of three decades of research on weight cycling involving dozens of studies. According to the panel, many of these studies were flawed or too limited in scope for drawing conclusions.

The task force's challenge to the body of research involving chronic dieting was not designed to support the practice. Clearly people who spend many years in an unsuccessful lose-gain cycle are not establishing the fundamental patterns upon which healthful diets are based. And indeed, yo-yo dieting may lead to depression and rebound weight gain simply by virtue of its discouraging prognosis. The main point is that people whose weight is at unhealthy levels should be encouraged to lose the extra pounds—even if they have tried and failed before. In the process, however, people should be encouraged to maintain a balanced diet and forego extremist plans.

Diets that are very low in calories and that promote dietary practices that cause deficiencies in essential nutrients are in abundant supply in the United States. The consensus among health professionals is that these diets are not healthy and usually not successful. The failure rate of low-calorie diets is estimated to be as high as 90 percent. Although statistics are not available regarding the percentage of dieters who have unhealthy weights, it is obvious that many people are consuming nutritionally deficient diets to match the lean-body standards of our culture. The intense social pressure to be thin has led to an entire population of weight- and food-obsessed individuals for whom losing 5, 10, or 20 pounds is a primary focus. Even if some of these people do have unhealthy weights, chronic dieting patterns are likely to cause greater health risks in the long run.

Are You Caught in the Thin Obsession?

For many Americans, the "thin obsession" is a way of life: Being thin is equivalent to being desirable, successful, and worthwhile. It is more important than talent, intellectual ability, personality, or any of the other factors that make humans attractive to one another. Take this test to find out whether you're a victim of the thin obsession:

1. The first thing you notice about other people is their weight.
2. You believe that people who are overweight are lazy, lack discipline, or don't care about themselves.
3. You believe that thin people are more attractive to the opposite sex.
4. Staying thin is a way of proving to yourself that you have discipline, stamina, and control.
5. At times, you have put off socializing, taking a vacation, interviewing for a job, or otherwise putting yourself in a public situation until you have lost a few pounds.
6. Even though you know that extreme dieting can compromise you nutritionally, you feel that it is sometimes worth it to lose weight fast.

7. If you gain any weight at all, you feel disgusted with yourself.
8. You don't think you'll ever be "too thin."

Examine your responses. The more times you answered "True," the more you are obsessed with body shape and weight.

Overcoming the 10-Pound Mindset

People who diet as a way of life do more than just limit their daily calorie intake. They spend an inordinate amount of psychological energy worrying about what they will, will not, or did eat. They develop a type of "diet head" that prompts them to set strict rules for how many calories they allow themselves per meal or per day and for which foods are "forbidden." The "diet head" may lead to daily weigh-ins and to extreme anxiety if the scale registers even the slightest upward fluctuation. It may also lead to a cycle of starving followed by overeating, and then guilt and self-disgust at one's lack of control.

Two University of Toronto psychologists, Janet Polivy, Ph.D., and C. Peter Herman, Ph.D., have coined the term "restrained eaters" to describe this population of people who are obsessively concerned about eating and overeating and who, as a result, are almost always dieting. They contend that the very rigidity of the restraint these people impose upon themselves causes them to end up losing control and overeating. In other words, once the dieter breaks the self-imposed "rules" by eating a forbidden food or consuming more than the allowed calories, what Polivy and Herman call the "what-the-hell" effect occurs, and they overeat.

The diet-obsessed segment of the population is not helped by the many conflicting messages they receive every day from the media. For example, one magazine ran an article entitled "Are You a Fitaholic?" as a way of helping people cope with an "addiction" to exercise, only to follow it several months later with a positive story about a woman who maintained her weight loss by combining five different exercise programs that took more than an hour and a half each day. Another magazine published, in the same issue, a feature about the dangers of anorexia and a diet plan that restricted calories to 800 per day.

Readers of popular magazines can also be confused by articles with titles like "It's No Longer 'In' to Be Pencil-Thin" that share pages with advertisements that use tall, thin models. And, although some of our favorite movie and television stars are showing more curves these days, not many average people can hope to look as curvaceously glamorous as they do.

These mixed messages contribute to a central problem that weight-obsessed people have: They lose touch with the normal body mechanisms that prompt people to eat when they are hungry and to stop eating when they become full. Of course, everyone overeats once in a while or, conversely, does not eat for one reason or another. But for chronic dieters, ignoring hunger pains, as well as feelings of satiety, is a way of life. They often pass up food they really want in order to keep their weight down and then eat beyond the point of feeling full when they do start eating.

Chronic dieters often feel deprived, not only because they so often avoid eating when they're hungry but also because they define foods as being either "good" or "bad." The "bad" foods are often those they find most pleasurable and therefore have to seek control over. They are incapable of participating in special occasions in a relaxed manner; a party or dinner out becomes an occasion to dread because the "bad" food temptations will be so great. While others around them are enjoying the pleasures of food, the chronic dieters are feeling deprived and depressed. If they do give in and allow themselves a forbidden food, they are ridden with guilt and even depression.

If you are a chronic dieter, the best way to control your diet is to drop some of the controls. Establish a normal eating pattern so that your hunger cues will return. Eat regular meals so you won't be thinking about food all the time. Stop applying "good" and "bad" labels to food. If a beloved food is not low in calories, don't deprive yourself completely. Rather, allow an occasional treat and limit the portion size.

You can also avoid feelings of depression and failure if you stop relying on arbitrary external measures of diet success or failure. For example, daily weight fluctuations are meaningless. Everyone's weight shifts slightly from day to day, but it is the balance of water that is shifting, not fat. Many women retain five or more pounds of water prior to their menstrual periods, but this weight gain is not related to the success or failure of a diet program. Besides, factors such as fat distribution and total body mass can't be recorded on the scale. People who are exercising and building muscle may even find that they weigh more, because muscle is heavier than fat. If you are trying to lose weight, you'll get a more accurate reading by weighing yourself once a week or even once every two weeks.

Options for Weight Loss

For those segments of the population who are above their healthy weight and need to lose, there are hundreds of diet options available. For some people, group support or structured programs are helpful. The best ones will include behavior modification and psychological support for those who need it. They emphasize sensible eating patterns and nutritious foods and avoid gimmickry or the promotion of special foods and supplements. They allow sufficient calories and encourage dieters to participate in exercise programs in conjunction with the diet. Occasionally, more extreme dietary procedures are needed. But, according to weight-control experts these extreme measures, such as gastric balloons or liquid-formula diets,

◆ NUTRITION QUIZ ◆
Do You Have the "Diet Head"?

Chronic dieters do more than just diet. They have a "diet head"—a set of self-punishing habits they use to control their food intake and their weight. Sometimes these habits are so ingrained that the dieters don't even realize they're obsessed about food. Might that be true for you? Take this quiz and find out.

1. How often do you diet in a conscious effort to control your weight? (a) rarely or never (b) sometimes (c) usually (d) always

2. Would a five-pound fluctuation in your weight affect the way you feel about yourself? (a) not at all (b) slightly (c) moderately (d) greatly

3. Do you feel guilty if you overeat or skip an exercise session? (a) rarely (b) sometimes (c) usually (d) always

4. How likely are you to eat less than you really want? (a) unlikely (b) somewhat likely (c) often likely (d) very likely

5. To what extent do you diet all day and then overeat at night, pledging that you'll start your diet again tomorrow? (a) never (b) occasionally (c) often (d) constantly

6. If you are on a diet and you eat a food that is not "allowed," do you then go on a splurge and eat other high-calorie foods? (a) never (b) occasionally (c) often (d) always

7. How frequently do you avoid bringing "forbidden" foods into the house? (a) never (b) sometimes (c) often (d) very often

8. How much food do you typically eat when you attend social events, such as parties or picnics? (a) just enough to feel satisfied (b) a little too much (c) enough to feel uncomfortable (d) enough to feel sick

9. How often do you weigh yourself? (a) hardly ever (b) once a week (c) once a day (d) more than once a day

10. How many times have you lost, and then regained, more than five pounds in the past ten years? (a) never (b) rarely (c) more than five times (d) more than ten times

This quiz was adapted from the "Three Factor Eating Questionnaire" developed by Dr. Albert J. Stunkard and Dr. Samuel Messick, published in the *Journal of Psychosomatic Research*. The more you circled "c" or "d," the more likely it is that you have self-punishing diet habits and excessive concern about your weight.

are usually warranted only if the excess weight poses a greater health hazard than the reduction method itself.

For people whose obesity puts them at high risk for disease, Optifast and other very low-calorie liquid diets might be an appropriate medically supervised treatment. Four out of five patients who stick with it (up to half drop out) lose an average of 40 pounds. Whether the weight stays off is another matter. Even when a liquid diet works in the short-term, long-term success is based on behavior modification and establishing healthful eating patterns.

Choosing a Safe and Successful Diet Program

Liquid diets and other extreme regimens are not appropriate for the average American. But it's easy to become confused by the plethora of weight-loss programs, all of which claim to have the method that "really works." In the next chapter, we introduce an approach that can help you achieve self-sufficiency while you learn how to structure a healthful, low-calorie, low-fat diet. However, if you are the type of person who normally responds better in group or structured environments, there are many different programs available to you. How to choose? We propose a checklist that includes three sets of questions: one set for your own personal evaluation of your goals and expectations, one set to use in a consultation with your doctor, and one for the directors of any program you might consider joining.

Questions to Ask Yourself

◆ What are your reasons for wanting to lose weight—are they health-related or mostly cosmetic? Your motivations are an important factor. If you equate a certain body style with specific benefits, such as a more successful career, a better love life, or just happier feelings in general, you are setting yourself up for potential problems. Although a diet and fitness program can be a positive motivating factor in getting other areas in your life moving, losing weight, in itself, will not guarantee that your life will change.

◆ Have you dieted before? If you are a "chronic dieter" who goes on diets once or twice a year, you may be setting yourself up for yet another defeat unless you address the issue of why other diets have failed. Chronic dieters cling to the belief that past failures are caused either by their own lack of discipline (which they're determined to overcome "this time") or by the programs they have tried, which have never been the "right" programs. The simple truth is that diet specialists have not yet discovered the one "miracle" diet that helps everyone to lose weight overnight. What you might have perceived as lack of discipline on your part was probably yet another diet hoax failing. One exercise you might try before pursuing a new weight-loss program is to chart your weight-loss history, noting the type of diet you went on, how long it lasted, how much weight you lost, why you stopped dieting, how long it took you to regain the weight, and what were the factors that contributed to your regaining. Use this chart as a basis for evaluating future programs. You're likely to find some trends in your experience—such as repeated failure with very low-calorie diets or greater success in group programs—that will give you a firmer grasp of what seems to work best.

◆ What do your parents, grandparents, siblings, and other relatives look like? Scientists know that genetic factors play a role in body shape, and there are some things that can't be changed. Many people who are not overweight by commonly used standards continue to diet in order to be thinner overall or to slim down thighs, legs, or hips. But you cannot simply point to a picture in a magazine and say, "I want to look like that person." No matter how much you diet, you cannot change your genetically given shape, any more than you can change the color of your eyes.

◆ Do you have special health considerations that must be discussed with your physician? Evaluate your personal medical history, as well as that of your family, to determine if you are at risk for heart disease, high blood pressure, or diabetes. Also note food allergies, gastrointestinal complaints, and medications you might be taking. Your ability completely to evaluate health risk factors will enable your physician to advise you better.

◆ What else is going on in your life? If you've just changed jobs, gone through a divorce, or are experiencing extra stress at work or home, decide whether you can cope with the added stress of changing your diet and exercise habits. If not, wait until you can get your circumstances under control. Even the elation that might accompany getting married or moving into a new house can make it difficult to focus on dealing with changes in lifestyle patterns.

Questions to Ask Your Doctor

◆ Does your current weight, medical history, and evaluation of risk factors make it necessary for you to lose weight for health reasons? There's nothing wrong with wanting to lose a few pounds for cosmetic reasons, but it should be viewed as an issue separate from health.

◆ Do laboratory tests indicate that you have special medical concerns, such as high cholesterol, high blood pressure, or high blood sugar? Are there any factors that would make certain diet approaches either good or bad for your health? Along with that, does your doctor have any recommendations of his or her own, or any literature available about effective programs?

◆ Also, be sure to let your doctor know if you have a history of bingeing to the point where you feel out of control, taking laxatives or inducing vomiting, or anorexia. You may have an eating disorder that should be addressed if you think you need to lose weight.

Questions to Ask the Program Directors

◆ Does the program provide a comprehensive approach that includes diet, exercise, and behavior modification? The most effective programs seem to be more well-rounded than simply helping you shed a few pounds fast.

◆ Is the program individualized? No single program works in the same way for everyone. Standardized diets that use the same format for everyone inevitably fail for those who don't fit the norm.

◆ Does the program make fantastic claims? There's no such thing as a diet that allows you to lose a huge amount of weight overnight while eating anything you want. Most diets that offer rapid initial weight loss are low-carbohydrate diets that have a diuretic effect. But losing water is not the same as losing fat, and such diets have no staying power.

◆ Is the program medically supervised? Don't hesitate to find out about the credentials of those who direct and monitor the program. Sometimes counselors are merely successful graduates of the program and have no medical or nutritional training. The presence or absence of trained medical personal (with expertise in weight control), nutritionists, dieticians, exercise physiologists, and behavior modification specialists will tell you a lot about a program's viability.

◆ Does the program relate realistically to your lifestyle? If you are not dangerously obese, your best course is to plan a gradual, steady weight loss—no more than one-half pound per week. This process will include developing new, more healthful eating habits. Many people fail on diets that require too much special shopping and preparation, or eating foods at times that don't fit their normal schedules. Some programs require that you weigh yourself daily, a practice that is both inconvenient and probably pointless. (Most metabolism and weight-control specialists believe that daily weighing tells you little about real fat loss.)

◆ Does the program recommend a nutritious diet? Never trust a program that emphasizes one or two "magic" foods, depends heavily on only one type of food (such as a high-protein diet), or otherwise deprives you of the nutrients you need.

◆ Does the program offer help with maintenance? Once you've lost the weight, the key is to keep it off. You will need maintenance support—not just behavior modification but practical guidelines as well, such as shopping and cooking advice.

◆ Can you afford it? There are many different kinds of programs in different price ranges. Some are quite expensive. Be sure to find out all the details in advance, such as what the program's guarantee is, whether you have to pay the entire amount up front, whether you'll get part or all of your money back if you drop out, and whether there are hidden costs for items like prepackaged foods or materials.

24

Take Charge of Your Weight Control

As a first step in your weight-loss program, you might want to try the Tufts Low-cholesterol Diet in Chapter 19. Because, by its nature, a low-cholesterol diet is going to be high in complex carbohydrates and fiber and low in saturated fat and cholesterol, most people will lose some weight on such a diet. It will also give you an appreciation of just how appetizing "healthful" food can be. The menus are fun to follow, and the recipes are delicious originals.

But even if you participate in a structured weight-control program in the beginning, your goal should be eventually to achieve self-sufficiency in managing a healthful diet. If you are a chronic dieter, this might be a foreign concept because you've grown so accustomed to others' telling you what you can and cannot eat. You may feel comfortable with the familiarity of that approach, even if the diets themselves have never worked for you. Maybe you're afraid that, left to fend for yourself, you'll lose control and fail.

On the other hand, it's likely that the more comfortable you become with selecting your own foods and managing your own eating and fitness plan, the less obsessed you'll become with food and the less likely you'll be to binge.

The following guidelines and food lists will help you begin to figure out how to construct a nutritious weight-loss plan on your own.

How Many Calories Do You Need?

Obsessive calorie counting is not the way to achieve normal, healthful dietary habits. And if you follow the guidelines for healthful eating, you'll probably find that your calorie intake automatically declines. Both human and animal studies have shown that when fatty foods are replaced by those high in complex carbohydrates, subjects consume fewer calories.

However, if you want to get a general idea of how many calories you should eat each day to encourage weight loss, note that there is a method for calculating this number individually. Many weight-loss programs place everyone on the same number of calories per day, but this practice is not very effective. People are different, and two people will have different results with the same number of calories.

As you calculate your calorie needs, don't forget that reducing calories too much will only create a slowdown in your metabolic rate and a tendency to retain water. Keep your calories at a reasonable level to encourage a slow, steady weight loss.

To find out how many calories you should consume to lose weight, you must first determine how many calories you need to maintain your current weight. To calculate this number, first you must estimate how many calories you require to maintain your normal bodily functions at rest—in other words, your Basal Metabolic Rate (BMR). Add to that the number of additional calories you use for your daily activities. The total becomes the number of calories you use to maintain your weight. You can estimate this number by using the following equation:

1. BMR = current weight x 10
2. multiply result x 0.30 (for daily activities)
3. add BMR number and activity number

It is estimated that the average sedentary American uses only an additional 30 percent of his or her calories on activity. If you are very active, you might want to raise your activity calorie level to 40 percent for a more accurate reading.

Once you know the daily calorie intake that keeps you at your present weight, you can lose weight by creating a negative energy balance—that is, taking in fewer calories than you use up. Specifically, to lose one pound of fat, you need to consume about 3,500 calories less than you use (by either eating less or engaging in more physical activity). We suggest that you do not cut your calorie intake below 1,200 calories per day. A better method might be to cut your calorie intake to your BMR, which means consuming 30 percent fewer calories per day. If you add exercise on top of this, you will increase the rate of weight loss.

At first glance, a weight loss of only a half pound a week may seem like very little, especially if you're familiar with the many diets that promise weight losses of five to ten pounds per week. But remember: On those diets you lose mostly water, not fat. And you probably didn't achieve or maintain long-term weight loss. If

EXAMPLE: HOW MANY CALORIES DO YOU USE?

Adult women: 140 pounds

$$140 \times .10 = 1,400$$
$$1,400 \times 0.30 = 1,420$$
$$1,400 + .420 = 1,820 \text{ calories}$$

you want successfully to achieve permanent weight loss, the slow, steady approach is your best and most nutritionally sound course. When you add a sensible exercise program, you can lose an additional pound or two a month.

Plan Your Weekly Menus

Construct your eating plans, using the following food lists as a general guideline. These lists are provided to give you a start. They are not intended to be rigid lists of "allowable" foods. To achieve your goal of becoming knowledgeable about foods and comfortable with the idea of managing your own diet, you need to avoid making "good" and "bad" food rules for yourself.

As you construct your weekly menu plan, follow these guidelines to ensure that you meet your nutrient requirements and are attentive to the recommendations for lowering fat and cholesterol:

Consume approximately 50 to 60 percent of your daily calories in the form of complex carbohydrates. Sources of complex carbohydrates include fruit, vegetables, breads, cereals, and legumes.

Consume 15 to 20 percent of your daily calories in the form of protein. These can be in the form of meat, poultry, fish and dairy foods, or vegetable proteins in a variety that fulfill complete protein needs.

Consume 30 percent or fewer of your daily calories in the form of fats. No more than 10 percent of total daily calories should be saturated fats. Saturated fats are high in many animal foods as well as in coconut and palm oils. Unsaturated fats are found in vegetable oils and margarine.

EXAMPLE: DAILY CALORIES FOR WEIGHT LOSS

Adult woman—Weight:	140 pounds
BMR:	1,400 calories per day
Activity:	1,420 calories per day
Total:	1,820 calories per day
(-0.30):	1,400 calories per day
Deficit:	1,420 calories per day[1]
Weight Loss:	Roughly 1 pound per week

[1]Does not account for increased physical exercise. To lose more, increase exercise rather than cutting calories further (see Chapter 25).

Consume no more than 300 milligrams of cholesterol each day. Cholesterol is found only in animal foods. (See Chapter 5 for cholesterol content of common foods.)

Limit your sodium intake to under 2,400 milligrams each day. In addition to common table salt, sodium is found in many processed foods and some seasonings.

While you're trying to lose weight, avoid alcohol. Its calories are "empty" in the sense that they supply no nutrients. On a controlled-calorie diet, you could end up wasting 20 to 30 percent of your daily calories with just a couple of beers or glasses of wine.

Assume a balance of essential vitamins and minerals by eating a variety of foods every day. Consume 2 to 3 servings of dairy foods per day; 2 to 3 servings of meat, poultry, or fish; 3 to 5 servings of vegetables; 2 to 4 servings of fruits; and 6 to 11 servings of whole-grain bread, cereal, rice, and pasta.

Refer frequently to the sections in this book on shopping for and preparing food. They contain easy-to-execute guidelines for making your meals interesting, healthful, and low in calories and fat.

Change Your "Diet Head"

Here are a few suggestions to help you avoid being obsessed by food and weight loss while you're dieting:

◆ Become active: Use the suggestions in Chapter 25 to find a regular program of exercise, preferably combining aerobic and weight-bearing exercise. Exercise will not only contribute to your fat loss but also increase your cardiovascular fitness, decrease your risk for osteoporosis, reduce the risk of diabetes, and reverse depression. Exercise will also increase your self-esteem and reduce your cravings for food.

◆ Stop weighing yourself: People with weight obsessions usually weigh themselves every day. Some even weigh themselves several times a day or after every meal. When you do this, you're just tracking the amount of water you lose and gain over the course of a day. Limit your weighing sessions to once a week. And don't forget that there might be times you retain a little water—women often do so before their menstrual periods, for example. You can even test to see if you're retaining water: Push your finger against your shinbone and hold it for a few seconds. When you take your finger away, the skin will bounce back if there's no water retention. A dimple will remain if you're retaining water.

◆ Don't make yourself miserable: If you're planning to attend a party or other special occasion, acknowledge in advance that you're going to splurge a little on a small dessert or other favorite food. If you go in with the attitude that you're not going to deprive yourself, you won't be as likely to binge.

◆ Drop the idea of "good food, bad food": Of course, if you're trying to lose weight, there are some foods that won't be a regular part of your diet. But your most successful route to life-time weight control is to avoid labeling any foods as bad. It won't harm you to have a treat once or twice a week. Calorie counting isn't, after all, a precise science. Eating 200 or 300 extra calories once a week isn't going to throw your diet off course. If it really bothers you, add some exercise—a better idea than cutting back on other nutrient-rich foods.

◆ Avoid unrealistic goals: It's good to have weight-loss goals, but try to keep them general and avoid linking them to important factors in your life. If you say, "I'm going to lose ten pounds before my vacation in Hawaii this Octo-ber," you are essentially saying that having a good time in Hawaii is dependent on your hav-ing lost ten pounds. Losing weight and getting fit is one way to improve yourself, but don't make it the requirement for your enjoyment in every other area of your life. If you're a chronic dieter, this tendency has likely been a part of your problem in the past.

◆ Focus on health, not weight: Except for those few people with medical complications, eating a healthful, well-balanced diet that is high in complex carbohydrates and low in fat and exercising several times a week will lead to weight loss and healthy weight maintenance. If you focus on improving your overall health and fitness instead of "going on a diet," you will most certainly benefit. And you may find, for the first time in your life, that you're enjoying yourself instead of suffering.

Can Less Fatty Be More Yummy?

If the prospect of a low-fat diet makes you feel glum, consider this. A group of 650 women in Seattle received instruction on how to reduce the fat in their diets and were then monitored by a psychologist, Deborah Bowen, Ph.D., at the Fred Hutchinson Cancer Research Center. Four years later, these women gave a lower preference rating to high-fat foods like cookies and potato chips than did a similar group of women who had not been instructed on how to follow a low-fat diet.

The women weren't just paying lip service to the idea of low-fat eating. Four out of five had managed to get their fat intake down from the typical American level of 37 percent of calories to 20 percent—and keep it there.

It's not that the women on the reduced-fat diets came to dislike the taste of higher-fat foods. In various tests they rated the mouth-feel and other sensory properties of fat as highly as the women who had not been fol-lowing a lower-fat regimen. What may have happened instead is that fat simply didn't agree with them anymore. Dr. Bowen notes that when people switch to a low-fat diet, too much high-fat eating can make them physi-cally uncomfortable—perhaps because fat increases the time it takes for food to leave the stomach and could thereby contribute to indigestion.

According to Richard Mattes, a scientist at Philadelphia's Monell Chemical Senses Center, a research institute devoted exclusively to the study of taste and smell, people may indeed experience a reduced taste for fat when they adopt a lower-fat diet.

Men and women in Dr. Mattes' study were divided into separate groups. Some were instructed not only to follow a low-fat diet but also to keep away from all sources of added fats, such as butter, margarine, sour cream, salad dressing, and the like. They were not allowed to have reduced-fat versions of those fatty items, either. So, in addition to being deprived of fat, they were also being deprived of the creaminess and mouthfeel of low-fat items that taste fatty. Others were told to follow the same diet but were allowed to eat reduced- and non-fat versions of the add-ons.

SAMPLE FOODS AND SERVINGS FOR A WEIGHT-LOSS DIET

Servings 100 Calories or Lower

Serving	Calories
1 medium apple	80
1/2 cantaloupe	80
10 seedless grapes	35
1 medium orange	90
1 peach	40
1 cup sliced pineapple	80
1 plum	30
1 cup strawberries	55
1 cup blueberries	82
1/2 grapefruit	50
3 small apricots	55
1/2 cup unsweetened applesauce	53
1 cup cooked carrots	50
1 cup cooked collard greens	65
1 cup cooked spinach	40
1 cup cooked summer squash	30
1 medium steamed artichoke	53
1 cup cooked asparagus	30
1 cup cooked green beans	30
1 cup cooked broccoli	40
1 cup cooked cauliflower	30
1 cup boiled eggplant	38
1/2 cup cooked green peas	67
1 slice cracked-wheat bread	65
1 slice whole-wheat bread	60
1 slice rye bread	65
1 slice French bread	72
2 bread sticks	86
3 rye crackers	72
4 saltines (low sodium)	52
4 wheat crackers	64
1 oz. bran flakes	90
1 oz. shredded wheat	100
1 corn tortilla	32
4 oz. tofu	82
4 oz. low-fat (1%) cottage cheese	82
1 oz. part-skim mozzarella cheese	80
1 poached egg	80
1 cup skim milk	85
1/2 cup vanilla ice milk	90

Servings 200 Calories or Lower

Serving	Calories
1 cup orange juice	110
1 pear	100
6 dried prunes	120
1 medium baked potato	145
1 cup cooked winter squash	130
1 medium baked sweet potato	160
1 medium bran muffin	110
1 English muffin	130
1 medium nut muffin	165
1 cup cooked farina	135
1 oz. corn flakes	110
1 cup cooked oatmeal	145
1 cup cooked long-grain brown rice	173
1 cup cooked macaroni	192
1 cup cooked egg noodles	200
1 cup cooked plain spaghetti	192
1/2 cup cooked lima beans	130
1/2 cup cooked navy beans	112
1 oz. sunflower seeds	162
1/2 cup part-skim ricotta cheese	171
1 cup low-fat (1%) milk	105
1 cup nonfat plain yogurt	125
3 oz. roasted chicken, skinless, white meat	165
1 roasted chicken drumstick, skinless	172
3-1/2 oz. water-packed tuna, no salt	127
3 oz. steamed shrimp	102
3 oz. broiled or baked oysters	133
3 oz. poached salmon	126
3 oz. broiled or baked salmon	149
3 oz. broiled or baked perch fillet	113
3 oz. broiled or baked sea bass	117
3 oz. broiled or baked flounder	101
3 oz. broiled or baked scallops	106
3 oz. broiled, lean, top loin	172
3 oz. roasted, lean, round eye	155
3 oz. broiled liver	137
3 oz. broiled, lean, veal steak	123

Servings 300 Calories or Lower

Serving	Calories
1 cup cooked spaghetti with tomato sauce	260
1 cup cooked lentil beans	210
1 cup low-fat fruit yogurt	230
3 oz. lean ground beef	217

After 12 weeks, both groups had managed to reduce fat consumption from more than 30 percent of calories to less than 20 percent. But only the first group—the one denied lower-fat imitations as well as high-fat foods—indicated a reduced preference for high-fat foods, and even for foods that only tasted fatty.

Dr. Mattes' conclusion is that if you go on a reduced-fat diet but continue to eat foods that have the sensory properties of fat, your preference for fat will remain. But if you reeducate your palate by eating fewer fatty-tasting items, you may actually come to prefer foods that aren't fat.

◆ NUTRITION QUIZ ◆
An IQ Test for Losers

Every other woman in this country as well as one in every four men—roughly 20 million people—are currently trying to lose weight. But despite the American preoccupation with shedding excess pounds, the fine points of how to do so healthfully and effectively are often misunderstood by even the most seasoned "losers." What is the safest rate of weight loss? Is cellulite harder to get rid of than other types of fat? What kind of exercise burns the most calories? To see whether you know the answers and other questions on "dieting down," take this quiz.

1. The recommended rate of weekly weight loss is (a) one half pound to one pound (b) one to two pounds (c) no more than five pounds.

2. Calories taken in at which time of day are the most likely to turn into fat in the body? (a) morning (b) dinnertime (c) just before bedtime (d) it doesn't matter; excess calories will become fat regardless of when they're taken in.

3. *True or false?* Cellulite is harder to get rid of than other types of body fat.

4. The best workout for losing weight and looking svelte involves (a) aerobic exercise such as jogging, dancing, and swimming (b) strength-training activities, like lifting weights or Nautilus training (c) spot-reducing exercises, such as situps and leg lifts (d) a combination of aerobic exercise and strength training (e) a combination of aerobic exercise and spot reducing.

5. Excess pounds on which part of the body pose the greatest health hazard? (a) the hips and thighs (b) the abdomen (c) the chest and upper arms (d) none of the above; all excess pounds, no matter where they're located, are equally bad for health.

6. *True or false?* After about two weeks of adherence to a weight-loss diet, the stomach shrinks, thereby decreasing the amount of food it can hold.

7. *True or false?* The first thing someone trying to lose weight should eliminate from the diet is high-calorie sweet food—cake, cookies, ice cream, candy, etc.

ANSWERS

1. (a) The federal government's *Dietary Guidelines for Americans* recommends that a "loser" shed no more than a half pound to one pound a week until his or her goal is reached. That's because the slower the rate of loss, the more likely the pounds will stay off. In addition, the more slowly weight is lost, the more likely the pounds shed will be made up of fat. Quick, early weight losses experienced on "crash" diets often indicate a greater loss of water and lean body tissue than of fat.

2. (d) For most people, it doesn't matter when food is eaten. If the calories taken in exceed the amount the body needs, they will be converted to fat. Some preliminary evidence does indicate that in obese people, heavy meals eaten at the end of the day are more likely to be

An IQ Test for Losers (cont.)

changed into fat inside the body. And other research suggests that excess calories taken in during regular meals are more prone to end up as body fat than extra calories nibbled throughout the day. Still, such evidence remains tenuous at best.

Those trying to lose weight, whether obese or just moderately heavy, would accomplish much more by concentrating on getting plenty of exercise and keeping excess fat and calories in the overall diet to a minimum than by worrying about what time of day they eat.

3. *False.* Cellulite is no different from "other types" of body fat. It simply is plain fat that has a dimply, waffly appearance because of the way the body deposits it. Consider that one of the places the body stores fat is directly under the skin in fat cells divided into compartments by strands of fibrous tissue. The more fat a particular body deposits in those fat cells, the more likely the compartments are to bulge and create the lumpy areas frequently dubbed "cellulite." But just like fat on other parts of the body, "cellulite" responds to diet and exercise.

4. (d) Although most people assume that aerobic exercise alone ranks tops in promoting weight loss because aerobic activities such as jogging and biking burn the greatest number of calories per session, exercise physiologists believe that the optimal regimen for losing weight and keeping it off involves a combination of aerobic exercises and strength-training routines. Preliminary research conducted by the National YMCA's strength-training consultant, Wayne Wescott, PhD, corroborates that viewpoint.

Dr. Wescott measured the weight and body compositions of a group of dieters who three times a week spent 30 minutes engaged in the aerobic activity of riding a stationary bike and compared them with the measurements of another group who, during their thrice weekly exercise sessions, spent 15 minutes cycling and 15 minutes strength training on Nautilus machines. Over the course of eight weeks, both groups lost weight, but the cyclers who included strength training lost more. They also gained more muscle mass, the primary advantage strength training confers on someone trying to lose weight and keep it off. The reason is that, unlike aerobic exercise, strength training builds significant amounts of muscle, which requires more calories to sustain itself than body fat and therefore causes a dieter to burn more calories than otherwise even when he's not exercising. That is, it appears that the more muscular the person, the more quickly he or she can lose weight—and the better able he or she is to keep it off over the long run.

That's not to say that would-be weight losers should forgo aerobic exercise and opt for strength training by itself. Aerobic exercise does burn the most calories minute for minute no matter what the body's lean tissue/fat composition.

Furthermore, only aerobic activity confers the important benefit of exercising the heart muscle and thereby enhancing cardiovascular fitness.

Note: Readers who think the best way to attain a sleek figure is through spot-reducing exercises such as leg lifts or sit-ups should be aware that such activities will not cause more fat to be lost from the area being exercised than from the rest of the body. Instead, fat lost as a result of "spot reducing" is taken from fat deposits throughout the body. However, exercising a specific group of muscles does tone and firm them, thereby giving them a leaner look.

An IQ Test for Losers *(cont.)*

5. **(b)** A growing body of evidence suggests that the "spare tire" created by excess fat around the abdomen poses a particularly high hazard to health because it raises the risk of ending up with problems such as heart disease and diabetes. In other words, where the body stores excess fat can be just as important to health as the number of extra pounds the body carries; two people could be the same height and weight, but differences in body shape could indicate that one is at a greater risk for disease.

    To check your body shape, measure your waist while standing relaxed, without pulling in your stomach.

    Then measure your hips around the buttocks, where they are largest. Finally, divide the waist measurement by the hip measurement to determine your waist-to-hip ratio. Ideally, the ratio should be less than one. In fact, 0.80 or less is the target for women. They tend to have proportionately smaller waists and larger hips than men, who should aim for no more than 0.95. Beyond those cutoff points, the higher the number, the greater the risk of health problems.

6. *False.* That the stomach shrinks when someone goes on a weight-loss diet is a common misconception. The truth is that it simply expands and contracts in proportion to the amount of food it contains at any given time.

7. *False.* Granted, because cake, cookies, candy, and other similarly sugary treats typically contribute lots of fat and calories to the diet and relatively little in the way of other nutrients, it makes sense for a person on a weight-loss regimen to cut back on those foods. Nevertheless, the belief that to lose weight it's necessary to swear off an entire category of foods is erroneous. Quite the contrary; the first step in creating a successful weight-loss plan is identifying dietary changes that you can make *comfortably*. It's true some people prefer going "cold turkey" and eliminating for a while particular foods that they find hard to stop eating once they've started. Generally, there isn't anything wrong with that. Others, however, may find it more suitable to just eat their "temptation" foods less often or in smaller amounts.

    The bottom line is that there is no one diet that will help everyone shed pounds. You have to discover what works for you, whether that means eating fewer candy bars, making a nightly after-dinner drink an every-other-nightly drink, and/or increasing your daily exercise. What's certain is that if it's a plan *you* feel okay about, it has the best chance of succeeding.

25

Build a Better Body

We include a chapter on exercise in a book about nutrition because exercise is such a vital part of keeping fit and healthy. Many studies have demonstrated that not only is exercise a good way to lose weight, it also is a key to basic health. Some of these benefits include cardiovascular fitness (with physical activities that increase the heart rate), a possible increase in bone mass that may diminish the risk of osteoporosis, and even a lessening of anxiety and stress. So, whether your goal is to lose weight, improve health, or both, exercise is the ideal companion to a nutritious diet.

Exercise: Separating Fact from Fiction

There are as many false ideas about exercise as there are about nutrition. One reason might be that, like diet, exercise has grown into a major industry, dedicated to selling fitness-conscious Americans on the idea that they "must" have special supplements, drinks, foods, lotions, equipment, and so on. Americans are gullible about buying into this promotion, not only because we're always on the lookout for a quick answer but also because we aren't very

well educated about exercise. Most of us learned about exercise in inadequate school programs, where the focus was on sports performance, not health. It's easy to see why we would be so filled with misconceptions. Let's look at some of the most common:

Fiction: No Pain, No Gain

Fact: If belief in this maxim stands between you and the decision to improve your physical fitness, you'll be relieved to learn that you don't have to push yourself until it hurts to enjoy the benefits of exercise. In fact, excessive exercise increases the chances of bone, joint, and muscle injury, not to mention making your workout seem more like punishment than pleasure.

For most people, simply exercising for 15 to 60 minutes, three to five times a week, will improve cardiovascular fitness and contribute to weight loss.

Cardiovascular fitness can be achieved if your heart is working at 70 to 80 percent of its maximum. Following is a list of the average 70 percent–capacity heart rate of people of various ages. Check yourself against the average this way: When you have completed your exercise, apply your fingertips to the artery on the inside of your wrist, just below the bone. Count the number of heart beats in a ten-second period and multiply it by six. That's the number of times your heart is beating per minute. Check yourself against these averages:

Age	Heart Rate at 70 Percent Capacity (Average)
20	140
25	137
30	133
35	130
40	126
45	123
50	119
55	116
60	112
65	109
70	105

If you think the weight-loss benefits won't be there unless you push yourself to the limit, consider this: If a 150-pound person spent one hour per day, three days a week, on a brisk walk, that would account for 900 calories a week, enough to lose about 13 pounds a year without even making one change in diet. What's more, most of those pounds come from stored body fat, not the lean body tissue that sometimes is lost with diet alone.

Fiction: Excess Weight Can Be Sweated Off

Fact: If this were true, we could all lose our excess weight by lounging around in saunas or steam rooms. Although it's not uncommon for exercisers who hop on a scale after a workout to find that they've lost weight, it's a result of perspiration. Once fluids are taken back in, that weight will return.

Fiction: Exercise Will Just Make You Hungrier

Fact: Many skeptical dieters think they'll grow so famished from exercising that they will eat back all they've lost. Ordinary exercise does not decrease appetite, but neither does it increase it. In one study, obese women at St. Luke's–Roosevelt Hospital Center in New York City followed a rigorous daily routine of walking a treadmill for a period of two months. Not only did they not increase the amount of food they ate, but they walked off enough calories to lose an average of 15 pounds each.

It should be noted that already-slim women who were also put on a treadmill routine did increase their calorie intake to compensate for the extra calories they were burning. But they did not raise their "input" over their "output" and gained no weight.

Fiction: Spot-exercising Causes More Fat to Be Lost from a Particular Part of the Body

Fact: If only that were true! Although the idea that fat-free thighs can be achieved by concentrating on leg lifts or that a flat stomach can be had through sit-ups alone is an enticing thought, it seems to be fallacious. Researchers at the University of Massachusetts helped dispel the notion about spot-reducing several years ago when they put a small group of college men on a four-week sit-up program. When they evaluated the results they found that the amount of fat in the men's abdomens was not reduced to any greater extent than the fat in their buttocks or bases of their shoulder blades. In other words, fat lost through spot-reducing is not selectively drawn from fat surrounding the area being exercised. Rather, it is pulled from deposits throughout the body. Happily, exercising a group of muscles at a specific spot on the body can tone and firm them, but if there is excess fat in that spot it won't be lost by concentrating on that area.

Fiction: Special Techniques Other Than Exercise Are Needed to Get Rid of Cellulite

Fact: Cellulite, that lumpy, dimply flesh that collects on the hips, thighs, and buttocks and is supposed to be particularly hard to "break up," does not even exist. It's nothing more than a name that clever marketers have given to fat that collects directly under the skin. Therefore, the claims that special exercises or products will "get rid" of it are completely spurious. The only way to smooth out those fat deposits is to follow the same kind of diet and exercise regimen that will get rid of fat all over the body.

Fiction: After a Certain Age, People Shouldn't Exercise

Fact: Tufts School of Nutrition physiologist William Evans, Ph.D., found just the opposite to be true when he conducted tests at the Tufts-USDA Human Nutrition Research Center on Aging. When he put men aged 60 to 72 years on a weight-lifting program, they markedly increased both the size and strength of their thigh muscles after just 12 weeks. Even a group of men and women averaging 90 years of age increased the muscle area of their thighs by about 10 percent. And the amount of weight they were able to lift went from an average of 17.6 pounds to 44 pounds.

Many of the participants—a number of whom relied on canes and walkers to move about—were able to walk a little faster, take longer strides, and get in and out of their chairs more easily. One 90-year-old woman reported that before "pumping iron" she was always tired and rarely lifted anything heavier than a quart of milk. But after getting involved in the program she found that she had more strength in her arms and legs, was capable of greater endurance during exertion, and had more overall energy. A man three years her junior who also participated in the weight-training program commented that "Psychologically, it's a good feeling to see that you're not deteriorating." Incidentally, Dr. Evans pointed out that elderly people who successfully strengthened their muscles at Tufts were eating well before they began. Had they not been, he believed, the outcome would not have been so dramatic.

Getting Started on Fitness

If you're new to exercising, the first thing to do is see your doctor for a complete physical checkup. Such an exam is particularly important if you have any medical complications, are over the age of 60, or have any muscle or bone impairments.

If you want to maximize both the fat-burning and cardiovascular effects of an exercise regimen, your best choice is an aerobic exercise program combined with strength training. Aerobic exercise keeps the heart rate up to the 70 or 80 percent level mentioned previously, in a sustained effort. Doing calisthenics, for example, is

---

FITNESS LEVEL SCORECARD

Dr. James Rippe, director of exercise physiology at the University of Massachusetts Medical School, developed this test to help people determine their level of fitness. Clock out a mile using the odometer in your car, then walk it as fast as you can and calculate your fitness score according to these guidelines:

	Time (Minutes: Seconds)	
	Male	**Female**
excellent	less than 10:12	less than 11:40
good	10:13–11:42	11:41–13:08
high average	11:43–13:13	13:09–14:36
low average	13:14–14:44	14:37–16:04
fair	14:45–16:23	16:05–17:31
poor	more than 16:24	more than 17:32

not aerobic because it involves stopping and starting. To gain the full benefit of aerobic exercise, it should be done a minimum of three times a week. In the accompanying box, examine the pros and cons of these favorite aerobic activities.

Strength training can be performed by people of all ages. Even the elderly have been found to benefit from it. A strength-training program for women conducted by Tufts showed substantial results, including a gain in muscle mass, muscle strength, overall conditioning, and balance. Participants performed simple exercises like leg lifts and sit-ups. Strength training exercises can be performed twice a week for basic fitness.

Most important, don't view exercise as an all-or-nothing proposition—that is, either you're out working up a sweat or you're parked in front of the television. Rather, think of it this way: You stand to gain even if you accumulate 30 minutes of moderate-intensity physical activity over the course of a day—for example, using the stairs instead of the elevator, gardening, raking leaves, or walking part way to work. Experts say that people who are extremely sedentary and begin such a moderate program can reduce the risk of disease as much as quitting smoking.

Tips to Make Your Workout Work

To get the most benefit from your exercise program and to avoid injuries, remember these points: Always warm up and cool down. Before you start exercising, make sure that your muscle tendons are stretched to give you more flexibility and avoid injury.

After exercising, reinforce the flexibility of your muscles by stretching again. During this period of reduced activity, your heartbeat will gradually return to normal. Here are two sample stretches:

◆ Knee bend: Place feet and knees together and squat down with your arms along the sides

HOW MANY CALORIES DO YOU SPEND EXERCISING?[1]

This list gives the average calories spent per hour by a 150-pound person.

Bicycling, 6 mph	240 calories
Bicycling, 12 mph	410 calories
Running, 10 mph	1,280 calories
Cross-country skiing	700 calories
Jogging, 5 mph	740 calories
Jogging, 7 mph	920 calories
Jumping rope	750 calories
Running in place	650 calories
Swimming, 25 yds./min.	275 calories
Swimming, 50 yds./min.	500 calories
Tennis, singles	400 calories
Walking, 2 mph	240 calories
Walking, 3 mph	320 calories
Walking, 4 mph	440 calories

[1]The calories spent in a particular activity vary in proportion to your body weight. For example, a 100-pound person would decrease these numbers by 1/3; a 200-pound person would increase them by 1/3.

of your knees and fingers on the floor. Straighten legs, leaving fingers on the floor and directing buttocks in the air. Repeat 8 times.

◆ Calf stretch: Stand 3 to 4 feet from a vertical surface (like a fence, wall, or tree). Lean forward against the surface, bending your arms and keeping your right heel firmly planted. As you lean forward, drop your right hip, stretching the right calf and bending the left leg slightly. Hold for 10 seconds, then reverse and stretch the left leg. Repeat 8 times for each leg.

While you're exercising, be sure to breathe fully: Breathing is an important part of the workout, and holding your breath will hold you back.

Inhale from the abdomen, expanding your chest with air, and then exhale, also from the abdomen, pushing the air out with a "whoosh." The rhythm of your breathing should coincide with the movement of your body. For example,

RATING THE AEROBIC WORKOUTS

The list that follows compares some of the most popular aerobic exercises in terms of the number of calories they burn, the muscles they exercise, the equipment they require, and other characteristics to help you choose the workout suitable for your needs. As you go over it, bear in mind that you don't need to choose one exercise and stick with it day after day, week after week. A more healthful method for both your body and your mind may be to vary your routine by alternating several different activities. That approach, known as cross training, not only lessens the risk of injuries that can result from repeating the same movements session after session but also prevents the boredom that often causes people to give up on physical activity.

Aerobic Dancing

CALORIES BURNED IN 30 MINUTES[1]: 183 to 237
BODY PARTS EXERCISED: all major muscle groups
EQUIPMENT NEEDED: good pair of sneakers; music
ADVANTAGES: Uses a variety of movements, thereby reducing risk of injury caused by repeating a simple motion over and over; adds to the pleasure of exercising for people who enjoy working out with a group.
SPECIAL CONSIDERATIONS: "High impact" dance routines involving vigorous jumping and bouncing may result in twisted ankles, knee injuries, and back pain; "low impact" workouts during which one foot is always touching the ground eliminate most of the jumping and other jerky movements that can cause injury.
Note: "Step aerobic dancing," during which the exerciser steps on and off a stair-step-sized platform to the beat of music, exercises the legs and buttocks particularly well but tends to aggravate knee problems—the higher the platform, the higher the risk of knee injury. (If you flex your knees at a 30-degree angle, as you would on a low step, the pressure on the kneecap is about one and a half times your body weight; if you bend your knee at a 60-degree angle, as on a slightly steeper step, the pressure is twice the body weight.)

Cycling

CALORIES BURNED IN 30 MINUTES (riding 9.4 miles per hour): 177 to 231
BODY PARTS EXERCISED: legs and buttocks
EQUIPMENT NEEDED: stationary or outdoor bicycle; helmet for outdoor bikers
ADVANTAGES: Less traumatic to joints than running or aerobic dancing because bicycle seat bears body weight; lends itself to family and group participation; helps maintain fitness when recovering from ankle, foot, or certain thigh injuries.
SPECIAL CONSIDERATIONS: Outdoor cycling that involves frequent stops and starts as well as alternating periods of cycling and coasting interferes with cardiovascular improvements; aerobic activity must be continuous to confer benefits to the heart. Open roads and bike paths allow for best chance of nonstop outdoor riding.

Cross-country Skiing

CALORIES BURNED IN 30 MINUTES: 210 to 276
BODY PARTS EXERCISED: the major muscle groups, particularly those of the arms and legs.
EQUIPMENT NEEDED: skis, boots, and poles; for indoors, machines such as a Nordic Track, which allow for the simulation of skiing's arm and leg movements.
ADVANTAGES: Low risk of injury because it involves fluid, gliding motions rather than bouncing, jarring moves.
SPECIAL CONSIDERATIONS: Requires excellent arm and leg coordination along with good balance; may be difficult to "get the hang of."

Rowing

CALORIES BURNED IN 30 MINUTES: 183 to 237
BODY PARTS EXERCISED: abdomen and large muscles of upper and lower body.

RATING THE AEROBIC WORKOUTS *(cont.)*

EQUIPMENT NEEDED: indoor rowing machine or boat or canoe.
ADVANTAGES: Like cycling, easier on the joints than running or aerobic dancing because the seat bears the body's weight; can be performed with one leg if the other is injured.
SPECIAL CONSIDERATIONS: none

Running

CALORIES BURNED IN 30 MINUTES (at 9 miles per hour): 342 to 447
BODY PARTS EXERCISED: legs
EQUIPMENT NEEDED: good pair of sneakers
ADVANTAGES: No special skills or equipment required; can be done any time, alone or with others.
SPECIAL CONSIDERATIONS: High risk of injuries to feet, knees, and ankles, particularly among those who try to run more than 35 miles per week and/or don't warm up properly; running or jogging on uneven surfaces such as grass or sand increases difficulty of stepping, thereby adding to strain on muscles.

Stair-Climbing

CALORIES BURNED IN 30 MINUTES: 213 to 279
BODY PARTS EXERCISED: legs, buttocks
EQUIPMENT NEEDED: stairs or, preferably, a stair-climbing machine such as StairMaster or Lifesteps.
ADVANTAGES: Exercising on a stair-climbing machine, as opposed to running up and down stairs in, say, a stadium, reduces impact to joints because the machine bears the body's weight.
SPECIAL CONSIDERATIONS: Locking arms on side rails of machine or leaning forward on equipment can significantly reduce calorie-burning potential; for every 10 pounds you support by leaning on the rail, you burn an estimated seven percent fewer calories.

Swimming

CALORIES BURNED IN 30 MINUTES (slow crawl): 228 to 297
BODY PARTS EXERCISED: all major muscle groups
EQUIPMENT NEEDED: pool
ADVANTAGES: Extremely low risk of injury because water cushions the body, protecting it from impact that could cause injury; particularly suitable for anyone with arthritis, pregnant women, those recovering from injuries, and older people.
SPECIAL CONSIDERATIONS: Beginners require a good deal of practice before becoming adept enough to swim a significant number of laps without stopping.

Walking

CALORIES BURNED IN HALF HOUR (normal pace): 141 to 186
BODY PARTS EXERCISED: legs, particularly calves
EQUIPMENT NEEDED: good pair of shoes
ADVANTAGES: Requires no special skills or equipment; easy for overweight, elderly, or previously out-of-shape people; not as stressful to joints as running or dancing.
SPECIAL CONSIDERATIONS: Walkers must keep brisk pace to reap full cardiovascular benefits; more time is needed to gain the same aerobic benefits from walking as from other exercises.
Note: Walking up and down hills and/or with a backpack increases intensity of workout.

[1]Source: American Heart Association.

if you are doing leg lifts, exhale as you lift your leg and inhale as you lower it.

If you are doing even mild weight-bearing exercises, be sure that you wear the proper shoes to provide the necessary cushioning and support. There are many kinds of shoes to choose from. The personnel at a sporting goods store should be able to explain the benefits of different brands and styles.

Don't push yourself: Start slowly and work up your speed and endurance over a period of weeks. If you try to do too much too soon, you'll suffer an injury or have so many muscle pains you won't be able to crawl to your next exercise session. Try to develop a slow but consistent three-day-a-week pattern.

Exercise for Strength

Aerobic exercise is important because it improves cardiovascular fitness. But we are learning that isotonics, also known as strength training, weight training, or resistance training, can also be very important for health and fitness.

Isotonics is crucial because it builds up muscle mass. The more muscle you have, the stronger you are, so that you can carry heavy packages or perform other tasks without becoming winded. Increased muscle mass also raises your body's metabolic rate, helping to "burn" calories more efficiently. The reason is that muscle requires more calories than fat to sustain itself.

Greater muscle mass also reduces the risk for developing diabetes, because the more muscle mass in the body, the less insulin it takes to get glucose out of the blood and into the tissues where it's needed for energy. Therefore, the body is less likely to use its insulin stores quickly.

Isotonics can raise HDL and lower LDL cholesterol and increase bone density to ward off osteoporosis. A study conducted at Tufts shows that it might even help mitigate the effects of rheumatoid arthritis.

A word of caution: Isotonics can cause injuries if the exercises are improperly performed. The best way to begin is to have a professional show you how to position your body and hold weights. Some people choose to pay for a couple of sessions with a health club instructor who is certified by the American College of Sports Medicine. Also, be careful not to do too much too soon. And always perform a thorough warm-up before beginning any exercise routine.

Walk for Fitness

You don't need expensive exercise equipment or the services of a gym to get fit. Walking has been shown to be one of the best all-around exercise regimens—making people feel more energetic, improving heart rate, reducing body fat, and raising "good" HDL cholesterol.

It isn't necessary to "power" walk, either, as long as you maintain a steady, moderate pace. Although slow walking does not have as many benefits as fast walking does, it can still improve fitness levels, especially for people who haven't engaged in any physical activity for a long time.

Walking also doesn't have to be limited to agreeable weather. A number of shopping malls across the country have walking clubs that allow people to get their indoor exercise before the stores open. The fee to join, if there is one, generally ranges from $10 to $20 and often includes a free T-shirt or other promotional item. Check with the management offices of your local malls to find one that has the program.

Nutrition Notes for Athletes

The serious athlete has specific nutritional and health considerations that might not exist for the more casual exerciser. Of primary interest to the athlete are maintaining top physical condition and gaining a competitive edge. To achieve the former, there is no need for the athlete to eat more than the balanced, healthful diet recommended for the average American—in spite of the fact that an entire industry of health supplements and dietary products exists. The sports industry has long promoted the viewpoint that the dietary needs of athletes are vastly different from those of normal people.

Certainly it is true that athletes must pay special attention to their diets, because nutrition is linked in a very direct way with physical stamina and performance. But it is important that athletes learn to understand their true needs to avoid sabotaging their health as well as to save money they might otherwise spend on expensive and useless supplements.

Carbohydrate Loading

One dietary practice, carbohydrate loading, may be beneficial if it is done properly. Carbohydrate loading means eating a diet that is very high in complex carbohydrates—about 65 to 70 percent of total calories—for four to five days prior to a sustained event that lasts more than two hours. This practice is common for marathon runners and long-distance swimmers, for example, who will be competing for several hours at a stretch.

Carbohydrate loading allows the muscles to store extra carbohydrate in the form of glycogen, a rapidly available fuel source that they and the rest of the body use to work. Normally, we have enough glycogen in our bodies to last an hour and a half to two hours of continuous exercise. So only athletes who go without a break for two hours or more really benefit from the practice.

To be effective, carbohydrate loading must be done properly. As the day of the event approaches, the athlete should gradually taper off the amount of exercise and do no exercise the day before. This time off will allow the body to hang onto the glycogen that has been formed from the carbohydrate so that it will be available during the event.

Carbohydrate loading is a practice that should not take place more than three or four times a year, and some experts recommend that it be done only under medical guidance because, taken to an extreme, it presents risks. In any case, it is a practice that has real value only in continuous endurance sports. It does not apply to stop-and-start games like basketball and football. If the event lasts an hour or less, the body has no need for the extra fuel supply.

Packing Protein

Because we know that protein is needed to build muscle and tissues, many athletes assume that large quantities of protein will make them more muscular. Some eat diets that are full of high-protein, high-fat, and high-cholesterol foods as a result of this misconception. Others take supplements of amino acids, the building blocks from which proteins are constructed.

Although research suggests that the protein requirements of some athletes, particularly marathon runners, may be higher than those of the average person, this finding should be considered in light of the fact that the average American diet already includes much more than the requirement for protein. For example, a single whole chicken breast provides 52 grams of protein, almost the entire RDA for the average adult male. The average diet can easily surpass this allowance. So athletes who need to consume more than the RDA for protein could do so very easily without consuming massive amounts.

Protein overloading comes with a number of risks, in addition to the well-known disadvantages of a diet high in fat and cholesterol. The body uses only so much protein at a time, and the excess is either burned for energy or converted to fat for storage. In either case, the nitrogen component must be stripped away and excreted through the kidneys. Overloading on protein can put the kidneys under stress.

The supplement industry lures athletes with

a variety of products, including protein powder, protein drink, and protein tablets, designed to increase protein consumption without adding fat and cholesterol. It's easy to see how athletes might be attracted to this idea. But, in fact, taking supplementary protein is a complete waste of money.

Fluids Are Essential

Vigorous exercise can mask the normal signals that tell us we're thirsty, and athletes lose a lot of water through perspiration. For this reason, they must take care to consume plenty of fluids, both before exertion and every 20 minutes or so during endurance exercise. Warm weather depletes body fluids further, so fluids should be consumed every 10 to 15 minutes. The best source of fluid is water.

What about sports drinks? The supermarket shelves are full of "power drinks" that promise to give athletes a competitive edge. In fact, sports drinks provide very little, unless an athlete is exercising vigorously for an hour and a half to two hours at a time. The reason is that it would take that long for the body to require the extra nutrients sports drinks provide, notably carbohydrates; the muscles already contain enough carbohydrate in a form called glycogen to fuel 90 to 120 minutes of activity. Furthermore, if you're concerned about losing and maintaining weight, be aware that sports drinks usually contain a fair amount of calories, usually in the form of sugar. The bottom line is that sports drinks might be helpful for heavy athletic activity, but aren't really necessary for weekend athletes or moderate exercisers.

Sports Supplements Should Be Avoided

Supposed "high energy" supplements containing vitamin E and certain B vitamins are a waste of money for those who meet their RDA through diet. There is no scientific evidence that an extra supply of these vitamins increases

endurance or prevents fatigue. The nutrients athletes need are in abundant supply in mixed diets.

Some people believe that athletes need to take salt tablets to replace the salt lost from the body through sweat. But consuming too much salt in the form of tablets will further dehydrate the body by lowering the level of water in the blood. Too much salt will also cause potassium loss, undermining the operation of muscle cells. There is rarely enough salt lost in sweat to require additional salt intake.

The best way to replace fluids lost through sweat is by drinking water. Only in very unusual cases (such as when five to ten pounds of weight are lost during the event) might salt replacement need to occur, and then it should not be in a concentrated dose but in a lightly salted drink or a small amount of salt sprinkled on food.

Potassium and magnesium, which are important for maintaining energy, body temperature, and the proper functioning of muscle cells, are also lost in high-intensity exercise, but again it is of no value to take supplements. Both are available in many foods. Potassium is found in dried fruits and nuts, bananas, potatoes, and oranges. Magnesium can be found in nuts, meat, fish, milk, whole grains, and dark-green leafy vegetables.

Beware cleims that supplements of chromium picolinate can reduce fat and build muscle strength. Rarely do people suffer a deficiency of chromium, and for others the supplement has no effect. It neither burns fat nor builds muscle.

Iron for Female Athletes

A condition known as sports anemia sometimes afflicts female athletes. The reasons for this low blood-hemoglobin level are not known for certain, but the condition tends to appear during the early stages of training. It is suspected that the culprits may include menstrual blood loss, poor iron intake, decreased absorption and increased loss of iron, expanded blood volume, decreased production or greater destruction of red blood cells, and inadequate dietary protein.

The best way to avoid iron deficiency leading to sports anemia is to consume plenty of iron in the diet. The best sources are animal products such as liver, meat, fish, and poultry.

Eating Disorders and Athletes

The popular image of an athlete is that of a vigorous, healthy person. But in recent years, specialists in sports medicine and collegiate athletic trainers have found an alarming incidence of young athletes who suffer from eating disorders, such as anorexia nervosa and bulimia.

What would cause a perfectly healthy young athlete at the peak of performance to reject food? The primary factor appears to be the extreme emphasis on leanness, both self-imposed and encouraged by coaches, in such weight-regulated activities as wrestling, lightweight crew, running, basketball, soccer, and figure skating.

Obsessive runners also seem to share some of the traits of individuals with anorexia nervosa. According to one study in the *New England Journal of Medicine*, these traits include extraordinarily high self-expectations, tolerance of physical discomfort, denial of the potential for serious disability, and a tendency toward depression as they struggle for a sense of identity and control.

Besides extreme emaciation, other symptoms of eating disorders include absence of menstruation in women, extreme hyperactivity and denial of fatigue, a bizarre preoccupation with food, trouble sleeping, and extreme paleness (a sign of anemia).

Poor dietary patterns are often found among bodybuilders who are judged for their physiques rather than for their athletic prowess. Research indicates that muscle builders develop their physiques through exercise and lifting weights (and sometimes by taking steroids), and not because of healthful diet practices.

To make their muscles bigger, bodybuilders often consume large quantities of protein, packing away huge amounts of meat and eggs and consuming protein drinks. But eating large amounts of protein does not build muscle; exercise, not diet, achieves that. As laboratory tests have shown, even animals on restricted diets will build muscle if they exercise.

In the month before competition, many bodybuilders subsist on diets that consist almost entirely of protein. According to Tufts sports nutrition expert William Evans, this is a dangerous and ultimately self-defeating practice. Carbohydrate is needed to provide energy for the grueling daily regimen of exercise bodybuilders put themselves through. If muscle carbohydrate stores become depleted, which will occur on a low-carbohydrate diet, bodybuilders will experience chronic fatigue.

Because eating disorders can have lethal consequences, it is important that athletes and their trainers recognize the dangers of pushing the goal of achieving leanness beyond the point where it will ultimately harm performance.

Ask the Experts: Tufts Answers Your Most Important Questions

Making Nutritious Choices

Q. Are there any nutritional differences between extra-virgin, virgin, fine, and ungraded olive oil?

A. None to speak of. The designations are related to variations in fragrance and flavor resulting from differences in the way oil is extracted from the olive. Extra-virgin olive oil, with its pleasant aroma and strong flavor, comes from the first "pressing" of an olive and is minimally pressed. If the olives are "cold pressed," a method that involves little processing and yields less oil, the finished product is even finer. The lower the grade of olive oil, the more pressings the olives have gone through to extract the oil and the more processing it has undergone.

Q. Are kosher meats too salty for people on low-sodium diets?

A. The koshering process, which involves treating raw meat and poultry with salt to leach out the blood, can give them twice as much sodium as nonkosher meat. However, you can remove some of the excess salt in kosher beef or veal without compromising the nutrients by soaking it in water for one hour before cooking, a pro-cess that does not seem to be particularly effective with chicken.

Q. Are the salt substitutes sold in supermarkets more nutritious than regular table salt? What about taste?

A. Salt substitutes consist primarily of potassium chloride, which differs from ordinary sodium chloride (table salt) in that potassium takes the place of sodium in the molecule. Although potassium is harmless for most people, individuals with kidney damage may have trouble getting rid of excess potassium, which can accumulate to toxic levels. Also, be aware that the taste of potassium chloride is distinctive and may take some getting used to. As an alternative to salt substitutes, you could consider making greater use of herbs and other seasonings that contain no sodium.

Q. Many recipes, especially for desserts, call for salt. Will the elimination of salt interfere with the success of the desserts?

A. Because salt is added to enhance flavor, if it's left out it will not interfere with the texture and quality of pie crusts, cakes, custards, puddings, and the like. It is even doubtful that you will perceive a difference in the taste. On the other hand, in the case of desserts made with yeast, it is necessary to add salt to control the rate of yeast fermentation and to help in the structure and texture of the finished product. And, when it comes to taste, you might notice the absence of salt in these recipes. The amount of salt used in most desserts and breads is not significant compared with the quantities we sprinkle on foods or consume when eating highly processed or salty snack foods.

Q. Is the salt content of foods the same as sodium?

A. No. Salt is about 40 percent sodium and 60 percent chloride—hence its technical name, sodium chloride. Only about one-third of the sodium in the typical American diet comes from table salt. You get the rest from sodium naturally present in foods and from the small amounts that are present in drinking water, as well as from salt and sodium added during food processing.

Q. What are egg substitutes made from?

A. Egg substitutes, which usually come in liquid form, are made primarily from egg whites, which means they do not contain fat and cholesterol, which eggs contain only in the yolks. In supermarkets, egg substitutes are stored in the frozen-food section. Look for small cartons with names like Eggbeaters or Scramblers. Or try Just Whites, a powdered egg white product. One quarter cup of egg substitute will generally replace a whole egg, both in egg dishes like omelettes and in baked goods and casseroles.

Q. Why is veal much higher in cholesterol than other cuts of beef?

A. Cholesterol is a fat-like substance that concentrates in the muscle (meaty portion) of an animal, rather than in the fat. Young animals have more muscle fibers because they are in a rapid growth stage, so they are greater sources of cholesterol than older animals. Veal is the flesh of one- to four-month-old calves.

Q. Is honey more nutritious than sugar?

A. Unlike refined sugar, honey does contain small quantities of essential minerals (mainly potassium, calcium, and phosphorus), but they're present in such minute amounts that they have little value for human nutrition. Honey and sugar have roughly the same number of calories per serving. The only major difference is that, whereas table sugar consists of pure sucrose, honey contains a mixture of fructose, glucose, and smaller amounts of other sugars.

Q. Because raisins, which are dehydrated grapes, are a good source of iron, does that mean that grapes are also a good source of iron?

A. No. Because grapes have much more water than raisins, the nutrients are not as concentrated. In fact, ounce for ounce, raisins have almost nine times the iron of grapes. Three-and-a-half ounces of raisins provide close to 20 percent of the USRDA for iron.

Knowing What's in the Package

Q. What do such terms as "sell by" or "best if used by" on food containers mean?

A. The "sell by" or "pull" date indicates the last day a product should be offered for sale on the supermarket shelf. Most foods are still good to eat up to a week beyond this date because manufacturers factor in time to allow for home storage.

The "best if used by" date marks the end of the period during which a food will be at peak freshness. It can still be used after this date, but it may be a little stale or lacking in some other quality that affects taste or texture.

The "expiration" date is the last day on which a food should be eaten. After that time, safety and quality are not guaranteed.

The "pack" date is the day a food is packaged or processed for retail sale. Its purpose is primarily to help companies and retailers rotate food.

All of these terms are used by food companies on a voluntary basis. The Food and Drug Administration has no regulations or guidelines on dating food for freshness.

Q. Is it true that significant amounts of nutrients are lost from milk stored in see-through containers? Is milk in an opaque carton a better nutritional buy than milk packaged in a plastic container?

A. Packaging food in containers that allow the light to pass through can promote a slow destruction of nutrients. In the case of milk, exposure to supermarket fluorescent lights can exert a dramatic effect on its vitamin A content. Studies of milk stored in see-through containers, either glass or plastic, have demonstrated that milk can lose as much as half its vitamin A content (and small amounts of its riboflavin content) in just a couple of days. Milk in paperboard cartons loses little of its vitamin A. But vitamin A is so widely available in other foods—fruits, vegetables, meats, cheeses, and eggs—that it is not likely that the nutrient loss from milk stored in see-through containers will be injurious to anyone's health.

Keeping Food Safe

Q. Why must crustaceans like lobster and crab be cooked alive?

A. Cruel as it may seem, throwing a still-moving lobster into boiling water reduces the risk of food poisoning. Meat from crustaceans, because of its unique texture, acts as a sponge for bacteria that tend to grow extremely rapidly once these sea creatures die. Because there is no way to tell if bacteria are present, it is wise to avoid eating crustaceans that have died before being

cooked. That should not be difficult, because public health policy forbids the sale of pre-killed crustaceans (other than shrimp) in fish markets and restaurants.

Shrimp, incidentally, does not have the same rampant bacteria problem as lobsters and crab. You can safely cook and eat dead shrimp as long as it has been handled under sanitary conditions and refrigerated.

Q. Will bay leaves cause harm if they are left in foods?

A. Bay leaves, often used to season soups and stews, are not nutritionally harmful. But their sharp edges make them a potential hazard. People have suffered perforations of the intestines by swallowing bay leaves. Be sure to remove them before serving or eating food.

Q. Why are certain types of ceramic cooking ware considered to be unsafe?

A. Lead is used in glazes that are applied to ceramic ware to create a smooth surface. When glazes are not applied correctly, or when the ceramic ware is not fired at a high enough temperature, the lead in glazes can leach into food. An accumulation of too much lead in the body over a period of years can lead to severe toxicity. At its most devastating, lead poisoning can lead to chronic illnesses of the nervous system, reproductive system, cardiovascular system, and kidneys. It is especially dangerous for very young children, who are affected by much smaller quantities of lead in their systems.

To avoid danger: Store food in plastic or glass containers; line ceramic bowls with plastic or foil to protect food; and don't use untested ceramics (especially products from Mexico, China, Italy, or Spain) to serve food.

Q. Are oranges that have a greenish color ripe? Are they safe to eat?

A. Such oranges have undergone a natural process called "regreening," which happens when a ripe orange fruit pulls some of the green chlorophyll pigment from the leaves and stem of the tree back into the peel. Regreened oranges are actually riper than others and often sweeter. And they're perfectly safe to eat.

Q. Will any harm come from eating peanut shells along with the nut?

A. Peanut shells are not meant to be eaten, and two physicians from Oregon Health Sciences University have presented some pretty convincing evidence of the potential danger that exists for people who do eat them. The doctors described the case of a young man who had a nightly snack of 15 to 30 peanuts with the shells. He came to them with complaints of long-standing abdominal pain, loose and frequent bowel movements, and painful defecation. Needless to say, he was advised to kick the peanut shell habit, and the intestinal symptoms gradually subsided. It's not surprising that shells can wreak havoc with your intestines when you consider that they're an abrasive used in grinding and polishing.

Q. Is barbecuing a safe way to cook meat?

A. The greatest hazard of barbecuing is that the cook will not use enough caution and get burned. Some people suggest that the barbecuing itself is dangerous, because the smoke, which is absorbed by the meat, contains benzopyrene, which, in its pure form, has been known to cause cancer in laboratory animals. However, in order to experience the same results, people would have to consume unrealistically large quantities of barbecued meat at a time.

Q. If the refrigerator door is accidentally left open a crack for several hours, will the food be harmed?

A. With the door open, your refrigerator runs constantly to keep its temperature setting. If it's set at 40°F or lower and running properly, your perishable food is probably still cold enough to be safe. If food is cold to the touch, it should be fine. The items you have to be most careful to check are raw meats and casseroles, especially if they are stored at the front of the refrigerator near the door.

Concerns of Life-Cycles

Q. What is the safest way for working mothers to store breast milk until they get home?

A. More and more new mothers are opting to breast-feed, even if they work outside the home. It is easy enough to use a breast pump to extract milk during the day, but how can the milk be most safely stored until the end of the day? Refrigeration is best, if you have access to a refrigerator where you work.

However, breast milk can be safely left at room temperature for about an hour, depending on the temperature. Unlike cow's milk, nonrefrigerated mother's milk is a poor breeding ground for organisms that can cause illness. The reason is that human milk contains appreciable amounts of protective substances, such as lactoferrin, that inhibit the growth of bacteria. To be on the safe side, mothers should store their milk in a cool place, out of direct sunlight.

Q. Do sweets and fatty foods increase the possibility that a teenager will have acne?

A. Scientists have found no evidence of a direct link between diet and adolescent acne. The notion originated with the premise that because adolescent acne is caused by an excess of oil in the skin, a diet that contained less fat would reduce this oil. But the oil in the skin is stimulated by the hormones, not by French fries. (The rare exception is when there is a clear-cut case of food allergy.) Acne occurs when follicles under the skin become clogged with oil. Bacteria under the skin feed on the oil and release toxins that spill out onto the skin's surface. The result: a pimple. Fortunately, treating pimples that crop up on the face, back, or other skin surfaces has been made easier by the recent development of a wide array of effective medications. Some of these new drugs are vitamin A derivatives—that is, compounds that are similar in structure to vitamin **A.** However, vitamin A itself will not "cure" acne and, in fact, can cause damage to the liver if taken in doses that far exceed the amounts people are likely to consume from foods alone. Only the medications prescribed by a dermatologist will do the trick.

Q. Is there a vitamin that prevents gray hair?

A. Although it's true that a deficiency of the B vitamin pantothenic acid causes gray hair in some laboratory animals, humans will not be spared the ravages of time by loading up on supplements containing this nutrient.

Understanding the Nutrition/Health Link

Q. Because cigarette smokers use 100 calories fewer a day than nonsmokers, won't people who quit smoking gain weight?

A. In 1988, the U.S. Surgeon General reported that a preoccupation with gaining weight plays a major role in influencing whether people start, continue, and even resume smoking after quitting. Apparently, young women are particularly apt to develop a nicotine dependency while trying to lose weight.

Smokers who quit usually gain an average of seven pounds—so the weight gain could not be called an unhealthful one. In fact, according to Jack Henningfield, Ph.D., of the Addiction Research Center at the National Institute of Drug Abuse, it is rare for former smokers to gain unhealthful amounts of weight. As Dr. Henningfield noted, "A few pounds of weight is a small price to pay for greatly increasing your chances of a longer, healthier life."

For those who are concerned, some evidence exists that nicotine gum might help minimize weight gain. A group of long-term nicotine-gum chewers monitored by experts at the University of London's Addiction Research Unit gained less weight than smokers who successfully quit without using it. This is not to say that transferring the dependence to nicotine gum is necessarily a good idea. But because chewing gum decreases exposure to nicotine and completely eliminates the harmful tar and carbon monoxide its users would inhale if they continued to rely on cigarettes, it's certainly preferable to smoking and might be a viable option for people who have trouble kicking the habit, either because they fear weight gain or for other reasons. Moreover, most users only need to use to the gum for three to six months.

Q. Are some foods more likely to cause heartburn than others?

A. Heartburn, an uncomfortable burning sensation in the chest that can occur when there is too much acid in the stomach, is a symptom of an underlying disorder called gastroesophageal reflux, a condition in which the contents of the stomach (including acid) flow backward into the esophagus. Although there is no proof that foods stimulate reflux, some substances are known to aggravate heartburn. These include coffee, alcohol, and citrus fruits, all of which make the stomach more acidic. Heartburn sufferers should also avoid fatty foods and chocolate, which interfere with contraction of the sphincter that separates the esophagus from the stomach. Other foods, such as spicy dishes, radishes, and cucumbers, may cause trouble for some people but not for others. Some doctors counsel their heartburn patients not to lie down immediately after meals. Remaining upright allows gravity to help in reducing the chances of a backflow, or reflux, of stomach contents.

Q. Are there any nutritional substances that can bolster the immune system?

A. Many essential nutrients, including vitamins B-6 and C and the mineral zinc, play a role in regulating the immune system. Researchers at Tufts have found that large doses of vitamin E also enhance immune responsiveness.

After giving one group of healthy men and women over 60 years of age a daily supplement containing several times the recommended dietary allowance for that nutrient, and another group a placebo, they found that the immune function of those who took the vitamin was significantly improved after just 30 days. The group taking the placebo had no change in immune function at all.

As provocative as the findings are, they are by no means a signal for everyone to start taking megadose supplements of vitamin E. Although the scientists were able to study much about immune function through a variety of specialized tests, they have yet to examine the direct relationship between vitamin E and the incidences of disease, such as cancer. In addition, they have not carried out long-term tests to find out if the effects last more than 30 days. Furthermore, The Finnish study challenged the notion of single nutrient benefits.

Q. Is it true that occasional fasting will eliminate toxins from the body?

A. Nearly every religion has encouraged fasting at one time or another, and fasting for a day or two every few weeks probably doesn't do any harm to a healthy person. But the alleged benefit, that the practice somehow "cleans out the system," is questionable. And fasting for more than a few days at a stretch could be quite harmful.

Ironically, although many fasters believe they are eliminating "toxic wastes," chemicals known as ketone bodies begin to accumulate in the bloodstream if they stop eating for too long. Ketone bodies are quite toxic and place a severe burden on the kidneys.

For some people, fasting can cause fatigue, dizziness, low blood pressure, and even depression. Prolonged fasting leads to a loss of protein from muscles and vital organs, as well as a depletion of the essential minerals calcium, phosphorus, sodium, and postassium.

The bottom line is that if your desire to fast is motivated by a desire to be physically healthier, you're probably choosing the wrong course of action.

Weights and Measures

Abbreviations

oz. = ounce
g = gram
lb. = pound
kg = kilogram
mg = milligram
µg = microgram
ml = milliliter
qt. = quart
tsp = teaspoon
tbsp = tablespoon

Volume

1 liter = 1.06 quarts
1 gallon = 3.79 liters
1 quart = 0.95 liter
1 cup = 8 fluid ounces
3 teaspoons = 1 tablespoon
2 tablespoons = 1 fluid ounce
16 tablespoons = 1 cup
2 pints = 1 quart
4 cups = 1 quart
32 ounces = 1 quart

Weights

1 ounce = 28.4 grams
16 ounces = 1 pound
1 pound = 454 grams
1 kilogram = 1,000 grams or 2.2 pounds
1 gram = 1,000 milligrams
1 milligram = 1,000 micrograms

APPENDIX C

The Nutrition Hotline

Food, Drug, and Alcohol Abuse

Action on Smoking & Health
2013 H St., N.W.
Washington, DC 20006
(202) 659-4310

Nonprofit legal action smoking group; provides general information

Alcohol, Drug Abuse, and Mental Health Administration Department of Health and Human Services
Parklawn Building, Room 12C-15 5600
Fishers Lane
Rockville, MD 20857
(301) 443-3783

Handles inquiries and supplies publications about alcohol, drug, and mental health problems

Alcoholics Anonymous World Services
468 Park Avenue South
New York, NY 10163
(212) 686-1100

Answers inquiries, makes referrals regarding AA groups in 110 countries

Alcohol and Drug Problems Association of North America
444 N. Capitol St., Suite 181
Washington, DC 20001
(202) 737-4340

Provides information, education, and referrals on drug- and alcohol-related problems

Alcohol Education for Youth
1500 Western Ave.
Albany, NY 12203
(514) 456-3800

Answers inquiries and provides education for the prevention of alcohol abuse among youth

American Anorexia/Bulimia Association, Inc.
133 Cedar Lane
Teaneck, NJ 07666
(201) 836-1800

Provides information and support for people with eating disorders and their families

Anorexia Nervosa and Associated Disorders, Inc.
P.O. Box 7
Highland Park, IL 60035
(312) 831-3438

Provides information and referrals for treatment of eating disorders

Bulimia, Anorexia Self-Help
6125 Clayton Ave., Suite 215

St. Louis, MO 63139
(800) 227-4785

Provides support and information for recovery from eating disorders

Center for the Study of Anorexia and Bulimia
One W. 91st St.
New York, NY 10024
(212) 595-3449

Provides support, information, and services related to the psychotherapeutic treatment of eating disorders

Children of Alcoholics Foundation
540 Madison Ave., 23rd floor
New York, NY 10022
(212) 980-5394

Supplies education and support for children with alcoholic parents

Drug and Alcohol Council
396 Alexander St.
Rochester, NY 14607
(716) 244-3190

Provides preventive education and primary intervention for alcohol and drug cases

National Anorexic Aid Society, Inc.
5796 Karl Road
Columbus, OH 43229
(614) 436-1112

Provides education, referrals, and services related to anorexia nervosa

National Clearinghouse for Alcohol Information
P.O. Box 2345
Rockville, MD 20852
(301) 468-2600

Supplies information, publications, and referrals related to alcoholism

National Council on Alcoholism
12 W. 21st St.
New York, NY 10010
(212) 206-2770

Provides referrals and information regarding alcoholism and its medical, pyschological, and sociological aspects

National Federation of Parents for Drug-Free Youth
8730 Georgia Avenue, Suite 200
Silver Spring, MD 20910
(301) 554-5437

Helps concerned parents prevent adolescent drug abuse

Office on Smoking and Health
Centers for Disease Control
Park Bldg., Rm. 1-10
5600 Fishers Lane
Rockville, MD 20857
(301) 443-1575

Answers inquiries, makes referrals, and publishes a bulletin related to smoking and health

Students Against Drunk Driving
10812 Ashfield Rd.
Adelphi, MD 20783
(301) 937-7936

Devoted to combatting deaths caused by drunken driving; offers education and information programs, as well as student–parent support

Food Policy, Safety, Labeling, Legislation

Center for Food Safety and Applied Nutrition
Food and Drug Administration
200 C St., S.W., Room 3321
Washington, DC 20204
(202) 245-1236

Provides information on nutrition, food, food technology, and food additives

Center for Science in the Public Interest
1501 16th St., N.W.
Washington, DC 20036
(202) 332-9110

Engages in research, education, and advisory services dedicated to improving the American diet

Clean Water Action Project
733 15th St., N.W., Suite 1110
Washington, DC 20005
(202) 638-1196

Promotes public interest in water safety through national education; provides information and referrals

Food and Drug Administration, Consumer
  Inquiries
5600 Fishers Lane
Rockville, MD 20857
(301) 443-3170

Answers inquiries and supplies publications related to food and drug safety and efficacy

Food Safety and Inspection Service Information
  Division
Department of Agriculture
14th St. and Independence Ave., S.W.
Washington, DC 20250
(202) 447-9113

Takes responsibility for meat and poultry inspection; provides consumer information and gives referrals

Public Voice for Food and Health Policy
1001 Connecticut Ave., N.W., Suite 522
Washington, DC 20036
(202) 659-5930

Acts as a national consumer watchdog organization that monitors food and health agencies and congressional committees charged with protecting public health

Illness and Disease Prevention and Treatment

American Cancer Society Medical Library
4 West 34th St.
New York, NY 10001
(212) 736-3030

Serves as a clearinghouse for information on cancer research, statistics, and public health

American Diabetes Association
505 8th Ave.
New York, NY 10018
(212) 947-9707

Provides information, education, research, and referrals related to diabetes

American Health Foundation
320 East 43rd St.
New York, NY 10017
(212) 953-1900

Engages in disease-prevention programs and public education and information services

American Heart Association
7320 Greenville Ave.
Dallas, TX 75231
(214) 750-5300

Answers inquiries, makes referrals, and offers reference services related to heart disease

American Lung Association
1740 Broadway
New York, NY 10019
(212) 245-8000

Engages in preventive efforts regarding lung disease; answers inquiries and provides educational materials

Association for Research of Childhood Cancer
3653 Harlem Road
Buffalo, NY 14215
(716) 838-4433

Provides support for parents of children with cancer

Centers for Disease Control
Office of Public Affairs
1600 Clifton Road N.E.
Atlanta, GA 30333
(404) 329-3286

Answers public's questions on health-related issues

Citizens for the Treatment of High Blood Pressure
1140 Connecticut Ave., N.W., Suite 606

Washington, DC 20036
(202) 296-4435

Engages in research and funding for treatment of high blood pressure; provides advisory services and conducts seminars

High Blood Pressure Information Center
2121 Wisconsin Ave., N.W., Suite 410
Washington, DC 20036
(202) 496-1809

Provides education, references, information, and seminars related to high blood pressure

Joslin Diabetes Center
One Joslin Place
Boston, MA 02215
(617) 732-2400

Provides research, education, and information on adult-onset diabetes

Juvenile Diabetes Foundation
60 Madison Ave.
New York, NY 10010
(800) 223-1138

Provides educational programs and information on adolescent-onset diabetes

Lipid Research Clinic
George Washington University Medical Center
2150 Pennsylvania Ave., N.W.
Washington, DC 20037
(202) 676-4152

Conducts reseach on blood lipids and lipoproteins and their relationship to coronary heart disease; provides patient services and referrals

National Cancer Institute
NIH Bldg. 31, Room 10A18
Bethesda, MD 20892
(301) 496-5583

Provides research, training, and information on all aspects of cancer prevention, detection, and rehabilitation

National Diabetes Information Clearinghouse
Box NDIC

Bethesda, MD 20892
(301) 468-2162

Supplies information, publications, and referrals related to diabetes

National Digestive Diseases Information Clearinghouse
Box NNDIC
Bethesda, MD 20892
(301) 496-9707

Provides information and nationwide referrals related to illnesses of the digestive tract

National Foundation for Cancer Research
7215 Wisconsin Ave., N.W., Suite 332W
Bethesda, MD 20814
(301) 654-1250

Distributes publications, makes referrals, and holds seminars related to cancer research

National Heart, Lung, and Blood Institute
Public Inquiries and Reports Branch
National Institutes of Health
Bethesda, MD 20892
(301) 496-4236

Answers inquiries regarding heart, lung, and blood diseases

National Kidney Foundation
2 Park Avenue
New York, NY 10016
(212) 889-2210

Provides education, information, research, and referrals related to kidney disease

National Osteoporosis Association
(800) 464-6700

Provides listings of bone density testing centers

Skin Cancer Foundation
475 Park Avenue South
New York, NY 10016
(212) 725-5176

Supplies education, information, and services related to skin cancer

Food Industry Associations

Food Marketing Institute
1750 K St., N.W.
Washington, DC 20006
(202) 452-8444

Serves as the association of supermarket retailers and wholesalers; answers inquiries and provides research information

Food Processors Institute
1401 New York Ave., N.W., Suite 400
Washington, DC 20005
(202) 393-0890

Provides information on food processing, labeling, safety, and policy

Grocery Manufacturers of America
1010 Wisconsin Avenue, N.W., Suite 800
Washington, DC 20007
(202) 337-9400

Provides information on the grocery industry, labeling, safety, and food quality

Milk Industry Foundation
888 16th St., N.W., 2nd floor
Washington, DC 20006
(202) 296-4250

Publishes research on milk and milk products

National Association of Wheat Growers
415 Second St., N.E., Suite 300
Washington, DC 20002
(202) 547-7800

Answers inquiries and distributes publications regarding the wheat industry

National Meat Association
734 15th St., N.W.
Washington, DC 20005
(202) 347-1000

Represents the meat packing and processing industry; answers inquiries

National Restaurant Association
311 First St., N.W.
Washington, DC 20001
(202) 638-6100

Provides information related to the food-service industry

Soy Protein Council
1255 23rd St., N.W., Suite 850
Washington, DC 20037
(202) 467-6610

Represents the food protein industry; provides information about research and government actions

Wheat Flour Institute
600 Maryland Ave., S.W.
Washington, DC 20024
(202) 484-2200

Provides information on wheat flour, nutrition, and diet

Nutrition and Health Information and Services

American Association of Retired Persons
1900 K St., N.W.
Washington, DC 20049
(202) 728-4880

Promotes education, welfare, research, and other matters related to the elderly

Beltsville Human Nutrition Research Center
Ag Research Service
U.S. Department of Agriculture
Room 223, Bldg. 308
Beltsville, MD 20705
(301) 244-2157

Answers inquiries and makes referrals concerning nutrient requirements and metabolism

Bureau of Health Care Delivery and Assistance
Health Resources and Services Administration
Public Health Service
Parklawn Building, Room G-05
5600 Fishers Lane

Rockville, MD 20857
(301) 443-2320

Oversees the provision of health and nutrition services; answers inquiries and supplies information

Community Nutrition Institute
2001 S St., N.W.
Washington, DC 20009
(202) 462-4700

Answers inquiries, conducts seminars, and distributes publications related to national nutrition concerns

Human Nutrition Information Service
Food and Consumer Services
U.S. Department of Agriculture
6505 Belcrest Road
Hyattsville, MD 20782
(301) 436-7725

Studies food and nutrition; answers inquiries

International Association for Medical Assistance to Travelers
736 Center St.
Lewiston, NY 14092
(716) 754-4883

Provides information on sanitary condi-tions and precautions for travelers around the world

Maternity Center Association
48 East 92nd St.
New York, NY 10028
(212) 369-7300

Provides prenatal education and services

National Health Information Clearinghouse
P.O. Box 1133
Washington, DC 20013
(800) 336-4797

Provides referrals from a database for more than 1,000 health-related organizations

President's Council on Physical Fitness and Sports
450 Fifth St., N.W., Room 7103
Washington, DC 20001
(202) 272-3421

Engages in development and education regarding national fitness programs

Tufts University Diet and Nutrition Letter
80 Boylston St., Suite 353
Boston, MA 02116
(617) 482-3530

Publishes a monthly consumer newsletter that reflects current nutrition research and guidelines

Index